Whether 'Tis Tru
Everything You Nee
Thought You K
You'd Ever Know is

♣ Did Patrick really drive snakes out of Ireland?
♣ What's the difference between the Gaelic, Celtic, and Irish languages?
♣ How are the Irish responsible for Thanksgiving Day?
♣ What do Michael Collins and Gerry Adams have in common?
♣ Who was the Irish Michael Jordan?
♣ What is a *seanchai*?
♣ Who were the Young Irelanders and why are they still such an inspiration?

. . . and much more.

Michael Padden is a trial lawyer with the Federal Defender Division of The Legal Aid Society in Brooklyn. He lives in Manhattan and travels at least once a year to Ireland, where he has lectured in the law department at University College, Cork.

Robert Sullivan, Assistant Managing Editor at *Life* magazine, has written for numerous publications, including the *New York Times, Outside, Travel and Leisure, Reader's Digest* and others. He lives with his wife and daughter in Mt. Kisco, New York, and New York City.

MAY THE
ROAD RISE TO
MEET YOU

EVERYTHING YOU NEED
TO KNOW ABOUT
IRISH AMERICAN
HISTORY

Michael Padden
and
Robert Sullivan

FOREWORD BY ROBERT F. KENNEDY, JR.

A PLUME BOOK

PLUME
Published by the Penguin Group
Penguin Putnam Inc., 375 Hudson Street,
New York, New York 10014, U.S.A.
Penguin Books Ltd, 27 Wrights Lane,
London W8 5TZ, England
Penguin Books Australia Ltd, Ringwood,
Victoria, Australia
Penguin Books Canada Ltd, 10 Alcorn Avenue,
Toronto, Ontario, Canada M4V 3B2
Penguin Books (N.Z.) Ltd, 182–190 Wairau Road,
Auckland 10, New Zealand

Penguin Books Ltd, Registered Offices:
Harmondsworth, Middlesex, England

First published by Plume,
a member of Penguin Putnam Inc.

First Printing, March, 1999
10 9 8 7 6 5 4 3 2 1

Ⓟ REGISTERED TRADEMARK—MARCA REGISTRADA

LIBRARY OF CONGRESS CATALOGING-IN-PUBLICATION DATA:

Padden, Michael.
   May the road rise to meet you : everything you need to know about Irish American
history / by Michael Padden and Robert Sullivan; foreword by Robert F. Kennedy, Jr.
      p.   cm.
   Includes bibliographical references and index.
   ISBN 0-452-27853-8
   1. Irish American—History.   2. Sullivan, Robert.
I. Title.
E184.I6P34   1999
973'.049162—dc21   98-42360
                                                                                         CIP

Printed in the United States of America
Set in New Baskerville and Pabst

To my parents, and in memory of Arby,
who truly loved being Irish and American.
—M.P.

To Caroline Rossi Sullivan,
may the road rise for you,
may the sun shine warm upon your face.
—R.S.

ACKNOWLEDGMENTS

The authors are deeply indebted to their supremely talented and hard-working editor at Plume, Deb Brody. We are indebted as well to our Hiberno-inclined advisers for all thoughts, encouragements, criticisms, hopes, and fears as we prepared *May the Road Rise to Meet You*: Kevin Doyle, Kieran Doyle, Tom Concannon, Terry Golway, and Peter Quinn. *Slainte,* boys.

Contents

CONTENTS

Foreword

I'm old enough to remember when being an Irish Catholic really mattered in politics. I recall a time when block-voting Irish still dominated America's urban political landscape from Boston to Chicago, from Tammany Hall to San Francisco. I recall the droves of nuns and priests and lay brothers who marched from the rectories, convents, and priories to campaign for Uncle Jack with the fervor of the Crusades. Those were the days when most people were saying a Catholic could never be elected President, and we believed a Republican couldn't be buried in a Catholic cemetery. I recall collecting—with my elementary school pals at Our Lady of Victory—some of the vast number of quarters doctored by anti-Catholics during the 1960 campaign with red nail polish to give Washington's wig the appearance of a Cardinal's red skullcap: an ominous warning against a papist in the White House. Among my earliest chums were Fays, Markhams, O'Donnells, O'Dwyers, and McNamaras, the children of the front-line troopers in the political battalions who won the White House for the first Irish Catholic American President. There were Irish politicians on both sides of my family for generations. We talked politics from the day we could speak.

Political passion came naturally to a deeply religious race for whom the distinction between political and religious martyrdom had blurred during 800 years of British occupation. From their arrival in America, the Irish took to politics as starving men to food, stifled as they were for centuries by rules that forbade them from participating in the political destiny of their nation. As early as 1691, statutes in Ireland prohibited Catholics from voting, serving on a jury, entering a university, becoming a lawyer, working for government, or marrying a Protestant. My own progenitors and those of most Irish American families were still in Ireland during that black February of 1847 when the pitiful announcement in England's House of Commons that fifteen thousand people a day were dying of starvation in Ireland so moved Queen Victoria that she donated five pounds to the Society for Irish Relief. So the Irish fled. "They are going, going, going," wrote the poet, "and we cannot bid them stay." They fled in the coffin ships and the Atlantic became, in Joyce's words, "as a bowl of bitter tears."

But many of them made it to America. And wherever they landed, they flourished. Fecund Irish mothers with little opportunity for fulfillment beyond childbearing had created an invading force that triumphed at law, politics, sports, literature, and business. No people were ever prouder than the spectacularly successful Irish Americans who returned to the Old World of humiliation and despair a generation later with heads high. Their cocky New World confidence was exemplified by the boxer John L. Sullivan who during his triumphant tour of the British Isles in 1887 cordially greeted the Prince of Wales: "I'm proud to meet you. If ever you come to Boston, be sure to look me up. I'll see that you're treated right." That day came for my grandfather, who must have relished the irony of recrossing the Atlantic as FDR's Ambassador to the Court of St. James.

Just how well the Irish flourished abroad is exemplified in the story of the nine youthful leaders of the 1848 Young Irish Rebellion whose death sentences Queen Victoria mercifully commuted to banishment in far wild Australia. The Queen was astounded to learn that Sir Charles Duffy, just elected prime minister of Australia, was the very same Charles Duffy she had deported twenty-five years earlier. Victoria ordered a commission to investigate the fate of the other eight Young Irish rebels. Thomas Meagher, the commission learned, was governor of Montana. Richard O'Connor was governor of Newfoundland. Mike Ireland was attorney general of Australia; his predecessor in that job, Morris Lyene, was also one of the nine. Thomas McGee, a member of Parliament in Montreal, was President of Council of the Dominion of Canada and minister of agriculture. John Mitchel was a writer and prominent New York politician whose son was mayor of New York. Finally, Terrence McManus and Pat Donahue were brigadier generals in the United States Army. Donahue and Mc-Manus were not the only Irishmen to flourish in the military. The race's acumen for politics was matched by its tribal aptitude for war.

I was brought up in the Irish Catholic tradition that the martial career was at least as noble as the political, if only for the opportunity it offered to display physical as well as moral courage. We knew every patriotic hymn and the fight songs for the Army, Navy, Air Force, and Marines. A portrait of Daddy's brother Joe in his Air Force uniform hung over the dining room mantel, the flak-filled London sky silhouetting his B-25. He had flown fifty missions before volunteering to pilot an experimental flying bomb that vaporized over the English Channel. His sister Kick, killed in a plane crash after the war, had flown to England to join the Nurses' Auxiliary at its outbreak. Her husband died heroically on the Maginot Line. My uncle Jack rescued his crew with a heroic swim when his PT boat was cut in two by a Japanese destroyer. We were reminded of their feats in our bedtime prayers, and from my father, a good military historian, we heard each night a dinner table rendition of Bunker Hill or some other battle that changed history.

The "Wild Geese" played a pivotal role in many of these engagements. Their tale typified the Celtic penchant for war. The legendary ferocity of these Irish officers and soldiers, forced from their native land after the Battle of the Boyne and scattered throughout the armies of the world, helped change the map of Europe. Fighting for the French, they broke the ranks of the English at Foutenoy, and for the Spanish, they bested the Germans at Melazzo. Often Irish soldiers died fruitlessly but, almost always, bravely. Irish Americans boast more Medal of Honor winners than any other immigrant group. During his 1962 visit to Ireland, President Kennedy presented the battle-torn flag of the Union Army's Irish Brigade to the Irish people. On a bitter cold day in December 1862, its 1,200 soldiers, their hats adorned by the green sprig, had borne the brunt of the Union Army's hopeless assault on the Confederate Heights at Fredericksburg. Only 280 survived. "Never," said an awestricken Robert E. Lee, "were men so brave." On a recent visit to the Little Big Horn battlefield in South Dakota, I took note that every man among Custer's butchered force bore an Irish surname. And the Irish soldiers sung of themselves,

> *War battered dogs are we,*
> *Gnawing a naked bone,*
> *Fighters in every land and clime*
> *For every cause but our own.*

Wherever they went, they brought their poetry. As the absence of a home army turned them into soldiers abroad, as the laws forbidding participation in politics turned Irish expatriates into politicians in foreign lands, so, laws forbidding the use of Gaelic language made this hardheaded race into poets in a foreign tongue.

That love of language distinguishes the Irish to this day. On our honeymoon in Dublin, my wife, Mary Richardson, and I were derided by a grizzled cabby as "philistines" because we were unfamiliar with certain obscure Irish poets whom he admired. We listened fascinated as two pierced and painted street urchins debated Harold Pinter's latest play with passion and eloquence. The Irish are the best-educated race on Earth. An Irish carpenter, the joke goes, asked to distinguish a joist and girder, is likely to reply, "Joyce wrote *Ulysses* and Goethe, *Faust*."

The Irish love of poetry was part of my own childhood. I grew up listening to and learning the poetry of Yeats, Keats, Tennyson, and Kipling. Each of my ten brothers and sisters memorized and recited poetry at dinner, a practice my own children now enjoy. On our frequent camping trips with friends, we often have fireside poetry duels. I've discovered the practice is widespread among Irish Catholic American families. My wife's cousins, the Ward brothers, with whom we often camp, know five hundred poems among them. Last Memorial Day, thirty campers, adults and children, sat around the fire on Magdalene Island in the Hudson River and listened to Kevin Ward win such a contest with his flawless recitation of T. S. Eliot's 120-line "Prufrock."

As an Irish American with five generations and an ocean's distance from Ireland, I am delighted that so much of the Irish legacy has percolated down through my bloodlines and family culture. Religious faith, the Catholic Church, and love of our Lady are still the central focus of our family lives. The love of politics and sense of duty to country, and the love of language and literature are virtues I consider part of my Irish legacy. Add to these the Irish hatred of oppression, their love of freedom, their admiration of moral and physical courage, and of course, the passion and desperate need of the Irish to believe in something worth dying for, and you have the best of the Irish character.

This book summarizes for Irish Americans what it means to be Irish and challenges us to live up to the best qualities of our race and history. These are qualities that I hope will flow into the next generation of Irish Americans, including my children.

—Robert F. Kennedy, Jr.

Introduction

Forty-four million Americans say they're Irish, and the claims of only a handful are blarney. (Annually on March 17, the number rises to 280 million.) Forty-four million, according to the 1990 census, with at least a dram of Irish in the blood. (And most of them are *legal*.)

The writer Reverend Andrew M. Greeley calls the United States "Great Ireland."

The Irish came, or their forebears did, by plane or boat (those who boost Saint Brendan as the first European in the New World would add animal-skin canoe). Some came to find a fortune that was elusive in the motherland, but many more came in flight from war or famine. They started coming in serious numbers before the colonies became our United States, and they were important early players in the European settling of the continent. Various calamities in Ireland during the seventeenth, eighteenth, and nineteenth centuries accounted for great bursts in their rate of emigration. From 1841 to 1860, during and immediately after Ireland's storied but all-too-real potato blight, 750,000 Irish immigrants poured into the urban ghettos of the eastern seaboard, and by the time this great transatlantic tide finally ebbed, one-quarter of the populations of New York City, Jersey City, and Boston were of Irish heritage. Said the social critic Orestes Brownson with confidence and prescience: "Out of these narrow lanes, dirty streets, damp cellars, and suffocating garrets, will come forth some of the noblest sons of our country whom she will delight to own and honor."

A century and more after Brownson, accountings can be made: Thirteen U.S. presidents have been Irish; more Congressional Medals of Honor have been awarded to Irish Americans than to members of any other ethnic group; captains of business (Henry Ford, W. R. Grace, William Randolph Hearst, Howard Hughes, Joe Kennedy, Andrew Mellon, James Concannon) have been of Irish extraction, as have giants of the labor movement (Elizabeth Gurley Flynn, Mother Jones, Mike Quill, George Meany). As Greeley writes: "In terms of education, income and occupational achievement, Irish Catholics are the most successful gentile group in American society. Their college attendance rate (among all people of college age) crossed the national average in about 1907 and has remained substantially above it ever since." The contributions of the Irish to western culture are legend in their enormity—consider merely the title of Thomas Cahill's sweetly boastful 1995 best-seller, *How the Irish Saved Civilization*—and this race did not leave its artistic impulse behind when it crossed the ocean. Composers Thomas Moore and Victor Herbert; actors Maureen O'Hara, Gregory Peck, Tyrone Power, Gene Kelly, Helen Hayes, Jackie Gleason, Walter Brennan, and Jimmy Cagney; musicians Tommy and Jimmy Dorsey, Bing Crosby, Hoagy Carmichael, and George M. Cohan; playwright Eugene O'Neill; fiction writers F. Scott Fitzgerald, Margaret Mitchell, Flannery O'Connor, John O'Hara, and William Kennedy; journalists Jimmy Breslin, Maureen Dowd, Pete Hamill, Jim Dwyer, and William F. Buckley; sculptor Augustus Saint-Gaudens; photographer Mathew Brady; painter Georgia O'Keeffe; architect Louis H. Sullivan—these were, or are, just some of the American artists who were not only proud of their Irishness, but allowed it to inform their work. Theirs are American creations, surely, but they are specifically Irish American as well. Take the writer Frank McCourt. His memoir *Angela's Ashes* is an Irish story, surely, but it is Irish American as well. As did the longtime leader of Ireland Eamon de Valera, the brothers McCourt set out on life's journey from Brooklyn. With poets and presidents alike, the bridge from the motherland to the States—in either direction—is a short and oft-crossed one.

That is a point: Even with assimilation, there has been scant diminishment of the Irish American community's sense of Irishness—its sense of self and Celt. To quote Greeley again: "In some respects the Irish, one of the early immigrant groups of America, have unintentionally, and often despite themselves, maintained greater cultural diversity and greater cultural distinction than groups that have come after them—in their family life, their attitudes towards achievement, their world view, their drinking behavior, and their political style. Irish distinctiveness continues unabated, with no sign that either generation in America or the decline of ethnic self-consciousness notably diminishes this distinctiveness."

Indeed, Irish newlyweds coming out of Saint Catharine's in Spring Lake, New Jersey, are sure to be toasted—eloquently, sentimentally, poetically—with Waterford raised high, and to be gifted with an Aran blanket or two. There will be Guinness at the reception as surely as there will be champagne. Senator Daniel Patrick Moynihan wears a tweed walking hat, and his choice is purposeful. Irish American priests are jailed for aiding in the Republican cause, and Irish American publicans sell contraband booze flown over from Shannon, while music available only "back home" spins on their Queens juke boxes. The kids who aren't doing the bars yet are holed up in their rooms, listening to the Cranberries, the Pogues, Black 47, U2, Sinead O'Connor, the Corrs, Elvis Costello. . . . (As their mothers and dads, desperately trying to relax, spin Enya or Altan or Clannad in the living room, even as they shout toward the bedroom, "Turn that down!")

In short: Irish Americans are in touch with Ireland. Many of them visit Ireland regularly, and they think about Ireland often. They enjoy going to movies produced by the thriving Irish film industry (*My Left Foot*, *In the Name of the Father*, *The Snapper*, *The Commitments*, *The Van*). They follow the political maneuverings of Gerry Adams with as much interest as they do those of Ted Kennedy, or his son Patrick, or his nephew Joe, the recently retired congressman. We talked about that bridge, which today grows even shorter: Aer Lingus is an ever-open artery to the heartland that is Ireland, and the country's erstwhile sons and daughters are never really far away.

Make no mistake, however: There is Irish and there is Irish *Americanism*. Most of the forty-four million are modernists, fully inculcated in the free world's dominant, frenetic late-twentieth-century society. Even as they hold dear their notions of what it is to have Irish blood, they very purposefully turn from the noxious actions of their kin. Most of the forty-four million deride the violence that has tormented the homeland, and most take offense at popular depictions of—or misconceptions about—the Irish. It's time to set the record straight on several matters. Greeley helps us quickly deflate three notions:

> *Irish Americans are conservative and racist.* Actually, the Irish are the most liberal non-Jewish ethnic group in the country and generally support integration and a woman's right to choose.
>
> *They're drunks.* No more so than English Americans, and they have a lower alcohol-problem rate than several ethnic groups from Eastern Europe.
>
> *They live in male-centric families.* In fact, Irish women are more powerful in the family than most women—in America *and* back home. According to a recent Common Market study, Ireland is the most feminist of all European Economic Community member nations.

So there. We are now agreed on three things about what it is or isn't to be Irish American at this grand point in time in this great, thriving country. Perhaps we can agree on many more by the time we finish this road, rising to meet us, that is our humble book. And having said that, let us quote the late Dennis Clark on Irish Americans, so that your authors have in pocket their preregistered *mea culpa, mea maxima culpa* for errors that might follow: "Almost anything you can say about them is both true and false."

And, oh, by the way . . . about that title: It is from an old Irish blessing, often used in the present day as an old Irish toast. The particular blessing that we have excerpted is a famous one, regularly offered at retirement, promotion, or going-away parties. It's a lovely verse, more lyrical and eloquent than most, if not as funny as some. The first stanza of the blessing seems stunningly appropriate to us— it succinctly defines the phenomenon of Irish Americanism:

May the road rise to meet you.
May the wind be always at your back,
the sun shine warm upon your face,
the rain fall soft upon your fields,
and until we meet again
may God hold you in the hollow of His hand.

That's what happened to the Irish in America.
The road rose
The breeze blew.
The sun shone and then the rain fell.
God has blessed the effort.

THE KENNEDYS IN AMERICA

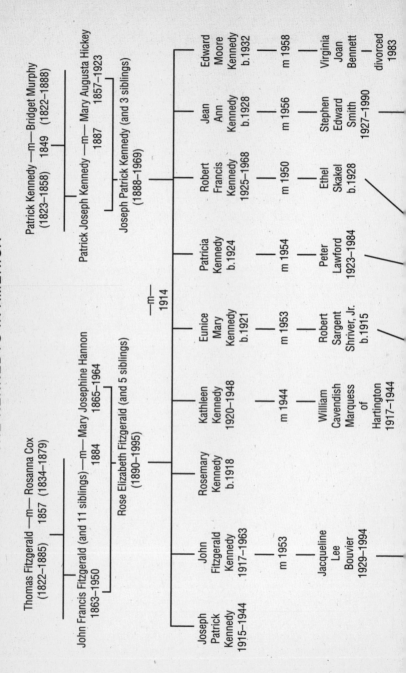

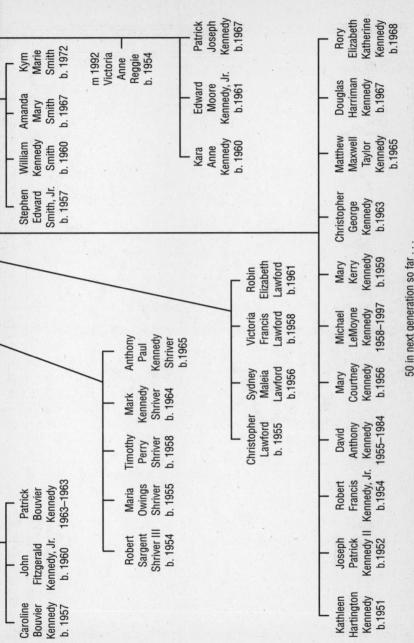

Traditional
Divisions of

ULSTER

CONNACHT
LEINSTER

MUNSTER

N

Atlantic Ocean

DONEGAL

NORTHERN
IRELAND

North Channel

Belfast

MAYO

SLIGO

LEITRIM

MONAGHAN

CAVAN

LOUTH

ROSCOMMON

LONGFORD

WESTMEATH

MEATH

Connemara

GALWAY

OFFALY

DUBLIN

Dublin

Irish Sea

CLARE

TIPPERARY

LAOIGHIS

KILDARE

WICKLOW

KILKENNY

CARLOW

LIMERICK

WEXFORD

KERRY

CORK

WATERFORD

St. George's Channel

IRELAND

ONE

Clannishness: Some Background

Who are Irish Americans?

When did most Irish come to America?

What kind of place did the Irish leave behind?

Who were the Irish before they came to America?

Who are Irish Americans?

They are descendants of people—or they are the people themselves—who hailed from an island in the North Atlantic and who, for reasons as negative as famine and as optimistic as opportunity, left their native land and landed in New York, Boston, and Philadelphia in the seventeenth, eighteenth, and nineteenth centuries (perhaps even in the fifteenth century or earlier, but we'll get to that later).

Or they are newcomers, winging in today to find fun or fortune, getting that green card and maybe even citizenship status, should they determine that the brave new world suits them.

Or they are native-born Americans so tied to the old land by immediate heritage that they seem far more Irish than Yank. **Eamon de Valera,** the dominant figure of the Irish State for much of the twentieth century, was born of Hispanic and Irish parentage in Brooklyn in 1882. **Frank McCourt** of *Angela's Ashes* fame is also Brooklyn born, though he's Limerick in his bones. The bridge between Ireland and America is a short one, well traveled in both directions. Definitions and sometimes even identities tend to blur.

Today Irish Americanism is generally perceived as something handed down by forebears from the primarily Roman Catholic Republic of Ireland, formerly the Free State of Ireland. This has everything to do with eternal religious and cultural divides between the northern and southern parts of the island, and with twentieth-century politics. The politics helps us to demarcate and to understand: The Republic of Ireland (founded in 1948), formerly the Free State of Ireland (established in 1921), *means* Ireland to those of ancient Irish heritage whose Irishness can be traced from the Celts through to the Catholics throughout the whole of the island (Northern Ireland not excepted). Northern Ireland, the country still formally aligned with Great Britain, is seen by Irish Republicans as both a real and symbolic manifestation of four centuries of conquest and persecution. By the second half of the sixteenth century, England had decided that Ireland must be brought in line with English ways—especially in matters of religion—and plans were made to fill the island with Protestants from England, Scotland, and Wales. Yeats's "war that ended in the Flight of the Earls"—the successful conquest of Ulster by British forces in the first decade of the seventeenth century—began the Protestant-minority domination of the Irish Catholic majority. There would follow, as the world knows, periodic Irish Republican (Catholic) resistance and intermittent war.

Of course there was war: Consider that during the so-called Protestant Ascendancy of the eighteenth century the country was ruled as a fiefdom by a minority that comprised but 10 percent of the sitting population. To this very day, many who are descended from Celtic Irish stock view their Protestant counterparts, even those who might have lived just as many generations on Irish soil, as the sons and daughters of invaders, usurpers, persecutors, vandals.

When the next step is taken from Irish to American soil, a certain irony creeps into this view. Under these rules, U.S. presidents Andrew Jackson, James K. Polk, Ulysses S. Grant, Woodrow Wilson, James Buchanan, Andrew Johnson, Chester A. Arthur, Grover Cleveland, Benjamin Harrison, William McKinley, and Bill Clinton would not be considered Irish American, descending as they did from the heavily Protestant North of Ireland. At the time of the signing of the Declaration of Independence, about one-sixth of the colonial population was of Ulster stock. Irish Americans face a perplexing question: Are these "patriots" not Irish Americans? And what do we make of Ronald Reagan, whose forebears were from Tipperary—but Protestant!

The question is particularly thorny when an American—whose history is steeped in ideals of egalitarianism, melting pots, and separation of church and state—gazes at it. When **John Rutledge** of South Carolina was named the second Chief Justice of the U.S. Supreme Court in 1795, he was considered a son of Ulster and therefore of Ireland. At the time, of course, Britain ruled all of Ireland (though opposition was ever present, as evinced by the unsuccessful United Irishmen's Rebellion of 1798). In our century, Britain presides in one part only, and "Ireland" in the other—a boundary has been drawn. So, two centuries later, Rutledge can be assigned to the Protestant, Northern, anti-Irish camp. He was not an Irish American, we (well, many of us) can claim. It's probably how Rutledge himself felt about it: His people were English not Irish; they traveled through Ireland to America; and now he, post-Revolution, was an American.

For the purposes of this book, we will take the standard view: Irish Americans are descended from those who feel well about Ireland, and the majority of these are linked to the Republic. But we will attempt to frame it, whenever useful, in a broader context. We will try to deal with *all* who were involved with America from that small island eleven miles off the British shore, and we will make distinctions where applicable. We'll tell you about the Scotch-Irish and their heavy impact on the nascent United States. And we'll tell you of the Boston Irish, and their imported contempt for all things Orange.

But when we speak of a sense of Irish Americanism, we are, it should be understood, speaking of that strain of Celtic Irishness that derives from the 95 percent of Roman Catholic Irish who inhabit the Republic. It is the relatives of these people who view themselves as Irish American, and they are the principal players in our drama.

A final note on this point: If the bridge from Dublin to Boston has always been direct, so too has the bridge from Belfast to London. Following the heavy emigration of Ulstermen from the north to the colonies in the eighteenth century, most of the Protestant Irish traffic has been with Britain, to which many Protestants have remained loyal. The Protestant Irish played a prominent role in the founding of the United States, and their descendants have continued to contribute to the American nation, but since the Revolution it has been the Catholic Irish who have set out for (or fled to) American shores at an always steady, sometimes rapid, rate.

When did most Irish come to America?

The greatest influx of Protestants occurred before the Revolution. Englishmen who found themselves in Ulster were, by nature, venturesome, and it is not surprising that some of them willingly became a big part of the colonial migration. As we shall see, many of these northern Irish and a few no less intrepid men from the south played significant roles in the founding of the United States. They fought bravely for American freedom against an English force made up of their former countrymen that included neighbors from Ulster. The American Revolution was itself a spur to immigration: British government troops that had been assigned to keep the peace in Ireland were reassigned to restore it in America, and many of them stayed on.

The Irish Catholic diaspora caused by the Great Potato Famine of the 1840s has never really ceased. While Irish marriage, birth, and death rates are similar to those of other European nations, the rate of emigration has always been much higher. Millions of principally Irish people are citizens of other countries, and the main target of Irish émigrés has always been America. During and immediately after the Famine (1845–1851), 1.7 million Irish landed in North America; at the turn of the twentieth century, they were still arriving at the rate of 500,000 to 1 million in each decade.

What kind of place did the Irish leave behind?

A lovely land, to be sure, but a troubled one.

Formerly a part of the Eurasian landmass—Ireland and England once coexisted!—the island is as far north as Labrador but lies in a temperate zone. Its interior central plain sits atop limestone and is surrounded by dramatic coastal highlands. The many lakes and bogs of the center make for serene scenery, while the wild, mountainous coasts of Cork, Donegal, Mayo, and Galway create fierce counterpoint only miles away. The island is only 302 miles long north to south, 171 miles wide east to west—about as big as Maine. Northern Ireland, with the awesome Mourne Mountains and the mystical seascapes of Portrush, surrenders nothing in beauty to the Republic: The fighting has never been over the sweetest parcel of land.

The Atlantic Ocean is no more than seventy miles from any location in Ireland, and therefore influences the island's weather each and every day. The southwesterly winds are usually mild—when they reverse, they can bring legendary tempests. The warm waters of the North Atlantic current keep everything moderate. The Gulf Stream is the fertilizer for palm trees on the south coast of Ireland, and on the off-coast "Garnish Island" of Glengarriff there are Italian-style gardens reminiscent of the Mediterranean. In January the temperature rarely drops to freezing, and in July it hardly ever gets above seventy. It does rain: thirty inches a year in the east to more than one hundred inches in some western areas. Of course, this keeps the fields lush and the livestock healthy.

It is, in another Irish irony, an exceedingly peaceful piece of land. That it has been disrupted so often and for such a long time by invasions and civil wars seems a violation of the natural order. But there it is.

Who were the Irish before they came to America?

Well, that will take a chapter or two to explain.

TWO

Ancient Ireland

What did the glaciers have to do
with who the Irish are?

How did those areas get deforested?

How big were the antlers of the giant Irish elk?

When were the first human settlements
made in Ireland?

What are the passage-graves?

What happened during the Bronze Age in Ireland?

Who were the Celts?

What is a druid?

Did druidic justice derive from a sense of honor among Celts or merely from barbarism?

What was the Fianna?

What is the difference between Gaelic, Celtic and the language Irish?

Is the word Ierne Irish?

What did the glaciers have to do with who the Irish are?

More than you might think, which is why we asked. Ireland experienced two large glaciations, maybe more, during the ice ages: One covered the whole of the island, and the other extended about as far south as Dublin. The glaciers rounded off the tops of mountains, and when they retreated they left "drift"—waste soils formerly frozen to the base of the ice—that was rich in limestone. When this topsoil was spread generally throughout the land, it made fertile what would otherwise have been impossible-to-farm areas heavy in granite and shale. The lush, farmer-friendly island owes its identity—its very greenness—to the glaciers.

A postscript: The glaciers also helped build the large peat bogs that made fire and fuel possible in deforested areas.

How did those areas get deforested?

The myth is that the rotten English came over and chopped down all the trees for shipbuilding. The English certainly did that, but many more trees were felled to make way for farming by the agriculturally inclined Irish.

How big were the antlers of the giant Irish elk?

Big.

Huge, in fact.

The antlers, perhaps the most prodigious ever to spring from a deer's forehead, were eight feet across; the animal itself stood six feet at its shoulders. By comparison the Alaska moose, the world's largest extant deer, has a shoulder height of up to seven and a half feet, but the American elk only grows to five feet high. The Lapland reindeer reaches four feet and our common white-tailed deer barely gets above three and a half feet at its shoulders.

Of what significance is this? Well, the abundant remains of Irish elk indicate that the early Stone Age hunter probably never reached Ireland. The massive elk roamed free and easy. The implication is that Ireland was untouched by man before the Mesolithic era, that transitional Stone Age period, 8,000 to 5,000 B.C., which bridged the Paleolithic and the Neolithic.

When were the first human settlements made in Ireland?

Probably about eight thousand years ago, perhaps even ten thousand years ago—a late debut for mankind in the prehistory of Europe. The settlers may have come by foot, crossing a Middle Stone Age land bridge from Scotland to Antrim, or they may have come by skin boats. These Mesolithic fishermen subsisted on the fruits of the sea as well as wild pig, fowl, and plants. Ireland was only sparsely inhabited during the Mesolithic period, and remnants that have been found there are mostly small flint blades.

Centuries later—approximately six thousand years ago—Neolithic farmers arrived. They continued the Mesolithic tradition of hunkering down near the sea but also moved inland. They were Ireland's first crop growers and spent their days tilling the soil and raising animals: enterprises identified with the island for millennia to come. The Neolithic people inhabited the entire island, and some took to the hilltops to build their shelters. Their tools—stone axes, looms—were sophisticated for the period. They altered the landscape, building stone walls, houses of substance, and many megalithic monuments.

What are the passage-graves?

Different burial patterns were imported by the Neolithic people from England to Ireland, many of them involving great stones, of which the passage-graves or passage-tombs are the most impressive and intriguing. They are beautiful, decorated, labyrinthian works of carved stone, usually set on hilltops or in cemeteries—as awe-inspiring and inscrutable as Stonehenge. On the Boyne River is a community of these tombs that is extremely eerie. The passage-graves, sometimes built with a solar orientation, were certainly a link to the gods—to transport the dead, to pay homage. They represent a vivid first chapter in Ireland's remarkable religious history.

What happened during the Bronze Age in Ireland?

The island was blessed with rich copper deposits from which to fashion cauldrons, tools, spearheads, and shields. Jewelry of copper, bronze, and gold was made in Ireland. Sean Duffy writes in *The Macmillan Atlas of Irish History*: "[T]he prehistoric goldsmiths' craft probably [reached] its peak at about 700 B.C. In fact, more gold-crafted objects survive from this period in Ireland than in any other country in western or northern Europe, and some objects of Irish type have been found in Britain and the continent, suggesting an active export trade."

Ireland was joining the wider world.

Who were the Celts?

Bob Cousy, Bill Russell, Larry Bird . . .

No, actually, the Celts were an Indo-European people that probably originated more than one thousand years B.C. near present-day Austria and Germany. They developed an Iron Age culture early on, and as they migrated east to west across Europe they wielded their weapons with barbaric flair. The Celts were not a single tribe but a network of tribes and were feared by the Greeks and Romans to the south of them: The Boii tribe from Bohemia invaded Italy in about 400 B.C. and sacked Rome in 390 B.C. (By 192 B.C., Rome had regained the upper hand with the Celts.) Through the first millennium B.C., the tribes occupied much of central and western Europe; they spoke several related dialects that are called Celtic—hence they are called Celts. As the tribes spread and migrated, much of what was Celtic was assimilated; the language and traditions survived most intact in far western Europe.

The Celts had arrived in Britain by the fifth century B.C., and in northern Ireland by approximately 300 B.C., probably by way of Scotland—certain evidences of Iron Age signposts like hill forts have been found in Antrim. The religious and cultural traditions they

MAY THE ROAD RISE TO MEET YOU

packed in with them defined Ireland for centuries and linger even today, whispering through the massive, usurping influence of Irish Christianity. It is important to note that the Irish Celts would eventually be *converted* to Christianity—not thrown out by a bunch of marauding Christians—and a converted people is never able to shut out the echoes of its origins.

Moreover, while Rome had conquered Britain by the first century A.D. and was exporting its version of civilization, a Roman plan to annex Ireland (there was such a plan, at least according to the historian Tacitus) was never carried out. Therefore, until the Vikings came in the ninth century, the Celts were on their own to grow deep roots of tradition and language in the Irish soil—and soul.

Early Celtic Ireland was divided into several separate kingdoms, or clans (*tuatha*), in the classically Celtic way. In each kingdom was a monarch, an aristocracy, and families who held serfs and slaves. Cattle, wheat, barley, and hay were commodities that fueled the exclusively rural society.

Celtic religion seems to be a spooky thing, full of night rituals, sacrifices, and ghosts. The sense of mystery inspired the title of an 1893 Yeats collection of supernatural writings: *The Celtic Twilight*. There were animal gods, to be sure, and probably human sacrifice. The Celts would move fast against an enemy and then fight with abandon, seemingly as careless with their own lives as with those of their foes. A deep Celtic faith in an afterlife was probably a factor in this reckless Celtic fury on earth.

What is a druid?

Webster's tries to tell us that a druid is "one of an ancient Celtic priesthood appearing in Irish and Welsh sagas and Christian legends as magicians and wizards," which of course implies that druids aren't real—but they were.

A druid was a member of a specific learned class among the Celts of Gaul, Britain, and Ireland—probably a priest of some sort. A druidic pupil would study for twenty years, committing the rules of druidism to memory. Julius Caesar claimed that the druidic order began in Britain and was involved with worship and spiritual rituals now deemed voodooistic, including sacrifices and the interpretation of oracles. But druids weren't seen as unduly spectral or even odd in their time; they were perceived as teachers, philosophers, judges. According to Caesar, druids rendered verdicts in Celtic disputes and

10

meted out penalties. They held quite a hammer: They could sever a perpetrator's link with the gods, since the Celts believed that spiritual communion was possible only through a trained mediator.

The druidic order had religious responsibilities that outweighed any governmental or educational duties. For the Celts, druids were the principal bridge between the natural and supernatural worlds. It is generally held that druids believed in the immortality of the soul. Certain aspects of druidic rites add the Halloweenish cast we associate with druidism: Druids worshiped in the forest and supposedly were able to predict the future. It was written that they practiced human sacrifice, either as propitiation to the gods or as a means of divining the future. While archaeological evidence of human sacrifice is scarce, it is generally accepted that druids were in charge of all manner of sacrifice made by the community.

In the heroic literature of Ireland, druids were often portrayed as wizards. They could see into tomorrow or whip up a frightful storm in a jiff. They were more potent than any mere British druid: They could pinpoint the proper moment to join in battle. (Interestingly, druids were not bound to serve in the military; they enjoyed many aristocratic privileges.) Cathbad summoned his fellow druids to help him raise black clouds to hinder an opposing force. Other druids raised mists to slow Saint Patrick.

As the Patrick legend indicates, Christians viewed druids as forces to be reckoned with and therefore depicted them as deceitful and villainous. The Romans painted a similar wicked portrait, citing their professed abhorrence of the druids' practice of human sacrifice. Romans may well have thought this a nasty bit of business, or they may have simply seen its opposition as a way to assail the power and prestige held by druids. As respected and educated leaders among the Celts, druids represented an entity that could conceivably unify Celtic tribes into a forceful nation; therefore, they had to be destabilized. Christians took the Roman tack in depicting druids as dark, deadly, and evil.

The picture of druids we have today owes much to their enemies' representations. In their time, those negative images were effective. Druidism faded in Ireland and elsewhere very shortly after the arrival of Christianity.

Did druidic justice derive from a sense of honor among Celts or merely from barbarism?

There was honor. Perhaps the best example of Celtic ethical values is found in "Instruction of a King," an ancient Irish poem supposedly written by **Cormac mac Airt,** the legendary lawgiver who died in A.D. 267. (The poem was probably written later, but because it's ascribed to Cormac its very intent is to convey a sense of Celticness. Although Cormac maintained that he eventually believed in the Christian God, his was certainly the pre-Christian, Celtic-chieftain era in Ireland.) Here is an excerpt:

> *I was a listener in woods,*
> *I was a gazer at stars,*
> *I was unseeing among secrets,*
> *I was silent in a wilderness,*
> *I was conversational among many,*
> *I was mild in the mead-hall,*
> *I was fierce in the battlefield,*
> *I was gentle in friendship,*
> *I was a nurse to the sick,*
> *I was weak toward the strengthless,*
> *I was strong toward the powerful,*
>
> *I was not arrogant though I was wise,*
> *I was not a promiser though I was rich,*
> *I was not boastful though I was skilled,*
> *I would not speak ill of the absent,*
> *I would not reproach, but I would praise,*
> *I would not ask, but I would give—*

For it is through these habits that the young become old and kingly warriors.

The poet presaged an era of Christian values, later in his poem:

> *Do not deride the old, though you are young;*
> *Nor the poor, though you are wealthy;*
> *Nor the lame, though you are swift;*
> *Nor the blind, though you are given sight;*

> *Nor the sick, though you are strong;*
> *Nor the dull, though you are clever;*
> *Nor the foolish, though you are wise . . .*

Feeling warm and fuzzy about the Celts yet? Well, here's how the poem ends:

> *If you be too harsh, you will be broken,*
> *If you be too feeble, you will be crushed.*

Now *that's* Celtic.

What was the Fianna?

It was a mythical band of soldiers in the employ of the mythical **Finn MacCool** (Fionn mac Cumhaill) in the mythical Fionn cycle of stories. The Fianna defends Ireland against forces both earthly and spectral. *The Oxford Companion to Irish Literature* describes the cycle: "One of the characteristics of the cycle is its frequent celebration of the beauty of nature, and birdsong, mountain, river, and seashore are frequently evoked in sensitive and vivid language." The Fianna lives out-of-doors, close to nature, the Irish way.

The cycle is set in the third century; in fact, Cormac is a character. But the stories were handed down orally for ages; St. Patrick is in there, too. What comes to us is essentially medieval literature about a Celtic time.

This slim volume of ours cannot delve into the great wealth of Irish mythology. The Fianna and the cycle are mentioned here to illustrate early in our text the great literary and storytelling traditions of both the Irish and Irish Americans, as well as the serious attention paid by the Irish to their tales. Eamon de Valera named his twentieth-century political party the Fianna Fáil, "Soldiers of Destiny." Can you imagine an American party named the Huckleberries after our own Finn, whose sense of right and racial justice we admire? No way, no how. But to the Irish, literature is air, it's breathing.

This passage from the cycle reveals how hard it was to become a member of the Fianna:

Not a man of them was taken till his hair had been interwoven into braids on him and he started at a run through Ireland's woods; while they, seeking to wound him, followed in his wake, there having been between him and them but one forest bough by way of interval at first. Should he be overtaken, he was wounded and not received into the Fianna after. If his weapons had quivered in his hand, he was not taken. Should a branch in the wood have disturbed anything of his hair out of its braiding, neither was he taken. If he had cracked a dry stick under his foot as he ran he was not taken. Unless that at full speed he had both jumped a stick level with his brow, and stooped to pass under one even with his knee, he was not taken. Also, unless without slackening his pace he could with his nail extract a thorn from his foot, he was not taken into the Fianship: but if he performed all this he was of Finn's people.

What is the difference between Gaelic, Celtic, and the language Irish?

The term *Celtic languages* refers to the tongues spoken by western Celts, including Celtberian (Spain), Gaulish (France and Italy), Gaelic, and British. Many forms of these languages have died out (for instance, the Pictish and Cumbrian varieties of British are long gone), but British survives today as Welsh and Breton, while Gaelic survives as Scottish Gaelic and Irish. The Irish language is frequently referred to as Gaelic, and that's understandable. The dialectal split into Modern Irish (or Irish Gaelic), Scottish Gaelic, and Manx Gaelic is only a few centuries old.

Irish Gaelic, known to linguists as Goidelic, is ancient. The history of the language's rise and decline is as much a political narrative as a cultural one.

Goidelic was an Irish export, not an import. The Celts brought their language to the island, then became one people with those who were already there. Over centuries, the newly assimilated Irish citizenry developed distinctions within their language and culture that were unlike any surviving in Britain or on the continent (where Rome's influence was spreading and being absorbed). When Rome's reach began to diminish, Goidelic-speaking Irish hopped from the island back to Britain. In the sixth century these "Scoti" became a real force in Wales, Argyll, and elsewhere. They burgeoned, and by the eleventh century Irish-speaking people dominated not only their homeland but all of Scotland, to which they leant a name.

The Anglo-Normans began to encroach, and, gradually, southern and eastern Scotland turned toward English. By the fourteenth century Goidelic was relegated on the British isle to the Highlands, the Hebrides, and parts of Galloway. Meanwhile, in Ireland, the native tongue was fighting a good fight against Anglo-Norman insurgency and was still dominant by the seventeenth century. Then London got nasty, and the Tudor and Stuart resettlements, capped by Cromwell's settlement and then the Penal Laws, made certain that the Irish learned class was an English-speaking one. By the mid-eighteenth century, Irish was gutter language in its own home state, spoken by only one-quarter of the population, the poorest of the people.

The demise of the language might have seemed sure at some point in the late 1800s, but death never came. Why, then, did Irish survive when Pictish did not? First, certain small southwestern enclaves remained untouched by the English onslaught. Second, the Irish language was, symbolically, at the very heart of Irish-English animosities. For obvious reasons, the native tongue became a flashpoint issue for Republicans: *They've usurped our land, our law, our language.* The Gaelic League was established in 1893 for the preservation of Irish; it sponsored classes, social gatherings that featured Irish dance and customs, the adoption of Saint Patrick's Day as a national holiday, and resistance in general. It opened a publishing house and by 1909 had printed 150 books. It put language on the national agenda.

In the twentieth century, the struggle to retain Irish has ebbed and flowed, much as the Troubles have. There seems little question, however, that this is, ultimately, a finger-in-the-dike proposition. According to the *Oxford Companion to Irish Literature*:

> In Britain and Ireland the [Celtic] languages survived to modern times but in an ever-decreasing geographical area. Welsh, with perhaps half a million speakers, is the best preserved, but is spoken by a mere 20 percent of the population of Wales. In Scotland, where there are about 80,000 speakers of Scottish Gaelic, the language has practically died out on the mainland but survives in the Hebrides. For Breton there are no reliable figures available, and estimates range between 20,000 and 700,000. In Ireland there is a similar disparity between a perhaps pessimistic estimate of 10,000 speakers living in the Irish-speaking communities and the certainly over-optimistic figure of one million. . . . The inevitable outcome of the decline indicated by these figures is that the Celtic languages will soon disappear as traditional community languages, whether or not they survive in some form among groups of individuals dedicated to their preservation.

Even with that elegiac note in mind, in areas of Ireland collectively known as the Gaeltacht, Irish Gaelic is used as an everyday language by ten thousand or more souls who are reaching back toward their country's beginnings.

Is the word Ierne *Irish?*

No, actually, it's Greek, or at least it was used by the Alexandrian Greek geographer Ptolemy. Writing in the second century, he offered the first detailed account of Ireland; his sources were probably Romans in western England who were familiar with Ireland. Ptolemy attempted to delineate tribes in various parts of the country, from the Dal Riata of Antrim down to the Erainn in Munster. The Greek name for Ireland, *Ierne,* probably is derived from Eiram Celts, which backward became a version of the Irish word from the country, *Eriu,* and finally *Eire*.

In the years just after the birth of Christ the Celts are in control of all of Ireland, but other peoples are becoming aware of the land. Everything from the Roman view of civilization to the Norman view of barbarianism to the very first whisperings of Christianity lay immediately east, just a few miles off the Irish shore. And all these things were bound to come across.

THREE

The Middle Ages: Christianity Comes to Ireland, and the Vikings Invade

(Meanwhile, the Irish Discover America)

When did the first Christians arrive in Ireland?

Who was Saint Patrick?

Was Ireland's revered Patrick actually English?

Did Patrick really drive the snakes out of Ireland?

If there were snakes, where would they have gone?

What writings did Patrick leave behind?

Did the efficiency of the Christian Irish movement depend on charismatic, heroic figures, such as Patrick and Colum Cille?

What were the Dark Ages?

How did the Irish save civilization?

Why didn't the Irish get credit for saving civilization before now?

What is the Book of Kells?

What was the Golden Age of Ireland?

What was an Irish monk's life like?

Who was Saint Brendan?

How large was the Viking invasion of Ireland, and what was its impact?

Who was Brian Boru?

When did the first Christians arrive in Ireland?

Hard to say, easy to guess. There may have been British and Gaulic Christian missionaries in south-central Ireland as early as the late fourth century; if there were, their impact was negligible. By the early fifth century, Rome's reach into England was tenuous, and so the Irish were not only trading with the northern provinces, but also raiding them. There were Christians living there, and the Irish certainly exchanged pleasantries. By A.D. 400, some Irish knew of Christ and the teachings being handed down in His name.

By the end of that century, all of Ireland would be aware, and much of it would be converted.

Although Palladius had arrived by 431, appointed by the pope to serve "the Irish who believe in Christ," a far more charismatic figure followed who would not only make Ireland aware, but who would, over time, make the world aware of where Ireland stood.

There were, to be sure, several bishops working in Ireland in the mid-fifth century. Palladius, Auxilius, and Iserninus independently barnstormed southeastern areas, while Secondinas traveled a bit farther north and east. Indeed, Christianity's reach into what is now the Republic of Ireland was accomplished early on by missionaries other than Patrick. He worked mainly in the northern half of the island.

While it is true that Ireland grew aware of Christianity within a century, the island did not fully embrace the movement with such expedience. In the seventh century there is still much opposition found in the written record. That such a record exists is due to the Christians. Christianity brought the written word to Ireland. Celtic traditions and even law had always been handed down orally; literature had been seen as an evil thing that could destroy memory. Now, shockingly, there was Latin on the page, and Latin schools were opening down the path from druidic ones. Some Irish saw Christianity as an intruder; to others it was a godsend.

What Christianity has meant to Ireland through the centuries is, of course, the whole story. What it meant at the time is that Ireland, which had always been just beyond the reach of the Empire—an empire that was now receding—had finally been touched by Rome. This European outpost, which received the word centuries after the barbarians, would become a flashpoint, even a cornerstone of Roman Christianity. The irony would certainly be appreciated in the pubs.

Who was Saint Patrick?

Patrick was a real man—he was not the Finn MacCool of Christianity. His *Confessio* and *Letter to the Soldiers of Coroticus* are real documents, though the *Lorica* (or *Breastplate*) *of St. Patrick* was surely not from his hand.

Based largely on the *Confessio*, his biography was embellished by those forwarding his mission after his time. His father was a municipal official and deacon on the west coast when Rome was in charge; his native name was Succat. He was captured at sixteen by Irish raiders and sent to Ireland "with many thousands of people" as a slave; he spent six years tending sheep and pigs for Milchu on Mount Slemish in Antrim. He escaped and fled back to England, then heard the "voice of the Irish" from the Woods of Voclut, calling him back: "We ask thee, boy, come and walk among us once more." He studied for the priesthood and arrived in Ireland with other

clerics. He gained quick renown by beating druids at various supernatural games, such as reversing eclipses of the sun and by driving the snakes out of Ireland. Early in the game, Patrick was larger
than life.

Patrick said he baptized thousands during his mission, and this is
probably true: The fifth century saw an amazingly large conversion
of Celts to Christianity. He ordained priests, he founded churches.
He gave gifts to kings and judges, and his success indicates that
bribery of the chieftain and even druidic classes must have been
something at which he was adept. He had learned to be tough at a
young age, and he exercised his learning.

History takes Patrick at his word for much of this story; however,
the first wave of monasticism in Ireland featured participants from
Brittany, Wales, and Italy, and "Patrick" could have come from any
one of these places. We know Patrick, or we think we do, yet his real
identity is shrouded.

In the west of Ireland there's a mountain topping out at barely
above twenty-five hundred feet. It's called Croagh Patrick, and on
Crom Dubh's Sunday, the last Sunday of July, the pilgrims climb its
scree sides on bended knees and bleeding bare feet to worship in his
name. At the base of the summit cone there's a monument to Saint
Benignus, where the pilgrims say Lord's Prayers and Hail Marys before proceeding on. (They circle as they pray, and each round is
called a *deiseal*.) More prayers are said at the summit, one after another *deiseal* made around "Patrick's Bed."

Why?

Because it's a fact, a certifiable fact: Patrick fasted here in 441. It's
a big old mountain that dominates the Mayo coast, and Patrick was
here, praying for the country and feeling the pain of his fast, in 441.

Ireland's a nation without enough certifiable facts—especially
happy or even moderate ones—and when you can seize upon a fact
that is at the very core of your being and belief, you grasp it hard
and firm.

A quick for instance: "Columbkille's Bed." There's a cross there in
the Glen of Donegal—and more, too. There's a Stone Age ring
called Saint Columkille's Chapel, and a seven-station trip to be
taken that marks Columbkille's (or Columba's, or Colum Cille's,
most properly) penitential route. There's all this, and there's a cult.
But it's nothing like Patrick's.

Why?

Colum Cille was real, too. Saint Columba was of the same clan as the O'Neills of Tyrone, and so is related (as we'll see) to both the great Brian Boru and the great John Fitzgerald Kennedy. He came to Donegal, founded a monastery, converted many Celts, and set up churches in Derry, Swords, Durrow, and Kells. He spurred a rising against the king up north in 561 and was defeated. In exile he founded a monastery on Iona. His order spread back to Scotland and Ireland. When he died in 597, he was about seventy-six years old. Colum Cille was immortalized in various "legends," not to mention in a play by Brian Friel. In gaeltacht Donegal he is as revered as revered can be, to be sure. But by and large, he's no Patrick.

Why?

Because . . . he's not real enough. Saint Columba seems mythic, whereas Patrick, never mind the snakes, seems real. The Irish, such tellers of tales, always have problems with this sort of thing.

Patrick left behind documents. Colum Cille left behind a poem, perhaps the first and certainly one of the most beautiful poems written for posterity in Ireland. It concerned how he wanted to be buried on Iona and can be seen as a precursor to Yeats's "Under Ben Bulben." Columba's prayer reads:

> *On some island I long to be,*
> *a rocky promontory looking on'*
> *the coiling surface of the sea.*
> *To see the shift from ebb tide*
> *to flood and tell my secret name:*
> *He who set his back on Ireland.*

He died on Iona, it is believed. Today we choose Patrick, because he seems less like a kind of Irish creation, less like a Finn MacCool, than does Colum Cille.

So be it.

Was Ireland's revered Patrick actually English?

Ah, glad you asked. Patrick could have been called British, but not English. In his day the British isle was peopled by Romanized Celts, whom we call Britons, and in its northern reaches by the un-Romanized Picts. Patrick was a Romanized Celtic Briton, certainly *not* an Englishman.

Did Patrick really drive the snakes out of Ireland?

Of course he didn't. There were no snakes. Most of what has been written or handed down about Patrick, including the idea that he was the exclusive or even principal courier of Christianity to Ireland, is debatable or even directly refutable. There's more charm than truth to the Patrick story, and the fact is Ireland has never been rich in Reptilia or Amphibia. The island has seen one species each of frog, toad and newt, and only one species of reptile: the viviparous or common lizard. No snakes at all, nor any sign that there ever were any. The Ice Age ended thirteen thousand years ago in Ireland, and although the land bridges existed for another eight thousand years, nothing slithered across that wasn't Celtic. Evidence indicates that snakes made it right up to the bridges but no farther. Five thousand years ago the last land bridge submerged and at least one reptile on the English side had missed the boat.

If there were snakes, where would they have gone?

A popular Irish American joke goes: After Patrick drove the snakes out of Ireland, they all went to New York and became cops. Brendan Behan saw them a generation or two later as judges.

What writings did Patrick leave behind?

Two.

The more famous and eloquent is the *Confessio*, Patrick's telling of his hard life and troubled times in Ireland and England. This brief excerpt has nothing to do with his own biography but tells the story of another:

> Among others, a blessed Irishwoman of noble birth, beautiful, full-grown, whom I had baptized, came to us after some days for a particular reason: she told us that she had received a message from a messenger of God, and he admonished her to be a virgin of Christ and draw near to God. Thanks be to God, on the sixth day after this she most laudably and eagerly chose what all virgins of Christ do. Not that their fathers agree with them; no—they often suffer persecution and undeserved reproaches from their parents; and yet their number is ever increasing. How many have been reborn there so as to be of our kind, I do not know—not to mention widows and those who practice continence.

Clearly, he was a master recruiter. It is said that while trying to convert a group of Irish, Patrick, though a great teacher, was having trouble explaining the concept of the Trinity. Noticing some shamrocks, he plucked one, and used its three leaves, held together in a unit, to get the idea across: "three in one."

Patrick never wrote about the shamrock, and no early account of the saint's life mentioned this sermon. (In fact, the first mention of the word itself came in the sixteenth century when the English herbalist John Gerard wrote that white and red clovers were "called in Irish *Shamrockes*." In fact, the Irish word *seamrog* means young clover, so Gerard was close indeed.) Yet the Patrick tale endures and is the most common explanation for how the shamrock, a simple but elegant clover (or, sometimes, a species of black medick or wood sorrel, either of which might also have three leaves and appear quite like a clover)—never flowering, ever green—became the national symbol of Ireland. Early in the eighteenth century, the cross of ribbons that used to be sported on Saint Patrick's Day was replaced by shamrocks tucked in hats, pinned to lapels. By the end of that century shamrocks were seen on Irish flags and badges; shamrocks were cited in the poetry of Thomas Moore (1779–1852). When George IV visited Dublin in 1821 he "blessed" the shamrock and wore a bunch of the plants in his hat. When Queen Victoria visited more than a half-century later, she wore a golden one emblazoned on her dress. She ordered, as well, that soldiers in Irish brigades sport the clover on Saint Patrick's Day in memory of comrades fallen in the Boer War.

By the way, contrary to popular legend, the shamrock is not unique to Ireland: This kind of clover is native to places from Scandinavia to the Caucasus Mountains and, in a nifty bit of symbolism, it is, like the Irish themselves, a naturalized alien in North America. And contrary to established belief, the shamrock is not the ancient symbol of the Republic—the harp is. The harp had been used for centuries in Leinster arms and flags, and in Tudor times it started to appear on Irish arms: a gold harp on a field of Saint Patrick's blue. Today it appears on Irish coins and on the presidential standard.

Did the efficiency of the Christian Irish movement depend on charismatic, heroic figures, such as Patrick and Colum Cille?

Yes and no. As with any missionary movement, charisma and leadership qualities are large pluses. But in the case of the Irish conversion, perhaps the most important factors were the number of monks who came, the general dispersal of them, and the specificity and power of their message. The quick success of Christianity's blanketing of Ireland depended on an influx of bishops and a general building of bishoprics. The fact that the early Christian churches were founded near ancient sites of spiritual importance—Patrick's center, Armagh, was very near the holy site at Amain Macha, for instance—suggests a strategy. The church movement meant to co-opt the Celts before converting them. It was very suggestive when, all of a sudden, monasteries bloomed in Ireland like lilies in the spring—and right where you had once gone to worship in your different way.

Irish Christian schools, which became quite the thing since they had the written word, were monastic. Monasteries became town centers; bishops took on the powers usually accorded mayors. Monks busied themselves transcribing, novices busied themselves learning.

This activity turned out to be a very good thing, for elsewhere in Europe the Dark Ages were descending. Once again, as when Ireland remained Celtic in the face of Romanism just across the sea, the small island's remoteness would assign it a unique role to play. And in this case, the assignment was all for the general good.

What were the Dark Ages?

The Dark Ages were a time in Western European history when the barbarians had the upper hand. If you don't distinguish between the Dark Ages and the Middle Ages—even the end of which was reasonably dark—this era stretches all the way from the fall of the Western Roman Empire (476) to the rise of Charlemagne, the Renaissance, the invention of printing, Columbus's voyage to America in 1492, the Reformation. At the beginning of the Dark Ages Christianity was a struggling religion; by medieval times it was a cultural, political, and religious force.

The darkest days of the Dark Ages were the fourth through seventh centuries, as barbarian cultures were not only routing Rome but also busily destroying the great art and literature that Rome had produced. This epoch was simultaneous with Ireland's shining hour, its Golden Age, its heroic moment when it saved civilization.

How did the Irish save civilization?

In 1995 Irish American **Thomas Cahill,** then the religion editor at Doubleday, flattered his ancestors with the presumptuously, marvelously titled *How the Irish Saved Civilization*. While he found welcome support in a community that already figured it had contributed everything worth saving anyway, Cahill and his eminently readable and often witty history found readers elsewhere, too. The account of how Irish monks and scribes, influenced by Saint Patrick himself, were responsible for preserving Western culture while Europe burned became a national best-seller. The longish answer to this particular question is to be found, presented with considerable charm, in Cahill's book—and we point you that way. The short answer, presented with considerable debt to Cahill, follows.

While learning on the Continent was being stifled and libraries were being lost forever, the manuscripts of Greek and Latin writers, both pagan and Christian, were being assiduously copied down by monks on the fabled "isle of saints and scholars," who would eventually set out with missionary zeal to relaunch civilization (as the West knows it) throughout Dark Age Europe—with a distinctively Celtic point of view. In other words, all that we know is Latin via Dublin.

Therefore, Saint Patrick gets the credit for creating the conditions that allowed medieval civilization to develop its spirit from Irish roots. He returned to Ireland as a missionary bishop around 432, which was just over twenty years after the sack of the city of Rome by Alaric the Goth. This was the salvo that led to the fall of Rome itself, which was of course the salvo that plunged the Continent into the Dark Ages. But in unconquered Ireland, Patrick is speaking out against the practice of slavery, which brought him to the island as a boy, and encouraging learning, asceticism, and the monastic life.

It was in the monasteries that the great heritage of Western civilization was faithfully and often artfully compiled and preserved, first for Ireland, then the Continent, then America, then the world. These arduously copied books were tied to the monks' waists—and they made their way back into a world that hadn't seen them for centuries.

And that is how, as Thomas Cahill explained at lovelier length, the Irish saved civilization.

Why didn't the Irish get credit for saving civilization before now?

Thomas Cahill blames a familiar foe. He reminds us that the history we are familiar with from schools and standard texts was written largely by Protestant English and Anglo-Saxon Americans. One writes, of course, from one's own vantage. Cahill asserts, "Just as certain contemporary historians have been discovering that such redactors are not always reliable when it comes to the contributions of, say, women or African-Americans, we should not be surprised to find out that such story tellers have overlooked a tremendous contribution in the distant past that was both Celtic and Catholic, a contribution without which European civilization would have been impossible."

What is the Book of Kells?

"The work of an angel, not of a man," said Giraldus Cambrensis from the great distance of the twelfth century.

It is the finest illuminated manuscript from the Golden Age. As Cahill writes, "From its earliest manifestations literacy had a decorative aspect. How could it be otherwise, since implicit in all pictograms, hieroglyphs, and letters is some cultural esthetic, some answer to the question, What is most beautiful?"

The Book of Kells is beautiful; moreover, in its day, it was highly influential. The monks at work on it employed not only a rounded script but also a more readable hand that, once it was seen on the Continent, became the script of choice. The Book of Kells has something to say about the way we read and write today.

It was compiled in the eighth or ninth century by three different scribe monks. It was said to be the gospel as preached by Colum Cille. It was kept in the monastery at Kells, County Meath—a monastery founded in 807 after the Vikings raided the nearby island monastery at Iona. The manuscript is a Latin copy of the four gospels; the initials are lavishly decorated; the beautiful illustrations are vibrant and elaborate. (The "Virgin and Child" and the "Arrest of Christ" are magnificent, but the masterpiece is the famous "Chi

Rho.") The paintings are complex; the masters who designed them were clearly assisted by a whole scriptorium of monks.

The manuscript was kept at Kells until at least 1192. Then the Columbian monastery there turned Augustinian, and the book began to move around.

It now resides in Trinity College, Dublin, where each day they turn a page to display the exquisite next one.

What was the Golden Age of Ireland?

The Golden Age is remembered even today as Ireland's shining hour. It is what the scholars and historians call the period we've just described, when there was peace on the island and a forceful, society-wide interest in language and learning. The fact that it is remembered romantically as the Golden Age has something to do with the abundance of clouds that have beset other eras, epochs, periods, and ages in the history of the Emerald Isle.

As soon as the Vikings ended the Golden Age, the Irish realized how great it had been and how much they had lost. A few lines from a ninth-century poem, "Ireland's Golden Age," written by Donatus of Fiesole, an Irish monk then living in Italy, reflect the view:

> *The noblest share of earth is the far western world*
> *Whose name is written Scotia in the ancient books;*
> *Rich in goods, in silver, jewels, cloth and gold,*
> *Being to the body in air and mellow soil.*
> *With honey and with milk flow Ireland's lovely plains,*
> *With silk and arms, abundant fruit, with art and men.*
>
> *Worthy are the Irish to dwell in this their land*
> *A race of men renowned in war, in peace, in faith.*

What was an Irish monk's life like?

For a small taste, sample this anonymous ninth-century poem called "The Hermit's Song," which is surely about an Irish monk and his view of the ideal monastery:

> *I wish, O Son of the living God,*
> *O ancient, eternal King,*

For a hidden little hut in the wilderness
That it may be my dwelling.

An all-grey lithe little lark
To be by its side,
A clear pool to wash away sins
Through the grace of the Holy Spirit.

Quite near, a beautiful wood,
Around it on every side,
To nurse many-voiced birds,
Hiding it with its shelter.

And facing the south for warmth;
A little brook across its floor,
A choice land with many gracious gifts
Such as be good for every plant.

A few men of sense—
We will tell their number—
Humble and obedient,
To pray to the King:—

Four times three, three times four,
Fit for every need,
Twice six in the church,
Both north and south:—

Six pairs
Besides myself,
Praying forever to the King
Who makes the sun shine.

A pleasant church and with the linen altar-cloth,
A dwelling for God from Heaven;
Then, shining candles
Above the pure white Scriptures.

One house for all to go to
For the care of the body,

Without ribaldry, without boasting,
Without thought of evil.

This is the husbandry I would take,
I would choose, and will not hide it:
Fragrant leek,
Hens, salmon, trout, bees.

Raiment and food enough for me
From the King of fair fame,
And I be sitting for a while
Praying God in every place.

Who was Saint Brendan?

He was a monk and the founder of a great monastery at Clonfert in the sixth century. And it's possible that he was the European who discovered America.

Pardon me?

Saint Brendan might have been the one to discover America.

Once more, please? A fellow named Brendan . . .

Yes. Brendan. First from the Old World to find the New. Got it?

And you will explain, of course?

Of course.

And, a word of caution before we plunge in: The founding might even have occurred before Brendan. It could have been made by pre-Christian Irishmen—Celts and such. Our story, then:

What American schoolboy or schoolgirl hasn't heard about the momentous discovery of the homeland by Christopher Columbus, the Italian navigator-sailor employed by Isabella of Spain, who sailed the ocean blue in 1492? Or, in more advanced history classes, that the Viking Leif Eriksson beat Chris to the punch by landing in Labrador around 1000?

Well, a case can and has been made for a far earlier Celtic voyage.

It has long been rumored that Brendan the Navigator—part-time monk, full-time adventurer—sailed his boat too far west one time and whacked into North America. The story of Brendan's quest for the "Land of Promise and of the Saints" has been translated into many languages, and in our time young sailors have tried to replicate Brendan's voyage in a similar handmade boat (and have got as far as Newfoundland).

Most historians will have none of it, but compelling arguments are forwarded at regular intervals by Hibernophiles. Take, for instance, the narrative as laid out in Robert Ellis Cahill's "Collectible Classic" pamphlet *The Old Irish of New England*. This is the most exciting.

Cahill rests his theory largely on a place he and others call Mystery Hill Caves in Salem, New Hampshire. The caves there closely resemble the little rock huts called beehives and the cavelike chambers that were tunneled into the earth by Celts building the passage-graves. Some of the Salem caves do resemble diggings of the Fir-Bolgs and the Tuatha De Danaan Celts who thrived before the colonization of the Milesian Celts hundreds of years before the coming of Christ. Other caves similar to those at Mystery Hill had been built by druids and the first Christian monks.

Cahill determined that he was dealing with more than coincidence, and then he came upon the work of William Goodwin, a retired insurance executive and amateur archaeologist from Hartford, Connecticut. Goodwin had already studied the half-mile of rock ruins and man-made underground chambers at Mystery Hill and, in 1937, had written an essay, "The Ruins of Great Ireland in New England," which had remained unpublished until 1946. It seemed to make great sense to Cahill.

Goodwin had concluded that the site was once a Celtic-influenced monastery built by Irish Christian monks in the tenth century. The professional archaeologists who looked into Salem at the time disagreed, saying the stone structures were nothing more than the food warehouses of colonial Americans, or possibly the tunnelings of indigenous tribes, or perhaps remnants of a Viking village.

But there was a rub: *Most* of the archaeologists, then and now, felt that the caves represented neither the work of colonial (seventeenth- and eighteenth-century) settlers nor that of the native inhabitants of the area.

One of the more interesting of Goodwin's finds was a large rock slab with a deep groove carved into its edge. This was recognized by

Frank Glynn, president of the Connecticut Archaeological Society, as an ancient "sacrificial table": The blood of the animals would drain into the grooves. Mindful that Celtic druids were adept at sacrifice and that the earliest Christian monks were regulars at the ritualized killings of animals, Glynn concluded that rather than being the site of a Christian monastery, Mystery Hill had been the home of Bronze Age druids who'd traveled to what is now New England as early as the third century B.C.

Wait a minute, wait a minute! This was about Brendan! Wasn't this about the Middle Ages?

Well, yes. We'll get back to Brendan. Glynn's is just one more theory. To continue:

In 1956 an engineer named Robert E. Stone from nearby Derry, New Hampshire, visited Mystery Hill and was fascinated by it. He purchased the site and proceeded to spend a lifetime exploring, studying, and excavating there. Among his discoveries were a stone shovel, a stone carving of an arrow pointing upward, and a bird with its eye and heart cut deeply into the stone for emphasis. In ancient Celtic symbolism, an arrow pointing up meant life; pointing down meant death. Birds and birdmen represented either reincarnation or life after death. The prominent heart could have alluded to a person's soul or spirit, and the eye might have been a sign of God or the sun. Working with a team of astroarchaeologists, Stone discovered that many of the standing stones scattered around his one hundred acres were actually astronomical alignment markers that could have been used to calculate the rising and setting of the sun—just like the ones known to have been built by prehistoric Celts in Newgrange, Ireland; Stonehenge, England; and Carnac, Brittany.

Through radiocarbon-dating of burned charcoal that was found two feet underground at Mystery Hill, Stone's team concluded that the date of construction of whatever community had been there was between 2000 B.C. and 2015 B.C. The Newgrange megaliths, tombs, and chambers date from about 2500 B.C. Under one of the mounds at Newgrange, hard by the Boyne River, is a seventy-nine-foot-long rock-walled passageway with three large rooms at its end. On December 21, the winter solstice, the day after the longest night of the year, the slanting sunlight beams directly into this passageway and lights up the chambers, which are completely dark every other day of the year.

Are you sitting down?

Mystery Hill also appears to have an ancient astrological laboratory, with monoliths that might have been used for solar and lunar alignments—the largest of which reflects sun on the summer solstice as well as the winter. And it was at the center of this biggest astro-lab that Goodwin found his sacrificial table.

We're not saying you have to believe all this.

What are you saying, precisely?

Well, that Irish Celts were the first from the Old World to reach the New.

Mystery Hill is not alone among New England sites with Celtic overtones. At Lowell, Massachusetts—where in the 1820s, for 75 cents a day, Irish immigrants would dig the canals that would fuel one of the Industrial Revolution's showpiece mill operations—there is, in Leblanc Park off West Meadow Road, a 167-by-60-foot mound with tall standing stones that are aligned to work the sunlight on the solstices. The locals call the place Druid Hill and believe that the Stonehenge-like construct was the work of Bronze Age Celts. In Danvers, Upton, and Hopkinton, Massachusetts, Celtic-type beehive huts have been discovered. According to local legend in Goshen, Massachusetts, in the 1700s two boys chasing a rabbit stumbled into a Gaelic-style "bothrain": a passageway with stone walls and a slab ceiling, covered with turf, with chambers at its far end—just like those at Newgrange. At Nahant, Massachusetts, overlooking the ocean, there's a stone chamber with a slab ceiling similar to megalithic wedge tombs found in Ireland, and six miles away at Lynn's Prospect Hill stands a seventy-ton granite capstone sitting on three smaller granite "legs" just like the dolmens in Ireland that are said to have marked the tombs of great Irish chieftains or the most powerful druids.

In a soggy bog outside Stamford, Connecticut, the ruins of thirteen stone huts were found long ago; locals suspect that they're Celtic and with good reason. In 1870 one of the last of the Stockbridge Indians told the Stamford town fathers that his tribe's oral tradition had long maintained that the huts "were here when my ancestors came from the west."

Writings in a cave at Ridgefield, Connecticut, have been identified by the American Epigraphic Society as ogam, an alphabet for the Irish language based on twenty-five characters represented with strokes and notches. Ogam was developed in the fourth century, it is believed, and examples of this writing are found on stones throughout Ireland and in Wales, Cornwall, and Scotland. There are more than 150 ogam-inscribed monuments in Ireland, most of them in the counties of Kerry and Cork in the southwest. Those writings seem to have been made from the fourth to the seventh centuries, and the language in them is primitive Irish. In myth, ogam was devised by Ogma of the Tuatha De Danaan Celts, but whatever its origins, it made its way to Connecticut. Besides the Ridgefield inscriptions, there are a dozen feet of ogam scratched into a boulder at Preston, on a hill overlooking the Thames Valley. Deciphered, it reads: "The heat of the sun from winter returns at the Equinox."

However, some of the ogam writings in Ireland date from the nineteenth century and were made by Celtic revivalists. Did the same thing happen in recent centuries in New England? It's possible.

What we do know is this: When a large seaside rock with ogam characters was found in Newfoundland only a few years ago, and "beehives" were uncovered not far away, Canada's national archivist declared, "There is no doubt that Irish monks reached our shores before the Vikings."

Are we back to the monks?

We're back to the monks.

Not much is made of a possible Irish Celtic arrival in the New World for two principal reasons: First, their traditions were oral and therefore no reliable history of their discoveries exists; second, if they *were* here, they had scant influence on those who came later to the area, such as the Indians and Pilgrims.

The monks, of course, had great literary traditions, and so it would be expected that we would have good documentary evidence of their comings and goings. That's what makes the Brendan the Navigator tale so inscrutable, even infuriating.

Can we finally *hear about* Brendan?

It's a terrific tale: Some fourteen hundred years ago an Irish monk named Brendan sailed west in search of the aforementioned "Land Promised to the Saints" (also translated as "Land of Promise and of Saints") that he had heard about from another Irish monk named Finbarr of Cork. Saint Brendan "the Navigator" set out from Dingle

Bay with a crew of more than a dozen men in a thirty-six-foot skin-covered boat called a curragh or coracle. When he returned to Ireland after seven years, he had many fascinating stories to tell about his adventures.

The oral traditions that had been handed down concerning Brendan were codified in Latin in *Navigatio Sancti Brendani*, written between A.D. 700 and 1000 (interestingly, the year Leif Eriksson made it to Newfoundland). The *Navigatio* was an influential and widely translated narrative; in it Brendan tells of encountering "mountains in the sea spouting fire" and floating crystal palaces, monsters with catlike heads and horns growing from their mouths, and "little furry men." Before dismissing Brendan's story as simply too Tolkien, consider Iceland's volcanoes, icebergs, walruses, Eskimos.

Brendan and crew drifted from one island to the next, "following God's stepping-stones," until they came to a large landmass where they stayed for many months. They called the place Saint Ailbe.

Their return voyage was made on an altogether different route, and they wound up in the Azores, whence they returned to Ireland. The voyage was deemed a great success, and news of the adventure gained great currency not only in Ireland but also on the Continent. Remember, Brendan was a monk and he was perceived by his fellows to be a truthful man. Shortly after he was deposed about his adventures late in the sixth century, he died.

It is believed that nine hundred years later, Christopher Columbus visited Dingle to obtain information about Brendan's trip before setting out on his own voyage of discovery. Certainly Columbus knew the *Navigatio*, and the map that he used when he sailed from Spain to the New World had a large landmass in the middle of the Atlantic Ocean labeled "St. Brendan's Island." In fact, the Spanish crown already had claimed sovereignty over the place—wherever and whatever it was—and many sailors before Columbus had sought it. Back then, no one scoffed at Brendan's claims.

In 1976 a sailor named Tim Severin and his crew set out from Ireland seeking to follow Brendan's "stepping-stones" (thought to be Scotland, the Hebrides, Iceland, Greenland, Newfoundland, and Nova Scotia—the "Promised Land" is New England). It turns out that this route is not only the one with the least open water if you are traversing the approximately three thousand miles from Ireland to America but also the very shortest route: Transatlantic jets use it on the Shannon to Boston leg. We know that Severin made it to the New World and we are left to wonder, Did Brendan? Could it have been Brendan himself or followers in his tracks who long ago set up camp at Mystery Hill?

Followers?

By the nature of their calling, Irish monks were missionaries—and missionaries are travelers. Furthermore, there was a good reason for these monks to hit the road: the Vikings.

Brendan's descendants in religion, seafaring, and exploration were a large group of monks called Culdees who had converted from pagan druidism and had busily spread the Christian word throughout Ireland until they were driven out by Norse invaders very early in the eighth century. The Culdees sailed their curraghs to Iceland, where they settled until they were driven out yet again by Vikings in the ninth century. When the Vikings colonized Greenland in 1007, they found remnant white cloth and religious articles that had been left behind by the Irish Culdees, who were on the move again.

According to the eleventh-century Icelandic historian Ari Thorgilsson, in 1009, while exploring the waters south of Greenland, Eric the Red and his Norsemen captured two boys "who spoke Irish" on an island; "three companions escaped by sinking into the ground." Perhaps into the long tunnel and subterranean chambers of a bothrain? The boys told their captors that their people had no houses but lived in caves or dens and wore white robes like those of the Irish Culdees.

How far did the Culdees travel from the eighth through eleventh centuries? If some of them did follow Brendan's route to Saint Ailbe when they left Greenland, it's logical that the Culdees would have settled as far inland as possible to avoid the seaborne Vikings, who had so beleaguered them by driving them from nest after nest.

So let's say that some of them got to the promised land of New England. To reach New Hampshire's Mystery Hill, Robert Ellis Cahill theorizes, they could have sailed up the Merrimack River—right through Lowell, by the way—and landed at what is now Haverhill, Massachusetts. From that area's highest point they could have spotted Mystery Hill just six miles in the distance and decided it was just the place to hole up. It certainly must have looked like an apt place to enjoy freedom to worship as they chose and set up their astrological laboratory. Later, after interacting with the Indians of the region, they could try out their old instincts of converting the heathen.

Is this simply wild speculation? Perhaps not. When the French first landed in Canada they were amazed to discover that the Indians there seemed to know more about Christ than they did. And as Columbus biographer Charles Duff notes, "Celtic words were used by pre-European American Indians." Furthermore, Merrimack, the name of the river that the Culdees would have maneuvered en route to Mystery Hill, may sound Indian, but the word in Irish means "merry stream." And when the Pilgrims landed in 1620, they learned that the Indians called what is now New Hampshire and Vermont Coos, which meant "crooked" for the rivers that twisted and turned through the north country's forests and mountains. In Old Irish or Gaelic *crooes* means "winding." In *Book of the White Mountains*, historian John Anderson writes that "the story of Mt. Washington is the story of its apparent capitulation to the white race. The Indians shunned the mountain because the Great Spirit lived there, and they called it 'Kan Ran Vugarty,' said to be Indian for 'the continued likeness of a gull,' sounding to us, however, suspiciously Celtic." Even the names of some New England tribes have an Irish lilt, such as Micmac and Mohican. *Mohagen* in the Irish language means "contained lowlander."

Finally, there is the legend, retold in John Spaulding's seventeenth-century *Historical Relics of the White Mountains*, of an Indian hunter lost in New Hampshire's woods with a thick fog setting in. He hears noises like thunder, then he hears chanting, then through the fog he sees "a great stone church, and within then, an altar, where from a sparking censor rose a curling wreath of incense smoke. Around it, lights dispersed a mellow glow, by which in groups before the altar appeared a tribe kneeling in profound silence. A change came in the wind, and down a steep rock trailed a long line of strange looking men, and they disappeared into the rent rocks."

If this old Native American tale is based on any kind of fact, then the "strange looking men" would have been the Culdee monks at Mystery Hill, disappearing into their bothrain tunnel and thence to the chambers, having finished their business of converting a tribe of Indians to Christianity.

Even if this evidence is not enough to convince you that it was the Irish who discovered America, you must admit that there is much that is eerily Old Irish in old New England.

How large was the Viking invasion of Ireland, and what was its impact?

The many-faceted invasion was large, and its impact was immense but not total—and not all negative.

The invasion—or invasions—began in 795, when raiders sacked island monasteries off the north and northwestern coasts of Ireland, on Rathlin, Inishmurray, and Inishboffin. Monasteries were often the first targets of the Norsemen: As antipagan places, they represented the Vikings' natural enemy, and monasteries were usually a community's economic stronghold. In a short poem written during the eighth or ninth century, a monk hears a storm brewing and takes solace, for the weather will protect him this night:

> *Fierce is the wind tonight,*
> *It ploughs up the white hair of the sea.*
> *I have no fear that the Viking hosts*
> *Will come over the water to me.*

But on many other nights, over the water they came. For four decades they picked away at the coasts, then plundered farther inland. They took Dublin in 841 and from there launched forays throughout central-eastern Ireland. Viking settlements were eventually established in Wexford, Waterford, Limerick, and Cork; the Vikings were threatening to take the whole island.

But Irish kings started to fight back, as was their way. In 851 Danes arrived in Dublin and started battling both Norse and Irish for control of certain sections. Things were getting complicated. The Vikings began to concentrate their insurrectionist efforts in Scotland and Iceland in the latter half of the 800s, and by the turn of the century they were weakened in Dublin to the point of being kicked out (in 902). They returned with a vengeance in 914, and ruled Dublin and much of York for two decades. Then their attention and power waned again, and the Viking wars were over by the middle of the tenth century.

So much for the fighting. What about the impact?

First, the wars served to turn Ireland into a place preoccupied with violence and turmoil rather than art and intellectual development. However, the "Viking Terror" did not overwhelm the island to any irreparable degree. Churches were sacked, but since the pagan invaders weren't pushing any great new religious agenda, the Church lived on. The Ostmen, as the new Norse-Irish were called, actually made positive contributions to society: the first Irish coinage; systems of weights and measures; many advanced technologies, including far better shipbuilding techniques; expertise in trading abroad; Scandinavian influences in arts and crafts; and the concept of "towns," which followed naturally and easily out of the recent monastery movement. The Vikings left behind sophisticated, strong, walled communities in Dublin, Limerick, Cork, and Waterford. They even left behind the English name for the island the Irish call Erin: *Iraland* is an Old Norse word. In his classic *The Story of the Irish Race*, Seamus MacManus—a Donegal man who, by the way, died in 1960 after falling from the seventh floor of a New York City nursing home—wrote, "The Viking age was by no means a starless night in Ireland, nor was society so horribly disorganized as is generally believed. It was a period marked by the lives of Irish chiefs of outstanding ability, of some of the greatest figures in Nordic history, and of women of unusual personality. Even in those days of terror and danger from foreign invasion, when an enemy fleet stood in every port and soldiers were encamped in many parts of the country, Ireland was still in the full current of European life. . . . In no other land in which these two peoples of such different culture came together did each learn so much from the other as in Ireland. In matters of agriculture and cattle raising the Irish were the teachers of the Norsemen, but in other purely material pursuits the civilization of the Norse was superior to that of the Irish."

So the invasion was a growth experience.

Now it is true, as MacManus admitted, that "the Viking invasions checked the normal development of Irish civilization, undid what the efforts of successive centuries had realized, and gave Ireland such a shock that learning scarcely ever fully recovered from it." And it's safe to say that, given the choice, Ireland would have opted to skip the Viking wars. But as unwanted conquests go, it could have been worse.

Who was Brian Boru?

Brian Boru succeeded his brother, Mathgamain, as king of much of southern Ireland in 976. He is regarded as the greatest of Ireland's high kings, as a vanquisher of Vikings (though he really wasn't), and as the man who first got people thinking about the island as one kingdom, one country, perhaps one nation.

He had consolidated his grip on the southern half of the isle by 997, and five years later had pressed his suit in the north and was named high king of the whole. In 1005 he started calling himself "Emperor of the Irish," and who was to differ? His forces defended his realm against a Viking-supported Dublin revolt in 1014, but Brian was killed in the battle.

For centuries—for a millennium, in fact—none would present to the world a vision of such a thoroughly unified Ireland as did Brian Boru.

FOUR

Troubles Brewing

Why did Pope Adrian IV give Henry II
dispensation to invade Ireland?

Who was Strongbow?

What does "beyond the Pale" mean?

What were the Statutes of Kilkenny?

Wasn't there a ship sailing far south of the
island at this time that was having some
impact in the New World?

What role did Henry VIII play in Irish history?

What was the Nine Year War?

*Were Irish involved in early English colonizations
by Sir Walter Raleigh and others in America?*

*Who were the Scotch-Irish and what did they have
to do with the settling of America?*

*Why weren't Irish from elsewhere in the country
going across in big numbers?*

What was the Rising of 1641?

Who was Oliver Cromwell?

*Did things get better for the Irish after the
restoration of the British monarchy?*

What was the Battle of the Boyne?

*Did the discord in Ireland in the late-seventeenth
and early-eighteenth centuries hasten Irish
emigration to America?*

Why did Pope Adrian IV give Henry II
dispensation to invade Ireland?

Certainly nationalism had something to do with it, as **Adrian** was
and remains history's only English pope. Adrian was surely aware
that whoever was in power in England, from the Romans right on
down to the sitting Plantagenet, **Henry II,** who was ruling the
post–Norman Conquest empire, had thought of invading Ireland.
And when Henry went the extra step of asking for a bull of legiti-
mation for such an annexing, Adrian was both predisposed and
properly placed to accede. In the fourth-century document *The Donation of Constantine*, the Roman emperor had bequeathed to the

pope jurisdiction over the whole earth, and despite the fact that this later proved a forgery, popes had behaved for more than five hundred years as if such dominion was their right. Adrian saw Norman rule in Ireland as a way of spreading Catholicism among the heathen. So for a variety of reasons, Henry's conquering of the strange Hibernian isle looked like an altogether reasonable and good idea.

Adrian issued his bull, *Laudabiliter,* in 1156. Henry looked westward and saw another kingdom to gather for his sons. He mulled.

Subsequently, Henry was accosted in France by **Dermot MacMurrough,** who had been expelled from Ireland in 1166 by the high king of Leinster **Rory O'Connor** (the usual quarrels: land grabs, abducted wives). MacMurrough swore fealty to Henry and in turn received permission to raise an army in England and plan an invasion.

Who was Strongbow?

He was **Richard FitzGilbert de Clare, Earl of Pembroke** (Wales) aptly called Richard Strongbow—Dermot's chief ally and ultimately his general in the second wave of the Irish invasion. By 1167 the hot-under-the-collar, swift-acting MacMurrough had already taken a swipe at Ireland with a small force of foreign knights. He continued to fight and was joined by Strongbow and a much larger militia in 1170. Together Dermot and Strongbow took Waterford and Wexford in August, and only weeks later they seized Dublin from the Vikings. (In those intervening weeks, Strongbow was given a reward by Dermot: his daughter Aoife's hand in marriage. Seen in context, the sacking of Dublin seems one of history's odder honeymoons.) After Dublin, the allied English army overran the province of Meath, then the kingdom of Breifne. Dermot died in 1171, and control of the kingdom of Leinster fell to his new son-in-law.

Now, Henry had always been wary of Strongbow; one of the reasons he asked him to join the Irish campaign was to get him out of England. When he saw Strongbow setting himself up as king of Ireland, he hurried to Waterford, seeking to make sure no kind of Irish nationalism got started. This was all supposed to be about England taking over Ireland, not England helping Ireland become an autonomous kingdom. In any event, in October of 1171 various Irish chieftains took a look at Henry's army and at the papal decree he was waving and allied with England in return for protection of their kingly interests. In Dublin Henry granted Leinster to Strongbow in return for Richard's renewed pledges of allegiance to the Crown.

That was the start of the Troubles. The English had come and conquered, and they've been represented on the island ever since.

What does "beyond the Pale" mean?

The Irish resistance to English colonization was largely ineffectual. Dublin filled with immigrants from Bristol, and English culture seeped into the countryside. Within a century, English ways had gained root in Irish sod.

Irish not willing to become English were pushed out. In the cities Crown areas were established where only transplanted Englishmen and those willing to adopt the dress, language, and customs of England could live. In Dublin the English-loyalist boundary extended twenty miles from the city center; this was the Pale. At its edge was a double ditch six feet deep with a palisade. Beyond the Pale were frustrated, disorganized Irish chieftains and assorted Anglo-Irish. Call it the birth of Irish Republicanism. But it didn't get off to a great start: Influence was extending outward from the Pale. Normans began intermarrying with Irish not only in the city centers but in the country. (Names of major "Irish" families—and of major Irish American families—that are actually Norman include Burke, Butler, Cusack, Darcy, Dillon, Fitzgerald, Fitzhugh, Lacy, Nagle, Power, Prendergast, and Roche.) There were some armed skirmishes—the English invasion casually pushed west and north throughout the 1230s and 1240s—but by far the most effective means of carrying the day was English assimilation.

By 1250 the Normans dominated all of Ireland save Ulster.

And then . . . they started to lose their grip.

Attacks on the king of England's capital in Ireland, Dublin, increased. In 1315 **Edward Bruce** of Scotland invaded Ulster with the intention of driving out English settlers, and defeated Crown forces as far south as Tipperary. Many English peasants went back home, allowing a general Irish reconquest of rural areas. As the fourteenth century progressed, more and more of the English "invaders" were using Irish in their daily speech.

Gaelic echoes were traveling on all four of the Irish winds, and it became clear to all that there was something smoldering here, a larger upheaval coming. The English sought to head it off.

What were the Statutes of Kilkenny?

At a parliament in Kilkenny presided over by **Edward III,** a set of laws was passed in 1366 that represented England's first attempt at legislating its dictatorial control of the Irish. Among the Statutes of Kilkenny were prohibitions against Englishmen in Ireland speaking the Irish tongue, intermarrying with the Irish, or fostering Irish children. Submitting to Ireland's traditional Brehon Law was to be considered high treason. Encouraging Irish storytellers and minstrels was deemed illegal. The statutes reeked of defensiveness: The English Crown wanted to make sure that it was not only subjugating the Irish but also preventing its own people from falling under the thrall of Irishness.

The statutes failed. This foray into cultural racism served to inform the Irish that the English were not going to allow them to be part of the empire, but were going to set separate rules keeping them out—and down. It let the Irish know everything they needed to know about English attitudes and intentions. Of course, such information foments resistance and even rebellion. The Kilkenny law can be seen as a precursor to apartheid, and while those rules might endure for a time, they are always overturned in the end.

In London there were increasing references to "the Irish problem"—how stubborn it was, how difficult to solve. Edward III and **Richard II** threw a lot of money at it; Richard even traveled to Ireland twice in the 1390s. Then there was a lull in English attention paid to Ireland. Then the Pale was expanded; by 1488 it had reached Dundalk. (The first time the term *Bloody Sunday* was used to conjure an unsettling incident in Irish history was when a group of English settlers picnicking beyond the Pale got themselves murdered for their pleasure by Irish nationalists.) At a parliament in Drogheda in 1494 more words were written emphasizing the low role of the Irish citizenry. The English Crown wanted to reassert dominion.

And then, in 1509, **Henry VIII** became king of England.

Wasn't there a ship sailing far south of the island at this time that was having some impact in the New World?

There were three ships, in fact: the *Niña*, the *Pinta*, and the *Santa María*. And if you don't subscribe to the story of Brendan the Navigator, then you should consider Galway native **William Eris,** or Ayers, the first Irish American. There's a claim often made in Hibernian circles that Columbus went to Galway to study Brendan's map. Maybe— but whatever, Eris hooked up with the great explorer and went across. The legend goes that Eris volunteered to stay in Hispaniola, and so was among the forty massacred by natives after Columbus headed home.

What role did Henry VIII play in Irish history?

First, he unified the many estates, counties, towns, and fiefdoms on the Emerald Isle into one kingdom. In 1541 he was named first king of all Ireland. (The kingship initiative was clearly another effort to de-Gaelicize the entire country.)

Second, he presided over the Reformation, which added religion to the stew that was and is the Anglo-Irish Troubles. When Henry split from Rome, England followed along toward Protestantism, but Ireland didn't. The Irish weren't diehard papists at the time and wouldn't have necessarily troubled themselves with Henry's marital woes and his problems with Rome. But Catholicism had, over time, become a part of Irishness—culturally as much as religiously—and now it became not only an institutional but a symbolic tradition to cling to as England, with its "Church of Ireland," tried to dictate again. The fray that had been English versus Irish now became English Protestant versus Irish Catholic. (The Irish also realized that England's immediate enemies, France and Spain, were Catholic. That was the camp for them.)

So here's the irony: The ferociously strong strain of Roman Catholicism that is *Irish* Catholicism was nurtured by the English king who went to war with all Catholicism.

What was the Nine Year War?

During the long reign of **Elizabeth I** in the second half of the sixteenth century, English rule was fortified throughout Ireland, though the Protestant Reformation gained no purchase. As the century wound down, resistance heated up once more. After several local rebellions by individual Irish chieftains—one of which was put down by **Sir Walter Raleigh**—a more formal conflict was joined in 1595. Although battles were fought throughout the country, the focus of the fight was in Ulster. The Nine Year War was all but over by

1603, and the result was a thorough Tudor conquest of Ireland. In the aftermath, the famous "Flight of the Earls" took place in 1607, and Ulster was left wide open for a new wave of English colonization. **James I,** now on the English throne, saw the opportunity and seized it. In January 1608 a plan was drawn up for plantations to be established in the province, grants were to be given to Scottish and English emigrants, royal officials, "deserving" Irish, and the English church. It was anticipated that many Scottish and English tenants would work the estates, but the plan didn't succeed, and this latest English attempt at dominion was foiled. Colonists just didn't arrive in the numbers expected.

However, this very purposeful land grab did serve to establish Ulster as an English province—in concept if not yet in fact.

Were Irish involved in early English colonizations by Sir Walter Raleigh and others in America?

A few took part. One was **Edward Nugent.** This account of Nugent's bravery is from the 1586 journal of Captain Ralph Lane, who had established camp along the shore in what is now North Carolina: "An Irishman serving me, one Edward Nugent, volunteered to kill Pemisapan, king of the Indians. We met him returning out of the woods with Pemisapan's head in his hands, and the Indians ceased their raids against the British camp."

Captain John White's journal from his 1587 voyage to Virginia mentions "Two Irishmen, **Darbie Glaven** and **Dennis Carrell**," who were left behind on Saint John in the Virgin Islands. It is unknown whether they shared Nugent's fighting-Irish spirit.

Who were the Scotch-Irish and what did they have to do with the settling of America?

Neither purely Scotch nor Irish, they were the first to carry a great quantity of blood, sweat, and tears from Ireland to America. In fact, their ancient heritage was Danish, Anglo, and Saxon, and they had been shoved into low and middle Scotland by the post-Roman invasions of England.

James I wanted to quell all the insurrectionist tendencies in Northern Ireland and sought to split and subdue Ulster by giving land grants. Some of these went to lowland Scots. By 1620 twenty thousand Scots lived on the Ulster plantations, and many displaced

Irish were in the bogs mounting guerrilla attacks against the usurpers. These Irish "woods kerns" were put down for good when fifteen thousand of them were killed in the uprisings of 1641.

In North America, British settlers had been trying to push their western civilization west—the first steady effort at Manifest Destiny—by luring poor Europeans, either desperate or adventurous or both, to the New World with that ever-golden promise: free land. Because of the raw terrain offered, and the dangerous Indian situation inherent, these pioneers were thought of by their sponsors, if not by themselves, as "disposable people."

The first wave of disposables were largely lowland Germanic, and to the great frustration of the English colonials, they found relative contentment east of the Blue Ridge Mountains—in the Piedmont land that remains so "Pennsylvania Dutch" in character today. There the westering movement stalled. The English turned their attention to the Scots of Ulster, who had been so recently engaged at this sort of thing: pushing a native group from its homeland and setting up an agrarian culture.

In 1715 the recruitment effort began in northern Ireland, and in the 1720s more than fifty thousand Irish, mostly Presbyterian, arrived on American shores (by the start of the American Revolution there would be as many as three hundred thousand of these "Scotch-Irish" in America). As might have been expected, they were by and large rougher and tougher than the Irish who stayed in Ireland. Among their numbers were a good many frustrated farm and mill workers who had the will to fight in their souls. Some even had a warrior pedigree: They were descendants of Cromwellian soldiers. All were of a long-battered race.

They squatted first on Pennsylvania land and learned early to be fierce in America by mixing it up with the Germans. Then, undeterred, they headed into the Appalachian Mountains: Indian country. An army of victims of centuries of persecution was on a forward, if disorganized, march, and it was a formidable thing. An old Scotch-Irish prayer goes, "Lord, grant that I may always be right, for thou knowest I am hard to turn." Scotch-Irish sayings include "Root hog or die," "Fish or cut bait," "The early bird gets the worm," "He who dallies is a dastard," and "To the victor belongs the spoils." America was about to discover the meaning of these adages.

Keep in mind that many of these people thought of themselves as Irish, the term *Scotch-Irish*, used by their sponsors and other "American" neighbors, was pejorative. It was almost precisely a century after their first great emigration that they began to think of themselves as Scotch-Irish, to distinguish themselves in their societal mind's-eye from the hordes of "Mere Irish," or Catholic Irish, beginning to arrive.

Scotch-Irish battles with nature, disease, and non-Scotch-Irish people (principally Native Americans) were constant and ferocious. The immigrants won some, lost many, and kept going. They were not "settlers" as the Germans had been; they didn't settle towns or valleys and left scant sign of their comings and goings. They were true American frontiersmen. **Sam Houston, Kit Carson,** and **Davy Crockett** were of Scotch-Irish descent; the mountain men were all but exclusively Scotch-Irish. Even the diplomats among them exhibited the rough-and-ready tendencies of a Scotch-Irish personality. **Andrew Jackson,** seventh president of the United States, was Scotch-Irish.

With long rifles and the felling ax, they moved on through the Creek Nation in Virginia, through the Shawnee, Cherokee, and Iroquois. Individually, if not collectively, the Scotch-Irish exhibited occasional sensitivity for those who came in their way. As Bil Gilbert notes in his exemplary history *Westering Man*, many of them spent "substantial, satisfying periods of their lives as Indians. They seldom were renegades who turned on other whites, but rather were realists who accepted the white conquest of the continent as inevitable. Most of them were leaders in the westering movement that was to bring this about—and were effective voices because of their rapport with their adopted peoples. However, personally and privately they were Indian lovers in many senses of the word." **Joe Walker,** who would help organize Independence, Missouri, and serve as its first sheriff, survey the Santa Fe Trail, and guide the first wagon train to California, was one of these men. Nine of his kin were killed by the Shawnee Black Wolf in 1786, yet he spent much of his life among Indians and had an Indian wife and family.

Once the Scotch-Irish were over the Appalachians, they were unstoppable. They paused but briefly in Missouri, then crossed the Mississippi and moved on to Colorado, Arizona, and eventually California. It had taken this race centuries to be transported from their various homelands to the rottenest part of Scotland, then to Ulster. It took the Scotch-Irish only a few decades to find their way across the Atlantic and but another half-century to reach the Pacific. To judge by their race across America, it seems the New World is what they had been seeking all along. They were better than good at the task their English sponsors had set for them. They were not merely disposable or necessary people to the richer white settlers, they were miraculous, heaven-sent people. And they were people who were staying.

Why weren't Irish from elsewhere in the country going across in big numbers?

America looked like another English colony to them, not a land of opportunity. Why travel an ocean to face the persecution you can face right at home?

But were some going?

Yes. New England town records show Irish on the rolls as early as 1621, even though it was illegal. Irish Catholics were "not allowed to set foot" in the region by law. But **Roger Williams,** who himself had been exiled by the Pilgrims, started letting them settle in Rhode Island, and strictures broke down—many Presbyterian Irish filtered in, and doubtless some Catholics snuck in. The Pilgrims began importing Irish convicts and, in particular, Irish girls to act as servants. For instance, in 1626 a ship heading for Virginia from Ireland was wrecked off Cape Cod and, according to the journal of Plimoth Plantation's governor **John Bradford,** "Most of her passengers were Irish servants." He took them into the plantation and later maintained that they "carried themselves very orderly all ye time they stayed. They helped plant crops and assisted in the harvest."

On March 15, 1636, the ship *St. Patrick* arrived in Boston with wools, livestock, and "wild Irish girls" who had come to find employment as servants for the Puritans. According to Governor **John Winthrop**'s journal, the captain of the ship, Palmer, had been ordered to "strike the Irish flag" upon his arrival; he had complied but "took this as a great injury." Palmer complained to the court, and the colonial lieutenant who had ordered the striking was called to testify. When his explanation proved insufficient, he was ordered to go and raise the flag on the ship himself "and acknowledge his error, so all the ship's company might receive satisfaction."

(John Winthrop's sister married an Irishman, George Downing of Dublin, who had arrived in Boston in 1638 at fourteen years old and had subsequently graduated from Harvard. Winthrop's widow, Martha, married John Cogan, also an Irishman and also a Harvard man. In March 1634 Cogan had become the first person to open a store in Boston, and his trade flourished: Upon his death in 1658 he left 175 acres of land to Harvard. So the Irish, though often shunted to the lower classes, were already rising.)

In 1654 another ship arrived in Boston, this one named the *Goodfellow*. The hundreds of Irish fellows and women aboard were quickly sold into servitude. **Richard Mather,** for one, was horrified at the influx, shouting that the Irish had been sent in a "formidable attempt of Satan and his sons to unsettle us." His fear of Irish papists was never cured; in 1688 he accused an Irish washerwoman named Glover of tormenting her neighbor's children, and of not answering the judge in English "but only in Irish, which was her native tongue." He carried the day, and saw to it that Glover was hanged as a witch on Boston Common.

"Cursed be he," wrote Mather's friend **Nathaniel Ward,** a clergyman and one of America's first authors, "that maketh not his sword starke drunk with Irish blood."

No wonder the Irish looked at the New World with a general feeling of foreboding.

What was the Rising of 1641?

The Rising of 1641 was engineered by **Sir Phelim O'Neill,** a native of Ulster, who rallied his fellows and seized Charlemont Castle. His military force pushed south and eventually gained the support of the "Old English" within the Pale. The Rising is interesting to study because of its confusion of alliances: Ulstermen allied with descendants of England living near Dublin who had not forsaken their Catholicism; English Protestant Royalists allied with Ulster Scots. Indeed, Sir Phelim, while fighting the English, claimed to be acting *for* the king. It shows that the religious and cultural affiliations of the Irish citizenry at the time were more than in flux—they were thoroughly befuddled.

There were various attempts at peace made during the decade, but the war begun by the Rising was still going on when Cromwell came on the scene in 1649.

Who was Oliver Cromwell?

Oliver Cromwell was perhaps the greatest villain in the Irish view of history. The havoc he wreaked upon the island in such a short span is astonishing even from a distance of more than three centuries.

After **Charles I** was executed on January 30, 1649, the Puritan zealot Oliver Cromwell was appointed Lord Protector of England. By August he was in Ireland, determined to have vengeance for reported atrocities against Protestants in the Rising of 1641, to quell all remnant insurrectionism on the frontier, and to finally convert every last Irishman to Anglicanism. Both sides had committed atrocities in 1641, but Cromwell's ruthless treatment of the Irish still shocks. First, there was the war. Using the cannon, a relatively new weapon of war—"Cromwell's Ironsides"—the Parliamentary army quickly gained control of the east coast of Ireland. Cromwell departed Ireland to fight in Scotland in May of 1650, but the force he left behind continued to effectively mow down Irish opposition. The English had won the war conclusively by the spring of 1653. Puritan preachers known as agitators who had accompanied Cromwell's militia continued their work of trying to eradicate all Irish Catholic traditions and rituals. As for saying mass, Cromwell promised, "where the Parliament of England have power, that will not be allowed of."

The campaign that followed was more devastating still. History had convinced England that tinkering with the Irish problem wouldn't work because these people were "indocile and averse from all civility and amendment," as Milton wrote. Said Cromwellian commander Michael Jones, "No lasting peace could be made but by removing all heads of septs and priests and men of knowledge in arms, or otherwise in repute, out of this land." And so the Irish were pushed off the good earth; known rebels lost their holdings outright, and others were shunted to the rocky region west of the Shannon. (Irish Catholics were told to go "to Hell or Connaught," indicating this impoverished beyond-the-Shannon land.) The Protestant minority, led by the new social class called the Protestant Ascendancy, now firmly controlled three-fourths of the island and ruled dictatorially. One hundred thousand Irish were sold into slavery and shipped to Jamaica and Barbados. Aftershocks of Cromwell's activities were felt elsewhere in the New World, driving "many Irish Catholics to Massachusetts," according to Scot Paradise in his *History of Essex County*.

Even some Cromwellians had difficulty with what they were witnessing. "It was their being cruel that makes us hate them so much!" wrote Vincent Gookin, a member of Cromwell's Parliament. "To punish them do not run into their sin, lest God punish thee."

God, or fate, would punish Cromwell, but not yet. The "transplantation"—a euphemism for genocide—led to widespread starvation and disease. Ireland's population, which had risen to nearly 1.5 million by 1641, fell to 616,000 by 1652.

Cromwell's comeuppance, hardly commensurate with his crimes, came in the form of an army coup. In May of 1660 the monarchy was restored in England as **Charles II** ascended to the throne. But Cromwell's dirty work in Ireland had been done effectively. Charles inherited a satellite kingdom with the Protestant Ascendancy now in control of most land ownership and all political power, lording it over a Roman Catholic peasantry that still spoke that strange, eerily beautiful Gaelic language. For the Irish, the road back looked impossibly long.

Did things get better for the Irish after the restoration of the British monarchy?

No. If anything they got worse. Charles II did return hundreds of Irish to their former holdings—the 1665 Act of Explanation forced some of Cromwell's grantees to give back a third of their land to "innocents"—but many more Cromwellian usurpers were confirmed in their ownership. Catholic Irish held three-fourths of the land in 1641, but now they owned barely one-fifth, and most of this in Connaught. Six-sevenths of the population was poor, existing at subsistence level, growing their own food, making their own clothes. Many of the dispossessed Irish became criminals in this new society, hiding in the forests, robbing the English. They were called rapparees, and were vigorously hunted.

Various restraints were put on the Irish economy and trade that served to make the country even more dependent on England. Screws were being tightened in a variety of ways. Religious persecution persisted. In 1672 it was decreed that Catholics could not be elected to the Dublin Parliament. Catholics were executed for treason in 1678. The heart and entrails of **Bishop Oliver Plunket** were burned publicly.

But then, in 1685, an avowed Catholic, **James II,** took the throne in England.

What was the Battle of the Boyne?

It was the crucial Orange-Green fight that is commemorated each summer in Northern Ireland with all manner of unrest and violence as Protestant loyalists march in celebration, while Catholics either grit their teeth or cast the first stone. Guess which side won in July of 1690?

The Catholic Irish were encouraged by the ascension of James II, the Catholic brother of Charles who was of French-Scot extraction. James quickly suspended anti-Catholic laws in Ireland and even appointed an Irish Catholic, **Richard Talbot,** as **Earl of Tyrconnel.** Tyrconnel raised an almost entirely Catholic army in Ireland. The times, they seemed to be a-changin'.

As the Catholics grew more hopeful, the Protestant Ascendancy, not to mention the Anglicans at home in England, were becoming concerned. James applied the brakes a bit. When Tyrconnel moved to undo the land partitions of the 1660s, James said, "Not yet." But perhaps it was already too late; James's Catholic leanings were causing more than mere grumblings among the aristocracy.

And then, in June of 1688, James became father to a son—a royal heir, a Catholic successor to the throne. That did it.

The English elite invited James's son-in-law, **William of Orange,** to seize the throne. During the Glorious Revolution of 1688, James fled to France. A year after that, he made his way to his power base. Tyrconnel's forces held all of Ireland except Derry and Enniskillen, and James arrived on the island on March 12, 1689. Memories of the massacres of 1641—some of them real, some of them conjured— prompted many Protestants to flee back to England.

For the first time in Irish history, the quarrel as we have come to know it today was straightforward: Irish Catholic natives would face off against English Protestant transplants. Clearly, much was at stake.

As if a formal act were needed to start the fighting itself, James summoned a parliament in June, and this congress proposed to dismantle Charles II's final land settlements. It proposed, in fact, to confiscate most property belonging to Protestants.

William of Orange—now William III—hadn't been wont to visit Ireland, but push had come to shove. Derry was secured by an English fleet in July of 1689; a month later William's army began massing in Ulster; several months after that, in June of 1690, the king arrived. He marched south and met James at the Boyne River. There, on July 1, he thrashed James's army. James did the habitual thing—he fled for France, this time from Waterford—where he would die in exile, the last of the Stuart kings. He left behind an Irish kingdom once more naked to conquest. William rolled on toward Limerick, to which he laid vicious siege. In October of 1691 the city surrendered, and the war was concluded with the Treaty of Limerick. With the battle lost, thousands of Catholic military men fled Ireland, just as James had, and joined armies in France. They were called the "wild geese" and their actions seem, in retrospect, indicative of a certain Irish ambivalence to put cause above expedience. We'll dwell on that further when we get to the great wars of the twentieth century, but for now let it suffice: The flight of the wild geese rendered it certain that Ireland would be docile as a new boot was stomped upon it by England.

The boot was heavy enough, even if lighter than Cromwell's. This time, the heel—ground in firmly—came in the form of the Penal Laws. Edward Wetenhall, Church of Ireland bishop of Limerick, was warning that the massacres of 1641 would be revisited if the Catholics weren't put down—*now!*—and firmly. Moreover, the theory went, if legislative burdens on Catholics were severe enough, they'd convert. And so, in 1697, the first of many years' worth of laws were passed that closeted and all but crucified Catholic worship in Ireland (at least, that was the plan).

A Penal Law enacted in 1703 sought to register the clergy and limit their numbers in Ireland—and sought further to deny recalcitrant Catholics any leadership. Other legislation forbade Catholics from educating their children as they chose, inheriting land, owning land, employing others, and bearing arms. The next year the Ascendancy, primarily Anglican, took care of its other group of malcontents, the Scotch-Irish of Ulster, largely Presbyterian. The Test Act of 1704 forbade Presbyterian schools and banned Presbyterian "dissenters" from public employment. The upshot was that a whole new wave of Scotch-Irish headed for America, joining the thousands who'd already been recruited. In 1727 three thousand Irish left for the New World; in 1769 the number was forty-four thousand. Almost all of these latter immigrants arrived with a deeply felt distaste for the English. Nothing could have made them happier than to learn that, within a decade, they'd have the opportunity to fight a real, fair-and-square war with the redcoats.

As for the Catholics, the wild geese had flown, and the Irish at home were powerless to resist the English. Although nearly a century of political docility followed, Irish Catholicism went stolidly, solidly onward. Their faith, which had been merely a cultural trapping useful as a symbol now and again, had hardened, through English opposition, into a religious reason for being. This faith became a spark that would light many a future flame and set off an occasional powder keg.

Did the discord in Ireland in the late-seventeenth and early-eighteenth centuries hasten Irish emigration to America?

Yes, especially among Presbyterians and even among Catholics. More significantly, some of the immigrants started to have an impact.

Robert Pollock of Donegal arrived in Maryland in 1672; his family would prosper, and his great-great-great grandson, **James K. Polk,** would become the eleventh president of the United States.

Irish-born **Thomas Dongan** would rise to become royal governor and grant New York colony its charter in 1686.

In 1704 **John Carroll,** who would become the first American Roman Catholic bishop, and his brother **Charles,** who would become the only Catholic signer of the Declaration of Independence, both of an immigrant family from Carrollton, Ireland, enrolled at the new Catholic Church school in Bohemian Manor, Maryland.

In 1715 the large Scotch-Irish influx began—and with it the heavy, pervasive impact of the Irish in America.

FIVE

Fighting Irish, Founding Irish

Who were the Friendly Brothers of Saint Patrick?

When was the first Saint Patrick's Day
Parade in New York City?

What role did the Irish play
in the American Revolution?

Who was the Father of the United States Navy?

What happened on December 31, 1775?

What happened on March 17, 1776?

Which other Irish characters played
a role in the Revolution?

Did Irish fight on the side of the British?

What was Lynch's Law, or Lynch Law?

What message is to be gained from the Irish role in the American Revolution?

Did any Irishmen sign the Declaration of Independence?

Were any of them above Catholic Irish?

And whatever happened to Charles Carroll's brother, John?

What role did the American Revolution play in the Irish revolt of 1798?

Who was Wolfe Tone?

Why is Wolfe Tone's widow buried in Brooklyn?

What is Vinegar Hill?

What role did the Irish play in the War of 1812?

With whom did the Irish side during the war with Mexico?

Should the Irish remember the Alamo?

What was—what is—the Ancient Order of Hibernians?

How many Irish came across in the years immediately before the Great Famine?

Who were the Friendly Brothers of Saint Patrick?

Well, they weren't his brothers and they weren't very friendly to their incoming colonial American brethren who wished to shuck off the yoke of the Crown.

Founded in 1768, the Brothers was a fraternal organization largely composed of Irish-born officers serving in British forces based in North America. The club held annual meetings, usually in New York City on Saint Patrick's Day. It is said that the Friendly Brothers, which bled into the Friendly Brothers of Saint Patrick in 1784, made no sectarian distinctions and welcomed all "fellow countrymen" arriving on American shores. But until the waves of Catholic immigration overwhelmed all standing Irish American clubs and cliques in the nineteenth century, the Friendly Brothers were friendlier to Protestants.

When was the first Saint Patrick's Day Parade in New York City?

In 1779 the Volunteers of Ireland staged the first Saint Patrick's Day Parade. The irony is that New York was held by the British at the time, and the Volunteers were a *loyalist* regiment. So the great shamrock-bedecked parade was an Orange one, not Green, in its origins.

Therefore: The first Saint Pat's fraternal organization in America and the first Saint Pat's Parade were sponsored by the Brits.

What role did the Irish play in the American Revolution?

A great one in both numbers and influence.

As would be the case for every conflagration in which the United States of America—or, in this instance, the aborning United States of America—would be involved throughout its long history, the fighting Irish would display their combative talents during the Revolution. This is particularly significant and proud-making, as the Irish in Ireland, for various political reasons that we will address later in this book, have not necessarily covered themselves in national glory in wartime, although many individuals and battalions from the country have performed valiantly.

Although there were many Scotch-Irish—not to mention English who'd been stationed in Ireland—who fought as redcoats, it is estimated that men of Irish birth or descent formed between one-third and one-half of Washington's forces, including 1,492 officers and 22 generals (15 of whom were in fact born in Ireland). Additionally, more than 25,000 men left Ireland during the war with the express intention of joining this fight against a common enemy, the English Crown.

Many of Irish ancestry rose to particular prominence:

- When asked to name the victim of the first volley at that precipitous event now known as the Boston Massacre, some Americans might cite Crispus Attucks. Attucks, half African and half Native American, was indeed felled. But among the others at his side in the bloody alley on March 5, 1770, was **Patrick Carr,** a recent immigrant from Ireland who took a musket ball in his belly and died an agonizing death nine days later. On the other end of the muskets, wearing their fine red coats, were seven members of the 29th British Regiment. Five of them were Irishmen recently arrived from Dublin.

- While he may not have fired the shot heard 'round the world in Lexington, Massachusetts, on April 19, 1775—no one knows who did, or even from which side it was delivered— New Hampshire's **John Sullivan,** whose father had emigrated from Limerick in 1723, has been hailed (and not only by Hibernians) as "the first to take up arms against the king." In 1774 Sullivan led a group of New Hampshire militia men in an attack on the British Fort William and Mary at Newcastle; his raid garnered gunpowder that would be used at the Battle of Bunker Hill six months later. For his boldness, Sullivan received a commission as major general in the Continental army, and later distinguished himself by leading his troops in a successful campaign against both the Iroquois and the Loyalists in New York State. After the war, John Sullivan went on to serve as chief executive of New Hampshire from 1786 to 1789, and his brother James, who also fought at Bunker Hill and who became the most decorated soldier of the Revolutionary War, was later elected governor of Massachusetts, serving in the first decade of the nineteenth century.

- At the Battle of Bunker Hill, which took place by and large on nearby Breed's Hill in Charlestown, Massachusetts, on June 17, 1775, no fewer than 276 Irish-born men were counted among the New England militia, and the greatest hero of the day turned out to be a regimental commander from New Hampshire named **John Stark.** Stark was second generation; his parents had emigrated from County Cork in 1720. He fronted a lot of men who were quite like himself in heritage and demeanor; with a reputation as fearless Indian fighters in the New Hampshire and Vermont woods, this thickly brogued force, mostly Irish or Scotch-Irish frontiersmen, took its position on the left flank of the main colonial force at Bunker Hill. Although the British eventually took the hill in what turned out to be the bloodiest day of battle during the entire war, it was the redcoats who suffered the greater slaughter: General Howe's army endured 1,054 casualties with 89 officers among then, while the rebels lost but 115 men, and saw 304 wounded and another 30 captured. The enormity of the day's losses caused British General Gage, who had watched the battle from nearby Boston, to make the prophetic observation: "These Rebels are not the despicable rabble too many of us have supposed."

It was Colonel Stark who expressed the sentiment "live free or die" that became a watchword in his time and remains the oft-misinterpreted New Hampshire state motto. (Many today see it as an adamantly conservative slogan, but Stark's complete, in-context musing was more philosophical, finishing with, "for death is not the worst of evils." It seems, in retrospect, like an expected declaration from an Irish rebel: true, brave, equivocal, poetic.)

(There is a small north country village named for the colonel. Stark, New Hampshire, only thirty miles from the Canadian border, is today home to four hundred souls. It used to sit on a train line from Maine to Montreal, and that made it busy; it has always had many mighty trees, and in lumbering eras that made it busy, too. During World War II, Stark was the site of a prisoner-of-war camp, and many Germans were interned there. The locals served as guards and volunteers. They treated the enemy with uncommon fairness; Dartmouth history professor Edward Koop wrote a fascinating 1988 book about this historical curiosity called *Stark Decency* [University Press of New England].

The people of Stark are proud of their past. In the 1980s, some of the former POWs began making their way back to the village to shake hands with those who had been their captors. There were tears all around, from old folks who, when young, had behaved in exemplary fashion. John Stark would have been proud.)

- In what has been called "the Lexington of the Seas," **Jeremiah O'Brien** of Machias, Maine, whose father had come from Cork, captured the British schooner *Margaretta* in Machias Bay in what was considered the first naval battle of the Revolution. O'Brien was commissioned as a Privateer and, along with his brother John, continued to harass the enemy in the sea war that he himself had begun.

Who was the Father of the United States Navy?

Long before Commodore **John Barry** was made the first head of the United States Navy, thereby earning the lofty title by which he is remembered in the history books, he followed the seafaring traditions of his native town in Ireland, Waterford, and shipped out of Wexford harbor as a cabin boy. By 1761, when he was fifteen, he had crossed the Atlantic and had found a new home port in Philadelphia. By age twenty-one he was captain of a schooner, and at twenty-nine he was commanding one of the first ships involved in transatlantic trade.

Already a patriot in his adopted country, Barry readily offered his services and considerable skills at the outset of the Revolution. As the commander of the *Lexington*, he was the first captain in the Continental navy to capture a British vessel when, on April 7, 1776—just a week shy of his ship's namesake's anniversary—he took the *Edward*. The *Lexington* saw much action as the naval war progressed, from skirmishes to full battles, and Barry even took part in at least one land assault.

Appropriately enough, Barry was at the helm of a Continental ship, the *Alliance*, in the last sea battle of the war, the March 1783 engagement with the British frigate *Sybill*.

When the fighting was ended and the country was born, Barry returned to the merchant seas. But then, the Constitution was adopted and the newly formed government of the United States of America decided that its future required the protection of an armed forces—not only an army but a navy. Barry answered the call and was commissioned on June 11, 1794, as senior captain of the fleet. Once this ultimate title had been bestowed upon him, Barry returned to the sea—no desk duty for him—as commander of the forty-four-gun frigate *United States*. He directed naval operations in the West Indies, where troubles with France were pivotal, and protected American commerce from increasing threats of piracy. He was on his way to the Mediterranean to deal with problems of a similar nature off the Barbary Coast when he became ill. He died on September 13, 1803.

John Barry was the most distinguished Irish American of his day. He is buried in the graveyard of Saint Mary's Church in Philadelphia, and statues both there and in Washington, D.C., honor him. His native land, too, takes great pride in Captain Barry of the U.S. Navy: There is a statue of him gazing out over the harbor of Wexford, the very harbor whence he sailed to glory as a boy.

And when Notre Dame plays the occasional game against Navy—as it did in a memorable away-game in Croke Park, Dublin, in 1996—Irish fans of American football have a hard time deciding who to support.

What happened on December 31, 1775?

On that New Year's Eve, Dubliner **Richard Montgomery,** a major general, became the first U.S. Army general officer killed in action.

What happened on March 17, 1776?

Well, of course, it was Saint Patrick's Day. It was also the day British troops evacuated Boston, and "Saint Patrick" was the password for General Washington's troops.

Evacuation Day remains an official holiday in Boston, whose many Irish Americans get a day off to celebrate . . . what? Freedom from British rule? The patron saint? Any and all?

Regardless, it's a fine excuse for a holiday.

What other Irish characters played a role in the Revolution?

You want a character?

How about **Hercules Mulligan,** the Irish-born "fashionable clothier" in the loyalist stronghold of New York City? From all appearances a good Tory, Hercules was, in fact, a rebel. British officers never hesitated to discuss troop movements and such when they visited Mulligan's shop to be fitted for new uniforms, and Hercules was listening carefully. Worse for the redcoats, he was making regular reports to General Washington. His information was sufficiently vital to the ultimate success of the American army that, when Washington returned to the city in triumph, the general publicly acknowledged the services of Hercules Mulligan, hailing him as an outstanding patriot and "a true friend of liberty."

That's all historical fact. Here's a little historical legend: It was Mulligan, they say, along with another Irishman named **Bill Mooney,** who, on July 6, 1776, toppled the statue of King George that stood at Bowling Green. The statue was melted down to make forty thousand bullets for Washington's troops.

Then there was **Colonel James Moore,** a descendant of Irish revolutionary hero **Rory O'More,** who won the Battle of Moore's Creek Bridge in North Carolina in 1776. This was one of the first big victories for the Colonials.

Then there was sharpshooter **Timothy Murphy.** At the Battle of Saratoga in 1777, he picked off two high-ranking British officers at long range.

Did Irish fight on the side of the British?

Yes, many did, and a few of them were Irish Catholics from the counties that today constitute the Irish Republic.

In fact, it was an Irish soldier who played one of the most highly symbolic roles in the birth of the American nation. It was a man named O'Hara—rather than, say, Cornwallis—who actually surrendered His Majesty's forces to General Washington at Yorktown on October 20, 1781.

General Charles O'Hara represented the third generation of English generals in a family that traced its roots to Sligo and Mayo. He'd spent his career in service to **King George III,** and had risen to second in command to **Lord Cornwallis** by the latter days of the war.

Distinguished for the fighting spirit he displayed after being wounded twice in the southern campaign, O'Hara was the only other British general present at Yorktown, and was the man to whom the overwhelmed Cornwallis turned when he decided to capitulate. O'Hara concurred with the decision—Hibernians will claim he did so reluctantly—and obeyed when his commander, pleading illness, sent him to Washington with the document conceding defeat at the hand of the rebel Yankees. O'Hara was taken captive but, as happened with the other officers, was promptly paroled. He dined that night with Washington (Hibernians will tell you cheerfully).

O'Hara returned to England and later commanded the British garrison at Gibraltar until he fought in the war with revolutionary France. He was taken prisoner again, this time by no less than Bonaparte. It is probable that no one in world history ever enjoyed more esteemed captors than did O'Hara, though there's no report of his supping with Napoleon. Eventually, he was returned to Gibraltar, where he lived out his life as the military governor without further history-making incident.

A strict disciplinarian, O'Hara apparently felt that his fellow Celts were a troublesome lot. In 1799, when his old mentor Cornwallis was Lord Lieutenant in Dublin, O'Hara told him not to send any Irish militia regiments because he had "too many Irish in Gibraltar already." As we will see, "too many Irish" would be something of a concern in the nascent United States as well.

What was Lynch's Law, or Lynch Law?

Charles Lynch was the commander of a volunteer regiment from Virginia during the Revolution. His ancestors, originally from Galway, had founded the town of Lynchburg, Virginia, where Charles had been a planter and a justice of the peace in the colonial era. When the loyalists and rebels were struggling for control of Virginia, Charles Lynch was dispensing a very personal form of justice. Conviction in Lynch's court meant summary punishment, and even for noncapital crimes that sentence could be death by hanging—thus the term Lynch's Law. The word *lynching* had entered the lexicon.

What message is to be gained from the Irish role in the American Revolution?

The men mentioned here as heroes in the colonial effort are just a few of the Irish who took part in this great revolutionary enterprise. Like their new country, they were intrepid. And they were fighting for both their former and present lands. They were seeking something that had seemed to be an elusive dream back home: If they couldn't be free as Irish living in Ireland, they would be free as Irish living in America.

Did any Irishmen sign the Declaration of Independence?

Eight of the signatories who affixed their John Hancocks to the document on July 4, 1776, in Philadelphia were Irish of one sort or another. **Matthew Thornton** of New Hampshire and **George Taylor** and **James Smith** of Pennsylvania were Irish born. The other five of Irish descent were **Edward Rutledge, Thomas Lynch, Thomas McKean, George Read,** and **Charles Carroll.** The secretary of Congress who adopted the Declaration was **Charles Thomson,** who had come to America as an indentured servant from Ulster. It was his duty to read the Declaration of Independence to the Congress for the first time. In 1789 he notified George Washington of his election as the first president of the United States.

The herald of America had arrived as a slave from Ireland.

Were any of the above Catholic Irish?

There was one Catholic: Charles Carroll. His grandfather, also Charles, had been named attorney general of Maryland in 1680 by the proprietor, Lord Calvert, and was founder of one of the most distinguished and prosperous Irish American families of the colonial era.

Charles Carroll is remembered not only for his signing but also for saying, "We must remember, and forgive." He was talking about the English in America, but surely he was referring to centuries of persecution as well. The Irish divisiveness over the "forgive" part has always defined Irishness and Irish Americanism. Not all Irish would see eye-to-eye with Carroll.

And whatever happened to Charles Carroll's brother, John?

John went on to become the first Roman Catholic bishop in the United States in 1790. (In 1808 he would be elevated to archbishop, also a first for an American Catholic.) But even before he became a bishop, he founded Georgetown University in 1789.

The Carroll brothers weren't the only Irish Americans having an impact at this time in and around the nascent capital city. Dublin-born architect **James Hoban** won a competition in 1791 to design what was then referred to as "the President's Palace"—later it would be better known as the White House.

What role did the American Revolution play in the Irish revolt of 1798?

An inspirational one.

The era was known as the Age of Revolution, and because the first revolution, which was based on high principles, succeeded so gloriously, it was bound to inspire others. The French Revolution took much of its original impulse, including its notions of democracy and equality, from the success of the American revolt. And Irish resisters to English rule took heart from both the French and the Americans.

During the eighteenth century in Ireland, anti-English sentiment was common in rural areas, and—à la Concord and Lexington—weapons were stored in various places. (When the Protestant Peep O'Day Boys tried to disarm County Armagh in the 1780s, they were met with resistance by the Catholic Defenders.) Middle-class Presbyterian Irish and Scotch-Irish were starting to listen to what Wolfe Tone was saying: Ireland could thrive only if it was a unified, nonsectarian, Protestant-Catholic land independent from English rule.

Ireland was starting to look like colonial America: restless, hot under the collar.

Who was Wolfe Tone? I thought that was an Irish band, the Wolfe Tones?

Well, it is. There's an Irish—or Irish American—band named after just about all famous Republican leaders, Republican ideals, or Republican days of reckoning: the Wolfe Tones, Black 47, Bloody Sunday. (U2 was an American spy plane, of course, but we'll get to that later.)

But to return to **Theobald Wolfe Tone.** He was a Protestant Dubliner born in 1763. In one of Irish American history's great ironies, Tone's father, a wealthy Dublin coach builder, disapproved of Wolfe's teenage ambition of joining the British army that was fighting the rebels over in America, and so the boy reluctantly headed for Trinity College instead, where he studied law. He was called to the bar in 1789. He tried his hand as a gothic novelist, then, in 1790, inspired by French revolutionary principles, he published the *Review of the Conduct of the Administration*, a harsh critique, followed the next year by *Argument on Behalf of the Catholics of Ireland*. From his thinking and activism—particularly his notion that his country "break the connection with England, the never failing source of all our political evils"—sprung a strong Dublin branch of the Society of United Irishmen. He proposed the term *Irishman* in place of Catholic, Protestant, and Dissenter. He fell into cahoots with William Jackson, and the two were discussing a possible armed raid of England when Jackson was arrested and jailed in April of 1795. Tone had an official place in the Irish parliament and so got off easier: He was asked to remove himself to America. He and his wife lived briefly in Princeton, New Jersey, but were unhappy there and moved to France. There, he got his insurrectionist dander up again and tried to talk England's natural enemy into an invasion of Ireland. He and the French tried their assault three times between December of 1796 and September of 1797, but were alternately foiled by weather and the English navy. Tone was captured, court-martialed, and sentenced to hang. His *Speeches from the Dock* contains some of Ireland's most moving prose regarding a utopian condition of Protestant-Catholic peace:

> I have labored to create a people in Ireland by raising three million of my countrymen to the rank of citizens. I have labored to abolish the infernal spirit of religious persecution, by uniting the Catholics and Dissenters. To the former I owe more than ever can be repaid. The services I was so fortunate as to render them they rewarded munificently; but they did more: when the public cry was raised against me—when friends of my youth swarmed off and left me alone—the Catholics did not desert me; they had the virtue even to sacrifice their own interests to a rigid principle of honor; they refused, though strongly urged, to disgrace a man who, whatever his conduct towards the government might have been, had faithfully and conscientiously discharged his duty towards them; and in so doing, though it was in my own case, I will say they showed an instance of public virtue of which I know not whether there exists another example.

While awaiting death—he had already lobbied for a firing squad over the gallows—Tone tried to cut his own throat and succeeded after a fashion: He died painfully of the self-inflicted injury days after the act. He is regarded as a great martyr but, more important, as an early, brave, and highly symbolic olive-branch bearer in the Protestant-Catholic clash.

While Tone was getting in trouble, then sprinting toward death, the United Irishmen were allying with the Catholic Defenders, and were starting to view themselves as a revolutionary army, not unlike the New England patriots. When they saw Tone's success in spurring French support and even action, they grew hopeful of an overthrow. Why wouldn't they? The U.S. effort had succeeded with French help.

So why didn't it work? Perhaps because of yet another Emerald Isle trademark: the Irish weather. Had a storm not foiled the first Tone-led French invasion in December of 1796, there might have been a general uprising of considerable strength and focus. It's highly hypothetical but can be argued: The misery of the next two centuries' Troubles might have been averted had the uprising become the second successful revolution of the Age of Revolution. Wolfe Tone might have been the American George Washington; the voyage across the Irish Sea might have seemed equivalent to boats crossing the Delaware. But as it was, the aborted mission to Bantry Bay put the English on alert, and authorities cracked down on arms and munitions holding throughout the island. By the time the revolutionaries did rise up, in the fighting of May 1798, they were a fragmented force and were put down by the Crown with relative ease.

The footnote is: The idealistic would-be rebels started to look at the newborn United States not only as a place of exile, as it had been meant for Tone, but as a Shangri-la of nonsectarianism and democracy. And the ocean was looking less wide. From Tone's day onward, Irish Republicanism would be fought not only from home but also by means of a shuttle (of philosophy, of diplomacy, of strategy, of talent, and of arms) that was built between Dublin and America as early as the eighteenth century.

Why is Wolfe Tone's widow buried in Brooklyn?

Under the exile order of 1795 Tone and his wife, the former Matilda Witherington, lived for a short time in New Jersey. Following Tone's death, Matilda and son William returned to America from Europe, becoming part of the pre-Famine Irish community in New York City. They moved to the Georgetown section of Washington, and **Matilda Tone** set about editing her husband's material. She is largely responsible for the fact that his light burns so brightly today. When she died in 1849, she was buried in Brooklyn, New York, where her only grandchild, Grace Georgiana Tone, lived. Grace married Lascalles E.

Maxwell and would raise seven children—the first substantial generation of Wolfe Tone's Irish American descendants.

In 1996 Irish President **Mary Robinson** traveled to Greenwood Cemetery where Matilda and other prominent Irish Americans are interred. She dedicated a restored white marble monument to Matilda Tone and to the spirit of 1798.

What is Vinegar Hill?

Vinegar Hill, outside the town of Enniscorthy in County Wexford, was where the decisive battle of the 1798 uprising was staged. It is also the name given to the section of waterfront Brooklyn, once called Irishtown, where the first immigrants to that part of New York settled. The area is near the old Brooklyn Navy Yard, where many an Irish American laborer helped build the battleships that served the United States in its several nineteenth- and twentieth-century wars.

What role did the Irish play in the War of 1812?

When the young American nation went to war again with Great Britain in 1812, the Irish among its citizenry were more than eager to enter this new fray against the familiar foe. They even recruited others of their kin to come from the homeland and get in a lick.

A son of Ulster named **John C. Calhoun,** representing South Carolina, was among the War Hawks in Congress urging a battle to end the British blockade of American ports. A self-trained and self-proclaimed military genius named **Andrew Jackson,** whose parents had emigrated from Carrickfergus in 1765, emerged from the battle of New Orleans a national hero. He was on his way to becoming the first Irish American president of the United States.

On the other side, however, was **Robert Stewart,** Lord Castlereagh of Ulster, directing the efforts of the Crown as England's foreign minister, and Major General **Robert Ross,** for whom an obelisk stands in Rostrevir (as well as in Halifax, Nova Scotia) in tribute to his taking of the city of Washington in 1814. It is said that Ross ate President **James Madison**'s dinner before torching the White House. He was later killed in the attack on Baltimore where, by the way, the words of "The Star-Spangled Banner" were first attached to the favorite marching melody of the Royal Inniskillin Fusiliers, establishing the Irish musical backbone of the future national anthem.

The sons of the Irish-born Father of the American Navy were active in the battle. **Oliver Hazard Perry,** whose mother was born in Ireland, became the greatest naval hero of the war when he defeated a British fleet on Lake Erie in September of 1813. He announced grandiloquently, "We have met the enemy and they are ours." A year later the British were trying once again to move their forces south from Canada by boat when they encountered **Thomas Macdonough** on Lake Champlain. By stanching the progress of the enemy and keeping New York and Vermont safe from invasion, the Irishman hastened the negotiations that ended the War of 1812. Macdonough's vital victory came only weeks before Jackson's at New Orleans, which is usually considered the last and conclusive battle of the war.

With whom did the Irish side during the war with Mexico?

Interesting question; complicated answer.

Since the early nineteenth century, the American government had tried to figure out a way of obtaining Texas from Mexico. While rejecting repeated offers to sell the vast area, Mexico encouraged the immigration of Americans, who steadily crossed the border to plant cotton and clear room for ranches. And Mexico reached north, with goodwill toward "Texans."

In the late 1820s, **James McGloin** and **John McMullen** secured a land grant from the Mexican government to establish the Irish colony of San Patricio de Hibernia about thirty miles northeast of Corpus Christi. The Mexicans looked favorably upon a settlement in Texas by Irish people who shared their Roman Catholic faith. McGloin and McMullen recruited about 250 settlers from Donegal, Leinster, and Connaught. In 1829 a group including Brennans, Carrolls, Conways, Dwyers, Faddens, Haugheys, and O'Dochartys established a farming and ranching community that, per order, was called San Patricio.

To Mexico City's dismay, the settlers who were officially living on Mexican soil actually considered themselves U.S. citizens. They resisted the rule of the Mexican Republic, not least because it forbade plantation owners from using slave labor. Even though special privileges were extended to American colonies such as Austin, where Anglos outnumbered the native population, Texas agitated for outright independence and achieved it by defeating Mexico in battle in 1836.

On Saint Patrick's Day of that year, San Patricio enjoyed, by order of General **Sam Houston** (himself of Ulster stock), the distinction of being the first county organized in the newly independent Texas Republic.

Most Texans wanted the region to become part of the United States, but because that country was equally divided between free and slave states such decisions were delayed. But finally, in 1845, U.S. President **John Tyler,** on his last day in office, secured the admission of Texas into the Union as its twenty-eighth state. Mexico protested, first vigorously and then violently, and war was joined; it would last until 1848. As many as half the soldiers in the United States Army were recent immigrants, most of them Irish and German volunteers who saw the war as an opportunity to earn a steady wage and escape the slum life of eastern cities.

Undoubtedly, the Irish immigrants who served in the war improved the group's overall status. Irish Catholics, suspected in America of being more loyal to their church than to their new land, benefited from the chance to prove their bravery and patriotism in service to the U.S.A.

Some politely declined the opportunity.

You mean the San Patricios?

Yes, the San Patricios.

During the Mexican War, up to three hundred American soldiers abandoned the United States Army led by General **Zachary Taylor** to fight for Mexico. Known in Spanish as the San Patricios, this Saint Patrick's battalion was motivated by solidarity between Catholics and opposition to slavery, as well as by promises of land and romance.

Who were these men? They were recent immigrants who had settled in the northeastern United States. Although many were not yet citizens, they had joined the army to gain acceptance as new Americans and to make $7 a month.

However, in the army they were met with treatment that was far worse even than what they had suffered in the nonconscripted world. Singled out for harsh discipline by Protestant officers, some were literally branded with the letter *D* when caught drunk or subjected to "bucking and gogging," a punishment in which the soldier was hog-tied for hours with a rag stuffed in his mouth. Others were flogged and placed in solitary confinement in a hole covered by a wooden door.

When they got to the border and found the Mexicans to be a peaceful people worshiping the Catholic way, they began to wonder what they were doing. Resenting their officers and hating the army that seemed to be using them as cannon fodder, they were easily tempted by the leaflets that were floated over by the Mexicans. The paper emphasized a shared Catholicism and offered the soldiers $10 bonuses and 320-acre tracts of land. Individually and in bunches, they switched sides—then banded.

They were led by **John Riley** of the seaside village of Clifton, County Galway, who had deserted the British army in Canada and had joined the U.S. Army before the Mexican War broke out. Fighting under a green flag with a gilded image of Saint Patrick emblazoned with "Erin go Bragh" on one side of it and the Mexican eagle on the other, they were an intrepid brigade. They were cited for their bravery even in American dispatches: one concerning the 1847 Battle of Buena Vista and another regarding their defense of the convent of Cherubusco later that year. Peter F. Stevens, whose history of the San Patricios will be published in the spring of 1999, claims that Mexican troops tried to surrender the convent three times, but each time the San Patricios pulled down the white flag, preferring to fight to the death. About a third of the battalion was killed, others escaped, and the rest were captured after they ran out of ammunition. Fifty of the San Patricios were taken to the final battle for Mexico City, at the Chapultepec Castle, where they were held in mule carts with nooses around their necks until the fighting was finished; then the Stars and Stripes were raised and the signal was given to hang all of them.

To the extent that they were remembered in the United States at the time, the San Patricios were recalled as drunkards, deserters, mercenaries, and traitors. However, in the mid-twentieth century, historians commemorating the hundredth anniversary of the war recognized them more as mistreated immigrant soldiers who found themselves on the wrong side of a fight that recalled Britain's domination of their own native land. They were also recognized, finally, as visionaries of a sort, for their complaints about slavery and about religious persecution.

Mexico lost 870,000 square miles of territory during the "War of North American Invasion," land that is now California, Arizona, New Mexico, Texas, and parts of Utah and Colorado. Having said that, Mexico still reveres its Irish American soldiers. To commemorate the fifty who were hanged, a new stamp was jointly issued by An Post, the Irish postal service, and the Mexican post office. The 32-cent stamp, designed by Mexican artist Lorenzo Rafael, depicts the Clonmachoise Cross: the Mexican crest with an Irish harp in the background.

Should the Irish remember the Alamo?

Yes, but—

When Mexican General Santa Anna, with forces far superior in number, overran the small garrison of 186 Texas volunteers (who did fight to the last man) at the old mission near San Antonio in 1836, much Irish blood was spilled. At least twelve of the Texas defenders were Irish born and another thirty-two, including Colonel **William Barret Travis,** the leader, and the legendary **Davy Crockett,** were of Ulster stock.

The caveat is: The sacrifice of these men at the Alamo provided just enough time for another Ulster-American, General **Sam Houston,** to regroup his forces at San Jacinto for the decisive battle that secured the independence of Texas.

And a postscript is: The Alamo had been founded as a Franciscan mission station in the early 1700s, but it had become a Spanish military post by the end of that century. It remained the property of the Roman Catholic Church until early in the twentieth century, when **Clara Driscoll,** an Irish American philanthropist, bought the property on behalf of the Daughters of the Republic of Texas, who operate it to this day as a shrine to Texan independence.

What was—what is—the Ancient Order of Hibernians?

It was founded in New York City in 1836, and from the 1850s through the 1870s it "enjoyed the most spectacular growth of any of the Irish societies," writes John T. Ridge in "Irish County Societies in New York, 1880–1914," his chapter of the authoritative 1996 book *The New York Irish* (Johns Hopkins University Press). These immigrant clubs, formed by other ethnic groups as well as the Irish, usually faded in size (or altogether) as their people were assimilated, as they became "Americans." Irish associations flourished in the latter half of the nineteenth century but, writes Ridge, "the typical life span of an Irish society in the mid-nineteenth century was no more than twenty-five or thirty years."

Not so for the AOH. Irish-nationalist in focus, this Catholic fraternal organization had an advantage over the "county" groups in that a Kerryman could join and so could a Meathman. Thirty-two Irish counties were represented in New York by the 1870s, and eighteen of them had their own county societies; by the end of that decade most of the clubs had folded. Meanwhile, the AOH prospered and spread. In the 1890s the AOH was even authorizing women's chapters; the first one was chartered in Grand Rapids, Michigan, in 1894.

In our time, more than a century and a half after its founding, the Ancient Order is most famous for trying—successfully, for the most part—to keep gay Irish groups from marching in its Saint Patrick's Day Parade in New York under the banners of their various organizations. But it must be noted that there is dissent even within the Hibernian fold. In 1991 Division 7 of the Manhattan Ancient Order of Hibernians split with the parade committee and invited the Irish Lesbian and Gay Organization to march under its banner. This caused a rift among AOH branches and didn't necessarily please John Cardinal O'Connor, but it demonstrated an Irish sense of sticking up for what one feels is right.

How many Irish came across in the years immediately before the Great Famine?

Perhaps as many as a million, though it's an often-ignored fact.

While the eighteenth century had seen waves of Scotch-Irish/ Ulster Presbyterian immigrants arrive in North America (about 250,000 individuals in all), only about 25,000 Catholics had made the trip by the Revolutionary War. (The first had done so in the seventeenth century, landing in Canada before moving south, because of ties between southern Ireland and France, whose Catholicism ruled in Canada. About 5 percent of "New France" was Irish.)

Now, as the centuries turned, the rebel instinct, fired by the United Irish Rebellion in 1798, saw many bright young Irish looking for freedom where they could find it. And they knew they might find it in the United States, already known as a "land of opportunity." **John Doyle,** an Irish immigrant in New York City by way of Philadelphia, wrote home to his wife in 1818: "It's a fine country and a much better place for a poor man than Ireland." During

the early days of the Industrial Revolution thousands
created in America. There were canals to dig, mills to
there would be railroads to lay. The Irish were the ba
sweat and muscle—behind the Erie Canal; they also built the great
Massachusetts mill town of Lowell, a shining-city-on-a-hill of early
Industrial America.

Between 1800 and 1830 perhaps 300,000 Irish Catholic immigrants landed on U.S. shores. The first Irish newspaper in America,
the *Shamrock*, rolled out in New York in 1810 (published by **Thomas
O'Connor,** a 1798 uprising refugee); four years later the Irish Emigrant Society was founded in the city to assist with the growing influx.
From 1830 to 1840, 540,000 immigrants headed for the United
States, and 44 percent of them were Irish (not exclusively Irish
Catholic, but Irish), many fleeing a cholera epidemic in the homeland. This was not a drop in the bucket for a developing country of
under thirteen million, almost all of whom were of English heritage,
and the Irish were greeted with hostility. Not only did their former
"countrymen"—including yet another wave of Ulster Presbyterians
traveling cheek-by-jowl with the Catholics in the same immigrant
ships—start calling themselves Scotch-Irish by way of distinction, but
general anti-papist sentiments among democratically inclined Americans escalated, in some cases, to violence. "Nativist riots" erupted in
Boston and Philadelphia. The first of these, in 1834, was particularly
ugly: A mob burned the Ursuline Convent in Charlestown, Massachusetts, to the ground. The Irish didn't take such things lying down, and
soon "fighting Irish" were getting a reputation in America—and it
wasn't a good one.

This was head-butting: While American society was unwilling to
graciously assimilate a new mass of strangers, the strangers themselves, hardened by centuries of clannish traditions and by a constant persecution that forced them to trust and rely on only their
own kind, didn't necessarily want to be assimilated. The Irish
wanted to remake Ireland in America, not be melted in the pot. To
survive and thrive in their new homeland, they would have to unlearn communal principles that once were the bedrock of their cultural being. This isn't news: Every immigrant group that would
come to America in the next two centuries would have to fight their
native instincts to varying degrees. But the Irish were the first to
confront this problem. And their greeting party was made up of
their enemies and former persecutors.

A last word about these pioneering Irish Catholic Americans: It wasn't all working and drinking and fighting and cursing. There were quiet moments, moments of reflection, and, indeed, silent tears. There was loneliness, exacerbated by the fact that they were unwanted. John Doyle told his wife more than "it's a fine country." He also wrote: "I am doing astonishing well, thanks be to God, and was able on the 16th of this month to make a deposit of 100 dollars in the bank of the United States. As yet it's only natural I should feel lonesome in this country, ninety-nine out of every hundred who come to it are at first disappointed."

It is assumed that Doyle—not to mention the forty thousand other Irish-born residents of New York City (by 1833)—sent some of his fantastic number of dollars home to Ireland. As has been noted, traffic between the two places, as well as between America and the Continent, was increasing greatly. Even by the nineteenth century, the world was becoming a smaller place.

On one of the many ships now heading east—from New York? Boston?—there was an invisible contagion. We know a lot about this fungus now: We know what it is about, how it can be stopped; we've given it a classification and a fancy Latin name—*Phytophthera infestans*. But back in the early decades of the nineteenth century, the contagion was a mystery, floating toward Europe like a specter traveling on the winds. It landed in Europe and did some damage in England. It crossed the Irish sea.

This contagion affected one particular crop, the potato. It caused general dismay wherever it went, because the potato, a vegetable originally brought north from the Andes of Peru in the sixteenth century by English venturers, had become a vital staple of the Western way of life—it was feed for both livestock and people. In fact, in poor Ireland by 1845, a place filled with landless peasants and struggling farmers, no fewer than three million of the island's eight million souls depended on this crop not only for their livelihood but for their life.

This was a precarious situation and everyone knew it. There had long been thoughts of turning the agricultural scheme toward a more balanced planting. But potatoes were so much more filling and nutritious than whatever else might be sown.

And now, from America, of all places—the beckoning golden land—on some anonymous ship or ships came a fungus that was destined to change the history of not only Ireland but the world.

SIX

An Ulster American Miscellany

*What was the impact of the earliest Irish in
America, their contributions, and their legacy?*

*Are there historical U.S.–Ulster ties
beyond these involving famous Irish and
Irish American personalities?*

*What was the impact of the earliest Irish in
America, their contributions, and their legacy?*

A marvelous question, for keeping straight the contributions of
Scotch-Irish, other Ulster Irish, Presbyterian Irish, and—finally—
Catholic, sons-and-daughters-of-the-Famine Irish is at the very heart
of an understanding of Irish American history. Let's pause and consider before we proceed.

As we've seen, America represented "a way out" for Europeans for
centuries. Increasingly (and for ever-increasing numbers) it came to
look like an escape from persecution to liberty, from poverty to the

77

promise of a better life. **John Dunlap,** the colonial-era publisher who founded *The Pennsylvania Packet*, America's first daily, wrote home to Ulster in the eighteenth century: "The young men of Ireland who wish to be free and happy should leave it and come here as quickly as possible. There is no place in the world where a man meets so rich a reward for conduct and industry."

As Dunlap's example indicates, not all of the Ulster émigrés were roughhewn hunter-gatherers like Davy Crockett (who could "whip his weight in wildcats and shoot six cord of bear in one day") or even Andrew Jackson. There were doctors, like the founder of abdominal surgery, **Ephraim McDowell,** who successfully removed a twenty-two-and-a-half-pound tumor from a Kentucky woman in 1809. Dr. McDowell's "name was so great and so honored in the Mississippi Valley a decade before the Civil War," wrote Mark Twain. There were publishers besides Dunlap, like the famous **Horace Greeley** of the *New York Tribune* who famously urged, "Go west, young man."

Some of these Ulstermen arrived in America in desperate straits; after the United Irishmen's Rebellion of 1798 fell apart, more than a few political refugees had to flee from no less a punishment than the hangman's rope. One famous exiled son of Ulster was **John Mitchel,** the nineteenth-century publisher viewed as seditious first by the British when he was in Ireland and then by the Union when he was writing pro-Confederate broadsides during the Civil War (a war in which he lost two sons). He is today honored in his homeland and in his adopted land as a man of courage and conviction.

The people of Northern Ireland are proud of their enduring links with America. They have carefully preserved the records, customs, and places that are a testament to the men and women who made many valuable contributions to the development of the United States.

So, then, before we turn our attention to the Catholic Irish immigrants who arrived in America from the larger section of the Emerald Isle, land that today comprises the Republic, here is a very brief rundown and wrap-up of the deeds and legacy of great Ulster Americans. We think of them, when we do, as vaguely European. But way back when, when they were playing their part—or in the present day, as they contribute still—they knew themselves to be sons and daughters of Ireland.

- In addition to the six Ulstermen cited in chapter 5 who either signed or, in the case of secretary to the Congress Charles Thomson, delivered the Declaration of Independence, there was a seventh involved with the great document: John Dunlap of Strabane, the publisher of *The Pennsylvania Packet*, who printed the immortal words.

- John Mitchel's *Jail Journal: Or Five Years in British Prisons* is a classic for Anglophobes. Mitchel County in Iowa is named after him. He is also remembered in Newry, Ireland, where he "came home" and died in 1875 after twenty-seven years in the United States.

- Among the many U.S. presidents with some Ulster blood are the trio who represent the country's only first-generation Americans to rise to the office: **Andrew Jackson, James Buchanan,** and **Chester Alan Arthur.** Arthur's ancestral home in Callybarckey, whence his father emigrated in 1816, today sports a memorial to the family. President James Buchanan's ancestors came from Deroran. His father was a descendant of George Buchanan, a Scot who settled in the town in 1674.

- **James Wilson** emigrated from Dergalt in or about 1807. On board he met a local girl, his wife-to-be in the new country. They begat and theirs begat. Thus was born Woodrow Wilson, who would be president.

- President **Ulysses S. Grant**'s great-grandfather, **John Simpson,** was born in Derginan in 1738 and left for Pennsylvania sometime around 1760. You can see Grant's heritage memorialized in Derginan. You can see his tomb, of course, on the Upper West Side of Manhattan.

- Union General **James Shields** was born in 1806 and emigrated in 1826. He defeated General **Stonewall Jackson**—the greatest of Confederate generals, also of Ulster stock—at Kernstown, Virginia. The Shields' family bank, the Altmore Loan Fund, still stands.

- **John Hughes** was first archbishop of New York. In 1850 he launched the grand design for Saint Patrick's Cathedral (called "Hughes's Folly"). He was a champion of poor Irish immigrants, and he was tough. When Catholic churches were burned in Boston and he was asked if they would burn in New York, Dagger John said with meaning: *Watch out for your own churches.* (He was called Dagger John because he used to embellish his signature with a cross which resembled a dagger and also because it seemed to suit him.) Hughes was born in Aughan in 1797 and emigrated in 1817. He made it his life's work to demand an equal share of the American dream for

Irish Catholics, and those who do know of him, particularly many from the New York area, regularly make return pilgrimages to pay tribute: There's a Hughes memorial in Saint Mac-Cartan's Church in Aughan, and Hughes's boyhood home has been re-created at the Ulster American Folk Park in Omagh.

A footnote: **John McCloskey,** the first American cardinal, and the immediate successor to Hughes in 1864 as archbishop of New York, was of an immigrant family from Dungiven.

And regarding that folk park: **Thomas Mellon,** patriarch of the fabulously wealthy Mellons of Pittsburgh, was born in a cottage in Omagh in 1813. Today, on the site, is the park, commemorating Mellon, Hughes, and the 250,000 other mostly Dissenter Ulstermen who sailed west in the nineteenth century.

- **Francis Makemie,** father of American Presbyterianism, was born in 1658; he worshiped in an Irish meetinghouse. He sailed to Virginia, where he was put on trial for preaching without permission. After his acquittal, he founded the first American Presbytery in 1706. He was a truly religious man and defender of religious freedom for all.

A footnote: The Reverend **James MacGregor** led an entire Presbyterian flock to New Hampshire in 1719. Why? Because these "Dissenters" also wanted freedom from persecution, and after the Crown had prevailed in the Siege of Derry (1689), dissent went out of fashion in Ulster. It is thought that Mac-Gregor's congregation planted America's first potato field. They named their town Londonderry, New Hampshire.

- **Alexander Campbell,** who was called the Sage of Bethany, emigrated from Armagh to Pennsylvania in 1809. There, with his father, he founded a new faith, the Disciples of Christ. Today, there are 1.5 million Disciples.

- **Cyrus McCormick,** the inventor of the mechanized reaper, an agricultural tool that was said at the time to be "pushing civilization westward at the rate of 30 miles a year," was born of Ulster stock.

- **Stephen Foster,** the Beautiful Dreamer himself—still perhaps America's best-loved songwriter (apologies to Irving Berlin)—was of Ulster stock.

- **Sam Houston**'s forebears immigrated in the eighteenth century. Houston avenged his fellow Ulster American Crockett and the others who died at the Alamo when his Texans routed the Mexicans and won independence. Houston was known as a great friend of the Indians and spoke fluent Cherokee.

- **Elijah Craig** of Georgetown, Kentucky, a preacher with Ulster roots, invented bourbon in 1788. It is said he did so because the popularity of Bushmill's whiskey demanded something of the sort in America among Ulster Americans. Bushmill's, the world's oldest legal distillery, situated then and situated still on a hill outside Portrush in far northern Ulster, had begun exporting to the United States in 1784, and a general thirst had developed. So Craig beneficently leaped into the breech.

    Today, turnabout being fair play, Bushmill's oak barrels come from Kentucky's bourbon region.

- In Portglemore in 1857, a baby named **Augustine Henry** was born. A billion trees today testify to his talent. The botanist introduced the fast-growing American conifer to the British Isles and utterly transformed its forests.

- **Alexander Brown,** Baltimore banker, was born in Broughshane in 1764. He emigrated in 1800 and founded the first U.S. merchant bank, then financed the Baltimore and Ohio Railroad. His birthhouse in Ireland is now a nursery for rare daffodils.

- **Timothy Eaton,** founder of the chain department store headquartered in Canada, learned his trade in Portglemore, Ulster, from 1847 to 1852. It is said that he worked sixteen hours a day and slept under the counter.

- What do **Mark Twain** and **Andrew Johnson,** the U.S. president who followed Lincoln and remains the only U.S. chief executive to be impeached (Richard Nixon resigning in the nick of time), have in common? Their forebears are thought to have come from Larne, in County Antrim. Johnson's grandfather emigrated from there around 1750. Samuel Langhorne Clemens's ancestors are thought to have done the same.

- **Belleck** was a potter, and today there are nearly ten thousand U.S. and Canadian collectors of Belleck's famous creamy pottery—so fragile it's translucent—which was first made in 1857. The worldwide Belleck Collector's Society headquarters are in Pine Brook, New Jersey.

- **Leif Crozier,** born in Newry in 1847, was superintendent of the Canadian North-West Mounted Police and responsible for curbing the power of Sitting Bull and Big Bear in his region.

- **John Macoun,** a naturalist, explorer of the Rockies, and surveyor for the Canadian Pacific Railway, was born in Maghenlam in 1831. He told the company to build the line across the Canadian desert, which they did. A peak in the Selkirks in British Columbia bears Macoun's name, as do forty-eight species of flora and fauna worldwide.
- Captain **Francis Crozier** of the Royal Navy found the Northwest Passage in 1848. He was born in Banbridge, Ireland. Also born in Banbridge was hymn writer **Joseph M. Scrivner,** the eventual benefactor of Port Hope, Ontario, who died in Port Hope in 1886, where he wrote "What a Friend We Have in Jesus."
- **Harry Ferguson,** the inventor of the tractor, was born near Hillsborough, Ireland, in 1884. His famous handshake deal with Henry Ford ended in a $250 million patent suit against the Ford Motor Company, which Ford won.
- **Catherine O'Hare** was the mother of the first white child born west of the Rockies. Her baby was delivered by Indian midwives in 1802. She herself had been born in Rathfriland, Ulster, Ireland.
- Another Ulster woman who made her mark in the far west was Hollywood film star **Greer Garson,** who was born in Castlewellon in 1908. She won an Oscar for her wartime film *Mrs. Miniver* (1942), a picture that boosted the British cause among Americans.
- The first Irish American in space was **John Glenn** (first of his countrymen to orbit the earth, too, in 1962). This son of Ulster went on to a distinguished career as the Democratic senator from Ohio, before returning to space in his seventies aboard the shuttle in 1998.

  The first Irish American on the moon was the first man on the moon, **Neil Armstrong,** who took his small step/giant leap in 1969. Armstrong's ancestors were from County Fermanagh.

  In 1971 **James B. Irwin,** also of Ulster heritage, drove the lunar rover on the surface during the Apollo 15 mission. His ancestors were from County Pomeroy.

  In blazing new frontiers, the astronauts carry on the Crockett tradition.

*Are there historical U.S.–Ulster ties
beyond these involving famous Irish and
Irish American personalities?*

Surely. For instance, we just gave you some flyboy links. Here's a fly-girl link: **Amelia Earhart,** nowise Irish, landed her tiny plane at Ballyarnet Field near (London)Derry in 1932. Thus ended the first solo flight by a woman across the Atlantic.

Here are but a few other examples:

- The last scheduled passenger voyage by a ship under sail to America was that of the *Minnehaha* in 1873. For thirteen years this copper-bottomed McCorkell clipper had made the Derry to New York City round trip three times annually. Even during the American Civil War she safely delivered a thousand immigrants a year on Union soil. The *Minnehaha* could sail home in only fifteen days.
- Since the Republic had problems with World War II and chose to stay on the fence, U.S. troops heading for the European theater arrived by way of Belfast in 1942. An obelisk in that city commemorates the fact. And transatlantic convoys during the war were guarded by U.S. lend-lease destroyers based in Derry, the largest of all United Kingdom escort bases.
- Linen was Ulster's greatest industry in the eighteenth and nineteenth centuries, with a million spindles spinning by 1900. American women coveted this stylish "soft look" linen and established the United States as a primary market. (When the auto industry got up and rolling in the second decade of the century, the linen was also sought for seat covers.) The linen trade opened the lines for a brisk twentieth-century import-export business with Northern Ireland, commerce that was uninterrupted by politics.

The point of it all is this: Contributions to American cultural, political, and industrial life by Irish Americans of Catholic ancestry are always saluted as contributions of "Irish Americans." Because of the age-old problems between northern Protestant Irish and Republic Catholics, the contributions of sons and daughters of Ulster often are not acknowledged. But when viewed without prejudice, it becomes evident that many with deep roots in the auld sod—albeit the auld sod of Ulster—have greatly impacted the birth, growth, and success of the United States. In some perfect world that we cannot yet see, when the Irish Troubles are but a memory, these people will once again be properly regarded as having been great Irish Americans.

SEVEN

Boston Bound (or, Philadelphia Here I Come!)

What was the Great Famine?

Did the British cause the Famine?

What was the Irish Rebellion of 1848?

Which of the Irish suffered most during the Famine?

So aid was being sent from America to Ireland?

What was the Famine like at its core?

Did all Famine refugees go to America?

What were the "coffin ships"?

Did all of the Irish who came to America settle on the East Coast?

What are the lasting aftershocks of the Famine?

Is there a museum in the United States where I might learn more about the Famine?

Who was Daniel O'Connell?

What was the Irish American attitude toward slavery?

Were there Irish in the South?

What part did the Irish play in the Civil War?

Who were the Irish heroes of the Civil War?

What was the Irish Brigade?

Who was Irish Bridget?

What was the U.S.S. Shamrock?

Who was Mathew Brady?

What role did the Irish play at the Battle of Gettysburg?

How were the Irish responsible for Thanksgiving Day?

What was the Conscription Act?

How bad were the Draft Riots?

What is the legacy of Irish American—At American interactions in nineteenth-century America?

What was next for the Irish in America?

What was the Great Famine?

The Great Famine—or the Great Hunger, as it is known to most Irish and as it is called in Cecil Woodham-Smith's famed 1963 history *The Great Hunger* (Harper and Row)—was the single worst depredation visited upon Catholic Ireland (Cromwell included) and, as it pertains here, the single greatest spur to modern Irish Americanism.

To set the scene: Despite the Penal Laws, Catholicism in Ireland was on the rise in the first decades of the nineteenth century. By 1840 there was a priest for every three thousand people. Meanwhile, the economy was in the tank. Beginning in 1810, a recession was felt throughout the island, but most acutely in the countryside. From 1821 to 1841 the proportion of the Irish workforce engaged in trade and manufacture fell by 15 percent; the country was becoming more reliant on agriculture. And the population was rising: to nearly seven million by 1820 (today, by contrast, it's only four million; Ireland is the only country in the European Community to experience a fall in population over the last century and a half). Authorities felt, however, that as long as the mass of agricultural laborers—56 percent of the workforce, most of them landless—could rely on the potato, the rising population was of scant concern.

And the people seemed to be staying: Ireland was not yet an emigrant nation; in fact, prior to the eighteenth century, it had a history of gaining steadily more people than it lost. Woodham-Smith estimates a 172 percent population gain from 1779 to 1841, while the population of England and Wales, by contrast, had grown at a rate of 88 percent.

Some Irish did start to leave: In 1827, for the first time in a half-century, the number of emigrants to North America exceeded twenty thousand, and in 1831–32 the number was higher than sixty-five thousand for the first time ever. (Most of these immigrants arrived first in Canada—not necessarily by choice, but because that passage was cheaper.) So emigration was on the rise but was not yet the national pastime: The Irish knew there were watery highways open, but things weren't so bad at home that they were compelled to hit the road.

Ireland was under constant threat of famine in those days. Between 1800 and 1845 there were no fewer than sixteen food crises, most of them caused by the weather. But the country was still producing enough food to feed its own and export a surplus.

Of all the crops for the fungus to hit, the potato was the worst possible choice for the Irish people. *Phytophthera infestans* proved to be not only incurable but also fast-traveling, thanks to a wet summer in 1845. It quickly decimated 40 percent of the crop. Things would get worse; the blight would hit again and again, and the potato crop would fail repeatedly between 1845 and 1851.

In Ruth Dudley Edwards's *An Atlas of Irish History*, there's a map showing percentage declines in Irish counties between 1841 and 1851, and it's shocking. By the time the famine struck, there were between nine and ten million people living in Ireland. Edwards's grim map shows population declines of 26 percent in Cork and Clare during that dark decade, 29 percent in Mayo and Sligo, and 31 percent in Roscommon. And once the famine finally ended, poor Irish continued to flee their ravaged land. Between 1845 and 1860, about 1.5 million Irish—25 percent of the population—would emigrate. Another million would die of hunger or disease. Without the famine Ireland's population would have risen to more than ten million by 1850. In fact, there were only 6.5 million souls left on the island by that year.

Did the British cause the Famine?

No.

Some Irish and Irish American historians have compared the Famine to the Holocaust, viewing it as England's purposeful "final solution" of its "Irish problem." But official British behavior before and during the Famine was marked by periods of everything from heartlessness to indifference to small bits of heroism, and there was never any attempt to inflame or prolong the Famine. During the horror, London continuously flip-flopped in its Irish policies, and in retrospect it is certain that this inconsistency did a lot of harm. But as for *causing* the Famine . . . The situation was itself the culprit: neglect of the fact that three of nearly nine million Irish were entirely dependent on a single crop and that fields not planted with potato were planted with cereal crops intended for export and hardly able to float an imperiled population. Yes, the English helped plant that seed, but the Irish were complicit in bringing about the state of affairs. The Irish could have turned their agricultural scheme toward more balanced plantings.

When the contagion came stealing in, the analysts blamed everything else: rain, the moon, an excess of cow dung. But soon the blight was so general—every Irish county was hit, and large sections of England as well—that it became clear a disease had spread through the fields. When the potato crop failed in 1845, British Prime Minister **Robert Peel** moved aggressively to forestall disaster in Ireland. He ordered shelters built for the farmers who would soon be destitute and shipments of corn from America rerouted to Ireland. Public works projects such as road building were begun. London seemed to be reaching out.

Peel is an interesting character in Anglo-Irish history. A conservative, he had been Britain's chief secretary in Ireland early in his career, and in that post he'd built a tough police force to keep the Irish in line. Older Irish will still call a cop a "peeler." Yet here he was, at the outset of the Famine, risking his standing in London by asking Parliament to lift trade restrictions—the Corn Laws—which set grain prices artificially high, too high for the Irish. Even Peel's own cabinet opposed him, and before 1845 was out, so was Peel as prime minister. The Whig **John Russell** was unable to form a government, and suddenly Peel was back in—and again he asked for reforms to help the Irish. So in June of 1846 he was ousted again, and Russell ascended. Few in Ireland realized at the time how unfortunate it was for them that tough old Peel's political career was over.

Charles Trevelyan, whom Peel had put in charge of relief operations in Ireland, had long disagreed with Peel regarding the Irish situation. Now he and Russell went their own way, which was a market-oriented one. As summer waned in 1846 he closed food depots and other aid operations. Then the crop failed again, and landlords started evicting tenants. Former farmers suddenly choked the roads of Ireland. (Today, it is said of the raggle-taggle tinkers who still color the Irish countryside: "They went on the road at the time of the famine and never came in again.") For a moment, Trevelyan seemed blind to the misery and continued shutting down relief projects. Then in the fall he reversed field and reopened a few depots—but not enough. In October a worker who had not eaten in many days died in Skibbereen, the first official victim of the Famine. He was followed by a million others, dying of starvation, exposure, and disease (typhus took its toll, as did cholera).

Eighteen forty-seven—Black '47—is remembered as the worst year of the Famine, but that's only because more Irish left that year than in any other; all of the years were awful. In 1847 the great **Daniel O'Connell,** told the British House of Commons, "Ireland is in your hands, in your power. If you do not save her, she cannot save herself." The government abolished the Corn Laws and relief operations geared up in Ireland again. The Quakers came with soup kitchens. Some Protestant missionaries offered food for conversion, and "soupers" were former Catholics who renounced their faith for a bowl. By the summer of '47 three million Irish were getting food from the British or from the missions every day. Meanwhile, Trevelyan was resolutely arguing that Ireland "must be left to the operation of natural forces." When the potato harvest of 1847 produced some crop, sympathies hardened again. Then the blight returned the next year—and in '49, and in '50—and the horror persisted.

In his book *Now and in Time to Be*, the Irish Australian writer Thomas Keneally uses a nice phrase to describe British attitudes and policies during the Famine: "criminal negligence." It's hard to prosecute that crime, but there it is. Keneally goes on to discuss how, despite facts, many Irish cannot get past the idea that their arch-enemy from across the Irish Sea inflicted the killing of the 1840s and 1850. He writes that "the Famine is central in the Irish imagination. Rightly or wrongly, it holds a place in the Irish imagination as the ultimate proof of Anglo-Saxon malice. It is to the souls of the Irish what the Holocaust is to the Jews." That's a nice distinction: The Famine, and the British role in it, torment the Irish *soul*, the Irish *imagination*, rather than the Irish intellect. The Famine and the British role in it bedevil the Irish, and always will.

Keneally continues: "Though the Famine might not have been anywhere near official policy, the questions which lie behind every famine, from Stalin's in the Ukraine in the 1930s, to Haile Selassie's in the mid-1970s and crazy Megistu's in the 1980s, still remain here: to what extent was it an act of politics, and to what extent was it an act of God? It is characteristic of all famines that people look for their explanation in terms of trials sent by the Deity—a crop fungus or a drought—without asking why systems have to be so run down in a given country that a shift of climate or a failed crop produces disaster for millions.

"The question of whether and to what extent the Famine was a willed attempt at genocide still—rightly or wrongly—teases the Irish mind."

What was the Irish Rebellion of 1848?

An uprising by middle-class, largely Protestant intellectuals who considered Britain to blame for the Famine. The revolt went nowhere, and one in 1849 didn't even get that far ("the rising in the cabbage patch," it is sometimes insultingly called). A sick and downtrodden population could hardly mount an insurrection. In *A Concise History of Ireland*, Maire and Conor Cruise O'Brien note: "In the Ireland of 1848 . . . a rebellion could only be a gesture, and a pledge for the future."

Which is interesting, because as the O'Briens also point out: "[I]n fact 1848 helped to establish the continuity of a revolutionary tradition; those who were to lead the rising of 1916 were lineal successors of the men of 1848; key figures among these 1916 men belonged to the Irish Republican Brotherhood, founded by **James Stephens** (1824–1901), one of the most determined of the 1848 rebels." Other leaders of the '48 rising, also known as the Young Ireland Rebellion, included **Thomas Francis Meagher**, **Thomas D'Arcy McGee**, and **John Mitchel**, who were transported to Australia, where they escaped and headed for the United States.

James Stephens, "the Fenian Chief," was devoted to the philosophy of Wolfe Tone, and from 1858 his organization had an American arm, the Fenian Brotherhood. The Fenian Risings of 1865 and 1867 were conducted by these groups with materials and even soldiers—some of them veterans of the American Civil War—crossing the sea. The Famine changed the dynamics of the Troubles in Ireland: With so many Irish immigrants in America, the United States became a behind-the-lines outpost of support for the Republican cause.

Which of the Irish suffered most during the Famine?

The westerners, in Connaught.

No, actually, we take that back. The *far*-westerners, nearing California.

It is a coincidence too extraordinary to believe: In the year 1847—

Black '47—an Irish American immigrant family was involved in the most infamous single episode of starvation in U.S. history. While thousands of Irish were dying of hunger back in County Carlow, eight thousand miles away, **Patrick** and **Margaret Breen** and their seven children were heading into the Nevada Rockies as members of the Donner Party. These settlers were seeking California, land of promise and plenty, and they had picked the wrong route. Trapped for three and a half months during the fierce winter of 1846–47, with little food to support them, surviving members of the Donner Party took to cannibalizing the dead in order to survive.

There had been eighty-one people in the party when it reached the Rockies in November 1846; only forty-five survived. Of the twelve families stranded, the Breens were one of two that made it out without losing anyone. Hibernians are quick to point out that the Breens behaved in exemplary fashion, perhaps even saving the lives of others by sharing their own food when supplies were dwindling. But the early Christian criticisms of the Celts—human sacrifice and cannibalization—come to mind when one envisions the family as it was found by a rescue party: sitting in a pit with snow walls twenty-four-feet deep, the bodies of four others around them, the flesh from the bodies already removed.

Now while we're on the subject of fascinating famine tangents from America's Wild West, let's look briefly at the Choctaw Indians. This was a tribe that knew what it was like to be victimized: Forcibly removed from their ancestral lands in Mississippi, they had lost nearly half their population during a six-hundred-mile death march to Oklahoma in the winter of 1831–32. Hearing of the Irish plight in 1847, the Choctaw raised $170 in relief funds and sent it to Dublin. By that time, the cries of the Irish were being heard worldwide, and many associations and governments were responding. But the Choctaw contribution still stands out, as was acknowledged in 1995 when Irish President Mary Robinson made a pilgrimage to the Choctaw Nation in Oklahoma to thank them for their generosity, while Choctaw artist Gary White Deer joined in a reenactment of the Black '47 famine death march from Doolough to Lovisburg, County Mayo. (In 1847 a group of hunger-ravaged Irish had walked the fifteen miles to petition the commissioners of Delphi Lodge for food.) White Deer sensed a "blending of spirits" between the Irish and the Choctaw. "It was very reminiscent of how the Choctaw had been treated. The hills around us were alive. They are a witness to what happened there. There were people walking with us who you could not see—spirits of the ones who had died."

He further observed: "The Irish never forget their heroes. . . . In Ireland there is a profound sense of loss, that feeling of there being holes in the national spirit, like in Native America. Our Choctaw people had just experienced dispossession, tremendous loss of life, extreme hardship and deprivation at the hands of the American government. The 1847 Choctaw donation to Irish Famine relief is a modern parable of giving, with lessons that each generation it seems must relearn. Its telling deepens your spirit and connects you in an interactive way to what I believe to be a kinship of cultures, Irish and Choctaw."

In order to better understand Irish culture and philosophy, White Deer served a three-month residency in Carogaholt, County Clare, when he painted a series of works like *The Buffalo of Connemara* that express an intimate connection between the Choctaw and Irish people. The paintings were displayed at the American embassy in Dublin. Upon returning to the United States, White Deer remained active in CAIT, Celts and American Indians Together, a nonprofit organization based at Iona College in New Rochelle, New York, that is dedicated to fighting world hunger.

So aid was being sent from America to Ireland?

Much. It's one of the reasons America so appealed to Famine refugees.

By 1850, word of Ireland's plight had spread around the world, and relief missions were mounted by many organizations besides the Quakers. The greatest and most helpful of these came from America. Justin McCarthy, a nineteenth-century journalist and member of the Irish Parliamentary Party, wrote in his memoir *An Irishman's Story*: "I can well remember the mingled sensations created by the sounding of joy bells from many steeples in the city of Cork, when the news went abroad that an American war frigate had come into the harbour heavily laden with food supplies wherewithal to resist the work of the famine. The mere thought that public rejoicing should have come to be associated with the arrival from across the Atlantic of donations of food for the starving poor whom the local authorities were not able to save from starvation, was of itself enough to fill the heart with a new and a keener sense of the misery surrounding us on all sides. Other countries followed the generous example of America. As a writer in one of the national newspapers said at the time, 'Even the heart of the Turk at the far Dardanelles was touched, and he sent us in pity the alms of a beggar.' "

What was the Famine like at its core?

Rwanda. Ethiopia. You've seen it on television.

Peter O'Leary, a Catholic priest who was a boy when famine hit County Cork, remembered in his autobiography, "Often, when the hunger was very severe, they'd have to rise and move out and head for the house of some neighbour (who, perhaps, would be as needy as themselves, or close to it) to see if they could get a mouthful of something to eat, which might take the frenzy of hunger off them."

The frenzy of hunger.

Others have tried to put it into words. A scholarly account is *The Great Famine*, by Desmond Williams and Ruth Dudley Edwards. For a more readable chronicle, there's Woodham-Smith's classic, *The Great Hunger*, cited at the beginning of this chapter. For a dramatic, powerful narrative, we commend Liam O'Flaherty's 1937 novel *Famine*, recently republished by David R. Godine Publishers of Boston.

For a brief, eloquent, even poetic take, we return to Thomas Keneally.

It is a reader's habit to have favorite writers, favorite books. Keneally, author of *Schindler's List* and more than a dozen other nonfiction volumes and novels, is one of our favorites. More than a century ago his grandparents, separately, "chose to launch themselves on the longest journey of the Irish diaspora—Cork to Australia." In 1990 Keneally traveled in Ireland, north and south. ("We people of the diaspora, whether from Australia or Michigan or the plains of Canada, get back here, returning ghosts, utterly confused and in need of guidance; and we see a place like Ballycotton, and recognize it straight away as a never but always known place.") His travelogue-cum-history-cum-meditation, *Now and in Time to Be,* is one of our favorite books, and since it has never been available in the United States, we go to it again so you can have a taste.

Keneally is remembering moments of epiphany in Ireland, "for instance finding a graveyard, fairly ill-kempt, in the Drum hills above Dungarvan, where famine victims were buried. The local community had spruced up the site and placed a memorial on the mute turf to mark a papal visit ten years back. Peasants on the road. Starving peasants always take to the road, in Ethiopia at the barbarous end of this century, in Ireland in the barbarous middle of the last. I stood on a hill like that and knew from what I had seen of the skeletal Ethiopians and Eritreans how the starved Irish looked on the edge of death. How hunger had impelled them along roads but now nailed them to this hill. Were they coming from the direction of Cork, or were they climbing out of Waterford County. Since this is not a regular churchyard, it means someone merciful brought all those who had died on the ascent to this spot for burial."

Did all Famine refugees go to America?

Most did, but many went to Canada, and as Keneally's family history indicates, others went as far as Australia. In fact, that country has quite a large Irish-heritage population today, thanks to the "transporting" of Irish convicts to the barbarous British penal colony there that began in the 1780s. (Between then and 1845, as many as sixty-five thousand Irish felons were transported, including some political prisoners—members of the United Irishmen, for instance, and those Young Ireland Rebellion leaders named above—and even Tom Keneally's wife's grandfather.)

Five hundred thousand Irish settled in Britain in the first half of the nineteenth century. In 1847 more than 320,000 Irish disembarked in the port city of Liverpool, some of them hoping to continue their journey east to the Continent or west to America, but many were destined to remain in the land of their enemy.

Herman Melville viewed the misery in Liverpool and remembered it when he wrote *Redburn*: "endless vistas of want and woe staggering arm in arm along these miserable streets." **Nathaniel Hawthorne,** Melville's friend and mentor, also chanced upon Famine-era Liverpool and viewed it less sympathetically, describing the Irish poor down by the docks as people "numerous as maggots on cheese."

What were the "coffin ships"?

The earliest of the immigration ships heading west from Ireland were overcrowded with thousands of already sick, dying, or dead peasants—and they earned this apt nickname. They landed in

Canada since the United States would not allow entry to the notorious vessels. Grosse Isle in the Saint Lawrence River, quite near Detroit, was begun as a Canadian disembarkation center but quickly became a hospice and burial ground for thousands of Irish refugees. In *The Famine Ships*, historian Edward Laxton details the plight of many vessels that traveled from Ireland to Grosse Isle, a teeming Canadian Calcutta. Here's Laxton's accounting of only one ship: The *Agnes* sailed forth with 427 passengers, 63 died at sea, 200 died on Grosse Isle, and only 150 pressed on into Canada.

In *The Great Hunger*, Woodham-Smith quotes Dr. Douglas, chief medical officer at the Grosse Isle station, as saying that every ship, without exception, came in with disease: "[I]n all these vessels cases of fever and dysentery had occurred." Today there is a plaque at Grosse Isle that reads, "In this secluded spot lie the mortal remains of 5,294 persons who, flying from pestilence and famine in Ireland in the year 1847, found in America but a grave." That's but a partial figure. More than ten thousand Irish would die on Grosse Isle, as would many Canadians infected with disease.

And many never made it even that far. In 1847 one hundred thousand Irish headed for Canada, seventeen thousand died en route, and another fifty thousand died upon reaching the promised land.

It was fated, of course, that even some better-regulated ships bound for American ports-of-call ended up as coffin ships. One, the *St. John* out of Galway, is remembered today because **Henry David Thoreau** stumbled upon her wreck on the Cape Cod beach of Cohasset. The brig had been done in by an Atlantic storm only a mile out of Boston Harbor, and as Thoreau watched the Massachusetts Irish pick through the *St. John*'s remains looking for kin, he openly despaired: "All their plans and hopes burst like a bubble. Infants by the score dashed on the rocks by the enraged Atlantic Ocean! No, no!" His account can be found in the classic *Cape Cod*.

Did all of the Irish who came to America settle on the East Coast?

Most did—it was where they landed, and they usually had no money remaining for a further move. But as with any diaspora of a refugee population, settlement was widespread. A family of sixteen headed out from Ballinascarty in Black '47 and landed in Quebec aboard a coffin ship having lost only one of its members—a good voyage.

They moved through Canada, then into Michigan, planting roots in Dearborn. The eldest son married, and in 1863 his eldest son was born: **Henry Ford**.

A priest from Wexford, **Father Thomas Hore**, had visited the United States in 1820 at age twenty-four. When Famine hit his homeland, he organized a massive emigration. He and 450 of his flock boarded the *Ticonderoga* in 1850 and headed for New Orleans, intending to eventually establish a community in Arkansas. But Arkansas didn't want the immigrants, and Hore searched for an alternative. A bishop in Dubuque, Iowa, pointed him toward Allamakee County, and there Hore bought three thousand acres on the cheap. By the time he returned to St. Louis to round up his parishioners, he found that some had already headed west in search of California gold, or had decided to stay where they stood. A dozen families accompanied Hore back to Iowa where, in March 1851, they founded Wexford. Father Hore spread his ministry in Iowa, traveled to Rome, then returned to his first Wexford, in Ireland, where he died in 1864.

Kate Kennedy was born in Meath in 1827. She and her sisters fled the Famine and landed in New York. When they heard of the California gold that had lured many of Hore's followers away—the rush started in 1849—the Kennedy girls went west. (A note about the gold rush, and about gold rushes in general: In 1859 two Irish prospectors who had been on the job for a while, **Peter O'Reilly** and **Patrick McLaughlin**, discovered the Comstock Lode. They sold out to the "Irish Four," **James Fair**, **James Flood**, **William O'Brien**, and **John Mackay**, who became the "silver kings" of Nevada. The Irish, so long destitute, were dreamers, dreaming of a quick fix, dreaming like Jackie Gleason of "the big one!" Dreamers are sometimes rewarded. Today, Irish Americans play Lotto or place a bet on the Irish Sweepstakes.)

In 1857 Kate Kennedy began teaching in San Francisco schools and in 1867 was promoted to principal. When her pay didn't rise accordingly, Kennedy protested, and gained the support of the famous suffragette **Susan B. Anthony**. In 1874 the California legislature, reacting to the Kennedy case, enacted an early antidiscrimination law guaranteeing pay equity for women. Today, a school in the Mission District of San Francisco is named for Kate Kennedy.

A huge Irish Catholic community was formed in Chicago. The mining town of Butte, Montana, was built by Famine Irish and their descendants. There were a million new Irish in this new land, so they went everywhere.

What are the lasting aftershocks of the Famine?

The western areas of the island hardest hit by starvation and disease were Irish-speaking, and so the language was devastated. Scholars view the Famine as the beginning of the end for true Gaelic culture, with subsequent rekindlings more romantic or political than real. Certainly very soon after the Famine, Ireland was an English-speaking country.

Ireland became a place where people married late. The early marriages that had been the norm and that had led to the population boom immediately preceding the Famine were now feared. The Irish didn't want large families, because there was no guarantee that a plague wouldn't revisit. Since they were so strictly Catholic, the Irish could find only one means of birth control: late marriage.

A change in the Irish character was seen by some. The gregarious Irishman was replaced by a grimmer, more hardened, and dour version.

And the foundation was laid for a dramatic change in English-Irish relations, a change much to London's disadvantage. So many Irish were now in America, they were bound to gain, over time, political influence and even power. (As politics turned out to be their chosen game, the power came sooner rather than later.) As America rose in the world, its voice could not be ignored. Downing Street had to listen if the White House called for an end to atrocities, or even for disunion. The O'Briens are strong on this point in their *Concise History*: "The famine may not have been a threat to the security of England, but it carried within itself the seeds of the destruction of the United Kingdom of Great Britain and Ireland."

Is there a museum in the United States where I might learn more about the Famine?

There is a stone on Atlantic Avenue near Faneuil Hall Marketplace in Boston commemorating the horror that was the Great Famine. It is the only monument anywhere in the United States to the plague that so greatly changed the face of two nations.

Who was Daniel O'Connell?

He was the dominant Irish political figure of the first half of the nineteenth century. He was a patriot but not a nationalist. He said he was a Catholic but not a papist. He was known as the Great Liberator.

We place him here, after the Famine but before the American Civil War, for a purpose. Although much of his work was done before the Famine, his influence was felt before, during, and, crucially for Irish Americans, after the blight.

At the turn of the nineteenth century, Catholics in Ireland had reason to hope that emancipation from the Penal Laws might be at hand. Although Protestant leaders in England and Ireland opposed liberalization, some, like **William Pitt,** were strong advocates for equity. Compromises were forwarded, but the bishops of Ireland and others said they would prefer exclusion to conditional emancipation. Daniel O'Connell was of this mind.

One of the first Catholic Irish lawyers—he was sent to the bar in 1798—he became a great success and then campaigned for emancipation for Catholics. He took the Catholic Association, founded in 1823, to remarkable heights of influence; in the elections of 1826, Catholics in Ireland voted into office M.P's sympathetic to their side. In 1828 O'Connell himself won election in County Clare, and to stave off sectarian violence George IV allowed a Catholic to sit in Parliament. In 1829 O'Connell won emancipation for his people, the great achievement of his life.

In 1830, O'Connell began fighting in Parliament to end the English-Irish union. He failed in this, but out of his politics and oratory the Young Ireland movement was born. This energetic group of nationalists would have influence in its time—in 1848, for instance—in times to come, and even today. O'Connell, meanwhile, would have influence in America.

"No sir, we are not what we were," O'Connell told the House of Commons in 1837. "We have caught the intonations of your rhymes. Englishmen, we are too like you to give you leave to keep us down. Nay, in some points we have surpassed you.

"We are an undecaying and imperishable people."

What was the Irish American attitude toward slavery?

ntislavery tradition that dates to the Council of Armagh (1177), which prohibited Irish trade in English slaves. In modern times, it's somewhat sound on an intellectual level, and this has much to do with Daniel O'Connell. In fact and deed, however, it's nothing to be proud of.

The Great Liberator, emancipator of Catholics, was praised by the revered American abolitionist **Frederick Douglass,** himself a former slave, for his efforts toward ending slavery in the United States. In 1840 O'Connell and sixty thousand other Irishmen signed the "Great Irish Address" urging Irish Americans to "treat the Negroes as friends and to make common cause among the abolitionists."

Douglass had escaped to freedom and become the publisher of the *North Star*, based in Rochester, New York. A legendary orator, he barnstormed the North, leaving thrilled crowds in his wake, as well as confrontations that bordered on riot. When he traveled to Ireland in 1845, he was already famous. Douglass viewed the effects of the Famine, and he met with O'Connell. The Irish statesman, for his part, had previously given up his wish to visit America precisely because slavery existed there. The two men shared their common views of justice and human aspiration.

> DOUGLASS: No transatlantic statesman bore a testimony more marked and telling against the crime and curse of slavery than did Daniel O'Connell. He would shake the hand of no slave holder nor allow himself to be introduced to one if he knew him to be such. When friends of repeal in the Southern States sent him money, with which to carry on his work, he with ineffable scorn, sent back what he considered the bloodstained offering, saying he would never purchase the freedom of Ireland with the price of slaves.

> O'CONNELL: I am charged with attacking American institutions, as slavery is called. I am not ashamed of this attack. My sympathy is not confined to the narrow limits of my own green Ireland. My spirit walks abroad upon sea and land, and wherever there is oppression, I hate the oppressor, and wherever the tyrant rears his head, I will deal my bolts upon it, and wherever there is sorrow and suffering, there is spirit to succor and relieve.

The message was not necessarily heard in America, and certainly not abided by, where Irish Catholics who had settled mostly in the northern cities suffered the same discrimination that had been put upon them by the British at home. They weren't going to worry overly much about the Negro. At the bottom of the social and economic ladder, they would naturally have to compete with any free blacks for positions such as laborer, house servant, or waiter—even sailor. Racial prejudice became a means to secure, then advance, social and economic status; the Irish knew that many employers considered the Irish a better bet simply because they were white, and they exploited this knowledge. Although in the North the initial turnover from black to Irish labor sometimes reflected good capitalist sense more than overt racial discrimination—for the newly arrived Irish, hungry and desperate, were willing to work for less than free persons of color—in the South Irish immigrants were sometimes preferred over slaves for reasons pertaining to nothing but race.

In his provocatively titled *How the Irish Became White*, published in 1995, Harvard University professor Noel Ignatien, tries to explain how the Catholic Irish, an oppressed race in their homeland, became part of an oppressing race in America. Defining the white race as those who partake of the privileges of white skin in this particular society, he traces the tattered history of Irish and African American relations and reveals how the Irish used labor unions, the Catholic Church, and the Democratic Party to help gain and secure their newly found place in the White Republic. Ignatien draws a powerful connection between the Irish American establishment's embracing of white supremacy and its "success" in nineteenth-century American society.

In his autobiography, Frederick Douglass came to lament the attitudes of O'Connell's countrymen in their new land. "Perhaps no class of our fellow citizens has carried this prejudice against color to a point more extreme and dangerous than have our Catholic Irish fellow citizens, and no people on the face of the earth have been more relentlessly persecuted and oppressed on account of race and religion than have this same Irish people," he wrote. "The Irish who, at home, readily sympathize with the oppressed everywhere, are instantly taught when they step upon our soil to hate and despise the Negro. They are taught that he eats the bread that belongs to them. . . .

"The Irish-American will one day find out his mistake . . . but for the present we are the sufferers. Every hour sees us elbowed out of some employment to make room for some newly arrived immigrant from the Emerald Isle, whose hunger and color entitle him to special favor . . . a ceaseless enmity with the Irish is excited against us."

O'Connell was well aware that most Irish Americans were not following his advice and example—in fact, they were turning venomously against it—and he referred to those who exhibited any form of antipathy toward black Americans as "depraved hearts."

The frustrating paradox of an abolitionist sentiment in Ireland countered by the behavior of the Irish in America was one thing. The behavior of the Irish in the North during the U.S. Civil War, some of whom became national heroes while others rioted against the draft because they could not bear to serve in any effort that might free slaves who could take their jobs, was quite another. This wasn't paradox or irony, it was a problem. For the Irish were in America now, and they were supposed to be Americans.

Were there Irish in the South?

Yes, but they were not always welcome. On Bloody Monday, August 6, 1855, an anti-Irish rally in Louisville, Kentucky, turned violent, and a priest and several Irish were killed. But then, such sentiment wasn't regional. The next year the Nativist American Protection Association terrorized the San Francisco Irish, lynching some. And the year after that, nativists torched a quarantine hospital on Staten Island to kill Irish immigrants.

The Irish dedication to their church and to their own kind played a part in their early unpopularity, but there was also the fact that they weren't particularly well prepared to be contributors to their new society, and so were resented. As Cecil Woodham-Smith writes in her seminal work: "The Irish famine emigration is unlike other emigrations because it was of a less-civilized and less-skilled people into a more-civilized and more-skilled community. Other immigrations have been of the independent and the sturdy in search of wider horizons, and such emigrants usually brought with them knowledge and technical accomplishment which the inhabitants of the country in which they settled did not possess. The Irish, from their abysmal poverty, brought nothing."

What part did the Irish play in the Civil War?

Wherever the Irish landed, they served (as the poorest and newest immigrants, they were used as cannon-fodder for both armies). Oftentimes, as we'll see at Gettysburg, the Irish fought on both sides. And sometimes they chose not to serve.

The biggest Irish contribution was to Northern forces. In 1861 most Irish Americans still lived in the Northeast or Midwest, and both regions were, of course, solidly in the Union. It is estimated that two hundred thousand Irish natives joined the Union army, and Irish made up entire brigades from New York, Pennsylvania, Indiana, and Iowa.

Who were the Irish heroes of the Civil War?

First, simply for dying, was Marine Private **Luke Quinn:** He was the only military man to be killed at Harpers Ferry, Virginia, in 1859. Also, early on: the many Irish in the 69th New York Volunteers, who took it seriously on the chin at First Bull Run in 1861. And another: Colonel **Michael Corcoran** who was captured at Bull Run and threatened with execution before being traded for a Confederate officer. He formed the Corcoran Legion and went on to better success as the war wore on.

For living, and winning: Brigadier General **James Shields,** born in Altmore in 1806, became the only Union general ever to defeat **Stonewall Jackson** (whose ancestral home, the Birches, was also in Ulster) in 1862 at Kernstown, Virginia.

For nobly defending: The several companies of Irish-born troops in Confederate service—commanded by the likes of Quigley, Mullen, Ryan, and Kennedy—who held Forts Jackson and Saint Phillip during the siege of New Orleans in May 1862, and the Confederate Irish troops who held back an overwhelmingly superior Union force at Sabine Pass in Texas in 1863.

In all, eight Irishmen rose to the rank of general in the Union army, which was commanded by a son of Ulster, **Ulysses S. Grant.** The Confederate army had five generals of Irish or, more likely, Scotch-Irish descent.

And then there was Brigadier General **Thomas Francis Meagher,** former Irish nationalist, still an Irish "convict" (albeit, an escaped one), freshly arrived in America from an intended incarceration in

Australia, about to become legendary as Meagher of the Sword, greatest leader of the greatest Irish brigade to fight in the Civil War.

What was the Irish Brigade?

The name has been applied to a number of fighting units in several wars whose soldiers had largely Irish surnames. An early IB—the first to make the name famous—was the troop of six thousand men who were shipped to France in 1692 to fight in the Williamite War. (The "wild geese" regiments discussed earlier were absorbed into the brigade in the eighteenth century.) The term *The Irish Brigade* was applied to a thousand Irish who fought against the Piedmontese in 1860, and it would subsequently be applied to Irish fighting for the Boers in South Africa in the 1890s, Irish fighting in the 16th British Division in World War I, Irish in the International Brigade during the Spanish Civil War, and Irish in the 38th Allied Division in World War II. In the United States, the Regimento de Hibernia under Colonel Arturo O'Neill helped Spain defeat the English at the Battle of Pensacola, and two Irish Brigades fought with the French forces at Yorktown, where colonial America finally defeated the British in the Revolution.

But the Irish Brigade that we're concerned with here was the 67th New York militia in the Civil War. Formed by County Sligo native Michael Corcoran from the 63rd, 69th, and 88th New York infantry regiments that served the Union, this Irish Brigade would come to include the 28th and 29th Massachusetts regiments, the 110th Pennsylvania, and surviving fragments of New York's 7th as well.

The "fighting Irish," as they called themselves, were led by a succession of commanders: Colonel **Patrick Kelley** (killed at Petersburg), Colonel **Thomas A. Smyth** (killed at Farmville), Colonel **Richard Byrnes** (killed at Cold Harbor), and Brigadier Generals **Robert Nugent** and, first and foremost, Thomas Francis Meagher. The unit distinguished itself in the battles of Bull Run, Antietam, and Chancellorsville. The most famous action of the brigade took place during the Battle of Fredericksburg, when it suffered enormous casualties in repeated gallant charges at Marye's Heights. At Gettysburg in 1863, so many were killed or wounded that the brigade vanished into the mists.

The brigade took on collective fame in its time and assumed legendary status in the years to come. And one individual, its first commander, Meagher, became a larger-than-life figure in the Irish American mind.

Born in County Waterford in 1823, Meagher was a vigorous nationalist and a leader of the abortive 1848 uprising. He advocated violence against the British, and this earned him not only O'Connell's ire—the Emancipator was urging peaceful means to an end—but the nickname "Meagher of the Sword." Sentenced to death for his part in the doings of '48, he saw this judgment commuted to transportation and, as mentioned, he was one of the convicts to escape in Australia and make their way to America. He landed in New York in 1852 and succeeded first at law, then as a newspaperman. He never stopped agitating for Irish independence. When the Civil War broke out, he helped Corcoran organize his brigade, one he would lead during its most famous action at Fredericksburg. Meagher asked that the Irish Brigade be allowed to withdraw from front-line duty for a time after the devastation of Fredericksburg, and when his request was denied, he resigned his command.

He had an evident charisma that allowed him to lead men in Ireland and America, and that made him attractive to the general population—hardly all Irish—after the war. In 1865 he became territorial secretary (a sort of acting governor) of the Montana Territory. He was one of a few Irish—including Colonel **William O'Neill** in Nebraska and **Father John Ireland** in Minnesota—who were, at this time, trying to lure more of their people west from the squalor of seaboard cities. Meagher boldly saw himself as "the representative and champion of the Irish race in the wild, great mountains." He never realized his dream as a colonizer, for, on July 1, 1867, he drowned in a fall from a riverboat. As if a final act had been needed to confer heroic stature, Meagher died before his time (albeit under mysterious circumstances; they say he was drunk).

Montana did receive its waves of Irish, of course, and with the copper-mine boom, towns such as Butte took on a profoundly Hibernian cast. (It was an Irish American, **Marcus Daly,** who struck copper there in 1876; see chapter 8.) Meagher is something of a patron saint among the descendants of these people. A statue of him astride a horse, sword held high, has stood in front of the state capitol in Helena since 1905.

Thomas Keneally is at work on a mammoth book about the Irish diaspora. For him, Thomas Meagher has proved to be a figure of immense attraction, traveling as he did from the Irish nationalist movement, to a prison ship bearing him far away, to a leadership role in one of world history's signal wars. We talked with Keneally about Meagher, the man and the legend:

> My two equal heroes at the moment are Schindler and General Meagher. He had an incredible ego, tremendous oratory; he was massively attractive to women; he was brave—he made his 'Meagher of the Sword' speech when he was only twenty-five—he was partially altruistic and partially self-serving. Heroes have a certain rigor of soul, a strength of personality, a lack of introspection to an extent—they *just do it*. Courage is certainly part of it, and acts of panache are definitely part of it: taking the mickey out of the system. The god of mischief influences our heroes. I think fatal flaws are important in a hero, too, flaws are definitely part of it all, and Meagher had all the faults and strengths of the Deity. That first summer of the Famine he started to stick into O'Connell, which was like attacking the figure of Moses. But that helps make him a hero, when we look back at it. He's human, and we want our heroes human, too. We want them to be like ourselves. Why did Christ have to become fully human? To be a hero. The Irish legend of Cuchulain: Here's an opportunistic cattle thief, great warrior, and we have the conversion of a cattle rustler into a demigod. That's heroic. I wouldn't trust a hero without flaws.
>
> So, then, Meagher was all of that. I think, in his time, he was like the young Kennedy. And of course he saved the Union on a particular day, at the Battle of Fair Oaks when the Irish Brigade held the river crossing two nights and a day. A legendary action!
>
> In Montana, a mystique attaches to him still. There was something about him. In the Celtic heroes, something enters them. Certain gods enter them. Catholics call it sanctifying grace. I think Meagher had it.

Who was Irish Bridget?

When her husband enlisted in the Union army's 1st Michigan Cavalry, **Bridget Diver** followed him on a campaign and served as a nurse. She often rode into action and had several horses shot out from under her. Her escapades included a memorable moment at the Battle of Cedar Creek when she galloped right through the enemy line. She would also, on occasion, rally the troops—as at the Battle of Fair Oaks, where she looked up from attending her wounded husband and yelled, "Arragh, goin' b'y! Bate the bloody spaleens and revenge me husband." This drove several retreating men back into the fray.

After the war Mrs. Diver, now more famous as Irish Bridget, continued her military career as a laundress, working for regiments engaged in the Indian campaigns.

What was the USS Shamrock?

It was a 240-foot steam-powered battleship christened—with a bottle of Irish whiskey—at the Brooklyn Navy Yard on Saint Patrick's Day in 1863. It had eight guns and was used on blockade duty along the Carolina coast during the Civil War.

Who was Mathew Brady?

Mathew Brady was America's most famous nineteenth-century photographer, and something of an enigma. We know he was of Irish descent, probably second generation, because he once said in an interview that his father was "an Irishman." Brady wrote no memoirs or diaries, and we know little of his early life. He was born in upstate New York and became interested in drawing. Despite the fact that he was nearly blind, he was fascinated by a new art form, photography.

He set up shop in New York City, and his reputation as a portraitist grew. In 1858 he opened the Brady National Photographic Gallery in Washington, D.C., near the White House. When the Civil War began, Brady saw an opportunity; he later claimed a spirit in his feet had said, " 'Go!' and I went." With assistants **Alexander Gardner** and **Timothy O'Sullivan**—who, in fact, took many of the pictures because of Brady's eye condition—he chronicled the efforts of the Union's Army of the Potomac. His September 1862 exhibit in New York, *The Dead of Antietam,* was a graphic, moving depiction of war's darkest side. "If he has not brought bodies and laid them in our dooryards," said the *New York Times*, "he has done something very like it." He was the world's great pioneer of war photography.

After the war, Brady returned to his portaiture. His several photographs of Lincoln, taken right up to the eve of assassination, are among his most famous.

Brady was all but penniless in his later years, having been ruined by the Panic of 1873. In 1895 he was hit by a carriage in the streets of Washington and died the following year.

What role did the Irish play at the Battle of Gettysburg?

At Gettysburg, Pennsylvania, in the summer of 1863, Irish Americans fought bravely on both sides. As was the case with most big battles of the war, there was more Irish blood on the Yank side of the line—and more blood spilled there. But even when seen against the backdrop of all the other major confrontations, Gettysburg was a seminal event for Irish American soldiers. There, the dramatic attempt at a breakthrough victory on Northern soil by Confederate General **Robert E. Lee** was foiled by Union forces commanded by an Irish American general, **George G. Meade.** And the largest and most famous unit to fight in this most bloody conflagration—seven thousand dead, forty-five thousand wounded or missing—was the Union's Irish Brigade.

The brigade had already suffered heavy losses at Bull Run, Antietam, and Chancellorsville and performed one of the most gallant (if futile) exploits of the war in charging the crest of Marye's Heights at Fredericksburg. It is too strong to say that these things pale in comparison to what happened at Gettysburg, but in retrospect they seem mere prelude.

So many of the Irish Brigade were killed or wounded at Gettysburg that the unit simply ceased to exist—its precious few unscathed survivors were assigned to other companies. The Irish Brigade died heroically, even as it was helping the Union army turn the tide. This did not go unnoticed, and today the courage and sacrifice of those who served in the brigade is commemorated on the Pennsylvania battlefield in a particularly poignant monument: a mourning wolfhound at the base of a Celtic cross.

How were the Irish responsible for Thanksgiving Day?

In the wake of Gettysburg, President Lincoln was moved to proclaim the first national day of Thanksgiving. Now, he may have proclaimed the day a commemoration of the 1621 feast at Plymouth, Massachusetts, but that had not, in fact, been the first celebration of Almighty gratitude staged by the Pilgrims. In the winter of their first year in America, these pioneers had been close to starving and were ready to give up on their new home. Then, a ship arrived bearing food that helped sustain the tiny colony. The day after the vessel's arrival— February 21, 1621—was designated a Day of Thanksgiving in Plymouth. The safe assumption might be that the ship had been sent from England or Holland, but the *Lyon* had set sail from Dublin. A food merchant in that city, whose daughter was the wife of a prominent Pilgrim, had chartered and loaded the boat.

What was the Conscription Act?

In an effort to replace recruits lost in battle, the Conscription Act of 1863 was passed in great haste. It was aimed squarely at family men, the only large source of manpower left untapped by the Union. Under the provisions of the new draft, no man could claim an exemption on the grounds that he was the sole support of his wife and children.

The Conscription Act met with strong resistance throughout the North, but nowhere was the resentment greater than among the immigrant Irish of New York City. They were incensed by a loophole that rendered the rich untouchable: A man could purchase exemption from military service for $300, or by hiring a substitute for some lesser fee to fight in his stead. Irish wives, mothers of large families, urged their husbands to battle it out in the streets rather than leave home. They knew that, if abandoned, their lot was to beg, steal, or live on charity. These options seemed untenable.

The first draft lottery took place on Saturday, July 11, 1863. On Sunday, the lists of those tapped for military service were published in the newspapers.

How bad were the Draft Riots?

As bad as can be imagined. Think Cromwell.

No—start with recent history. In 1992 most Americans watched with deep concern as images of Los Angeles smoldering flashed across their television screens following the not-guilty verdicts delivered in the case of police charged with beating Rodney King. To some, it seemed the worst example of the ugly violence that recurs in inner-city America. For others, there were worse memories: Watts in the sixties; Newark, Detroit, and Harlem in the fifties; Tulsa, Oklahoma, in 1921, where a thousand homes burned, forty city blocks were leveled, and scores were killed. Surely one of these was the most violent riot ever.

However, if you add up all the damage, they pale in comparison to the Draft Riots of 1863. The death toll of all American race riots in the twentieth century falls far short of the two thousand killed during the Draft Riots of 1863 in New York City. And there was property damage of $5 million (in 1863 dollars!): It remains the worst civil disturbance in American history—and most of the rioters were Irish.

It started on the hot, humid Monday morning of July 13. Just ten days after the battle of Gettysburg, where Irish Americans had done so well, a rally had been called in Central Park to protest the freshly proclaimed Conscription Act. The first military draft in our nation's history was opposed by many in the North as an illegal expansion of federal power. For the poor and working classes, largely Irish, an additional infuriating component was that drafted men could send substitutes off to fight in their places or buy a waiver for $300.

There was also a racial issue behind the demonstration. Some trade unionists were opposed to Lincoln's Emancipation Proclamation because they feared competition for jobs from the four million freed slaves. This argument was pumped up by the right-wing, pro-Confederacy press, which was not confined to cities south of the Mason-Dixon Line. In New York, this bigoted point of view had been reinforced when black laborers were used to break a longshoremen's strike in March of 1863. Furthermore, the Conscription Act limited the draft to male "citizens," and since blacks weren't citizens, they could not be drafted. So not only would drafted men be fighting to bring about a situation that could ultimately cost them their jobs, but even while they were off fighting, those jobs might be stolen out from under them by stay-at-home blacks. Or so the issue seemed to many lower-class whites.

On that heavy summer morning, the demonstrators marched from Central Park downtown to the U.S. Provost Marshal's Office at Third Avenue and Forty-seventh Street. Along the way, some men broke into a hardware store and stole broad axes; others cut telegraph lines. Then a group of Irish women with crowbars began tearing up the Fourth Avenue railroad. The same was done to the Second and Third Avenue lines. The crowd was becoming a mob.

The Irish surged out of the Five Points, Mulberry Bend, Hell's Kitchen, and the Upper West Side. They set forth to burn, loot, and even kill. They attacked the draft offices, the New York Tribune Building (looking to murder its liberal Republican editor, Horace Greeley), the mansions on Lexington Avenue, the Negro Orphan Asylum on Fifth Avenue and Forty-third Street where, fortunately, 237 black children were led out the back way even as the rioters were screaming "Burn the niggers' nests!" and setting torch to the building.

Over the next four days, an estimated fifty to seventy thousand men, women, and children participated, three fourths of them not even subject to conscription. Most were armed with primitive weapons: bricks, paving stones, clubs. They moved through the city in groups of up to ten thousand, and the sight of them swarming down a wide avenue—filling it wall-to-wall, as far north as the eye could range—was blood-chilling to the authorities.

Eventually, nearly all of Manhattan above Mulberry Street fell into the hands of the mob. Police were concentrating their efforts south of that line, hoping to protect business and financial interests. Uptown law-enforcement detachments were taking cover in their station houses.

Federal troops, some fresh from Gettysburg, were called in. It took six thousand soldiers plus batteries of field artillery—lined up hub-to-hub, loaded with grapeshot and canister—to clear a bloody path through the rioters. The tide did turn on the fourth day. Facing volleys fired by trained infantry, cavalry charges, and artillery barrages, the dissidents gradually melted away.

The draft proceeded without further protest from the tenement districts, and New York was peaceable enough for the duration of the war. Thousands of men who had fought in the streets in July 1863 answered their summonses and fought in the Union army later that same year.

Upon the occasion of the 1992 riots in L.A., Irish American columnist Pete Hamill looked back down the trail of American urban violence and focused on 1863. He wrote in the *New York Post*: "All of this was long ago. . . . But the Draft Riots make a point that must be underlined: Blacks don't riot, Latinos don't riot—the poor do. And if the poor are sufficiently brutalized, ignorant and alienated they are capable of obscene atrocities. Many Irish-Americans now grow huffy with self-righteousness at the riots in Los Angeles and other cities. They should read some history. The Draft Riots remind us of one large fact: No race, no nationality and no religion has a lock on virtue."

What is the legacy of Irish American–
African American interactions in
nineteenth-century America?

It sometimes seems that Daniel O'Connell and Frederick Douglass shared blood ties—Douglass was called "the black O'Connell" in his time—but we know this to be a poetic, metaphoric leap. However, the Irish American and African American populations, finding only themselves and each other at the low rung of the socioeconomic ladder once the war was over, were bound to find some kinship—specific as well as metaphoric.

A brief listing of links is in order at this point, for the Irish were neither strictly racist à la the draft rioters nor strictly utopian à la O'Connell. Even as the rioters were rioting, the Irish Ladies Anti-Slavery Society was sending money from Ireland to America to aid the fight for freedom; it was a fine thank-you, for during the Famine, the abolitionist movement—and in one case a group of "negro slaves"—had sent money to Ireland. In short, it's all very complicated.

The ambiguous intersection of the Irish American and African American experiences is illustrated by the following:

- Jesuit **Patrick Healy,** born to a native of Roscommon who had illegally married a Georgia slave woman, became the first black American to earn a Ph.D. and was president of Georgetown University. His brother **James Healy** became America's first black bishop in 1875.
- **Muhammad Ali**'s maternal great-grandparents were a free black woman and a County Clare immigrant.
- The Color Green: Writer **Alice Walker**'s great-great-grandfather was Irish.
- The Reverend **Martin Luther King, Jr.,** had an Irish great-grandmother on his father's side.
- New Dealer **Frank Murphy,** a white attorney general, Supreme Court justice, and NAACP board member, once recognized discrimination as "the most un-American . . . thing in our life today."
- Justice **William Brennan** made it a crusade in our century to expose the racism inherent in the death penalty.
- When **Autherin Lucy** sought enrollment at the University of

Alabama thirty-five years ago, campus chaplain **Emmet Gribbin,** a grandson of Irish immigrants named for the Irish patriot **Robert Emmet,** was a voice of conscience and even endured physical attack on campus.

- Archbishop **Patrick O'Boyle**'s invocation opened the famous 1963 March on Washington.
- Women such as the Student Nonviolent Coordinating Committee's **Connie Curry** (first-generation Irish Protestant) and **Mary O'Neil Good** (third-generation Irish Catholic) organized and struggled in the Deep South during the earliest days of the civil rights movement.
- Tex-Irish **John Howard Griffin** first lived and then wrote *Black Like Me*, opening a window into the world of Jim Crow.
- With *The Other America*, **Michael Harrington,** born of a "very lace curtain" Irish family in St. Louis, forced his country to confront its "race class condemned [by] heredity to be poor."
- **John F. Kennedy,** false starts aside, first used the Oval Office to cast segregation as a moral issue and initiated the most important civil rights legislation of this century. His brother Robert, as attorney general under both JFK and Lyndon Johnson, was, if anything, more dedicated to the cause, marching in the South, bringing the law to bear in the South.
- **Kevin Doyle,** a philosophical son of Justice Brennan, worked tirelessly for mostly black inmates on Alabama's death row and is currently the New York State Capital Defender. When receiving a citation as one of *Irish America* magazine's Top 100 Irish Americans in 1996, he reminded his audience that it wasn't so long ago that they, the Irish, were the poorest of America's poor, the ones facing the gallows.
- New York Yankee shortstop **Derek Jeter** and singer **Mariah Carey,** who dated one another briefly in 1998, each have Irish and African blood.

So, what to make of all this? Only that things are never as straightforward as they seem. We could just as easily have made a list like this that would serve to condemn rather than elevate the Irish American role in matters of racial justice. Indeed, as Doyle himself tells us, "Lest heads swell when considering names like Kennedy, Harrington and O'Boyle, remember the name Connor, as in **Eugene 'Bull' Connor**, the racist sheriff who epitomized a virulent, poisonous Southern attitude toward integration. And when school desegregation came

North, and **Judge Garrity** issued his order in Boston, the Irish of that city did not exactly cover themselves in glory. We Irish have all profited from the fair wages and opportunities stolen from generations of African Americans.

"Most importantly, genuine equality still eludes America. There is plenty of opportunity to better the home that we Irish have the good fortune to share."

What was next for the Irish in America?

The ladder. The climb.

Now, the Irish would try to fight their way up. They still weren't liked, and no one was reaching out to them. And they were hardly prepared: Twenty percent of New York's Irish were unskilled laborers in 1855, while only 3 percent of other immigrants in the city were unskilled.

We'll end this chapter detailing the great turning point in modern Irish American history where we began it, with Mrs. Woodham-Smith's *The Great Hunger*:

> Irish emigrants, especially of the famine years, became, with rare exceptions, what their transatlantic environment made them, children of the slums, rebuffed, scorned by respectable citizens and exploited by the less respectable. The Irish were the most unfortunate emigrants and the poorest, they took longest to be accepted, longest to become genuinely assimilated, they waited longest before the opportunities the United States offers were freely available to them.
>
> The story of the Irish in the New World is not a romantic story of liberty and success, but the history of a bitter struggle, as bitter, as painful though not as long-drawn-out, as the struggle by which the Irish at last won the right to be a nation.

EIGHT

The Fightin' Irish in the Wild, Wild West

Did everyone already in America
detest the incoming Irish?

How was the assimilation of the Irish different
from that of other ethnic groups?

How far west did the Irish settle?

Did the Irish fight the Indians?

Were all the Irish in the West Indian-haters?

Were there Irish gunslingers in the West?

Who were the Gallagher Brothers?

Who was Marcus Daly?

Who was John A. O'Farrell?

Weren't the Molly Maguires miners?

Who was Edward Doheny?

Who was John Concannon?

Who was Annie Moore?

*Did everyone already in America
detest the incoming Irish?*

Not quite. The great nineteenth-century poet Walt Whitman, for one, did not:

Far hence amid an isle of wondrous beauty,
Crouching over a grave an ancient sorrowful mother,
Once a queen, now lean and tatter'd seated on the ground,
Her old white hair drooping disevel'd round her shoulders,
At her feet fallen an unused royal harp,
Long silent, she too long silent, mourning her shrouded hope and heir,
Of all the earth her heart most full of sorrow because most full of love.
Yet a word, ancient mother,
You need crouch there no longer on the cold ground with forehead between
  your knees

O you need not sit there veil'd in your white hair so disevel'd,
For know you the one you mourn is not in that grave,
It was an illusion, the son you love was not really dead,
The Lord is not dead, he is risen again young and strong in another
  country,
Even while you wept there by your fallen harp by the grave,
What you wept for was translated, pass'd from the grave,
The winds favor'd and the sea sail'd it,
And now with rosy and new blood,
Moves to-day in a new country.

How was the assimilation of the Irish different from that of other ethnic groups?

Most significantly, it was the very first such assimilation. It must be remembered that the "United States" was—pre-Famine, pre-freeing-of-the-slaves, pre-westward-expansion-into-Indian-territory—a homogeneous community of white, Anglo-Saxon Protestants of English descent. Give me your tired, your poor wasn't yet part of the picture. The Irish were the original wretched, huddled mass thrown upon North American shores. Therefore, the country would be finding its way as it went about this immigration game. What the United States learned from its experience in assimilating the Irish would be useful later as Italians, other Europeans, Latins, and Asians followed. Parts of the Irish American life—first stop is the slums, for instance—would be common to all trailing ethnicities. But it was worse for the Irish because there were so many of them.

There were, to be sure, certain advantages to being so large a refugee migration. The Famine and its aftermath sent so many Irish to North America—perhaps 1.7 million—that these new citizens instantly constituted a significant minority of the American population and started to impact the culture and mores of their new land by the sheer force of their presence. (For example, the Irish all but created the Catholic Church in the United States.) By 1860 the Irish represented more than one quarter of the population in New York City and Boston, and nearly half of all the foreign-born population in the country. (There were thirty-five thousand Irish in Boston in 1850 and three times that many by 1855.) Some in the United States must surely have regretted that the Founding Fathers had, in their wisdom, set the nation up as a democracy—a system under which such a large group could play the game and lift itself up—but it was too late to do much about that.

Because the Irish were such a big contingent, it was easier for them to stick together and retain ethnic identity than it was for subsequent immigrant groups arriving piecemeal. By staying "Irish," they stayed in touch with Ireland (which was not, of course, very far away—certainly closer than most of the countries exporting emigrants to America). As the Irish American historian William D. Griffin, author of *A Portrait of the Irish in America* and *The Book of Irish Americans*, writes: "The Irish in America were distinguished by more than their sheer volume of immigration and the breadth of their settlement and occupational activity. What set them apart from almost all other ethnic groups was their continuing commitment to their native land." This commitment allowed Irish Americans to impart a sense of Irishness to certain American institutions—politics, the inner city—and it also allowed them to influence events "back home." Several post-Famine drives for Irish nationalism, while fought on the ground by groups such as the Irish Republican Army, were steered with help from Boston, Brooklyn, and even Washington, D.C.

So, there were some advantages, but the daily reality for most travelers in the first great waves of Irish immigration was poverty, violence, chaos. Life was harsh in the squalid ghettos of those early American cities. These poor people had jumped from the frying pan and were now in the fire. The famous transcendentalist **A. Bronson Alcott** was moved to condemn the heartlessness of a system seemingly dedicated to keeping its lowest class down when he encountered the Boston slums, then almost exclusively Irish, on July 31, 1870:

> I pass . . . as I ride into the city and return, squares of newly built tenant houses erected on lands which the high tides can hardly fail to overflow and every rain inundate—near a slaughterhouse moreover, rendering them unfit for human dwellings at any season. The capitalist doubtless pleads his legal right to use his money or lands in any manner he please, and the poor occupant perhaps considers him a benefactor in furnishing a shelter even in such unwholesome quarters, while he can pay his rent for it; though his wife and children, if not himself, fall victims to his surroundings, unless they chance to be sound and virtuous.
>
> Cities, like Cain, may not hope to shield their crime by legislation, excusing themselves from being their "brother's keeper" thereby, nor hold any guiltless who disregard, for gain, the health, comfort, or virtue of a single citizen.

And the conditions in Boston were relatively pleasant when compared with the wretchedness of New York's tenements.

The Five Points section of the Lower East Side was a horrid, swampy slum well before the famine Irish came across. When the poor and sick of Ireland disembarked at the adjacent South Street Seaport, many could go no farther and so added new clients to an already teeming ghetto. During and after the Civil War, Irish gangs proliferated, and the Five Points became New York's most dangerous, murderous quarter. The Bloody Ould Sixth Ward, which comprised eighty-six acres, a territory bounded by Broadway, Canal Street, the Bowery, and Park Row—today, ironically, the hub of the city's principal agencies for the administration of justice, with the state Supreme Court building, the New York City Criminal Court building, and the U.S. Federal District Court building cheek by jowl—was a place into which you simply did not venture unless you had to. But you *did* have to if it was your home, as it was to 3,435 Irish families at the time of the Civil War. The next most populous ethnic group in the Five Points, the Italians, were represented by only 416 families.

The Old Brewery, called Coulter's Brewery when erected in 1792 on the bank of the "collect"—a miasmic lake—was the heart of the Five Points and, when it was converted in 1837 (having become so dilapidated it was of no further use), it was the most notorious tenement in the city. The "Den of Thieves" was one room in the Brewery, and "Murderers' Alley" was 'round the back. The Brewery housed up to a thousand people, a sad tenancy that was half Irish, half black. Rape and incest were accepted facts of life.

The gangs lived and worked the tenements. Beginning before the Civil War and flourishing after, the Forty Thieves, the Kerryonians, the Plug Uglies, the Dead Rabbits, and (slightly farther north in the Bowery) the Bowery Boys, the True Blue Americans, the American Guards, the O'Connell Guards, and the Atlantic Guards wreaked havoc on southern Manhattan. Any Irish with dreams of a better life in America realized that if those dreams were to be realized, they had to get out of the slums, they had to get away from these . . . these fellow countrymen. For everyone, even reformers, realized the slums were never going away. "The slum is as old as civilization," wrote the muckraker **Jacob Riis,** himself an immigrant (Dutch) who made it his life's work to better the lot of New York's poor. "Civilization implies a race to get ahead. In a race there are usually some who for one cause or another cannot keep up, or are thrust out from among their fellows. They fall behind, and when they have been left far in the rear they lose hope and ambition, and give up. Thenceforward, if left to their own resources, they are the victims, not the masters, of their environment; and it is a bad master." A cruel master: When a cholera epidemic swept through Gotham Court, successor to the Old Brewery as the city's worst tenement (aka "Sweeney's Shambles"), one fifth of the thousand tenants were killed in a season; one third of the 183 children born that year died within weeks.

There's no telling precisely how many first-generation Irish fell victim to the urban slums of the nineteenth century, but while the number would be staggering, it would still not imply the immensity of such a tragic, painful social circumstance.

While sheer numbers made it certain that the Irish would forever be a part of the cities that they landed in, the intolerability of the urban situation made it certain that the Irish would begin to seep and even leap out of the slums, given half a chance. Recruiters like Thomas Meagher were singing siren songs of clean air and opportunity in the West. The California gold rush in midcentury drew thousands of Irish, and other subsequent ore strikes made silver and copper miners out of thousands more. The Indian wars provided jobs. The mountain-man lifestyle appealed to hundreds of the Scotch-Irish, and the best of them, such as Joseph Walker, became pioneers to the Pacific. Horace Greeley, an Ulster American, said *go west*, and many of the Irish did. They built the Erie Canal. (The idea behind the canal had come from **De Witt Clinton,** by the way, the New York governor who was descended from Protestant Irish immigrants.) In 1869 they completed the Transcontinental Railroad (not only did Irish supply much of the labor, they numbered among them a man named Jeffers, whose son would become president of the Union Pacific in 1937). The National Road from Pennsylvania into Ohio was built by newly landed Irish attracted to America by the promise of a $6-a-month wage. They kept coming: In the 1870s nearly a half million more Irish immigrants arrived in the United States. They took power: **"Honest John" Kelly** succeeded **William Marcy "Boss" Tweed** at Tammany Hall in 1874, signaling Irish control of New York politics that would last for more than fifty years. (Tammany pol **George Washington Plunkitt,** son of Irish immigrants, said of his success in America: "I seen my opportunities, and I took 'em.") In 1886 **Hugh O'Brien** became the first Irish Catholic mayor of Boston. They kept coming: In the 1880s, 650,000 more Irish immigrants arrived in the United States. They still were hated: **Thomas Nast**'s cartoons in *Harper's Weekly* depicted the Irish with apelike features, and the nativist and Know-Nothing movements—with political philosophies based on little more than a hatred of immigrants—gained steam. They kept coming: Nearly a half million more Irish immigrants arrived in the United States in the 1890s.

And they kept going, as did their new country, into the West.

How far west did the Irish settle?

To Chicago, certainly, although Chicago's Irish population was established from the first, just like Boston's and Philadelphia's and New York's.

A fellow named McCarthy, who was one of the Wild Geese, visited Chicago as early as the seventeenth century. He was in the French army, and the area was controlled by France. When Fort Dearborn was built in 1803, an Irish-born Catholic named **John Whistler** did the building and then served as its first commander. You might not think that **Sauganash,** who settled with the Potawatomi tribe in the 1820s, was Irish, but in fact his Christian name was **Billy Caldwell** and he was the son of an Irish-born officer in the British Revolutionary army and an Indian mother. Caldwell had served as Tecumseh's right hand before moving to Chicago. Today there's an affluent Chicago neighborhood named after him. It's called Sauganash, not Caldwell.

Beginning in 1836 with the building of the Illinois and Michigan Canal, Irish flooded LaSalle and Chicago. Old animosities festered in the New World: In 1838 men from County Cork battled those from Ulster until the militia was called in. When the canal project went broke in 1842, workers were given land in exchange for already rendered service. And that is how the Irish came to settle here in considerable numbers.

Around this time, as might be imagined, the Chicago slums were up and festering. On the North Side an Irish Town not unlike Boston's or New York's was established, in the felicitous if not happy words of Thomas J. O'Gorman, writing in the Spring 1996 issue of *The World of Hibernia* magazine, "more bubonic than bucolic." The "Kilglubbin" area, as the region on the Chicago River's north branch became known, saw constant brawling between County Connaught men and County Munster men, County Galway men and County Mayo men. Ireland was Ireland, wherever it went.

The building of the transcontinental railroad transformed and uplifted Chicago. Meatpacking, grain-packing, and shipping all became centered in Chicago; and the unskilled Irish flocked—make that swarmed—into the city. In 1850 six thousand Chicagoans had been born in Ireland, 20 percent of the population. By 1890 seventy thousand had been born there, and Windy City citizens with at least one Irish parent who was three generations deep numbered 215,000.

This suggests dominance, but the Irish were *not* dominant. "Why do our police reports average two representatives from Erin . . . to every one from any other inhabitable land," wrote the *Chicago Tribune* in 1853. "Why are the instigators and ringleaders of our riots and tumults, in nine cases out of ten, Irishmen?" In 1855 the *Trib* upped the ante: "Who does not know that the most depraved, debased, worthless, and irredeemable drunkards and sots which curse the community are Irish Catholics?"

And then, on Sunday, October 8, 1871, at about nine o'clock at night, a fire began—it was said in the cowbarn of Catharine O'Leary at 137 Dekoven Street. It was said, the cow did it. The Great Chicago Fire killed three hundred, left ninety thousand homeless, caused damage in excess of $200 million. Never mind that all manner of late-twentieth-century books replete with new evidence prove that the O'Learys didn't start the fire. At the time, the vilification of the O'Learys—and of all Chicago Irish—was as intense as the blaze itself.

The Irish had been at play in Chicago. In 1866 a thousand of them had even invaded Canada, hoping to set up a new nation of sorts (as we'll see in the chapter on Fenian involvement and Irish nationalism that follows this one). But now, they were in trouble. As Chicago struggled to come back from the devastation, Irish Chicagoans—chastened, if unjustly so—joined hands with their fellows as simply Chicagoans. The fire was the font from which a curious, particular, proud Irish urbanism flowed. Irish American politicians ran—and won—in council elections and then citywide. The great architect **Louis Sullivan** designed many of the great buildings that rose once the ashes had been swept out. The Chicago Irish, proud of their city—prouder of their city, perhaps, than of their old country—helped lay the new bedrock of Chicago.

But, of course, many of them got out of town.

Did the Irish fight the Indians?

Yes, in considerable number, even though they, in particular, might have had reason not to.

American Indians, like the Irish, were threatened with something like extinction by the mid-1800s. While the Irish had suffered the Famine, the Indians, over the course of two centuries, had been ravaged by disease, starvation, and the unceasing press of white oppressors. The European colonization of this New World, the Manifest Destiny of white settlers, was the Indians' Holocaust.

But whatever kinship existed among the downtrodden, one fact remained: The Irish were white. In "The Perils of Pat" (*Irish America* magazine, 1993), Peter Quinn, the noted Irish American historian, speechwriter, and novelist, writes about his grandfather's exploits on the American frontier. Patrick Quinn took part in frequent encounters with bands of Apache Indians who had been, according to his 1941 obituary, "on the warpath along the border. He was one of the crew on the train that carried Geronimo, leader of the Apaches, into captivity." Writes his grandson: "The irony of an Irishman helping drive forward the same process of colonization in America was one we never considered."

Lands set aside for the Indian were often subsequently reclaimed by whites as the United States expanded westward. This led to fighting, of course. The superior post–Civil War army that fought the "Indian wars" was largely Irish. No fewer than thirty-one of Custer's force of 265 7th Cavalry troopers who were killed at Little Bighorn on June 25, 1876, were Irish born, and many more were second-generation Irish Americans.

Here's a strange historical footnote regarding that battle: One body of the 265 was neither scalped nor brutalized by the Indians. It was that of the Irish-born commander of Company I, **Myles Keough.** Who was Keough, and why was he spared mutilation?

He was a Catholic from County Carlow, and at Saint Patrick's College he proved good with horses. He was a mercenary in Africa and then, in 1860, he joined Pope Pius IX's papal army and fought against the Italian forces seeking unification. For his service he was awarded the *Medaglia de Pro Petri Sede*. Keough the adventurer saw the Union army as the next good thing and sailed for America. He saw front-line action, killed more than a few Confederates, and, after a brief peacetime demobilization, joined the newly formed 7th Cavalry in September of 1866 (eventually, natives of Ireland would make up nearly one quarter of the six hundred men in the regiment; the company took for its regimental march the Irish air "Garry Owen"). On the fateful day, Keough's company fought just left of Custer's own; according to some reports, Keough was among the last to fall. And, then, he was left unmarked. Why? Well, it is known that he was wearing a medal around his neck, and if it was the splendid *Medaglia* given him by the pope, then it is possible the superstitious Sioux were wary of mutilating this strangely blessed man.

Another footnote regarding Custer's Last Stand: It was massacres such as Little Bighorn that prompted the Irish American General **Philip Sheridan** to proclaim, "The only good Indian is a dead Indian."

Were all the Irish in the West Indian-haters?

Not quite. The makeup of Custer's 7th Cavalry is as good an example as any that there were many Irish and Irish Americans engaged in the wars against the Indians. But while most Irish probably shared Sheridan's harsh sentiments, there were others in the nineteenth century who exhibited rare vision and compassion in matters relating to Native Americans. An early advocate of the rights of Native Americans was **Thomas Loraine McKenney,** a veteran of the War of 1812 and grandson of an Irish immigrant, who served as superintendent of the Indian Trade Bureau from 1816 until its dissolution in 1822, then as head of the Bureau of Indian Affairs in 1829. He lobbied for them with Presidents Madison, Monroe, Adams, and Jackson—most often to no avail. He battled federal corruption in Indian trades and tried to stop the illegal sale of alcohol to the tribes. But he faced the formidable opposition of tradesmen, including the tycoon **John Astor,** whose lucrative fur business involved routine exploitation of the Indian. When Congress passed a law forbidding all but foreign trade on the frontier, Astor used French boatmen to cross the border from Canada to continue trade with the Indians, many of whom were being coaxed out of their goods for the price of a bottle of whiskey. The foreign-trade loophole had been put into the trade act by congressmen who'd been greased by Astor, and McKenney was powerless to fight it. McKenney was, however, able to secure passage of the Indian Civilization Act of 1819, which appropriated $10,000 a year for the development of Indian schools.

McKenney's downfall came during the term of the first Irish American president, Andrew Jackson. Jackson had scant concern for Indian rights and drove for the removal and relocation of tribes occupying the southern and eastern quarters of the United States, tribes including the Creek and Choctaw, who had fought alongside Jackson's own soldiers at the Battle of New Orleans in the War of 1812. In 1830, after several heated confrontations with McKenney, Jackson dismissed him as head of Indian Affairs.

McKenney's respect for Native Americans is memorialized in a collection of portraits that he commissioned of the nation's leading chieftains, painted when the Indians would come to Washington during treaty negotiations. Although the original 128 artworks were destroyed by fire while on display at the Smithsonian Institution in 1865, the collection lives on in a book: *The McKenney-Hall Portrait Gallery of American Indians* (Crown, 1972), which includes a history of McKenney's life and times.

Another nineteenth-century champion of the Indian was County Cavan–born **Thomas Fitzpatrick,** who had negotiated the 1851 Treaty of Fort Laramie that deeded to the Sioux, Cheyenne, Crow, Arapaho, and other tribes the Black Hills Land where, in 1874, gold was discovered—which meant that the white man wanted the land back, which led to the 7th Cavalry's ill-fated visit to the area, which led to the Little Bighorn, which led to the death of so many Irish and Irish Americans.

After coming to the United States as a seventeen-year-old in 1816, he went west and began a career as a beaver trapper on the Missouri River. He became a famous mountain man and fur trader and served as a guide to California-bound pioneers. Although in his early days he was frequently engaged in hostilities with Indians, Fitzpatrick gradually earned the respect and even friendship of many erstwhile enemies. He softened in his own views and eventually served as Indian agent for the upper Arkansas Territory from 1846 to 1854. He was known by the Indians as "Broken Hand," after the result of an earlier battle with the Black Foot tribe. While fleeing an attack, Fitzpatrick rode his horse off a forty-foot cliff and landed in a stream below. He turned to shoot at the Indians and his rifle misfired, blowing off three fingers of his left hand.

Despite that little drama, Fitzpatrick—a guide, after all, and in fact the first to lead a wagon train to California, having delivered ninety-eight emigrants from Westport, Missouri, in 1840—was said to be fiercely opposed to frontier violence. He reasoned that the United States could deal with the influx of whites into Indian Territory in one of two ways: by fighting a bloody campaign or by trying to coexist. He suggested remuneration as a way to make peace with the natives. This kind of thinking got him fired as an Indian agent, but he was rehired in time to organize the Great Indian Council of 1851 between the Plains tribes (only the Comanche boycotted) and the American government. The treaty that Broken Hand cinched, which involved a payment of $50,000 and which established definitive boundaries between the Indian nations, allowed the United States to build forts and roads in Indian territory. It also made depredation by either side a punishable offense. It was, in short, a treaty bound to be broken.

Fitzpatrick's efforts were undone by a consensus represented by Indian-haters like General Sheridan. Sheridan's parents had also come from County Cavan to New York, where the future Union war hero was born in 1831. Maybe the Sheridans had known young Tommy Fitzpatrick as a boy, back in the old country.

Sheridan, seeking nothing but dead Indians, became one of the most brutal, successful, and famous of all Indian fighters. He saw Manifest Destiny where Broken Hand Fitzpatrick had sought harmony on both sides.

And then there was **John Boyle O'Reilly,** a crusading Irish American journalist, who looks enlightened and heroic from our vantage but drew the ire of his own people at the time by sticking up for Indians, Jews, and blacks—particularly Indians.

Born near Dowth in 1844, he was yet another fervent nationalist, and his Fenian activities got him arrested in Ireland and sentenced to death. Like Thomas Meagher, O'Reilly saw his sentence commuted to transportation, and, like Meagher, he escaped the Australian penal colony and hitched a ride on a whaler headed north. He arrived in the United States in 1869 and began his agitating as a Boston journalist. As editor and owner of the Boston *Pilot*, he became, according to the historian William Shannon, "the foremost spokesman of his generation."

He was already on the record as being pro-Indian when news of the massacre at the Little Bighorn made its way east. Writing in the *Pilot*, O'Reilly offered a contrary view. He saw Custer as a fool, the Sioux as champions. In the aftermath of the battle O'Reilly kept up his drumbeat for better treatment of the Indians and was chastised by many of his own for doing so.

But, clearly, not *all* of his own. The *Boston Post* said of him: "He is one whom children would choose for their friend, women for their lover, and men for their hero." The 1890 obituary in *Harper's Weekly*, which had routinely opposed him, said O'Reilly "was easily the most distinguished Irishman in America. He was one of the country's foremost poets, one of its most influential journalists, an orator of unusual power, and he was endowed with such a gift of friendship as few men are blessed with."

In Dowth, there's a not dissimilar tribute. On a Celtic cross put in place in 1903 there's an inscription in Irish: "John Boyle O'Reilly, hero, poet, orator, true Irishman, lovable, famous. He endured great torment at the hands of the big crow on behalf of Ireland. He had always hoped in his heart to be buried in this spot among the hills and plains where he was born and which he loved so dearly. God grant eternal rest to the soul of one who enhanced the reputation of his country."

O'Reilly is, in fact, buried in Holyhood Cemetery in Brookline, Massachusetts.

Were there Irish gunslingers in the West?

Were there ever! A great many of the outlaws in the Wild West— gunslingers, crooked sheriffs, other ne'er-do-wells—had more than a drop of Irish blood in them.

Perhaps the most famous outlaw in the American West was **William Bonney**, immortalized as Billy the Kid. It is believed that he was born with the less-menacing name Henry to an immigrant named Catherine McCarthy—or McCarty—around 1860 in the Irish slums of New York's Lower East Side—perhaps in the Five Points itself. Nothing is known of Henry's father. When his mother married a man named William Antrim, the boy became known as Billy Antrim, Jr., and also Kid Antrim.

After being raised in various Midwestern towns and gunslinging his way to the frontier—he is said to have killed his first man, Frank Cahill, while still in his teens—he hooked up with a gang of characters with names like O'Fiollard and McCloskey and O'Keefe. He wound up in the midst of a power struggle between rival land-owning and business factions in Lincoln, New Mexico. He was on the side of a rancher named Tunstall, a father figure to Billy (who was by now known as "William Bonney") against an Irish mafia of sorts headed by a Murphy and a Dolan. Laurence Murphy had been born in County Wexford, James Dolan in County Galway, so you can see how the pot is melting for the Irish: Here's a corrupt business collective headed by Irish natives who controlled a sheriff named Brady, who in turn had a gang of deputized thugs that included a Riley and a Boyle, about to enter into what would come to be known as the Lincoln County War, and the best young hired gun on the other guy's side is a second-generation Irish kid from the Manhattan ghetto. Isn't America grand.

When Billy's benefactor—who was English, by the way—was cut down by a Murphy-Dolan posse, the Kid retaliated by killing Sheriff Brady. He and his Irish mates from the Tunstall camp killed four more Murphy-Dolan associates during a three-week spree. Then the U.S. Army, which also was controlled in that area by the Murphy-Dolan machine, sought to intervene, and that episode in Billy's career came to a close with a wild shootout in Lincoln. Many of the Kid's confederates were killed, but he managed to escape.

Billy the Kid's gang went about their horse-thieving, cattle-rustling ways until yet another player with an Irish surname, Garrett, became sheriff of Lincoln County in 1880. **Pat Garrett** made it his highest priority to catch the Kid, and he did this after a two-day siege near the charmingly named Stinking Springs, New Mexico. Billy was sentenced to hang by a judge in Murphy-Dolan employ, but before the judgment was meted out he escaped from jail: During a meal, he used his free hand to deck a guard, killed the man with his own gun, killed another, stole a horse, and rode into the sunset.

He was at large but a short time. Garrett was informed that Billy was hiding at Fort Sumner, an abandoned army post. He surprised Billy there and cut him down with several shots. Billy the Kid was twenty-one when he died; he claimed, by that age, to have killed more than twenty men. In the century after his death he would be portrayed variously as a romantic Robin Hood–like outlaw, a degenerate psychopath, a lost soul in search of a father, and a guy who found himself in the wrong place at the wrong time.

The truth is elusive. What facts are known lead to one conclusion that might say something about the Irish American experience at that time: With so many second- and third-generation Irish being born and raised in the abject poverty of urban slums, gang warfare and other forms of lawlessness were ever at hand. They didn't look like evils, they looked like options. For many Irish kids—just as for poor black, Italian, Latin, and Asian kids to come—they looked like a way out.

In *The Book of Irish Americans*, William D. Griffin looks for something deeper in the legend: "Beyond all of these Hibernian surnames, there is something very Irish about the whole epic of Billy the Kid. The story of the warrior youth who comes out of the wilderness to take part in a struggle between battling clans is reminiscent of ancient Irish tales. So too is his implacable quest for revenge against those who killed his 'father,' including the slaying of the slayer. The band of comrades, with a price on their heads, defying all odds and enjoying the support of the countryfolk, raises echoes of the Irish experience. And, at the end, there is the martyrdom of the young hero, who goes to his death unarmed (Billy was not carrying a gun) as if welcoming his doom. Whatever the prosaic reality of Henry McCarty's life and death, the story of Billy the Kid, romanticized over the generations, has attained a sagalike quality that gives it a peculiarly Irish aura."

Who were the Gallagher Brothers?

They were not criminals like Billy the Kid or the James Gang. Not all Irishmen in the postwar West were Indian fighters, mountain men, or gunslingers.

The Gallaghers were three Irish American brothers who found themselves in Colorado in 1876 and, with no mining experience, decided to give prospecting a try. They struck silver and, almost overnight, the town of Leadville rose up—it would become nearly as big and bustling as Denver in the decades after the Gallagher strike. (Leadville used to boast that it had the hottest red-light district in the West. It also had a nice opera house, which still stands.) The Irish poured into burgeoning Leadville; one of the mines that opened was called the Maid of Erin. The Gallaghers watched the boom for a while, then sold their stake for $225,000. They could have become much richer had they stayed longer. They had been lucky indeed, but when it came to mining savvy, they were no Marcus Daly.

Who was Marcus Daly?

Marcus Daly was the greatest of many great Irish prospectors and miners. He built Butte, Montana, into a vital city.

Hailing from Ballyjamesduff, County Cavan, he headed for America in 1856 when he was fifteen. He spent five years in New York, then headed west, where the found-by-Irish Comstock Lode was issuing forth. The Walker Brothers of Salt Lake City hired him, and sent him to Butte in 1876 to look into a silver-mining operation there. Daly said "buy," and added $5,000 of his own money to the deal. Daly sold out his interest in the Alice Silver Mine for $30,000, and at that time the Walkers and everyone else thought Butte was just about tapped out. Daly didn't think so, and bought the Anaconda Silver Mine, where he sank a shaft in a dormant area. He struck . . . copper. Daly wasn't happy. But then, the deposit kept coming in, and coming in, and coming in. Daly bought the mineral rights nearby and opened up shop.

Daly was a fair man, and word of this spread quickly, attracting workers, many of whom were Irish. He paid $3.50 a day, much more than Irish could earn elsewhere. Certainly mining was a primary occupation among the Irish in the second half of the nineteenth century, and a lot of places had become targets for Irish Americans hoping to escape the slums, but Butte was something different. Daly was Irish, he was one of them. He was a leader, a good man who seemed to know what he was doing. He was paying a good wage; he seemed to care. By the turn of the century, Butte had become an Irishman's mining mecca: twelve thousand of Butte's forty-seven thousand people were either Irish born or first-generation Irish Americans. To be sure, Daly played favorites: There were 1,250 Irish-born miners in the Anaconda Mine in 1894 and only 365 English born, even though the English still outnumbered the Irish in Butte. But such bias seemed gentle compared with what had transpired through history, and as Butte evolved into Irish Town, no one seemed to notice or mind.

Daly was a pace-setting Irish American in many ways. He was a benevolent boss who helped his own. He was a politico: Vigorously Democratic, he gave **Williams Jennings Bryan** nearly one quarter of his campaign funding for an unsuccessful 1896 run for the White House. He was combative: He fought fellow copper magnate W. A. Clark for control of the state's Democratic party.

Daly was a piece of work. You can get a sense of that—and him— today by visiting his summer place in Hamilton, Montana, which is now a National Historic Landmark. The Daly mansion is twenty-four thousand feet of Georgian Revival opulence, with twenty-four bedrooms, fifteen bathrooms, and seven fireplaces faced with Italian marble. It is the final monument to the Copper King, and it is fitting.

There's a statue of Daly in Butte, at North Main and Copper. It is by the famous sculptor Augustus Saint-Gaudens, who also was Irish.

Who was John A. O'Farrell?

He was a much more modest Daly.

John A. O'Farrell was the very first citizen of what is now Boise, in what was one of the last states to be settled by whites, Idaho. An Irish native, O'Farrell was a miner: He had been to California during the gold rush of 1850, and by the 1860s he was moving toward the Rockies with his wife. In 1863 they built their log cabin—Boise's first house, if you discount the Indians' adobe huts—and soon after a wagon train delivered several of his wife's relatives from the Philadelphia area. The O'Farrells' little settlement attracted other prospectors, and soon there was a town. The army decided the growing community needed a frontier post, and that's how the future state capital got rolling.

The O'Farrells were staunch Catholics. One day, it is said, Mrs. O'Farrell hailed two missionaries who were headed for Oregon and invited them in. There, in the cabin, the first Mass in Idaho was said.

John did well in ore, both in California and in Idaho. His family finally lived in a finer house on Franklin Street in Boise. It wasn't Daly's digs—but then, what was?

Weren't the Molly Maguires miners?

Yes, they were. Coal miners.

That is, if they existed. Some say they were as real as leprechauns.

The many popular accounts of the Molly Maguires have ranged from Sir Arthur Conan Doyle's Sherlock Holmes novel *The Valley of Fear*—Holmes pitted against the mysterious, elusive Mollies—to, more recently, a 1970 film starring Sean Connery and Richard Harris, wherein the Mollies are depicted as a ruthless band of criminals carrying out a reign of terror in the Pennsylvania coal mines of the 1870s.

Let's say, for sake of argument, that the Molly Maguires in America were real. (In a moment, we'll explain why their existence might have been useful to the mine owners if, in fact, they were not.) The Pennsylvania Mollies were an offshoot of a rural secret society in Ireland. The original organization had been built to protect poor Irish tenant farmers from oppressive landlords, and the name of the group—call it a gang—derived either from a particularly heroic woman in their midst or from the fact that the boys sometimes wore women's dresses during their raids as a means of disguise. Perhaps they wore the dresses in tribute to the woman? Facts concerning the original Mollies are just as elusive as those regarding the American branch.

The Molly Maguires had reached into the United States by mid-century and established a trade union–style function. The Irish in the coal mines of Appalachia and the Alleghenies were working sixteen-hour days in deplorable, terribly unsafe conditions. Their English or Welsh bosses—*charming* to have the old order in the new world—cared little that those Irish who weren't dying in cave-ins were succumbing to black-lung disease. The Molly Maguires, miners and associates of miners among them, offered protection to the mass of laborers in Pennsylvania just as their forebears had offered it to Irish farmers. Lacking the means to give any kind of practical help through negotiation, they used intimidation and sabotage to convey their message to management. They can best be understood by comparing them to other, more famous organizations: They were like a little mafia for their kinfolk. And if it was true, as mine management claimed, that they were linked to the local Ancient Order of Hibernians, then they stood in relationship to that respectable institution rather as the Irish Republican Army stands in relationship to the political party Sinn Fein.

The Mollies expanded rapidly after the Civil War, and hundreds of acts of violence and arson were ascribed to them. When a massive strike hit the Pennsylvania coalfields in 1875, it was said that the Mollies had organized it. Then the murders started. Schuylkill County was not a place where life had tremendous value in those days; in the 1860s and 1870s, as many as 150 murders went unsolved (most of them blamed on the Mollies, of course). But there definitely was an uptick in homicide in 1875, and the mine owners decided to do something about it. They called the Pinkerton Detective Agency.

Jim McKenna arrived in the mines at about that time. Did he witness the murders? Did he concoct his behind-the-scenes account? Did he, perhaps, commit them himself? It doesn't matter now. What matters is that he was really **Jim McParlan,** an Irish American from County Armagh, employed by the efficient Pinkertons as an undercover agent. He was seen by reporters of the day as "the epitome of the swashbuckling, generous, roguish, charming, devil-may-care Irishman," and this might account for his quick acceptance in the pits. McParlan said that he became an intimate friend of the Molly Maguire leaders and of AOH lodge officials. All the while he was gathering evidence.

McParlan said this during the Molly Maguire trials of 1876. At the two trials—one in Pottsville, the other in Mauch Chunk (today called Jim Thorpe, Pennsylvania)—twenty Molly Maguires were sentenced to hang. Ten died on the same day—June 21, 1877—and ten more were sent to the gallows by the end of 1879. The swashbuckling, roguish McParlan was hailed as a hero.

History has allowed another side of the story to emerge.

By any standards, pit conditions in the mines were atrocious. For example, 112 workers were killed and another 339 permanently injured in the Pennsylvania mines in 1871. There was no labor protection, and one quarter of the twenty-two thousand miners were seven to sixteen years of age. Cheap labor, cheap working conditions: It was incumbent upon the Irish to try to change such a situation, but it was just as important to the mine owners that the status quo be maintained. When the Irish grew more and more dissonant, as exhibited in the strike of 1875, and as natural leaders began to emerge among them, the owners perceived the threat.

The reputation of the ghostly Molly Maguires among the law-abiding citizenry of Pennsylvania was not good, and the owners exploited this. They stoked the story of a terrorist gang of immigrants conspiratorially backed by the local Ancient Order of Hibernians. This line of reasoning was popularly received, and it was the very heart of McParlan's testimony.

The owners did all they could to assure themselves of convictions. The prosecution team was made up of mine owner Asa Packer's buddies, and Packer picked the judge himself. Irish Americans were bumped from the jury pool one after another. Nevertheless, the first trial broke down without a verdict. So McParlan enhanced his narrative, probably perjuring himself, and the death sentences were secured.

Many twentieth-century labor historians and two good books on the specific subject—*A Molly Maguire Story*, by Patrick Campbell, a descendant of one of the hanged men, and *The Molly Maguire Riots*, by Walter Coleman—lay out the revisionist view clearly: The mine bosses wanted to destroy the workers' leadership and realized that the leadership was being organized within the Ancient Order of Hibernians, so they wanted to destroy that, too. **John Kehoe,** the alleged leader of the Mollies, was a senior official of the AOH, and four others who were hanged were AOH divisional officers or county delegates. The trials were a travesty, and there was no evidence the Mollies existed. The twenty who were doomed were not necessarily criminals (a 1993 "retrial" in Pennsylvania freed them all) but rather martyrs of the American labor movement.

In 1978, shortly after the hundredth anniversary of John Kehoe's death, his great-grandson petitioned the Pennsylvania Board of Pardons to "remove the stigma that hangs over my family." His argument for reversal of sentence was buttressed by the testimony of historians and lawyers. A month after receiving the filing, the governor of Pennsylvania signed a posthumous pardon for Jack Kehoe and declared: "We can be proud of the men known as the Molly Maguires because they defiantly faced allegations that made trade unionism a criminal conspiracy. These men gave their lives on behalf of the labor struggle." A struggle in which future Irish Americans like George Meany and Mother Jones would play such a large part.

So, then, the Molly Maguires are vindicated—if, of course, they existed at all.

Who was Edward Doheny?

Born in Fond du Lac, Wisconsin, of Irish immigrants, **Edward Doheny** had gold fever as a teen, and after a near miss at wealth in Arizona—he registered his claim improperly—he hit it big in New Mexico. In 1892, in Los Angeles, he saw brea—a black tar used for fuel—being carried to and fro and wondered if oil might be nearby. In Westlake Park, he and a partner struck black gold: the first to hit oil in California.

Doheny was a tycoon overnight. But he is best remembered for his part in a scandal. His company leased the "Teapot Dome" area of Wyoming from the Interior Department in order to access its oil; in exchange, Doheny was to provide a substantial supply of fuel. There was a problem: Doheny had bribed Interior Department officials, most notably Secretary Albert Fall, to the tune of $400,000 in order to obtain the leases. Fall went to jail as a result of the Teapot Dome scandal, while Doheny lost millions in penalties—plus his good name.

Who was John Concannon?

John Concannon was a native—a super-native, if you will—of Ireland, born in the lonely, lovely Aran Islands off the west coast, a place where only Irish was spoken, in the first years of the Famine. He is proof that not all Irish immigrants who ventured west of New York in the latter decades of the nineteenth century became engaged in (1) the shooting of Indians; (2) the shooting of one another; or (3) the mining of minerals.

Concannon came to Boston, worked for a while in the Singer Sewing Company factory, returned to the Arans, married, returned to America, and migrated west. He worked as a shepherd in Oregon, then as a traveling salesman. By the 1880s he had saved enough, and he bought forty-seven acres of land in Livermore, California. He decided to try his hand at wine making, of all things.

He learned a little about the trade at the University of California at Berkeley. Most heartening, he learned that the soil in northern California was a lot like that of, say, the Bordeaux region in France. He imported vines, and, after a bit of failure, they took. Bishop Alemany of San Francisco started ordering his sacramental wine from the Concannon Winery, and this would be the vineyard's saving grace during Prohibition. Today, the winery is the oldest continuously operating one in the state, your Gallos and Mondavis included.

Who was Annie Moore?

She was a wonderful representative of all that was Irish and Irish American in the nineteenth century. **Annie Moore** became a member of one of the great families of her old land. By the luck of her arrival date, she became a significant symbol for her new home.

While approximately twelve million immigrants to the United States passed through the Ellis Island Immigrations Centre between 1892 and 1954—and it is estimated that 45 percent of all Americans today can trace their ancestry to at least one of them—the very first of these scared, desperate people was a young woman from Ireland. On January 1, 1892, thirteen-year-old Annie Moore arrived aboard the SS *Nevada* from Queenstown (now Cobh) in County Cork. With her were brothers Anthony, eleven, and Philip, seven. They were all on their way to join their parents, Matt and Mary Moore, who had come to New York earlier with their eldest son, Tom. Annie and the younger brothers had been cared for by Matt Moore's sister in Cork until the parents could afford to send for them. And now that time had come.

The three Moores had been living at 32 Monroe Street in Brooklyn, but with the family whole they soon had to move, and they relocated to Indiana. There, the tall and beautiful auburn-haired Annie met Patrick O'Connell, a descendant of the Great Liberator himself, Daniel O'Connell. The first person through Ellis Island had met an heir to all that was Irish. Love ensued, and the two were married in 1898 in, of all places, Waco, Texas.

The O'Connells had eight children before moving even farther west to Clovis, New Mexico, where they came to own a hotel and restaurant near the railroad station.

Annie passed away in 1923.

NINE

Irish Nationalism: The American Role

Could we begin this chapter with the national anthem, please?

The Young Irelanders have been mentioned as inspiration in Ireland's long march toward nationhood. Just who were they?

Who were the Fenians?

How did the funeral of an Irish American become a rallying point for the Fenian movement?

Didn't an Irish American army invade Canada?

How did the Fenian movement fare in Ireland?

What was the Fenian Ram?

What was the Orange Riot?

What was Clan na Gael?

Who was Charles Stewart Parnell?

Did Clan na Gael suffer when its friend Parnell fell?

Who was Eamon de Valera?

Who were the Black and Tans?

Where was de Valera during the war?

Who was Michael Collins?

How was Collins killed?

Does Michael Collins, the movie, tell the real story?

What happened to de Valera after Collins' death?

Ireland didn't fight in World War II?

Were there Hitler sympathizers in Ireland?

What happened to de Valera after the war?

*What happened to the nationalist movement
after the establishment of first the Free
State and then the Republic?*

Who is John Hume?

Who is Gerry Adams?

Could we begin this chapter with the national anthem, please?

Certainly, at least with a pertinent verse from "A Soldier's Song," the national anthem of the Republic of Ireland:

> *Soldiers are we*
> *Whose lives are pledged to Ireland.*
> *Some have come*
> *From a land beyond the waves . . .*

The Young Irelanders have been mentioned as inspiration in Ireland's long march toward nationhood. Just who were they?

As the Famine raged, the revolutionary tradition of 1798 reasserted itself in the Young Ireland movement. Founded in 1842 by a group that included the northern Protestant publisher and future supporter of the Confederate States of America, **John Mitchel**—called the Wolfe Tone of the movement—the YI's stressed cultural nationalism and rejected the narrow exclusivity of Daniel O'Connell's Catholic Repeal Association. Seeking help for a revolt, a contingent that included **Thomas Meagher** traveled to the Second French Republic in 1848. There, they got little more than words of encouragement—nothing like the material help Wolfe Tone had found in France—but they did bring back an enduring symbol modeled after the French tricolor: the green, white, and orange flag that would eventually represent the Republic of Ireland.

The Rising of '48 itself was, as we noted in chapter 7, nothing short of a fiasco. But it did serve to point the way to a future and help spread the gospel of Irish Republicanism to North America and Australia. How? Directly. Leaders such as Mitchel and Meagher and several others we'll meet in this chapter were arrested and either exiled to America directly or transported to Australia as convicts. Both Mitchel and Meagher were in the latter category, and once Down Under they escaped to New York, where they found careers as journalists. There, Mitchel published his *Jail Journal*, which would inspire future Irish nationalists. He moved on to a farm in Tennessee and became an outspoken supporter of slavery, while Meagher, as we know, rode into battle for the North under the banner of a gold harp and shamrocks on an emerald field. Political kinfellows in the old country, they were at swords' points in the new, and yet they were both still dedicated Irish nationalists.

Mitchel returned to Ireland, where he was elected to Parliament. He died soon thereafter.

Meagher was recognized for his wartime efforts when President Andrew Johnson gave him that Montana posting, which lasted until he fell into the Missouri River.

We start here, with material that is somewhat reiterative, because from Mitchel and Meagher and the energetic philosophy of the Young Irelanders extends a lineage that includes Wall Street financiers backing Irish revolt, radical priests shipping arms to the IRA, a future president of the Republic born in Brooklyn, licit and illicit comings and goings too numerous to mention, and aid and comfort from U.S. presidents and Speakers of the House.

The Young Irelanders got booted, they landed in America, and neither Ireland nor America has been quite the same since.

Who were the Fenians?

In 1856 a secret federation of former Irish Confederation and Repeal Association members united in the Phoenix Society. It was formed in Ireland by **Jeremiah O'Donovan Rossa,** who believed that the well-being of his country depended entirely on one thing: ousting the British. The Phoenix Society evolved into the Irish Republican Brotherhood, established in Dublin in 1858 by Rossa and **James Stephens.** The Brotherhood vowed to use physical force to free Ireland from British rule, if necessary.

Simultaneously, its American wing was established in New York by **John O'Mahoney.** This was the Fenian Brotherhood. O'Mahoney was a prosperous Irish Catholic, and an Irish-language scholar steeped in Celtic mythology. He named his organization after the legendary warriors, the Fianna, who'd fought under the chieftain Finn MacCool.

The alliance of the two organizations was a defining moment in the Irish nationalist struggle. From that point on Ireland would no longer be on its own as a small, impoverished outpost struggling in the shadow of the world's foremost military and economic power. A third party would have to be reckoned with—the United States, the world's soon-to-be ascendant nation with a million Irish immigrants ready, willing, and increasingly able to use their votes and spare pennies on behalf of the people they had left behind and the cause that they had not.

The word *Fenian* became, to opponents, descriptive of the international conspiracy that the Irish nationalist movement was evolving toward. In our day, British soldiers on Belfast streets have been wont to tell "Fenian bastards" to move along, and the Irish American rapper Seanchai (Chris Byrne of Black 47) has emblazoned on his promotional T-shirt a refrain from one of his songs: UNREPENTANT FENIAN BASTARD.

The official newspaper of the Fenian movement, published in Dublin, was *The Irish People*. Its often anticlerical nationalist views were attacked by priests and institutional employers, but its circulation grew. The Catholic Church in Ireland, under the leadership of Paul Cullen, was particularly opposed to the Fenian movement because it seemed a threat to Cullen's own political organization, the National Association, which promoted Catholic middle-class rights. The more privileged groups in Ireland opposed the Fenians because the middle class and better-off tenant farmers believed their well-being was tied to British rule. So no one liked the Fenians except the Fenians—and philosophers rich or poor who thought Ireland should be free from Britain.

How did the funeral of an Irish American become a rallying point for the Fenian movement?

In December of 1860 one of the exiled Young Irelanders, **Terrence McManus,** who had given up a promising career in the shipping business to take part in the Rising of '48, died in poverty in San Francisco—but he was not allowed to rest in peace. The publicity-hungry John O'Mahoney proposed sending the body back to Ireland after a long tour of the United States. The train carrying poor, dead McManus made stops for viewing in all areas where the Irish American population had put in a request, and the body did not leave for Ireland until September of 1861. In a world that has seen a lot of out-of-control Irish wakes, this was the strangest. To add insult to injury, when McManus finally did reach Ireland, Father Cullen refused to bury him at the cathedral in Dublin.

At that point, the Fenian affiliate, the Irish Republican Brotherhood, held a wake for McManus at the Mechanics Institute building (which would later become the site of the Abbey Theatre). More than fifty thousand nationalists followed the coffin to Glasmerion Cemetery, where a priest from Mayo presided over the burial. Along the way, the McManus processional continued making stops at spots sacred to the revolutionary cause in Ireland—the house wherein Robert Emmet had been hung, for instance, and the house where Wolfe Tone's body had lain before burial, then the house where Lord Edward Fitzgerald had been wounded in 1798.

The long, bizarre funeral of a destitute Irish American immigrant named McManus worked as well as O'Mahoney had hoped it would: It proved to be a great psychological victory for the Fenians in both the United States and Ireland over the anti-Fenian church hierarchy.

What Irish nationalism needed at that point, since there was no war yet, were rallying points.

Didn't an Irish American army invade Canada?

Yes. It invaded Canada twice, an episode every bit as odd as the waking of Terrence McManus.

In October of 1865 an American Fenian named **Thomas W. Sweeney** was appointed secretary of war of the Irish government-in-exile, as the Fenian movement in the United States was now thinking of itself. This gave Sweeney a full portfolio, for he was still a brigadier general in the Union army, in whose service he had lost an arm and had come to be considered a hero of the Civil War. Observing that the Irish Republican Brotherhood was unprepared to mount an offensive against the British in Ireland, Sweeney proposed the raising of a private army in the States, made up largely of Civil War veterans. He wanted to invade Canada, because of its formal alliance with England.

Armed with U.S. Army surplus equipment and buoyed by a postwar anti-British sentiment (remember: Britain had backed the Confederacy), Sweeney looked to be building some kind of real force. The United States apparently wasn't going to step in; there was indifference in the Andrew Johnson administration, which no doubt felt indebted to the Irish for the role they'd played in the Union cause.

The battle for an Irish Republic in North America began on May 31, 1866, when eight hundred soldiers under the command of **John O'Neill** crossed the Niagara River from Buffalo and planted the American and Fenian flags in the Canadian village of Fort Erie. He claimed the land for the Irish Republic in exile. The first skirmish, on June 2, was a complete rout of a part-time Canadian militia that was caught off guard.

Meanwhile, Washington had come to the realization that it really couldn't countenance a war with a peaceful neighbor. Generals Grant and Meade (the Irish American of Gettysburg fame) were dispatched to end the nonsense. They began to patrol the Niagara River and cut off supplies and reinforcements to O'Neill and his men. The Fenian army was stranded and so headed back into the United States, where they were arrested.

President Johnson issued a proclamation on June 6 forbidding any American citizens from taking part in further raids on Canada, and one day later, on Grant's orders, Meade and his men confronted General Sweeney in Saint Albans, Vermont, where he had been preparing his own assault. He, too, was placed under arrest. In all, some seven thousand Fenian soldiers were taken into custody by Meade, who had once been the commander of many of these prisoners. When the captives reached New York en masse, they were told they could return to their American homes. Tammany Hall's Boss Tweed and New York City mayor William Hoffman, each with an eye to the increasingly significant Irish vote, agreed to pick up the tab for all that rail fare.

The dismantling of the Fenian invasion was a devastating blow to the Irish American nationalist movement: It was beginning to look like they'd never be able to set up their Irish state *anywhere*. But old dreams die hard, and old, crazy dreams die hardest. The Fenians would organize one more ineffectual invasion of Canada in 1870, and this would come to a similar end. Meanwhile, Canada, so shaken by the unexpected blow from its friendly neighbor to the south, moved to unite its vast provinces into a single nation. In our time, we can see the problems this has caused: Quebec wants to be free of Ottawa just as badly as many in Northern Ireland want to be free of London. For forcing French-English union upon a country where union was unnatural, blame the Irish. The ironies never end.

How did the Fenian movement fare in Ireland?

Not very well.

In February and March of 1867 the Irish Republican Brotherhood led insurrections in Kerry, Cork, Tipperary, Limerick, Dublin, and Clare. They were, for the most part, attacks on barracks of the Royal Irish Constabulary. But with so many IRB leaders either on the run or already in jail, the offensive was rudderless and a military failure.

However, while armed insurrection was going nowhere, nationalist sentiment was growing. In November, when three Brotherhood members were hanged in Manchester, England, for murdering a policeman during the bombing of a prison van carrying Fenian leaders, many Irish people united in vocal support. The "Manchester Martyrs" were honored in the song "God Save Ireland," which quickly became the unofficial national anthem of Ireland.

In 1869 O'Donovan Rossa was elected to Parliament from Tipperary, but he could not take his seat as he was in prison for Fenianism. He refused to wear a prison uniform and demanded recognition as a political prisoner. When Parliament formally disqualified him from office, Tipperary elected another Fenian who'd just been released from jail. Between the lines, Ireland was cracking; anger was rising like lava.

The legacy of the Fenian movement would be a resurrection and repackaging of the nonsectarian ideals of Wolfe Tone and the United Irishmen of 1798. It would also mark a turning away from the pacifism preached by Daniel O'Connell—who had been, after all, the founding father and philosopher king of Young Ireland, and who remained a hero to all nationalists.

Fenianism in America and Ireland implied the right of the Irish people to use force to gain freedom.

What was the Fenian Ram?

In 1873 **John Philip Holland** of County Clare left the Christian Brothers in Ireland and traveled to Boston to join his brother, an exiled Fenian. Before signing on with the Brothers, his ambition had been to go to sea, and now over the waves he sailed with a head full of ideas about naval warfare. From studying every sea battle of the Civil War and reading all else on the subject that he could find, Holland surely possessed as much knowledge of navigation—particularly submarine navigation—as any man living. He was also a superb draftsman and engineer, and so he was dangerous: Given the chance, he could put his knowledge to work.

He offered his design of a submarine—one propelled by a screw that was activated by a pedal—to the United States Navy. It was dismissed by the secretary of the navy as the "fantastic scheme of a civilian landsman!" However, the Fenian movement in the United States realized that the power of the British Empire depended largely on its maritime supremacy. It financed Holland's building of a vessel that, it was hoped, would be a genuine threat to the British navy. With $6,000 from the Fenians' "skirmishing fund," Holland built his sub and began testing it in New Jersey's Passaic River. This prototype was a success. The Fenians gave Holland more money and Holland built a bigger boat. The *Fenian Ram*, modeled after a dolphin's contours, was christened at the foot of West Thirteenth Street in New York in May of 1881, but divisions within the Fenian leadership and squabbles about ownership left the sub stored in a lumber shed for many years. It was finally unveiled in 1916, but only to raise funds to help Irish who were suffering repression after the Easter Rising.

First, they try to take over Canada—*twice*—then they get it in their heads that they can bring down Britain with a submarine. They actually get the sub *built* but let it molder. Today the *Fenian Ram* sits on display in West Side Park in Paterson, New Jersey. It is a deftly executed prototype for the nuclear submarines of today.

As for Holland, he finally sold a sub, his sixth, to the U.S. Navy in 1900. The USS *Holland* dove and rose for ten years before retirement. By that point, its inventor, too, was out to pasture. When submarine production became big business in the first decade of the twentieth century, Holland began to realize the terrifying potential of his invention. He put away designing for good, took to studying aeronautics, playing music, and teaching Gaelic to children of Irish descent in Trenton, New Jersey. He died shortly before the outbreak of World War I, which was a good thing. He didn't live to see German U-boats acting out his very worst fears.

What was the Orange Riot?

It was said at the time that the Wednesday of the Orange Riot in New York—July 12, 1871—was the bloodiest day in American peacetime history. More than fifty people were killed in a street riot on the border of Manhattan's Chelsea and Hell's Kitchen neighborhoods.

The Orangemen in New York, pro-Britain Irish, had been preparing for their annual celebration of the Battle of the Boyne. That year, the Fenians were intent on violently opposing it. If this sounds similar to the annual summer Marching Season tensions in the cities of Northern Ireland in our present day, that's understandable: The same historical event was being commemorated, the same religious and political differences were creating the tension.

It was a hot summer day; trouble was thick in the air. The previous year's Orangemen's picnic at Elm Park had been attacked by Irish of the Green persuasion, with the result of a few cracked heads and blackened eyes. Now, the somewhat better organized and far more belligerent Irish Nationalists were proclaiming that the Orange would not get off so lightly. The newspapers had published the rumors: Ten thousand Catholics were arming themselves. Leaders of the Orange societies let it be known that five thousand of their own would carry weapons as they marched. By their reckoning, their right to march was as sacred as the opposition's right to its Saint Patrick's Day Parade (long since having shed its initial Orange sponsorships and now flagrantly Green).

Little was done by the city fathers to prevent mayhem. The attitude of the largely Anglo-Saxon middle and upper classes was that if the Irish Catholics, whose draft riots were fresh in mind, needed another stern lesson from the police and militia, then let them have it.

Roman Catholic Archbishop John McCloskey sent a letter to his priests instructing them to urge their parishioners at Mass to "array themselves on the side of peace and order and allow the Orangemen to parade." Even the Fenian firebrand O'Donovan Rossa risked his standing within the movement by urging leaders of his and other Irish organizations to let the Orangemen have their celebration. Interfering with the parade, he said, would be "unworthy of Irishmen and Americans."

On Monday, July 10, Mayor A. Oakley Hall ordered Police Superintendent J. J. Kelso to cancel the police department's permit for the Orange parade, then he rescinded his own order. Instead, he put in place 800 police and 2,300 militia to protect the 160 Orangemen who finally showed up to march. When these men left the confines of Orange Society headquarters at Twenty-ninth Street and Eighth Avenue, flanked by rows of armed escorts—rifles, bayonets, and nightsticks at the ready—no one knew what hell might break loose.

At first, little happened. Frustrated protesters could only throw bricks and stones from the roofs of tenements along the avenue. But then a shot rang out—perhaps a soldier accidentally discharging his rifle—and a militia regiment responded by firing indiscriminately into a crowd that included women and children. In the riot, besides the 50 who were killed, 105 suffered gunshot wounds and 169 were arrested.

The *New York World* editorialized that "New York has been disgraced by a street fight in 1871 over the merits of an Irish battle fought in 1690," while the *London Times* blamed the trouble on the "combative temperament of the Irish manifesting itself in the New World." Horace Greeley's *Tribune* pointed out that one of the more far-reaching aspects of the riot was that Tammany Hall's Boss Tweed was losing his grip. Tammany had long claimed to be the protector of the poor and defender of the faith, and to have control of all things that happened in the streets of New York. But now the police and militia had cut loose at the crowds. Tammany had pressed the mayor to pull the permit and had lost that fight: The machine had been overruled by a mere state governor. This would cost Tammany: In the next election, the slum vote was split between Tammany and the Democratic reform slate; as a result, a Republican ticket was voted into state office. Tweed, through ballot stuffing, was one of the few Tammany candidates to avoid the backlash and defeat his opponent, none other than O'Donovan Rossa. But Tweed had been arrested for fraud just eleven days before the election, and he was cooked. He soon fled the country.

What was Clan na Gael?

Founded in the United States in 1867 by **Jerome Collins,** an Irish exile who was the meteorological and science editor of the *New York Herald* (he wrote America's first newspaper weather forecast), Clan na Gael (Family of the Irish) was an even more secretive society than the Fenians, which had been infiltrated by spies since its earliest years. It was an oath-bound group with Masonic-type rituals, and it met in the shadows of New York's Irish American subculture. Its major objectives were the liberation of Ireland from British rule and the promotion of Irish culture in both the old land and the new. Clan na Gael's many activities included raising funds and weapons to forward the fight for independence.

From 1871 forward, **John Devoy,** a former Fenian and yet another exile, dominated Clan na Gael. Devoy is a seminal figure in the story of Irish Americanism, as is made clear in Terry Golway's 1998 biography *America's Greatest Irish Rebel,* to which our short account of Devoy and the Clan owes much.

Devoy was born in County Kildare in 1842, the grandson (according to family legend) of men who had fought in the Rebellion of 1798. His experience would stretch from the Famine through his financing of the Easter Rebellion in 1916 to the birth of the Irish Free

State in 1921 (he would die in 1928). His father had been a supporter of Daniel O'Connell, and Devoy was raised a patriot. He studied Gaelic and would sneak out of mass early to join his friends for an afternoon of singing nationalist ballads. When he was eighteen he joined the fledgling Fenian movement as a member of the Irish Republican Brotherhood. Committed to the violent overthrow of British rule but in need of military training, he rejected a chance to join Meagher's Irish Brigade only because he thought the American Civil War would be over in a matter of months. He opted instead for the Army of the French Republic, and that was a mistake. He was garrisoned in Algeria, where he saw no action.

Returned to Ireland, Devoy began trying to subvert the 60 percent of the British army that was of Irish heritage, looking toward an insurrection. He and other Fenians were arrested, and Devoy spent the next five years in jail until he and fellow rebels, including O'Donovan Rossa, agreed to live anywhere except within the United Kingdom of Great Britain and Ireland in exchange for early release. The obvious choice was New York, the burgeoning capital-in-exile of the imagined Irish Republic. In 1871 Devoy and his mates entered a city of one million people that was now one-fifth Irish, with 37 percent of the population having at least one Irish-born parent. Devoy settled in the charming Five Points slum and almost immediately joined not only Clan na Gael but the Marx-inspired International Workingman's Association. He found work as a reporter for the *Herald*. Meantime, he started sketching a plan to rescue Irish nationalists who had been transported to the prison colony in western Australia. With help from his friend in Boston, the journalist John Boyle O'Reilly, he arranged for Clan na Gael to purchase a ship called the *Catalpa*, which sailed to Australia, picked up six escaped Fenians, and beat it back to Manhattan—where the Irish American community staged a parade of welcome. This triumph of the shadowy Clan na Gael was heard of in Dublin and London.

In 1877 Clan na Gael formed an alliance with the Irish Republican Brotherhood and established a joint directory of individuals who could help with the fight: a transatlantic Rolodex of Irish sympathizers. Many prominent Americans, such as **T. V. Powderly** of the Knights of Labor, had given their calling cards to Clan na Gael.

In the winter of 1878–79, as a result of falling prices, crop failures, and wet weather in Ireland, the rural population was threatened with disaster similar to, if on a smaller scale than, that of the Great Famine. Bankruptcy, starvation, and the eviction of small farmers were again a prospect. Irish Party leader **Charles Stewart Parnell** saw the land question as a good way to rouse the masses.

Who was Charles Stewart Parnell?

He was "the uncrowned king of Ireland," but pretty much an Irish American in bloodlines. His mother's father, nicknamed "Old Ironsides," was an American admiral who sank two British warships off the coast of Portugal near the end of the War of 1812. His great-grandfather had fought in the American Revolution. His mother, Delia had been born in America and had married the British-born squire John Parnell; they became landowning Protestants in County Wicklow. As for Charles himself: He was well educated, respected by his peers, and had been elected to Parliament in 1875. In this dire time, he took up land-ownership reform as his cause.

Clan na Gael and the Irish Republican Brotherhood also saw land reform as a useful vehicle for encouraging large-scale revolt against the British and slid toward Parnell's Irish Party. John Devoy and the Clan rented Madison Square Garden in New York for a speech by Parnell in the fall of 1879, which indicates the enormity of the Clan's pot of gold.

Michael Davitt, who had founded the Mayo Land League in 1879 (it shortly would become the National Land League with Parnell as its head), traveled to America and met with Devoy and others in Clan na Gael who wanted their own pipeline to the Irish masses. Together they formulated the New Departure Plan. Parnell and his supporters would start arguing for home rule while Clan na Gael and the Irish Republican Brotherhood would prepare for revolution. The Clan and the IRB recruited and radicalized among the Irish by campaigning for fair rent laws, a tenant's right to sell his interest if evicted, complete abolition of the landlord system, and establishment of a peasant proprietorship. Parnell would eventually add to the menu a formal call for home rule by the year 1882. When Britain refused, as Britain certainly would, a revolt would be ignited. That was the plan.

To briefly emphasize just how transatlantic all this was: The Land League in America was concocted by these Irish nationalists—each club in one place needed a sister club in the other—and became one of the best-organized and most intelligent critics not only of land-lordism in Ireland but also of out-of-control capitalism in America. As president of the U.S. Land League in the 1880s, Chicago lawyer

Alexander Sullivan was probably the most powerful Irishman in America. On the side, he ran a well-oiled political machine that placed hundreds of Clan na Gael men in dozens of government agencies, especially the police department. Sullivan also controlled hundreds of thousands of dollars that were earmarked for Parnell's use or for terrorism.

And there was terrorism. When two bombs went off in the London underground, Westminster asked Washington to crack down on the "dynamite press" in the United States, meaning *The Irish World*, O'Donovan Rossa's *United Irishman* and two Brooklyn-based tabs, *Ireland's Liberator* and the unsubtle *Dynamite Monthly*. When bombs went off in the Tower of London and in Parliament, creating panic, they had indeed been planted by teams of Irish Americans.

But, remarkably, the efforts to end landlordism in Ireland proceeded in a statesmanly fashion where it most mattered—in Ireland. The period of mass resistance on this issue extended from 1879 to 1882. There were boycotts and rent withholdings. While most methods aimed at reform involved moral suasion, some bits of violence against landlords did occur. (Were the mysterious Molly Maguires at work again?) But there was no war, no new rising. In 1881 a Land Act passed that promised to wreck the old landlord system and guarantee farmers stable tenure at fair rent. But the act was not perfect, and when Parnell and other Irish Party leaders opposed it because it did not include tenants in arrears, they were jailed. In March of 1882 British Prime Minister Gladstone visited Parnell in prison, where they agreed on a modified Land Act. In their agreement, known as the Kilmainham Treaty, the arrears would be taken care of and all prisoners would be released. Thus the land war ended.

The "quiet revolution" by which ownership of land slid from landlord to tenant in Ireland at the turn of the century came off with much less difficulty than anyone would have guessed—less, perhaps, than some agitators would have liked. It set Parnell up as a considerable hero, and put him in a good position to continue the big fight: home rule.

And then he fell for **Kitty O'Shea,** and thus he would fall from power.

When Captain William O'Shea was divorced from his wife, Parnell was named at the trial as corespondent. This was the unveiling of what had been a longstanding affair. Such news wrote *fini* to political careers in places like Ireland, but Parnell tried to hang on to the leadership of the Irish Nationalist Party. His recalcitrance derailed the home-rule campaign, and so "the uncrowned king of Ireland" leaves a dual legacy. His enacted reforms improved the lot of farmers, and his reformist ideas certainly boosted the nationalist sentiments that were flourishing anew in his time. But for carrying on his risky affair and for not leaving the stage gracefully so that others could get on with business leaves many wondering if he didn't ultimately set back the cause of Irish independence.

Support in the United States for the Irish Party was less enthusiastic after the fall of Parnell; the flow of money to Ireland dried up considerably. When **John Redmond** tried to revitalize the Irish Party after Parnell's eventual departure, the United Irish League of America was founded in 1901 to support him, eventually covering most of the party's expenses through the Irish elections of 1910. But a lot of steam had gone out of the charge toward home rule.

Did Clan na Gael suffer when its friend Parnell fell?

It was already suffering. Those bombs had gone off in England (Clan na Gael was blamed), factions within the clan were squabbling, money was tighter. Parnell's scandal certainly didn't help.

The organization was reborn a bit in 1900 when the Boer War gave it something useful to oppose. (The British waged a savage three-year battle for control of South Africa's natural resources.) Irish Americans denounced the war in mass meetings organized by Clan na Gael. Some got so carried away, they volunteered to fight with the Boers. The United Irish Society, a Chicago-based coalition of Irish organizations, agitated against the war. Both the Republican and Democratic parties began writing planks for the 1900 election that would denounce the war. President McKinley, descended from Protestant Irish, took note of the fervency of the opposition and said he would try to mediate an end to the war; his fear of an allied electorate of Irish Americans, German Americans, and anti-imperialists no doubt spurred his concern. Nothing came of his mediation, but the effectiveness of organized Irish American protest was made clear—not least, to Irish Americans.

Larger war questions were to come for the Irish, the Irish Americans, and other Americans as they looked at the Irish. In world wars, everyone is supposed to pick a side. But in each world war, every Irishman had to ask himself: Is the enemy of my enemy my friend? Then he had to ask further: What's the right thing to do?

Consider World War I: When Redmond agreed to support England's efforts against Germany, he angered Irish nationalists and destroyed the United Irish League of America, which had supported Redmond's Irish Party. (Redmond was hoping that playing nice with Westminster would make Westminster feel kindly regarding Irish home rule after the war.) Fenian doctrine held absolutely that Britain's difficulty was Ireland's opportunity; Clan na Gael condemned Redmond at its 1914 fall convention. The Clan wanted the United States to remain neutral, while the Ancient Order of Hibernians supported the Germans. Absent the inchoate evil that Germany would embody a quarter century later, many Irish felt no moral imperative was at stake. John Devoy wrote in the *Gaelic American* that Irish hopes for liberty would be best served by a German victory.

Meanwhile, however, Irish Americans with no time to debate, fought in the U.S. services, and more than 270,000 Irishmen—40 percent of the adult male population—fought in Britain's armed forces. "Long Way to Tipperary" was everywhere in the air, and it was the rare Irish village that didn't see a son killed. The final irony or paradox—take your choice—is that large numbers of Irish nationalists had actually enlisted with Britain because, like Redmond, they thought such noble behavior would serve to bring home rule as a reward once the war was over. Meanwhile, members of the Ulster Volunteer Force felt the same way: If they pitched in during this time of need, London would certainly reward the Protestant north by keeping a firm hand on the whole of Ireland.

In 1916 Clan na Gael was able to provide money and weapons in support of the Easter Rising in Ireland against British rule, and this made the clan happy indeed: a cause without ambivalence.

Who was Eamon de Valera?

He was an Irish American who became the dominant character in the Irish Republic's twentieth-century passion play.

Considered by some to be the most Irish of Irishmen, **Eamon de Valera** was in fact born in New York City to immigrant Spanish and Irish parents. His father died shortly after his birth and his mother sent young Edward (as he was christened) to be raised by his grandmother in County Limerick. A gifted student, he was educated on scholarships and became a mathematics teacher. A passing fancy for the priesthood had to be abandoned when he fell in love with his

Irish teacher, Sinead Flanagan, whom he married in 1910. Learning Irish had not only inflamed his amorous passions but also fanned his nationalist fire, and he joined the Gaelic League and the Irish Volunteers. His command of the Boland Mills garrison during the 1916 rising was an important role.

The Easter Rising—or the Rising of 1916—or the Easter Rebellion is an event of equal consequence to, say, Gettysburg or Antietam in America. The Ulster Volunteer Force had bet correctly vis-à-vis participation in World War I: There were no signs that Britain was going to give up Ireland, even though Westminster had promised Redmond that the subject of home rule was being considered. The rising was supposed to occur nationwide, but because of poor planning among the Irish Volunteers and sheer bad luck, it erupted only in central Dublin. The battle was fierce, but finally disastrous for the insurgents. The rising had started on April 24 and was quashed by April 29. Several rebel leaders not killed during the shooting were executed afterward; **James Connolly,** wounded during the firefight, was shot in a chair since he couldn't stand upright when facing the firing squad.

The reaction in America was intense. The usually pro-British mainstream press was horrified by the summary executions. Poets and writers rallied in Central Park on behalf of "the poets of Dublin," and thousands demonstrated at Carnegie Hall against the reprisals. Representative **W. Bourke Cochran,** who was a friend of and, as an orator, an inspiration to Winston Churchill, addressed the crowd: "For thirty years I have been one of those who had believed that it was the part of prudence for Irishmen to forget—aye, seek to forgive and try to forget—the wrongs of the centuries in the hope that better days were dawning . . . and now, behold the consequences of this attempt. The vilest murders ever committed in Irish history are fresh before our eyes. The noblest Irishmen that ever lived are dead, dead by the bullet of British soldiery, shot like dogs for asserting the immortal truths of patriotism."

Next on the list to be executed for his part in the rising was de Valera, but before he could be killed the outcries had been heard across the Atlantic. General **Robert Maxwell,** the commanding officer of the British garrison in Ireland, realized that shooting a native son of the United States would damage relations between America and England horribly—and at a time when England needed help with the war against Germany—and he ended the executions.

The year after the rising, de Valera won a by-election to Parliament in County Clare as a candidate from **Arthur Griffith**'s newly formed nationalist party Sinn Fein (Ourselves), of which he soon took charge. When Sinn Fein saw fit to set up its own assembly, the Dail Eireann, purportedly in place of Westminster, de Valera became its president. Of course the establishment of the Dail was regarded as an illegal act by Britain, and this was the genesis of the Irish War of Independence, which would last until 1921. It was a strange fate for an American boy: to find himself in a George Washington situation in his mother's homeland.

The War of Independence, fought on the rebel side by guerrilla warriors and on the Crown side by the Royal Irish Constabulary and a few special forces such as the Auxies and the Black and Tans, lasted from 1919 to 1921. As with another, earlier Revolutionary War against rebel guerrillas, things didn't go very well for England. The war would end with "the Treaty," which created the Free State of Ireland—a new nation autonomous from Great Britain.

Who were the Black and Tans?

They were an affiliated force of the Royal Irish Constabulary that executed their missions during the War of Independence with a particular viciousness. They were not, as many Irish nationalists claim, British jailbirds assembled to wreak havoc in Ireland, but ex–World War I soldiers lured back from demobilization in 1920 by the promise of money and action. Whence their nickname? Once the war was on, there simply weren't enough RIC uniforms for all the forces, and so this gang went about in khakis. Admittedly, **Michael Collins** and his Volunteers—now called the Irish Republican Army—didn't shrink from potshot and assassination, but even by IRA standards the Black and Tans were a ruthless bunch. Decades later, mention of their name sends a shiver up the spine of an Irishman, as the authors of this book learned, while attending, not long ago, a literary reading on the decorous Upper East Side of Manhattan. In the audience were various Irish and English and Irish Americans, as well as some just-plain Americans. The reading had an Irish slant and was generally well received. But there were odd moments, not the least of them when the evening's host, apparently of English descent, mentioned during his introduction of tonight's guest that he himself had dressed for balance—tan sports coat, black slacks—since the forthcoming words were sure to be so very Green. The audience laughed politely.

Later, at a Greenwich Village restaurant, the honoree, your two authors, and the host were engaged in pleasant conversation about how well the benefit had gone. Everyone was in agreement on the point, but the honoree said that he felt compelled to mention that, on the occasion of a presentation on the Holocaust by a Jewish scholar, it might have been inappropriate for the master of ceremonies to sport a swastika on his lapel.

We three rocked on our heels for thirty seconds or so, drinking in the point.

Where was de Valera during the war?

At first, in jail. By the time the Dail held its initial congress, de Valera was in prison in England for creating the Dail. His daring escape therefrom was orchestrated by Michael Collins, and was followed by a trip to America. De Valera claimed Ireland's interests would be best served if he could coax the United States to Ireland's side in the battle for international recognition. He was unsuccessful with President **Woodrow Wilson,** who was perhaps still upset that, as you'll learn in the next chapter, **Eugene O'Neill** had thrown a beer bottle through his window at Princeton. (Devoy once said of Wilson: "He hates the Irish with the implacable hatred of the Ulster Orangeman—the stock he comes of.") But while Wilson let him down, de Valera was greatly bolstered by the outpouring of support and money from Irish Americans.

De Valera returned to Ireland after nineteen months, rejoining Collins, who had been waging his bloody guerrilla war. When greeted with news of many great successes under the Big Fella's leadership, de Valera responded coldly, "We'll see who's the Big Fellow."

Who was Michael Collins?

Michael Collins was born in 1890 in County Cork, a hotbed of Irish nationalism. As a youth he was a fellow traveler with any who might want to drive the English out of Ireland. Released from prison after fighting in the Easter Rising, he organized the "Irish Volunteers," a band of rebels that was the forerunner of the Irish Republican Army. Collins's boys fought with astonishing success during the War of

Independence. After the Bloody Sunday killings of 1919, in which several special agents from London were eliminated one by one, the Big Fella, as Collins was known, grew into that Irish fireplace favorite: *A Living Legend.*

Eventually the British offered terms and Collins, as part of the negotiating team sent to London, accepted for the Republic. Under the treaty, the Brits would keep the North and the Irish could set up a Free State in the rest, as long as they pledged a loyalty oath to Westminster. Collins's adherents maintain that Collins took what he could, while hoping to get more—the north, perhaps absolute independence—at a later date. "Freedom to achieve freedom," as Collins put it.

De Valera saw the threat Collins posed to his own leadership. This certainly had been behind de Valera's refusal to take Collins to London for the preliminary negotiations after the July 1921 truce, and some say it led to de Valera's sending Collins for the ultimate negotiations. By then, the pragmatic de Valera surely realized that Unionist intransigence in the North would not allow the creation of a complete Irish Republic, and that whoever came back with half a loaf would be doomed. In this thinking, he sent Collins in his own place as scapegoat, to negotiate the treaty he fully expected, but could then publicly rail against.

De Valera's rhetoric in resigning from the Dail when the Collins treaty was ratified, and his further rhetoric on the stump, stoked the fire that led to civil war—a war that claimed the lives of so many of de Valera's former comrades, including Michael Collins.

How was Collins killed?

When Collins returned to Ireland he found some support for the treaty—the Irish were hungry for a homeland, even a parceled one—but equally strong sentiment that he had betrayed the cause. De Valera denounced the settlement, then sided with militant antitreaty forces. Suddenly, IRA was fighting former IRA, reconstituted as the Irish Free State army.

Yes, the Irish went through their revolutionary war and then their civil war within half a decade.

In 1922 Collins, recklessly and for uncertain reasons, went home to Cork, now a hotbed of antitreaty recrimination. There he was shot and killed in an ambush.

'Twas born to be a movie.

Does Michael Collins, *the movie, tell the real story?*

The story behind the much heralded 1996 movie reads like a great Irish saga of old. It adds some insight to how the Irish view de Valera and Collins. And the film was underwritten by a big Hollywood studio, so it's an Irish *American* tale as well.

"Yesterday's terrorist is today's statesman," said director **Neil Jordan** upon winning the Venice Film Festival's top prize for the film. "I make no apology for that." A mite defensive? Forgive him; he had cause to be gun-shy. It seemed that every time he opened his mouth about his epic biopic, he was barraged not with questions about **Liam Neeson**'s gigantic performance or **Julia Roberts**'s *interesting* accent, but with criticism for glorifying a back-alley killer, or for playing fast and loose with history. His inquisitors professed to be shocked that an Irishman might be putting an artistic gloss on the facts.

What were the facts? Well, first, the facts at the time of the film's release were that a breakdown in the Irish peace talks, renewed sectarian violence in the north, the TWA crash off Long Island, and the Atlanta Olympics bombing had all conspired to create a more skittish world theater in which to launch *any* film about a real-life guerrilla warrior, albeit one already seventy-four years dead. That Collins was seen by some as the father of modern terrorism—Mao studied his methods, adopting many—assured that the release of a Collins film would be something of a hot item. So hot, alleged one British tab, that Warner Bros. was delaying release of the film in Ireland so as not to add any fuel to a fire.

But there really was nothing much to worry about. Yes, sure, the Irish are a people known to riot over the opening of a Synge play, but as Maol Muire Tynan, a political reporter for the *Irish Times*, put it, "Ireland has a very young population today, and Michael Collins's name doesn't really provoke any real emotion. I think that we've probably grown up enough not to get too excited. People will go along to enjoy the movie the same way they went along to see *Braveheart*—it's like a western, but it has little to do with history."

If Neil Jordan might have been calmed by Tynan's assessment, he wouldn't have been made happy by it. "I challenge anybody to make a historical movie more accurate," he said of his *Collins*, and that was a challenge worth investigating. So we did.

Our opinion is that the movie baldly seeks to write—rewrite?—

history, and its point of view does, in fact, have a bearing on every-thing that has happened in this Irish century, and everything that is happening today. As has been mentioned, Collins was killed by the same Irish Republican Army that he had helped create, and as with, say, the death of John F. Kennedy, the killing of Collins has long been barnacled with rumor and suspicion—suspicion that has con-tinuing significance since Collins is eternally tied to the IRA and to the Troubles. The Irish have asked themselves for three-fourths of a century: Was Collins a traitor? A martyr? Was he executed for cause, or cold-bloodedly murdered? Who ordered the killing?

Neil Jordan, speaking from his home in Dublin, told us: "His am-bush is kind of our grassy knoll."

In *Collins*, Jordan put forth his personal theory. The director's scenario was that de Valera, a man who went on to become the three-term prime minister and president for fourteen years of the Repub-lic of Ireland, all but pulled the trigger that killed Michael Collins. Jordan, whose concentration at City College in Dublin was history, knows that this is a controversial take on affairs and thinks it's part of the reason no Michael Collins movie has been made till now. "For years, filmmakers wouldn't touch this story," he said to us. "De Valera was alive, of course, and also—lots of people didn't want to admit that the roots of this Irish state were born out of a certain kind of violence."

A few did try. John Huston nearly made a Collins film years ago and, more recently, Robert Redford, Michael Cimino, and Kevin Costner all mounted efforts. Even as "Dances with Druids" was com-ing to naught, Jordan was at work on his script. "I'd been interested in all this stuff forever," he said. "I realized that with these characters you could tell the whole story of the foundation of the Irish state. I started working on the *Michael Collins* script way back in 1982." But he couldn't get it made, not least because Neil Jordan wasn't yet *Neil Jordan*—the famous, *Crying Game* Neil Jordan—and Liam Neeson was the pre-*Schindler* Liam Neeson. "Neil asked me to play the part eleven years ago," Neeson told *Irish America* magazine when the film was in production. "It has taken up until this year for all of us to achieve that bit of clout to warrant David Geffen and Warner Bros. putting the money into it, so it's been a long road." The money—$28 million—was peanuts for an epic, but Jordan con-vinced Neeson and others—Alan Rickman (scenery-chewing as de Valera), Aidan Quinn (fine as Collins's friend Harry Boland), Stephen Rea (terrific as the informer Ned Broy)—to work cheap.

Out of nowhere, Roberts, noted Irish-guy date, asked to play Kitty Kiernan, Collins's love (she did so with a brogue that falls slippingly from the tongue). Suddenly, the Collins project was a *Lawrence of Arabia*–style canvas with a *JFK*-style ending and Julia Roberts spooning with Liam Neeson, directed by Mr. Crying Game. Green light, baby.

Where this vehicle would head after passing go was all in Neil Jordan's head. For instance: Just before *Michael Collins* went into production, a major new Collins biography by Tim Pat Coogan was published. Tim lived just down the road a piece, so Neil hired him as a historical consultant. It didn't work out. "I separated from the film in a very unhappy way," Coogan told us, speaking from his home in Dublin. "I saw the script and parts were grossly inaccurate historically. I would say to Neil, 'This has to change.' And Neil had a standard response— 'Oh, yes, well, we'll see.' The worst was the Bloody Sunday sequence. That was Michael Collins's defining moment, as he held together when everyone else cracked. But Neil had this technique he took from *The Godfather* where he goes back and forth to the killings around Dublin, and then to Michael romping near bare-assed with . . . what's her name? Julie Roberts! That sequence is very offensive to many Irish, but Neil was sticking with it. He'd been gobsmacked by Coppola!" (Gobsmacked, which is not Gaelic, means something akin to "smitten by"—at least in this context.)

Coogan left the production; Jordan made his film. When Coogan was asked about the substance of Jordan's eventual ending—the implication that de Valera might have okayed the assassination—he said, "If I had been a consultant still, I wouldn't have let it stand." In his biography, Coogan quotes a member of the ambush team saying that, in fact, de Valera tried to talk the shooters out of the shooting. "Now, I don't like de Valera, but it was not proved that he was involved in the killing and, in fact, it was not true. In my book I make it clear that his finger was not on those triggers. Dev had tried to dissuade them that morning. The killers told him to get stuffed, and he flounced out in anger. If Collins's people ever knew for sure that Dev had complicity in the murder, he would've been dead.

"I guess Neil's been gobsmacked not only by Coppola but by Oliver Stone."

Jordan denied the charge, was offended by the insinuation. "I've seen the kind of imaginative license Oliver Stone takes with American history, and this is nothing like that," he told us. "Half the lines in our film are spoken dialogue that these people truly said in life. The circumstances of what happened that day in Cork have always been murky."

Said Neeson: "The whole period is like an oyster shell that we're only beginning to pry open. It's about a certain period, from 1918 to 1922, but it's also about the British oppression of Ireland for seven hundred years. To try to telescope that into a feature film is some achievement. But I strongly believe that we've retained and highlighted the spirit of the truth."

Though they protest about spirit of the truth, the moviemakers know what they did at bottom: They declared Collins a hero, de Valera a villain. Collins as a silver-screen good guy represents, at the very least, an oversimplification of the truth: He was not a one-woman man, he was not entirely cause-over-ego, and he was not above cruelty. "Collins would target spies and take them out ruthlessly," said Tynan of the *Times*. "Collins was unsentimental about such things, especially for such a young man."

Jordan, Collins acolyte, defended the Big Fella, and thereby his film. "I wouldn't draw any comparison between Collins's IRA and the current one," he said, for instance. "Collins ran a guerrilla war against an enemy, not the indiscriminate bombing of civilians."

Before letting the controversy and questions about *Collins* go, we approached one more expert, this one an Irish Australian, our old mate Tom Keneally, a man who, via *Schindler*, knows something about the cinematizing of historical fact—the responsibilities and punishments heir to. Also speaking from Dublin (everyone was in Dublin at that time, it seemed), where he was researching his history of the diaspora, Keneally said, "I don't know if it's *dangerous* to present these notions as historical fact in a film. There is a level to which people suspend the literalness of things when they go to a movie.

"But of course," he continued, "in Ireland, some people take this all very seriously. It has a fretful effect on the older folks in Ireland who haven't forgotten these things. It's caused a lot of fretfulness."

It did, in 1996, in Ireland—though not nearly so much fretfulness as that year's reignition of the Troubles, with shootings and bombings in the north marking a loud end to a six-month cease-fire. In America, the movie simply bombed. Not enough people knew who Michael Collins was, and too few cared to find out. But the fact remains: Even if de Valera set him up for the antitreaty recrimination, even if de Valera sentenced him to death, Collins's generalship during the War of Independence and his signature on the document in London signaled the birth of a state after seven centuries without one, and that birth of a state would quickly evolve into the birth of a nation.

What happened to de Valera after Collins's death?

All good things, eventually.

First, his side lost the civil war, and he spent a short time in jail. But then he reentered Irish politics and gained prominence as a statesman in the Free State that he himself felt was insufficiently large and insufficiently free. In 1926 he broke with Sinn Fein to form his own party, Fianna Fail (Warriors of Destiny), which gained a majority in the 1932 elections and would dominate the nation for much of the remainder of the century. De Valera would serve as taoiseach (prime minister) from 1937 to 1948, from 1951 to 1954 and from 1957 to 1959, then as president of Ireland, a largely ceremonial role, from 1959 to 1973. Along the way he would grant government pensions to those IRA men who had fought against the Free Staters in the civil war. But then, when those who never accepted partition simply would not put down their guns, he would outlaw the IRA via the Offences Against the State Act of 1939. He would write the 1937 constitution that loosened ties to Britain. He would rename the Free State *Eire* (see chapter 2). He would enshrine Catholicism as something of a state religion. He would lay claim to all thirty-two counties on the island, while limiting the area of jurisdiction to the twenty-six counties that were truly his, "pending the reintegration of the national territory." He would start slowly, in short, and then revert to his old, bold self.

In essence, the rise of de Valera, a former revolutionary, to his position of primacy and respectability in the Free State put a lot of other revolutionaries out of business. Not just the now-banned IRA, but nationalist organizations in the United States as well, groups that had once sponsored Parnell and de Valera's speaking engagements. "John Devoy's influence over Clan na Gael begins to wane with de Valera's dominance in Ireland," said Terry Golway, Devoy's biographer, in an interview for this book. "De Valera could clear the field of rival leaders. He viewed Irishmen everywhere as his constituency. 'Whenever I wanted to know what the Irish people wanted, I had only to examine my own heart,' he once said, and I'm sure he assumed, because of his place of birth, that he understood

Irish America as well. This view left little room for John Devoy. De-voy was followed in Clan na Gael by **Joe McGarrity,** a de Valera devotee—he even named his son after him—but McGarrity became disillusioned by de Valera's break with the IRA."

By the late 1930s, de Valera was putting constant emphasis on Ireland's independence; he didn't need clans and leagues and brotherhoods to do this for him. He was so dedicated to the cause, he was adamant that his country remain neutral during World War II—a stance that, it must be said, was supported by most other Irish.

Ireland didn't fight in World War II?

Individual Irish did, even side by side with English in Great Britain's forces. And Irish Americans did by the thousands, as we'll see in chapter 12. But Ireland did not.

In April 1938 British Prime Minister **Neville Chamberlain** gave back to de Valera the so-called treaty ports like Cobh, the former Queenstown, which had remained a British naval base under the 1921 treaty. The following September, with the outbreak of hostili-ties between Great Britain and Germany, de Valera took a hard posi-tion: As long as Northern Ireland remained British, Ireland could not and would not join any coalition of which Britain was a member. No Irish army, no ports. This position was maintained even after the United States entered the war in 1941, when Irish American politi-cians—not to mention all the proud Irish American soldiers and sailors—implored the homeland to enter the conflict.

Winston Churchill, who succeeded Chamberlain as prime minis-ter in 1940, reacted to the Irish stance with a mixture of incompre-hension and cold fury, particularly as the loss of the treaty ports had put Britain at a disadvantage in her battle with German U-boats in the Atlantic. The British, who had spoken with a benevolent attitude about Republicanism for the Free State only so recently, now mur-mured about invasion. But de Valera would not be budged, nor would he consider a return of the treaty ports.

It should be noted that Irish "neutrality" leaned heavily toward the Allies. When airmen from Allied forces crash-landed in Ireland—once involving a U.S. Air Force general who came down in 1944 with a plane scheduled for the D-Day invasion—they were driven to the northern border and handed back to their own side, while German fliers were interred in Curragh Camp for the duration. If the Allied planes were serviceable, they were refueled and sent on their way, often with holds full of eggs, butter, and milk. British Observer Corps members were allowed to station themselves on the Irish coast, and no attempt was made to interfere with the recruitment of thousands of Irishmen into Crown forces. When Belfast was bombed in 1941, de Valera sent fire engines from the Free State to help. (Dublin itself was accidentally bombed by the Germans that year, resulting in great loss of life.)

Nevertheless, stated neutrality was stated neutrality, and the issue brought Anglo-Irish and U.S.-Irish relations to their nadir in 1945 when the American-born de Valera, in a gesture he tried to explain away legalistically, signed the book of condolences at the German Embassy when Hitler killed himself. Was he being insolent? Plain stupid? Churchill singled out de Valera for abuse in his VE-Day speech: He just could not comprehend the degree of Irish bitterness.

Most historians feel de Valera missed a crucial point: Hitler was evil, at least as evil as Cromwell. It's not saying animosities have to be set aside, it's that some things are bigger than animosities, and some things have to be repelled. For de Valera not to see, by 1945, that what Hitler had done and was doing to powerless victims (Poles, Slavs, especially Jews) paralleled what had been done to the Irish by the British was willful blindness. In the United States, de Valera's expression of sympathy for Hitler hurt him far more than any duplicity he might have exhibited toward Michael Collins.

Of course, there are other views. Marxist historian Thomas Alfred Jackson, who had been a protégé of James Connolly, considered England's refusal to undo the partition as the root cause of Ireland's stubborn but reasonable neutrality. He also saw, and said he could understand, why Irish public opinion was with de Valera. This was another imperialist war, felt the Irish, and none of their business.

Most of the world felt otherwise, and Irish progress in the twentieth century was set back by its recalcitrance.

Were there Hitler sympathizers in Ireland?

The term *sympathizer* is too strong, but in 1933 a fascist-style "Blue Shirts" movement was led by **Eoin O'Duffy,** a former police commissioner who had been fired by de Valera. The Blue Shirts were clearly influenced by Mussolini and his idea of the corporate state; their avowed aim was "to promote and maintain social order." O'Duffy always denied having dictatorial ambitions, and he would have made an unlikely Fuhrer or Duce, but de Valera was sufficiently alarmed by the posturing of the Blue Shirts to set up the so-called Broy Harriers, named after their first leader, which was a special police auxiliary force made up of ex-IRA men. Ultimately, the Blue Shirts movement amounted to little, the group's most significant achievement being the sending of a division to help General Franco in his war against the Spanish Republic.

What happened to de Valera after the war?

If he was in any way a villain in the fall and death of Collins, then it seems sweet justice that Ireland's final tie with Britain was not severed until after de Valera had been voted out of office for the first time. In 1948 he lost at the polls; in 1949 the Free State's dominion status was rescinded, and the Republic was born. No more pledging of allegiance to the Crown.

In his later and largely ceremonial role as president of Ireland, de Valera would, in 1963, welcome John F. Kennedy, the president of the United States, back to the land of his ancestors. He would be recognized as the longest-living statesman of the twentieth century. He would be revered by those who backed him and wondered at by those who didn't. He would come to personify the independent Ireland as much as he always did the independent Irishman. He died in 1975.

In a book such as this which celebrates or commemorates so many Irish Americans, de Valera stands out as a most remarkable American Irishman.

What happened to the nationalist movement after the establishment of first the Free State and then the Republic?

It never completely went away because many felt, as did de Valera, that the Free State simply was not a whole nation. However, de Valera's outlawing of the IRA certainly had an effect. In the words of Irish American Constantine FitzGibbon in his book *The Irish in Ireland*, de Valera was "consistently and even brutally hostile to the 'new IRA' who were ready to use force in order to reunite all Ireland," and so the militants were driven far, far underground. Then, during World War II, the IRA received a subtle signal that it might be okay to start marching again, and the group did. When there was an upsurge in Irish nationalism in the 1960s and 1970s, there was a corresponding uptick in trouble—or the Troubles.

The IRA had been outlawed in the Free State in 1939, but when the organization set off bombs in Great Britain in the 1940s, the Free State government remained mum. That seemed like encouragement, and so the IRA got back in business. In 1954 the IRA launched attacks in Armagh. From 1956 to 1962 the IRA staged regular border attacks.

Nineteen sixty-nine is usually viewed as the year "the most recent Troubles" began. That year the People's Democracy March from Belfast to Derry was followed by a series of explosions. That year, as well, Irish American supporters got back in the game.

Michael Flannery, a veteran of the Irish civil war, had emigrated from County Tipperary in the 1920s and had served for decades in various Irish organizations in New York, including Clan na Gael. In 1969 he was a founder of Irish Northern Aid (NORAID), which quickly became the highest profile American organization supporting the Republican movement in Northern Ireland. Flannery had been born on a farm in North Tipperary in 1902, had joined the Irish Volunteers at age fourteen in time to fight in the Easter Rebellion, had joined the IRA and had fought against the Treaty during the civil war, had been imprisoned for two years, and had gone on a thirty-nine-day hunger strike to protest brutal prison conditions. In short, he was the real deal. His forty-one years in the actuarial department of Metropolitan Life Insurance did nothing to gloss his image; he was brought up on gun-smuggling charges as late as 1982. The next year, when the Saint Patrick's Day parade committee selected Flannery as grand marshal, Governor **Hugh Carey** and Senator **Daniel Patrick Moynihan,** both Irish Americans, refused to march, and **Terence Cardinal Cooke** would not receive this man of violence on the steps of Saint Patrick's Cathedral.

The point is this: After 1969, men of violence like Flannery returned to the fray in New York and Boston as well as in Belfast and Derry. The incidents piled up:

In 1970 the Dublin Arms Trial led to splits in Sinn Fein and the IRA, with provisional factions the result. In 1971 **Ian Paisley**'s Democratic Unionist Party was founded in the north; the first British soldier was killed by the IRA in Belfast. In 1972, after yet another Bloody Sunday—this one in Derry, in January—direct rule was imposed in the North. In 1974 a bombing in Dublin claimed several lives. The Guildford and Birmingham bombings followed in November and December. In 1976 the British ambassador was killed in Dublin. When the IRA bombed a County Down restaurant in 1978, twelve were killed. In 1979 **Earl Mountbatten**, the war hero—the hero from a war that Ireland had refused to fight, a point not lost on the British—was killed in County Sligo. Eighteen soldiers were killed in County Down. In 1981 **Bobby Sands** and other IRA hunger strikers died in H-block, prompting international sympathy if not outrage. In 1987 eleven were killed before an Enniskillen service on Remembrance Sunday. In the 1990s the toll since 1969 climbed to over 3,000, then to over 3,100, then to over 3,200.

In 1994 the IRA and Loyalist paramilitary groups announced a cease-fire. In June of 1996 the IRA killed a policeman in the Irish Republic, then set off a bomb in Manchester, England, that injured more than two hundred people. In 1997 the group announced another cease-fire.

In 1998, history was made. Even as unexploded pipe bombs were being found in London, even as Orange Order parades were being banned in Northern Ireland, even as ten Catholic churches were being torched in the North (and four Protestant churches were being set afire in retribution), even as three young Catholic boys nicknamed Tavish, Marky, and Ace were being killed in Ballymoney by a sectarian arson attack on their mother's home—even as all this terrible business-as-usual was going down in and around Ireland—a peace accord was signed, referendums were held that showed overwhelming support for the plan, and a Northern Ireland Assembly of 108 lawmakers was established, elected, and seated. On April 10, after twenty-six months of negotiations in Belfast, the treaty hammered out by mediator **George Mitchell**, former U.S. Senator from Maine, was signed by officials from the North and the Republic. Then, on May 22, the settlement was endorsed by voters in both parts of the island. As part of the agreement, the Assembly was elected on June 25 and convened the next week, marking restoration of local government in Northern Ireland, something lacking since Britain imposed direct rule in 1972 and began to pull all strings from London. In electing their new parliamentarians, many voters in the North—Catholic and Protestant both—turned away from old loyalties to support new ideas. Whether the center can hold is yet uncertain; the Rev. Ian Paisley, whose Democratic Unionist Party won twenty seats in the Assembly elections, has pledged to block anything the governing body tries to accomplish that might draw the North closer to the Republic. But few would argue that the accord, the vote and the Assembly have given Ireland its best chance at peace in many a year.

Before we leave the topic we thought we'd introduce you to two players who might still be around by the time you read this book. If they're not, you should know of them anyway, for they've already made contributions worth noting—no matter what history and fate conspire to decide for Ireland.

Who is John Hume?

John Hume is one of the founders of what might be called modern Ulster.

In 1968 he was a French teacher in Londonderry who made a little political hay by leading, along with **Ivan Cooper,** a march to protest discrimination against the city's three-fifths majority Catholics by the Protestants who controlled Derry's government. Inequities in housing and employment were being maintained by statutes that were overseen by the two fifths of the city's population that, by virtue of some nifty gerrymandering, was allowed to elect 60 percent of Derry's board of governors. The Royal Ulster Constabulary hosed Hume down with purple dye during that demonstration, then arrested him. Thereby and instantaneously was he granted status and notoriety—and some measure of influence.

As things quickly got worse in Derry, Hume's public persona grew. In 1972 thirteen protesters were shot dead in the city by British paratroopers; Hume's was the loudest outcry against the massacre. Loudest, yes, but also the most measured, which was a crucial difference. Slowly, this former schoolteacher became a singularly prominent Catholic advocate for peace. He spoke out against the Irish Republican Army and its tactics, and sought to assure the United States—through visits with Presidents Carter, Reagan, Bush, and Clinton—that the Catholics of the north were antiterrorist. He all but actively courted the disapproval of both Protestant Unionists and Catholic supporters of the IRA—not least among these, **Gerry Adams.**

So it was a surprise move when, in 1993, he entered into secret talks with Adams to try and revive the dormant—some said, dead—peace campaign. Their hushed efforts, conducted at Hume's small house in Derry, led to the on-again, off-again IRA cease-fire and, perhaps more important, to the very public negotiations of June

1996. "These have been twenty-five very difficult years," Hume told the *New York Times* that May, on the eve of the peace talks. "There have been many tragic moments. I think we have the best opportunity now in our history to achieve peace."

Hume was nominated for the 1995 Nobel Prize for Peace, but did not win. He told the *Times*: "The only prize I want is peace for my people." In the summer of 1998, Hume was chosen first deputy minister of the Northern Ireland Assembly.

Who is Gerry Adams?

He's the fellow the *Times* no longer bothers to couch as *perhaps* linked to the IRA, but rather introduces, in articles datelined Dublin, as "Gerry Adams, the head of the political wing of the Irish Republican Army. . . ." Adams is, in fact, the president of Sinn Fein, and has been since the 1970s when he was one of a group of young turks who overthrew the party's old guard, claiming it was too soft with Britain and demanding an end to the cease-fire then in place. Adams is a complicated man in a tricky situation. He has had to be tough enough to keep IRA militants behind him, but conciliatory enough to keep his seat at the peace talks and stay in good with administrations in Washington, Dublin, and London. A Catholic, he was born in West Belfast to a Republican father who was shot and then imprisoned by the Royal Ulster Constabulary in the 1940s. In October of 1964, sixteen-year-old Gerry was walking home from school when he saw Reverend Ian Paisley, in his early years as a public advocate of union, start a riot by tearing down an Irish tricolor. Fifty were hurt in the melee, and Gerry Adams was an activist before he reached home.

People like Paisley consider Adams a terrorist because of his early years in the movement (British Intelligence reports have him rising as high as battalion commander in the IRA). Adams was jailed twice—in 1971 and 1973—before he came in from the streets and became a tie-and-blazer politician. Even as he tries to find a solution, he does not deny that he and people like him have been part of the problem. "I think we all have been in situations where we have directly contributed," he told the *New York Times* in 1996. "But in terms of the contributions which we make to the conflict, I do think we have to accept and we ought to express regret for the fact that each of us has hurt and each of us has been hurt." The reporter pressed Adams as to how he, a Catholic, could resolve being a revolutionary with the commandment against killing. "It's been written that the Catholic who is not a revolutionary is living in mortal sin," Adams replied with a laugh. "I've engaged in public debates with the bishops on a whole range of issues. There's always an uneasy relationship. Parnell once wrote: Our religion we can take from Rome, but our politics we get at home."

With those politics, Adams enhanced Sinn Fein's public standing in the Republic somewhat even as he has kept the IRA in line—again, somewhat. And he worked his way to the table for the peace talks, no small feat. But he's even now playing a very dangerous political game. People in the North certainly would like to kill him; he sleeps in a different safe house every few nights, and in 1997 a relative of his was gunned down outside a bar after there was renewed IRA activity in the North. Moreover, Adams's signature on the accord may come to seem middling to his more militant friends, and they will want to kill him, too. There is graffiti in Ireland that seeks to give Adams his marching orders as the quest for lasting peace continues: GERRY, REMEMBER MICHAEL COLLINS.

TEN

The Lit'ry Life
(and Other Artsy Pursuits)

Whence the Irish literary tradition?

What is a seanchai?

What is the Irish American literary tradition?

Who is Leon Uris?

Who is Frank McCourt?

What about other writers of nonfiction?

*Among the writers, why haven't you
mentioned Eugene O'Neill?*

*Did Irish writers in Ireland take note of the
Irish experience in America?*

170

Who were the famous players in O'Neill's plays?

*Were there famous Irish American
actors before Helen Hayes?*

*Who were the dramatic actors in
Hollywood?*

*Have Irish Americans made similar
contributions in music?*

Who is Mick Maloney?

*What other Irish American contributions
to the arts have there been?*

*Is there a conclusion to be drawn about
all these Irish American artists?*

Whence the Irish literary tradition?

If we're talking about the Irish literary tradition—the language Irish—then we're referencing one of the oldest vernacular literatures in Europe, with written records from the sixth and seventh centuries. When we were discussing Gaelic languages and the Celtic tongue back in chapters 2 and 3, we briefly discussed the ancient ogam writings developed in the fourth century, and the oral traditions whereby heroic tales were handed down by the pre-Christian Celts. Certain Cuchulain exploits were sung before they were written. Folklore is as rich in the Irish tradition as it is in any other ethnicity's. Mythical tales, adaptations of international legends, and humorous narratives are all part of the Irish folk tradition, and the greatest of Irish writers—Yeats, for instance—did not hesitate to dabble in the form: It was never seen as pedestrian, always as elevating and even artistic.

Well before there was Irish literature, there was an Irish literary state of mind and the basis for an Irish tradition of storytelling. It's safe to say that Irish literary expression is at least as old as the Christian era.

Among the early authors, **Adamnan,** the abbot of Iona in the seventh century, stands out, not only as a writer but as a visionary: In his *Life of Colum Cille* he made an appeal for peace during Easter regardless of ecumenical differences of opinion. That was a monk who saw Ireland whole; he is today regarded as a saint in the Irish Church.

The arrival of the Christians brought Latin thought to the mix. The Normans added culture. And then, near the end of the seventeenth century, the English language took over, becoming the predominant means of expression even for Irish writers in Ireland. As with uprisings generally in Ireland, there have been several linguistic ones—minirenaissances of Gaelic speech and writing, including the one now ongoing. But in a painful irony, it must be said that the most famous Irish writers did their most famous writing in English, the enemy language.

As with most things Irish, there are two ways to look at this because you can reasonably argue: They did it better than the other fellow. Okay, spot them Shakespeare and Milton. But since then, wouldn't they love to claim Swift, Goldsmith, Burke, Edgeworth, Thomas Moore, Wilde, Shaw, Yeats, Joyce, Synge, O'Casey, Beckett, George Moore, Behan, O'Flaherty, O'Faolain, O'Conner, Flann O'Brien, Joyce Cary, and, in our time, Brian Friel, Edna O'Brien, William Trevor, Benedict Kiely, Seamus Heaney, and right on up to Roddy Doyle? And then there are the scribes who play with journalism—Conor Cruise O'Brien comes to mind—who can scribble with anyone.

We would like nothing better than to digress on each of the aforementioned. We'd like just as well to talk about Irish writers from around the world, like our special friend, the Aussie Thomas Keneally—whose Irish *American* novel, *Confederates*, is considered by the writer Peter Quinn "the best book on the Civil War ever written" (which opinion, as we'll soon see, discounts another big and pretty famous Civil War novel with an Irish perspective).

We'd like, further, to insist that everyone must read Jonathan Swift's *Gulliver's Travels*, Wilde's prose and plays, Yeats's poetry and prose, Joyce's *Portrait*, *Ulysses*, and stories ("The Dead" every Christmas), Beckett's *Watt* and plays, the stories of the O'-boys named above, the stories of Trevor, the poetry of Nobel Prize winner

Heaney, Friel's *Dancing at Lughnasa*. We'd like to tell you of the Abbey Theatre and the little graveyard under Ben Bulben where Yeats rests as horsemen pass by. We'd like to do all that.

But our efforts here are supposed to regard Irish America, and so, having done brief spadework that might lead to some small understanding of Irish and Irish American writers and artists—and having said that, if you want a concise education on any of the above, a good source is *The Oxford Companion to Irish Literature* edited by Robert Welch, professor of English at the University of Ulster at Coleraine (Clarendon Press, Oxford, 1996)—we will now turn our attention. Let it suffice: No country as small as Ireland has as great a literary tradition. The island has been a garden of the *seanchai*.

What is a seanchai?

A *seanchai*—or *seanachie*, or *shanachie*—is a storyteller. He's a conduit of "old lore" (*seanchas*) or ancient knowledge (as the *Oxford Companion* tells us). The *seanchai* was, classically, a player in the oral traditions, but in recent centuries the term has come to mean a teller of tales short and long, serious and whimsical, painful or joyous, true or false, folkish or etymological, said or written, rhymed or not: a talented jack-of-all-trades wordsmith, with a natural twinkle in his eye. He's the one at the campfire reciting ballad poetry, telling of Dan McGrew. He's also **William Trevor,** building one of the greatest volumes of finely crafted stories the twentieth century has seen.

What is the Irish American literary tradition?

It is a tormented beast, with some of the most famous Irish American writers shunning or ridiculing their heritage, while others try to understand it and even celebrate it. It's also a relatively late-blooming thing among Irish Catholic writers, and this might be part of the reason some of the most famous (F. Scott Fitzgerald, John O'Hara) shunned their religion and, sometimes, their heritage. Andrew Greeley had a theory; "If [they] left the community, it was in part because there was no room for them in the Irish Catholicism of their young adulthoods. The ancient Celtic art of telling tales and singing songs was negatively reinforced until very recently in the Irish Catholic community. No parents wanted to raise their sons to be novelists and their daughters to be poets, and everyone was suspicious of the parish priest who wrote books." Priests like Father Greeley, we might add.

In the nineteenth century, there were writers in the United States of Irish extraction who seemed wholly un-Irish. Two literary and academic giants of turn-of-the-century America were the James brothers, philosopher William and novelist Henry, who were grandsons of an Ulster Irish immigrant. Their father, Henry Sr., son of the Ulsterman, was a free spirit, something of an eccentric, actually, and had seen to it that his boys were schooled not only in New York, Boston, and Newport but in Paris, Lyons, Geneva, and Boulogne. The brothers did most of their growing up in Europe, and Henry settled on the Continent for good in 1876 ("At last I live!"). **Henry James** lamented that the United States, his native land, lacked the "tone of time" that he so loved about England, and that he captured in his many masterworks: *Portrait of a Lady*, *The Bostonians*, *The Europeans*, *The Golden Bowl*. The ever-philosophical **William James** was more in tune with his Irishness—at least he wasn't shy about it—and sister Alice was more in tune yet, but Henry James reeks of London, though Irish blood ran in his veins. Irish Americans can claim him if they want, and it is that way with several other Irish American writers. The great mid-nineteenth-century poet and storyteller **Edgar Allan Poe** was descended from Ulster Irish as well, but the terrain he described in his writing is no more Ireland than it is America, unless you claim that it extends from the supernatural side of Celtic tale-telling (which, of course, you can do). When the mid-twentieth-century novelist **Thomas Wolfe,** to name a third descendant of northern Irish, looked homeward, it was to America's South, and to a family of southerners for whom Irishness didn't play much of a role, unless in the way their attitudes had been formed in great part by Scotch-Irish traditions (which, of course, they had been).

Henry James—along with **Mark Twain, William Dean Howells, Stephen Crane** (the "genius boy" whose 1893 novel *Maggie: A Girl of the Streets* is a vivid portrait of a young Irishwoman in New York's slums; "On the Bowery," Crane said, "I got my artistic education"), **Theodore Dreiser,** and **Edith Wharton**—is remembered among the most famous American novelists of the late nineteenth century. Hardly remembered at all is **Finley Peter Dunne.** While James was evoking things English, Dunne was capturing the heart and soul of Irish America at the turn of the century. As the poet Eamonn Wall (of Creighton University, Nebraska) wrote in his essay "The Irish

Voice in American Fiction": "Dunne celebrates the gifts of the Irish—intelligence, range of interest, loyalty to Ireland and to the United States and to families in both countries, and their quite inimitable gift to turn the raw material of language into sparkling conversation." Indeed, in his "Dooley" books—*Mr. Dooley in Peace and War* (1898), *Mr. Dooley in the Hearts of His Countrymen* (1899), and others, Dunne created, within the confines of Martin J. Dooley's saloon in "Archey" Road (actually, Archer), a place where the Irish mind-set and patois were precisely, lovingly observed. There were laughs in the Dooley books, and wisdom as well; the great critic Howells, among others, recognized this at the time. The literary historian Van Wyck Brooks wrote in *The Confident Years: 1885–1915* that Dunne was among those responsible when "the 'American language' took shape in the words of writers of various races who concurred in their use of an English that was no longer England's." From *Observation by Mr. Dooley* (1901): "I know histhry isn't thrue, Hinnissy, because it ain't like what I see ivry day in Halsted Street. If any man comes along with a histhry iv Greece or Rome that's show me th' people fightin', gettin' drunk, makin' love, gettin' married, win' th' grocery man an' bein' without hard-coal, I'll believe they was a Greece or Rome, but not befure. Historyans is like doctors. They are always lookin' f'r symptoms. Those iv them that writes about their own times examines th' tongue an' feels th' pulse an' makes a wrong diagnosis. Th' other kind iv histhry is a post-mortem examination. It tells you what a counthry died iv. But I'd like to know what it lived iv." Dunne, a journalist not a historian, wrote about his own times and place—the small houses holding large, turn-of-the-century Chicago Irish families—and today those times are gone, and so is general memory of Dunne.

Henry James would never have set foot in Dooley's saloon—in fact, upon visiting Chicago in this era, he drank in the tenements and warehouses and he declared, "What monstrous ugliness!"—and that would have been fine with Dunne. "Dilute Englishmen, the dudes around New York," Dooley called such as James, "enfeebled literary men, around Cambridge and New Haven." Dunne was joined in his contempt of highfalutin literary ways back East by fellow Chicago reporter and novelist **George Ade,** whose marvelous and funny books contain no "long Boston words" or any "first-class language." William Dean Howells greatly admired Ade's writing, as did Mark Twain. But Howells and Twain were brave exceptions, as

Brooks observed: "In the East the ancient bond with the Anglo-Saxon mother-country had scarcely been diminished as yet in literary circles." Brooks called it "Eastern Anglomania."

Do not doubt that Mr. Dooley's creator shared each and every one of his barkeep's sentiments. "I dislike and distrust the English government and the classes that control it because I am of Irish blood, because I have suffered in my own family from their cruelty, and especially because I believe they are as much the enemies of this country today as they were one hundred years ago, forty years ago or ten years ago," Dunne wrote in a letter to **Theodore Roosevelt** in 1904. As the letter implies, Dunne was political. His Mr. Dooley went on a campaign against the imperialism of Roosevelt and Mahan at the time of the Spanish-American War, and Dunne was read aloud at cabinet meetings in Washington much as Artemus Ward had been cited by Lincoln during the Civil War. "Big business is much like murder," said Mr. Dooley at one juncture, and at another: "The Supreme Court follows the election returns." Dooley was vox populi; Dunne was always with the little man.

Why do we go on at such length about Finley P. Dunne? Because he, with James, sets up nicely the Irish American literary problem. Whether descendant from the north or south of the island, are we proud of who we are, or are we ashamed? *Is my heritage lower-class, and if I use my heritage in my writing, then is my writing second-rate?*

The most famous of all Irish American writers, **F. Scott Fitzgerald,** is, like James, in no way famous as an *Irish American* writer. We would argue that this is to misread him. Yes, he went to Princeton; yes, he was ashamed of his mother and others of his own people; yes, he bolted the Church early; yes, after having Amory Blaine as protagonist of his first novel (*This Side of Paradise,* 1920) he stuck with Protestant Americans as heroes and villains until the Bradys took center stage in his final novel (*The Last Tycoon,* 1941). But what is he saying about all the WASP revelers of the Jazz Age, all these flamboyant American royals? He's clearly not applauding the excesses of the time. Aspirants to the glittery set are shunned or disillusioned. His is an appraising eye, viewing from the verandah—and it's a damning, Irish Catholic view.

In his journal, Fitzgerald once wrote of growing up in Saint Paul, Minnesota: "At the top came those whose grandparents had brought something with them from the East, a vestige of money and culture; then came the families of the big self-made merchants, the 'old settlers' of the sixties and seventies, American-English-Scotch, or German or Irish, looking down somewhat in the order named—upon the Irish less from religious difference . . . than from their taint of political corruption in the East."

This is a point to be emphasized about the larger Irish American (not exclusively literary) experience in the early twentieth century: The Irish had been in the United States long enough and in such numbers to have reason for not only pride (Thomas Meagher, say, or John Boyle O'Reilly) but also shame. Irish Americans had misbehaved (in the neighborhood saloon, in Teapot Dome, and in Tammany Hall). A bright young man like Fitzgerald might not want to call himself Irish American, for reasons wholly other—nowhere near so Anglo-centric or aristocratic—than those of earlier eastern belletrists. In 1933 Fitzgerald wrote a letter to another Irish American writer who was having large problems being an Irish American writer, John O'Hara: "I am half black Irish and half old American stock with the usual exaggerated ancestral pretensions. The black Irish half of the family had the money and looked down upon the Maryland side of the family who had, and really had, that series of reticences and obligations that go under the poor old shattered word 'breeding.' . . . So being born in that atmosphere of crack, wise crack and countercrack I developed a two cylinder inferiority complex. So if I were elected King of Scotland tomorrow after graduating from Eton, Magdelene[,] the Guards, with an embryonic history which tied me to the Platagonets [*sic*], I would still be a *parvenue*. I spent my youth in alternately crawling in front of the kitchen maids and insulting the great." As did so many Irish Americans in this century. The race, battered for centuries at home, had now been battered for a bit in its new land, called low-class and no-class. And yet this race had joined the team. The race didn't know whether to laugh or cry.

And it still didn't know whether to fully invest in the team—call itself "American"— or keep the word *Irish* as a modifier. Consider **John O'Hara:** If Fitzgerald had a two-cylinder inferiority complex, then the author of *Appointment in Samarra* (1934) and *Butterfield 8* (1935) was running full throttle on a V-6. "O'Hara reveals a mixture of ambivalence and hostility to his ethnic background," wrote Eamonn Wall, putting it mildly. "As many commentators have pointed out, O'Hara preferred to caricature Irish Americans rather than confront his own past." Certainly Pal Joey is not a character Irish

Americans would take to their hearts. But other critics have said that, as with a more subtle reading of Fitzgerald, O'Hara is commenting on the Irish American condition as life presented it to him. Born in Pottsville, Pennsylvania, in 1905, O'Hara dreamed of blending in, dreamed of going to Yale, dreamed of filling out the Fitzgerald résumé. But his father, a doctor, died young, and the dreams were dashed. Is Pal Joey an expression of his anger and frustration? Is O'Hara the Irishman-as-Eternal-Outsider, perhaps the Irishman-as-Eternal-Victim? The Irish American writer William V. Shannon, who continually criticized O'Hara for spending too much time with the Protestant circles that bedeviled him, also wrote: "One hears speaking through his work the inarticulate, half-strangled, half-conscious rage and resentment of every Irish man and Irish woman who has ever been turned down for a job in an old-line Protestant law firm, ever snubbed for the 'sin' of having gone to the wrong college, ever left out of a fashionable party, ever patronized for wearing slightly wrong clothes." And the novelist Peter Quinn, speaking during an interview in New York, feels that, although both Fitzgerald and O'Hara forwent their Irish Catholicism, the religion absolutely informed their writing: "It's interesting to me that the two keenest observers of the twenties and thirties were outsiders—their Irish Catholicism put them on the outside, looking in—whether that's the way they wanted it or not." Quinn feels that the authors mightn't have even realized what was happening: "I've always felt Jay Gatsby was an Irish character."

It has been speculated, regarding Fitzgerald, O'Hara, and many other Irish American writers, that they feared too small an audience for a narrower, strictly Irish view. We'll mention quickly that the Irish are the greatest book-buying people on Earth, that Dunne was immensely successful in his time, that Eugene O'Neill sold a few tickets, and that William Kennedy not to mention Frank McCourt have peddled their pages in the current day. Even contemporaneous with Fitzgerald and O'Hara was an Irish writer achieving great critical and popular success by writing from an openly Irish American view. **James T. Farrell**'s *Young Lonigan* (1932), *The Young Manhood of Studs Lonigan* (1934) and *Judgment Day* (1935) are realistic depictions of gang life in Chicago's streets. Farrell came from those streets but pulled himself up, even to attending that bastion of traditional intellectualism the University of Chicago, which at the time was all but off-limits to Irish Catholics. Upon graduating, Farrell returned whence he'd come, perhaps too much so. The critic Alfred Kazin wrote in *A Writer's America* (1988): "Farrell's social science approach to his own experience was exceptional [but his] doggedness in repeating his early life story in dozens of volumes finally sank him—his mind was simply not interesting enough to feed an interminable personal history."

As in Ireland, England, or anywhere else, the writing biz in the United States is conducted on two parallel tracks, one seen as high, the other as low, one called artistic, the other demeaned as "popular." Occasionally there comes a Fitzgerald or Hemingway—or, briefly, Farrell—who can have it both ways. The point we want to make is this: There's an awful lot of Irish Americanism in Margaret Mitchell's *Gone with the Wind*, which appeared in 1936 and knocked *Studs* a notch lower on the best-seller lists. Also, though it is seen as a grand romance today—*popular*—it was both popular (a million copies sold in its first six months, though the Depression howled) *and* acclaimed (a Pulitzer Prize) in its time.

Margaret Mitchell was, like Fitzgerald and O'Hara, an outsider: thoroughly Catholic and half-Irish (maternally) in the South. Her mother's grandfather had been with Wolfe Tone and had fled to France before landing in America around 1820. He joined a community of Irish Catholics in, of all places, Taliaferro County, Georgia. He married, and by 1854 his estate included seven daughters, three thousand acres and thirty-five slaves. One of the daughters, Anne, married John Stephens of the 9th Georgia Regiment, and it is the conjured memory of this brave Irish American woman (who really did protect the family home) and this dashing Irish American Civil War captain that gives *Gone with the Wind* much of its drama and verve. Mitchell, who died at age forty-nine after being struck by a taxi in Atlanta in 1949, always denied family connections in the novel, but it's clear her grandmother inspired Scarlett O'Hara, and Ireland inspired some of the book's grander themes. Land is the only thing that lasts on Tara, a plantation bearing the name of the place where the high kings of Ireland once presided.

Other books than *Gone with the Wind* were written earlier in this century by Irish American women. **Betty Smith**'s *A Tree Grows in Brooklyn* was an immense success when it appeared in 1943. It's a lovely telling of the Irish immigrant experience: The Nolan family of the novel lived in the Williamsburg slums of Brooklyn from 1902 until 1919, and the book belongs, primarily, to the daughter Francie. The scenes wherein the father sings Irish ballads as he waits tables in a restaurant linger years after reading. The book moves at a southern novel's pace, and, in fact, Betty Smith lived and wrote in Chapel Hill, North Carolina.

More than a million copies of *Tree* have been sold and the book is hardly a secret. Now here's a sleeper that's a true gem: **Mary Doyle Curran**'s 1949 *The Parish and the Hill* is a similarly marvelous evocation of an immigrant family in the Northeast. An Irish-born wool sorter makes his way out of County Kerry to a New England mill town and begins a slow, difficult, ultimately successful rise. It's truer than the clichés, truer even than Lonigan's gangs or O'Hara's drunks. It's what really happened for so many Famine-era and later immigrants, and the novel is wonderfully well written.

Then there was **Flannery O'Connor.**

We would like to posit: While such as Farrell, Smith, Curran, and (to come) Edwin O'Connor, William Kennedy and Alice McDermott are Irish American twentieth-century writers who tell stories, and wonderfully, with clearly Irish scenes and clearly Irish American themes, O'Connor may stand as the greatest of all Irish American writers in capturing a spiritual Irishness. This seems strange to say, for O'Connor, like Wolfe, is always regarded as a southern regionalist, and she is rarely included in synopses of Irish American writers. But the heart of O'Connor's fiction—the sudden violence, the codes of honor, especially the Catholicism—peg her as an Irish modernist, a daughter of Yeats. "I write the way I do because (not though) I am a Catholic," she wrote in a letter in 1955. "This is a fact and nothing covers it like the bald statement. However, I am a Catholic peculiarly possessed of the modern consciousness, the thing Jung describes as unhistorical, solitary and guilty. To possess this within the Church is to bear a burden, the necessary burden for the conscious Catholic. It is to feel the contemporary situation at the ultimate level. I think that the Church is the only thing that is going to make the terrible world we are coming to endurable; the only thing that makes the Church endurable is that it is somehow the body of Christ and that on this we are fed. It seems to be a fact that you suffer as much from the Church as for it but if you believe in the divinity of Christ, you have to cherish the world at the same time that you struggle to endure it. This may explain the lack of bitterness in the stories." So she was a sophisticated Irish American Catholic writer able, because of a true faith (as opposed to an instinctual one), to see life as a passionate play with redemption at its core;

she could get by the bitterness, much as Yeats did, as Joyce did, and as Frank McCourt would do. In a world under God, rough things happen: That's an Irish slant.

Mary Flannery O'Connor was born in 1925 and would die only thirty-nine years later of lupus. The maternal and paternal bloodlines in her family were strongly Irish, exclusively Roman Catholic—an exceeding rarity for a family with roots in Georgia dating back to the early 1800s. (Early on, one of O'Connor's great-great-grandfathers had settled in that same Taliaferro County Catholic commune that had welcomed Margaret Mitchell's forebears.) As a girl, Flannery was educated in Catholic schools. When her father, whom she revered, died young—also of lupus—Flannery, only sixteen, saw her faith put to the test. It deepened and took on a richness. By the time she was ready to write, after graduating from Georgia State College for Women and the writing program at the University of Iowa, hers was a complex and, especially in the South, unique voice. When her disease was diagnosed, she returned to the family farm in Milledgeville to write in peace and to raise her peacocks. Her reputation, which has grown since her death, is based on two slim novels, *Wise Blood* (1952) and *The Violent Bear It Away* (1960), and especially upon short stories such as "A Good Man Is Hard to Find," "Good Country People," "Revelation," and "The Life You Save May Be Your Own."

Her stories, like Faulkner's, sound southern. But as Michael Meyer wrote in an in-depth study of the writer in his *Bedford Introduction to Literature* (fourth edition, 1996): "O'Connor's stories are rooted in rural southern culture, but in a larger sense they are set within the psychological and spiritual landscapes of the human soul." This puts them in league with Yeats, Joyce, even Beckett (though the soul may seem unnourished there). And that's our claim for Flannery O'Connor: That she, perhaps above all American writers, was an Irish writer, in the strong tradition of trying to discern God's plan. (Or in a Celtic sense, the gods' plans.)

"It's interesting, most of the Irish American writers early in the century just weren't that influenced by the great literary traditions in Ireland," says Meyer, speaking from Storrs, Connecticut, where he is a professor of English at the state university. "They were interested in local matters, more concerned with the younger, native country. They were finding their own voices, and I don't think these people were reading Joyce and Yeats and so forth. The ones that came later—yes, sure, they had gone to that school. Donleavy, certainly, saw himself in an Irish tradition rather than Irish American. And William Kennedy sure has read his Joyce."

John Patrick Donleavy stands out as an oddity in this procession of Irish American writers. Born in Brooklyn, New York, the son of an Irish-born firefighter, he studied at Trinity College in Dublin after World War II. In Ireland, he met a fellow American, one Gainor Crist. The freewheeling Crist inspired the character Sebastian Dangerfield in Donleavy's rollicking first novel, *The Ginger Man* (1955), set in Dublin's Bohemia. The language and action were racy enough that the book had to be published first on the continent, à la *Ulysses*, which certainly pleased Donleavy since Joyce and Flann O'Brien were clear inspirations. As with other literary scandals, the hubbub over *The Ginger Man* turned its author into an overnight sensation. J. P. Donleavy, who became an Irish citizen, wrote several more novels—some set here, some set over there—essentially dining out on *The Ginger Man* for near a half-century (his 1994 autobiography is entitled *The History of the Ginger Man*; there's a saloon in New York called The Ginger Man). But to read the book today is to conclude: J.P. was no James Joyce. Much more successful than this American who tried to be Irish were the Irish Americans who wrote what they knew.

Such as **Raymond Chandler,** descended from Ulsterfolk, who made art out of the crime novel. (Noel O'Hara has written a book, not yet published, on Irish American writers, and in it he posits the notion that two Ulster Americans, Poe and Chandler, essentially invented the detective genre—and that the darkness of their stories was bred in the bones. Certainly black humor, sudden death, and horrible twists of fate—not to mention all manner of other grotesquerie—were the heart and soul of the ancient Irish sagas and folktales.)

Such as **Edwin O'Connor,** who knew Boston pols and wrote about them with celebratory panache in *The Last Hurrah* (a brazenly unveiled telling of the James Michael Curley story that became a big film with Spencer Tracy in the lead) and *The Edge of Sadness* (which won the National Book Award).

And such as **Mary McCarthy,** who incisively examined the clashes of will and heritage among smart, modern American women in *The Group*. Such as, in our time, **J. F. Powers,** who writes of that most Irish American institution, the clergy, with compassion, insight, and wit.

Such as **Andrew Greeley,** the priest from Chicago who writes about everything under the sun. We've read his borderline pot-boilers, his studies of younger people's views of religion, and his lively, highly opinionated books on Irishness (*That Most Distressful Nation* and *The Irish Americans: The Rise to Power and Money*) and, forgive us, we like 'em all. From the last mentioned, here's Greeley on the subject at hand: "To oversimplify a vast and complex literary tradition, Irish writers tend to be lyrical, mystical, grotesque, hopeful, innocent, and deeply sympathetic with nature."

Such as **Thomas Flanagan,** whose huge historical novels are all of the above and grandiose to boot. A summer spent on the beach with Flanagan's great trilogy, *The Year of the French*, *The Tenants of Time*, and *The End of the Hunt*, will afford the reader much entertainment even as it provides a detailed and accurate view of Irish history.

Such as **Peter Quinn,** whose epic of the civil war era, *Banished Children of Eve*, is every bit as informed as Flanagan's work; you can feel New York burning during the Draft Riots.

Such as **Mary Gordon,** who wonders, in *Final Payments* and other novels, whether life is better within or without the confines of Irish Americanism (her concerns and complaints sometimes seem O'Haran).

Such as **Elizabeth Cullinhan,** who in *House of Gold* and her story collection *Yellow Roses* expresses sympathy for an Irish Catholicism yet extant in the towns of Long Island, even as she exposes problems and flaws.

Such as **John Gregory Dunne,** who, actually, isn't our cup of tea, but who, in *True Confessions* and other books, has looked at the Irish as they walk through a world gone modern around them. (That's our problem: Dunne's Irish Americans seem archaic, stereotypical, not as with-it as the people they walk amongst.)

Such as **George V. Higgins,** who *is* our cup of tea, and whose Boston characters from Eddie Coyle to the attorney Jerry Kennedy are part Chandler, part Edwin O'Connor, and, in their speech (Higgins's dialogue crackles), part Finley Dunne.

Such as **Alice McDermott,** our current favorite. Beginning (for us) with *That Night* in 1987, progressing with *At Weddings and Wakes* five years later, and culminating with *Charming Billy* five years after that, McDermott has shown herself to be a post-modern magician, a daughter of Joyce who can create characters beguilingly real and plots seemingly simple but almost astonishingly compelling. Her theme is "the current of loss after loss that was adulthood"—and there are indeed many disappointments in life and love along the way—but her books are somehow buoyant. As with Flannery O'Connor, there is no time for bitterness. But neither is there time, in McDermott's writing, for sentimentality. Her stories are true, and true to their time.

And especially such as **William Kennedy.**

Now, Kennedy, like McDermott—and to certain and lesser extents, other contemporary Irish American writers—has gone to school on the great Irish writers of earlier in the century; it's interesting how modernist devices and techniques forwarded by Yeats, Joyce, and Flann O'Brien have been accepted over time and have now been adopted by descendants living abroad. **Michael Stephens** (*Brooklyn Book of the Dead*) writes about what he sees in his native land, but owes more to Irish literary traditions than American. And William Kennedy has shown himself, in his Albany cycle, to be a master of the kind of stream of consciousness and blending of interior and exterior monologue that were once Joycean experiments. Kennedy also has a great narrative sense and a wonderful tale to tell. Albany encapsulates the Irish American struggle to rise in the nineteenth and twentieth centuries, and the assorted Phelans who come and go in *Legs*, *Billy Phelan's Greatest Game*, *Ironweed* (which won the Pulitzer Prize), *Quinn's Book* and *The Flaming Corsage* are variously charming, hysterical, passionate, destitute, sad, bold, courageous, honorable, and tormented, even tortured. With the possible exception of *Quinn's Book*, each novel is as good as the last, or the next. That's a thing about Kennedy: Each book is a weave within itself, and the whole is a weave. It's rough, like the wool in an Aran sweater, and beautiful like linen. William Kennedy, for our money, is the greatest Irish American writer since Flannery O'Connor.

There are writers with Irish surnames working other veins today—**Tim O'Brien**'s novels of Vietnam are wrenching and eloquent, **Mary Higgins Clark**'s thrillers are books neither of our mothers can put down, **Tom Clancy**'s techno-thrillers are what they are (he's better-selling than Stephen King and John Grisham, by the way)—but we barely mention them, since as we saw with Henry James and Finley Dunne, some writers are concerned with the Irish American condition, while others are Irish Americans who write. As the millennium bears down, this is fine; it's proof, as if any more were needed, of advanced assimilation. But while these American writers might be talented, they are not in the tradition that started with Dunne being able, in but a few paragraphs, to make his reader *feel* what was different about Irishness.

As here (we can't resist just one more), from "The Grady Girl Rushing the Can," contained in the collection *Mr. Dooley and the Chicago Irish*:

"Mr. McKenna hopped from the car and went in to find Mr. Dooley sitting comfortably behind the tall stove which was steaming from the reservoir atop. Mr. Dooley was partaking contentedly of an aromatic mixture of a golden color, slightly flecked with Vandyke brown, in which a bit of lemon peel was floating.

" 'Is it cold, I dinnaw?' said Mr. Dooley, laying down his glass.

" 'Oh, no,' said Mr. McKenna, rubbing his ear; 'it isn't cold. I dropped in to get an umbrella. I'm afraid I'll get sunstruck of I go along without one.' "

Dooley absorbs his friend's sarcasm, "calmly chasing the lemon peel around with the spoon."

Who is Leon Uris?

Leon Uris is a popular American novelist living in New York, the author of *Exodus, Mitla Pass, Mila 18, QB VII,* and *Topaz,* among others, who fell in love with the idea of the *seanchai* and, in 1976, spun a large, romantic, and hugely successful novel called *Trinity* about Ireland from the Famine to the Rising of 1916. Uris's fictional Conor Larkin was the epitome of a strong, noble Irish revolutionary. Less successful than *Trinity* was its 1995 sequel, *Redemption,* starring Conor's wild nephew, Rory Larkin.

We'll take Thomas Flanagan.

Who is Frank McCourt?

Frank McCourt is at the center of the most remarkable story in the recent Irish cultural renaissance. In an era that has seen the pop of U2 and the Cranberries soar, the New Age mood music of Enya sell in the tens of millions worldwide, the step-dance extravaganza "Riverdance" sell out everywhere from Dublin to New York to London to Sydney, Irish films such as *My Left Foot* and *In the Name of the Father* become huge critical and box-office hits—in even such an era, it is astonishing that a school teacher from New York in his sixties, with no previous book to his name, would see his memoir about an impossibly hard-bitten childhood in Brooklyn and, especially, Limerick sell and sell and sell and sell and sell, while winning the Pulitzer Prize for biography. "I'm amazed," McCourt himself has admitted. "I thought it was a modest book, modestly written, and that it might have a modest reception."

Angela's Ashes traces the family McCourt—the drunken father, the tragic mother who gives the book its title, the younger brother (Malachy, now an actor and also a memoirist, whose *A Monk Swimming* was a 1998 best-seller), the other siblings who died in infancy and some who did not—from the time of Frank's birth in Brooklyn through tenement life, the return to Ireland, the destitution there, the boy's coming of age, and his escape to the United States at nineteen. Page after page there is tragedy, but the book doesn't read sad. Its magic lies in two things: the voice McCourt found—an observant child's voice, though the prose isn't childish—and that lack of bitterness, even as fate howls at the family McCourt.

Angela's Ashes followed another fine Irish American family tale, one that should not be left in the dust. **James Carroll**'s 1996 book, *An American Requiem: God, My Father and the War That Came Between Us*, which won the National Book Award for nonfiction, shares little in subject or style with McCourt's book. For one thing, it happens over here, not over there. But it is nonetheless exceptional. McCourt and Carroll could be heralding a golden era of the Irish American memoir (we're promised more from McCourt, anyway, who is at work on a sequel to *Angela's Ashes*). Already, the two men have joined a long and proud tradition of Irish autobiography that, just in our century, extends from Yeats through **Sean O'Casey, Brendan Behan,** and **Frank O'Connor** to William Trevor.

What about other writers of nonfiction?

As evinced in the career of the aforementioned Peter Quinn, the Irish love of words has found expression in the world of oratory. "That's it exactly," says Quinn, who was raised in the Bronx, New York, "the love of words. My father was in politics, and I knew as a kid that one of the ways you were judged was words. One of the ways you held your own was telling stories." Quinn is now the chief speechwriter for Time-Warner, and has previously written for an Irish American governor of New York, Hugh Carey, and an Italian American governor of New York, Mario Cuomo, who is thought to be one of the great postwar orators. "My heritage absolutely informs my writing. And it was no different writing for Cuomo than for Carey," says Quinn in an interview. "Cuomo's an outer-borough Catholic, and no matter what you were ethnically, part of you is Irish if you went to those schools." Quinn notes that Irish American **Peggy Noonan** wrote with great effectiveness for Irish American Ronald Reagan, "the great communicator." And he adds that this isn't simply a recent burst of Irish American masters of rhetoric: "Certainly the Tammany politicians were big orators, not to mention the Irish nationalists themselves. Even the English learned from some of these guys. Winston Churchill said his speech-making was influenced by Bourke Cochran, who was a turn-of-the-century U.S. congressman who was said to be a great orator."

Another words-and-politics game with a strong Irish American tradition is journalism. As Terry Golway wrote in *The Irish in America*: "Irish writers flocked to a trade that rewarded literacy and street-smarts." Golway pointed out that, by the 1870s, the *New York Herald* had more than two dozen Irish immigrants on staff, and the field "was not completely closed to women. One of the most fabled journalists of the late nineteenth and early twentieth centuries was Elizabeth Cochrane, better known to her successors as **Nellie Bly.** The daughter of an Irish American (and Protestant) judge in Pennsylvania, she won fame and stardom in the highly competitive world of New York journalism as a feature reporter for Joseph Pulitzer's *New York World*." It was Bly who famously went 'round the world in seventy-two days, just to have something to write about.

In the twentieth century it would be hard to find a journalist more influential than **Edward R. Murrow,** descended from northern Irish. He started as a radio reporter for CBS in 1935, and his dispatches from Britain during the German blitz of World War II made him famous. During the 1950s and early 1960s, Murrow was ubiquitous on CBS television with his *See It Now* and *Person to Person* programs. He then served as director of the United States Information Agency. A longtime chain-smoker, Murrow succumbed to lung cancer in 1965 at fifty-seven years of age.

Today the descendants of Bly and Murrow are legion: **Francis X. Clines** and **Maureen Dowd** at the *New York Times*; **Mary McGory** at the *Washington Post*; **David Nyhan,** and **Kevin Cullen** of the *Boston Globe*; **Jack McKinney** of the *Philadelphia Daily News*; **Jim Dwyer** and **Mike McAlary** at the *New York Daily News* (Dwyer won his Pulitzer Prize at *Newsday* for coverage of the situation in Northern Ireland). And there are descendants, too, of Finley Peter Dunne: journalists turned novelists who, in their fiction and nonfiction both, capture the life of Irish Americans around them. Three New Yorkers are prominent in this category: **Pete Hamill, Jimmy Breslin,** and, most recently, **Anna Quindlen.** Quindlen won a Pulitzer for her *New York Times* column—always written from a feminist perspective and sometimes from an Irish American one—before she resigned from the paper and began writing books. Her most recent novel, *Black and Blue,* was a best-seller in 1998. Jimmy Breslin, too, won a Pulitzer Prize for his columns about New York City. Breslin is a very significant figure in modern reportage. Born in 1929, he started out as a sportswriter, switched to cityside, and became an avatar of the "New Journalism" being practiced by Tom Wolfe and others. A champion of the oppressed, Breslin didn't just take on issues in his columns, he created characters. So it was natural for him to tackle the novel, and he did, beginning in the early 1960s. *The Gang That Couldn't Shoot Straight*, *Forsaking All Others*, and *World Without End, Amen* are peopled by low-life, lovable Irishmen who delight Breslin's fans while seeming cartoonish to his critics (Greeley, for one, feels they're stereotypical and ring false).

Pete Hamill, like Breslin, is a native New Yorker. Born in Brooklyn in 1935, he is a New York gadfly journalist, sometimes a columnist and sometimes the boss. He was editor of the *Daily News* until he and media mogul Mort Zuckerman, a truly odd coupling from the start, finally tired of one another in 1997. Hamill's Irishness informs his journalism (he, like Dwyer of the *Daily News* and Cullen of the *Globe*, follows the Troubles more assiduously than most Dublin reporters). It is also the heart of his novels and his eloquent reminiscences. In *The Gift* (1972) Hamill recalls his father "singing about some long-gone island and his own sweet youth." His most recent novel, *Snow in August*, was published in 1997, and in that same year he contributed a lovely essay, "The Interrupted Narrative," to Michael Coffey and Terry Golway's *The Irish in America*. "My parents' myths were not my myths," Hamill wrote, thinking about their Irishness and his Americanism. "My father remembered music hall songs and clandestine meetings of Sinn Fein. He remembered playing soccer on the fields of Belfast. My mother remembered British army patrols and their boots crunching the streets of the Short Strand. . . . I had other memories and different myths. My mythic figures were named Batman or Captain Marvel, Roy Rogers or Jackie Robinson."

Another Irish American journalist/columnist/novelist is **William F. Buckley, Jr.** Born in 1925, educated at Yale, he gained fame as a conservative thinker while still in his twenties. He is cofounder and editor of the conservative journal *The National Review*, and longtime host of the PBS show *Firing Line*. The reason we separate Buckley from Breslin, Quindlen, and Hamill is not because of his politics—though they are as different from theirs as night is from day—but because his novels are thrillers that do not attempt to say anything about Irish Americanism. More germane to the discussion at hand is Buckley's 1997 book exploring his profoundly felt Catholicism.

And before we leave the topic of great Irish American reporters of—and commentators on—the American scene, let's not forget one of the greatest. **Walt Kelly** was born in 1913, and for millions of Americans his daily newspaper feature was essential to their understanding of Washington, of the world, of life itself. Kelly's feature was, of course, *Pogo*, the comic strip set in Georgia's Okeefenokee Swamp, where the 'possum and his pals seemed the sanest creatures on Earth.

Among the writers, why haven't you mentioned Eugene O'Neill?

Well, we could say we hadn't got to playwrights yet. Or we could say we've been saving ourselves. Either would be true.

Eugene O'Neill is the titanic Irish American literary figure. He was born in 1888, the son of a touring actor who had married up in class, and his childhood was difficult, with constant moves and a constant tension between the "peasant Irish Catholicism" of his father and the more sophisticated religious ideas of his mother, Mary Ellen O'Neill. This isn't even to mention his mother's drug addiction.

O'Neill attended Catholic boarding schools, then Princeton for a year, then left to see the world. He worked as a merchant seaman and lived an alcoholic's life. He attempted suicide at least once and perhaps three times. By the time he settled down to write, he obviously had matters to write about.

His first play, *Bound East for Cardiff*, was staged by the amateur troupe the Provincetown Players in Massachusetts in 1916, and later that year on Broadway. In 1920 his first full-length play opened on Broadway, and between that year and 1943 twenty others, plus several shorter plays, followed. O'Neill won an unprecedented four Pulitzer Prizes for drama and, in 1936, became the only American dramatist to win the Nobel Prize for Literature. He died in a Boston hotel in 1953, withdrawn from the world, a player in an O'Neill tragedy.

That's the résumé.

Behind it are sound and fury, starting with James and Ella O'Neill's tremendous fights in the cottage in New London, Connecticut, as witnessed daily by their youngest son. James was a Famine immigrant from Kilkenny who often bragged that the O'Neills had been the most powerful clan in Ulster. He named his son after Eoghan O'Neill, a Celt-descended warrior born in 1590; Eoghan actually translates as Owen, but if you'd told James, he'd have raged bloody murder at you. The playwright would subsequently push this family tradition, naming his son Shane after a Celtic chieftain and his daughter Oona, which is a Gaelic name.

By the time he got to Princeton, O'Neill was well out of control; it is said he threw a beer bottle through University President Woodrow Wilson's window. His Irish Catholic sense of guilt knew no bounds, as he believed his difficult birth had led to his mother's morphine addiction. His years as a seaman could well have been his last but for yet another tragedy, this one a godsend in disguise. Contracting tuberculosis in 1912 forced him to clean up his act. That led him to Cape Cod, and to his calling.

O'Neill's work was, from the first, antithetical to Irish Catholic stage traditions in America, which involved baggy-pants vaudevillians and comically drunk micks. Not everyone understood; after sitting through his son's first Pulitzer Prize winner, *Beyond the Horizon*, James O'Neill asked, "What are you trying to do, make the audience go home and commit suicide?"

James is lucky he didn't stick around for the whole oeuvre. *Desire Under the Elms* featured a husband and wife who wanted anyone but one another, with an ineffectual son watching from stage left. *Ah, Wilderness!*, O'Neill's only comedy, might have made Dad happy for a while—until he realized that it was his son's lament for a youth he never had, a longing for a family that laughed and talked together, something as foreign to him as Timbuktu. *The Iceman Cometh* would certainly have mystified the father, as would *Hughie* and *A Moon for the Misbegotten*. O'Neill's themes were family and God, the first he so badly desired, and the second as well—though he could believe in neither. Ed Shaughnessy's 1996 biography of O'Neill, *Down the Days and Down the Nights*, talks about O'Neill's longing for faith, and his unconquerable resistance to it. Peter Quinn synopsizes: "He was a very unhappy unbeliever. He wanted to believe." He was an Irish

American who tried to soak in the lessons, religious and cultural, but who had been presented with a reality so overwhelming, it shattered him. Daily.

Long Day's Journey into Night—America's *Hamlet*, America's *Lear*—which was the undisguised story of the O'Neills (call them the Tyrones, if you choose), won him his fourth Pulitzer. Posthumously. Just as well. James wouldn't have liked it, and acclaim such as that for a play such as this might have been too much even for Eugene.

How could he so assiduously bear witness in his youth, digest, then so openly cry out loud? O'Neill wrote a letter to his son in 1945: "The critics have missed the important thing about me and my work, the fact that I am Irish." He ultimately wrote as many as seventy plays, and among the many he destroyed, never having seen them mounted, was a cycle of nine that hoped to tell the tale of the Irish in America. The title of the cycle was *A Tale of Possessors Self-Dispossessed*.

Did Irish writers in Ireland take note of the Irish experience in America?

Certainly. In one instance, a playwright who was as great as O'Neill wrote of the Famine, and of the manner in which some Irish hoped to use the opportunity provided by the United States to have vengeance on England. The passage became so famous it is the reason most Irish prefer the terms *The Hunger* or *The Starvation*, as they imply British complicity. This is from **George Bernard Shaw**'s *Man and Superman*:

> MALONE: Me father died of starvation in Ireland in the black 47. Maybe youve heard of it.
> VIOLET: The Famine?
> MALONE [with smouldering passion]: No, the starvation. When a country is full o food, and exporting it, there can be no famine. Me father was starved dead; and I was starved out to America in me mother's arms. English rule drove me and mine out of Ireland. Well, you can keep Ireland. Me and me like are coming back to buy England; and we'll buy the best of it.

But back to O'Neill: Who were the famous players in O'Neill's plays?

In our time, **Jason Robards,** a smidgen Irish, is the one most closely associated with the work. It's worth noting that those who perform O'Neill admirably share aspects of the playwright's past. "I came from a family that closely paralleled O'Neill's," Robards wrote in *The Irish in America*. "My father had given up his greatest talent for the Hollywood scene, and O'Neill's spent his energy playing a crass Count of Monte Cristo all over the country. His mother was vacant, there and not there, as was mine, and I understood that." Robards has starred in six O'Neill plays in early and later years; he played Jamie in the original cast of *Long Day's Journey* in 1956 (which included Florence Eldridge as the mother and Fredric March as the father), then revisited the play twice more in his career, each time as the father.

Significantly, the first U.S. performance of that masterpiece was at the Helen Hayes Theater—significantly, for Hayes, born in 1900 in Washington, D.C., was the O'Neill of actors. Her grandparents had been Famine immigrants—the grandfather was a romantic drunk, who hoped to translate Shakespeare's works into Irish, the grandmother helpless to do anything about her husband. Hayes's mother, a classic stage mother, was a refugee from this unhappiness, hungry for success in America. She pushed her pretty daughter toward acting, which was fine with Helen, who was ambitious from the start. Hayes took her mother's maiden name professionally, and dove in.

Helen Hayes, eventually the First Lady of the American Theater, first did O'Neill on radio when still in her teens. She was cast as the lead in *The Straw*, which the playwright considered "far and away the best and truest thing I have done." The year was 1920, and O'Neill, with casual success behind him, was not pleased that this . . . *nobody* . . . had the lead. After he heard her reading, though, he telegrammed: "It is seldom that a playwright has the privilege of hearing his character realized exactly as he had imagined it. Tonight, you have given me that." Helen Hayes played a lot of O'Neill before her final role in one of his plays: as Mary Tyrone, his mother and some of hers, in *Long Day's Journey*. She was magnificent.

"To play O'Neill," wrote Robards, "is to plumb the depths of the Irish tragedy and to share its poetry as well. To play O'Neill is to be an honorary Irishman." Or, in Hayes's case, an honest one.

Were there famous Irish American actors before Helen Hayes?

Oh yes, including a precious few you'd be proud of.

The earliest Irish American performing tradition was vaudevillian. "Stage Irishmen" were clowns and drunks. In music halls across the land, stumblebums with thick Irish accents were in great demand. Worse, there was a tradition of Irish comics parodying blacks that had started with the minstrel shows of Irish Americans **Daniel Emmett** and **Thomas Rice.** Rice's dance was called "Jump Jim Crow." (In a later era, the clown tradition would be cleaned up by **Emmett Kelly,** named after the Irish patriot Robert Emmet. In the twentieth century, Kelly had a decades-long run as the world's most famous clown with the Ringling Bros. and Barnum & Bailey Circus.)

Not nearly so offensive in retrospect as the minstrelsy, though traveling the same circuits at the time, were the family routines: the **Three Keatons** (which included the great comic genius Buster, whose films are still considered among the finest and funniest made by an American) and the **Four Cohans** (whose little one was George M.). "Vulgar, cheap, ill-mannered, flashily dressed, insolent Smart Aleck" was the *New York Times*'s appraisal of boy George. But the audience came to love Cohan's patriotic music ("Yankee Doodle Dandy," "Grand Old Flag"), his dancing, his comedy. "There's a style of Irish comedy that goes all the way back," says Peter Quinn. "Cohan and Keaton up through Gracie Allen—she started as a step dancer in vaudeville—and Fred Allen on the radio—his real name was Frank Sullivan—up through Jackie Gleason and even Denis Leary today. It's shared with Jewish and black comedians, and it sort of looks at authority and says, 'screw you.' The ultimate example: the Keystone Kops. Mack Sennett was Irish."

Born Michael Sinnott in 1880, **Mack Sennett** went on to become the legendary director behind hundreds of Kops comedies. He directed more than a thousand films, including ones made by Keaton, **Charlie Chaplin,** and **W. C. Fields.** (A brief note regarding Chaplin, before passing: He married Eugene O'Neill's daughter, Oona, at a young age—hers—and under scandalous circumstances—both of theirs. Oona's father disowned her at that point. Not exactly Irish American history, but something we felt you needed to know.) Sennett, like **Fred Allen,** was a bridge-building Irish American. These comedians led Irish-heritage performers from nineteenth-century vaudeville—a world they both knew—toward the twentieth century of movies and, in Allen's case, radio. In the pre–World War II years Allen was, as Terry Golway wrote, "the Irish rebel of radio—without seeming to be anything more than a generic American, or a generic Bostonian in any case. For fifteen years, he carried on a conversation with millions of listeners who came to regard him as the Irish Will Rogers, sharing Rogers's folkish dissent but adding a sharper, more pointed twist. He was topical, political, tastefully disdainful of the leaders of the day." He was, in short, an electrified Finley P. Dunne.

Before we leave the subject of Irish American comedy, we cite one man who humored the younger folk. **Walt Disney** was descended from County Carlow immigrants; his Protestant Irish ancestors were on the island as long ago as the sixteenth century. In America, he built an empire on the back of a mouse. In 1930 he became the first Irish American to take home an Oscar, when he won for best short subject.

Who were the dramatic actors in Hollywood?

There have been many Irish Americans among the greats, and many influential Irish American directors as well. Taken in the order of their birth, they sketch a history of Tinseltown:

- **Walter Brennan** (1894–1974), one of the finest character actors ever, won three Academy Awards as Best Supporting Actor. Remembered by baby boomers as TV's Grandpa McCoy, he had earlier distinguished himself as a scene-stealing sidekick. In 1970 he was inducted into the Cowboy Hall of Fame for the work he had done in westerns, directed by the likes of . . .
- **John Ford** (1894–1973), who was born Sean Aloysius O'Feeney to County Galway immigrants in Portland, Maine. He got booted out of the University of Maine for punching a fellow student and headed west in 1914. He won his first of four feature-film Oscars for an Irish film, *The Informer*, based on the Liam O'Flaherty novel. He made a star out of John Wayne with the 1939 classic *Stagecoach*, the first of fifteen collaborations between the two men. (Ford used to run something of a stable: Wayne, Victor McLaglen, and the Irish actor Barry Fitzgerald were in film after film.) Most of the Ford-Wayne

films were horse operas, but when the director and his star triumphantly returned to Ireland to make *The Quiet Man* in 1951—Ford had been thrown out of the country thirty years earlier for providing aid and comfort to the Irish Republican Army—they created what many believe is the finest Irish movie of all time. John Wayne's depiction of strong, kind, irresistible Sean Thornton was Ford's dream of himself. Ford also made the towering film adaptation of John Steinbeck's *The Grapes of Wrath*, a film implicitly if not explicitly Irish. "Wandering on the roads to starve," Ford said of his movie. "Part of the Irish tradition."

- **Pat O'Brien** (1899–1983) was the grandson of immigrants, and he wore it on his mug. In more than a hundred movies he rarely played anything but an obvious Irishman. He was a cop a dozen times and a priest perhaps that many. When he made a television series it was called *Harrigan and Son*. It's a lovely bit of confusion that surrounds his most famous role. In *Knute Rockne—All American* he played a Norwegian-born coach to Irish American Ronald Reagan's George Gipp, who also, like Rockne, had not been of Irish heritage. But O'Brien and Reagan made the two Notre Dame football legends appear Fightin' Irishmen indeed.

- **Spencer Tracy** (1900–1967) could play anything. He could play comedy, as he did in *Father of the Bride* and *Father's Little Dividend*, and as he did opposite the love of his life, Katharine Hepburn, in nine films including the classics *Desk Set* and *Pat and Mike*. He could play strong, as in *Judgment at Nuremberg*, or vulnerable, as in *The Old Man and the Sea*, or dramatic, as in *Inherit the Wind*. He could play Irish, as in the screen adaptation of Edwin O'Connor's political novel *The Last Hurrah*. Tracy won back-to-back Best Actor Oscars in 1937 and 1938 by playing a Portuguese-American fisherman in *Captains Courageous*, then Father Flanagan in *Boys Town*. No actor had that kind of range, that kind of talent. A footnote: Tracy and Hepburn never married. Tracy, a Catholic, would not divorce his wife.

- **James Cagney** (1899–1986) *did* portray a real Irish American in one of his most famous pictures, *Yankee Doodle Dandy*, the 1942 biopic about George M. Cohan. The film was a breakthrough for Cagney as the erstwhile tough guy got to smile, sing, and dance. He did them all, particularly the last, spectacularly well, and won the Oscar for Best Actor. Theretofore he had played one gangster after another, thanks to an image forged by his terrifically menacing performance in *Public Enemy*. Thereafter he could play whatever he wanted, including a marvelous late-in-life turn as the police commissioner in *Ragtime*.

- **Marion Morrison** was born in Winterset, Iowa, in 1907, grew up to hate horses, and made sure that he escaped military service during World War II so he could keep his career as "John Wayne" charging uphill. Garry Wills, the Pulitzer Prize—winning historian whose 1997 book, *John Wayne's America: The Politics of Celebrity,* looked at both the real man and the icon, told us in an interview: "John Wayne is a fictive hero. Very large, very mythic—but a hero of the imagination." He was something of an Irishman of the imagination, too. He was mostly Scotch-Irish on his father's side, English Irish on his mother's, although his maternal grandfather, Robert Emmet Brown, was yet another Irishman named for the great patriot of 1803. Marion's father was retiring, his mother a hellcat: a classic, domineering Irish mother. Marion, nicknamed Duke after his dog, would run away from home several times to escape domestic firestorms. The family moved to California, and Duke Morrison secured a football scholarship to the University of Southern California; while there, he started working at Fox studios, where he met John Ford. Their famous collaborations would come later, but meanwhile big Duke's career was launched, and a new name given: John (because it sounded American) Wayne (after Revolutionary War hero Anthony Wayne). This icon of the imagination, this questionable Irishman, was suddenly the epitome of masculine Irish Americanism. His career as perhaps the greatest American film star of the twentieth century is well known and documented. As to his Irishness, a solid view was offered by John A. Barnes in his book *Irish American Landmarks*, when he visited John Wayne's birthplace in Winterset: "While his characters were rarely explicitly Irish, Irish Americans certainly viewed him as one of their own. His strong, independent, yet charming demeanor—especially in *The Quiet Man*—came for many to symbolize the assimilated, yet still ethnically identifiable, first-generation Irish American."

- **Tyrone Power** (1914–1958) was the great-grandson of an Irish actor famous in London for playing comedy. Power listed toward more dramatic—and, indeed, melodramatic—fare. His handsome figure swashbuckled through more than forty films including *The Black Rose* and *Blood and Sand*. Power was only forty-four when he died; he's one of those actors you just can't envision old.
- **Anthony Quinn,** born in 1915, is one of those actors you envisioned old before he was old. As an over-the-hill fighter in *Requiem for a Heavyweight*, as Kazantzakis's sage in *Zorba the Greek*, in *Viva Zapata!* and in *The Shoes of the Fisherman*, he always brought weight and the wisdom of age to his roles. You could win a lot of money laying bets on Quinn's Irishness, but it's certifiable: His father was exclusively so, his mother was Mexican.
- **Jackie Gleason** (1916–1987), remembered as a television comedian and musical-variety host, was a sensational serious actor as well. Watch him closely as he hastens Quinn's fall in *Requiem for a Heavyweight*. Watch him fence with Paul Newman's Fast Eddie in Robert Rossen's *The Hustler*. Gleason, the Babe Ruth of bon vivants, was also a musician: His Jackie Gleason Orchestra cut forty albums of best-selling lounge music in the 1950s and early 1960s. And, yes, the Great One was arguably the biggest and best funnyman of the postwar era. His series *The Honeymooners*, with Art Carney playing Ed Norton to Gleason's Ralph Kramden, is not just classic television, it's classic comedy.
- **Gregory Peck** is the son of a woman who had emigrated from County Kerry. He himself was born in San Diego in 1916. He has been nominated for the Best Actor Oscar five times and he won it for *To Kill a Mockingbird*. He fell in love with his mother's native land while filming the epic *Moby Dick* there, and lived for a time in County Galway in the 1970s. Peck had a cameo in the recent cable-television remake of the Herman Melville classic. This time, they saw fit to film it in Australia. Needless to say, it wasn't a patch on the original.
- **Maureen O'Hara,** born in Dublin in 1920 as Maureen Fitz-Simons, emigrated in 1939. She was an Irish beauty of a different, darker type than, say, Grace Kelly, but the camera loved her no less. She could play comedy (the original *Miracle on 34th Street* is so much sharper and more sophisticated than

the recent remake) or drama (*How Green Was My Valley*). If every Irish American boy wanted to grow up to be John Wayne, it was in part because when Wayne burst into that cottage in *The Quiet Man* and swooped up the girl as the wind blew a gale—the girl in question was Maureen O'Hara.

- **Carroll O'Connor** was born in New York City in 1924 and, fifty years later, was the most watched and talked-about actor in America in his role as the bigoted Archie Bunker on television's *All in the Family*. By bringing the nation into the Bunkers' living room, this Norman Lear comedy brought issues such as racism and family values into living rooms from Maine to California. Lear and O'Connor were both liberals; they knew precisely what they were doing, even if their message was sometimes misinterpreted. O'Connor has become passionate not just about politics but about Ireland: He has studied at the National University there and has acted on stage throughout the country. He has done other TV series—*Archie Bunker's Place*, *In the Heat of the Night*—but none have had the impact of *All in the Family*. Archie Bunker's living room furniture, including the famous chair, is on display at the Smithsonian Institution.

- **Grace Kelly** (1929–1982) was a princess before she became one. She came from a prosperous, gifted family in Philadelphia (something that cannot be said of a lot of Irish). Her great-grandfather, a pig farmer in Ireland, had emigrated in the 1860s and built the bricklaying company upon which a family fortune would rest. Her father, Jack, ran the firm and became an Olympic-champion rower; her uncle George became a Pulitzer Prize–winning playwright; her uncle Walter became a successful song-and-dance man. But it was Grace who became the legend, in films such as *Dial M for Murder*, *Rear Window*, *High Noon*, and *To Catch a Thief*. She won the Best Actress Oscar for *The Country Girl*. In the mid-fifties she was wooed and won by Prince Rainier of Monaco and became true royalty. (Charming footnote: The Prince got from the Kellys a $2 million dowry.) Grace Kelly died in a car accident in Monaco; she had been at the wheel.

- **Edward Burns** is the future. This young man's 1995 film *The Brothers McMullen* won the big prize at the Sundance Film Festival and went on to a successful theatrical release, announcing Burns as a talented actor and director. The film, made on a shoestring, is a romantic comedy investigating Irish American life in the modern suburbs. Assimilated yet still Irish, the brothers wonder at the world as they fall in love with Jewish girls as easily as Irish girls. The recent Irish film renaissance—*Cal, Hear My Song, The Crying Game, My Left Foot, The Commitments, Circle of Friends, In the Name of the Father, The Snapper, The Van* (just to give you our favorites)—has been often commented upon, as has the Irish American cultural renaissance heralded with great prescience as early as 1981 by Andrew Greeley in his book *The Irish Americans*. Edward Burns stands at the intersection of these rebirths, and at the far end of a continuum that began with John Ford heading west from Maine. From there, Burns gazes at the twenty-first century.

Have Irish Americans made similar contributions in music?

Yes.

Irish American achievements in song started, as we have noted, with the descendant of Northern Irelanders **Stephen Collins Foster,** whose popular, melodic music was heard across the land after the Civil War, and is still heard today. Then came **George M. Cohan,** whose fervently patriotic songbook seemed to be shouting that the Irish were just as red-white-and-blue as the next guys. Interestingly, a century later, no music seems more *American* than that of Foster and Cohan.

Victor Herbert was born in Dublin in 1859 and was a cellist with various symphonies before he accepted the directorship of Pittsburgh's orchestra in 1898. He took to composing, and his operettas—*Babes in Toyland, Naughty Marietta*—were great successes. Herbert was also the first American to compose a movie score.

Another Irish-born performer making beautiful music in the early decades of the twentieth century was **John McCormack,** the famous tenor from County Westmeath. He was trained as a member of a Roman Catholic choir in Dublin and debuted in London in 1907. He was an instant opera star, triumphing in Milan and elsewhere on the Continent, and finally in the United States. McCormack gained American citizenship in 1917. He became a recitalist after the war (his acting abilities had always been slight) and continued to sell out concert halls in Europe and America until his retirement in 1942. In the late 1920s he returned to live in Ireland, and in 1928 Pope Pius

XI named him a papal count. McCormack's recordings of traditional Irish songs—many, such as "Oft in the stilly night" and "The Meeting of the Waters," from *Moore's Irish Melodies*—have been beloved by generations of Irish and Irish Americans.

While McCormack was recording the age-old songs, **Hoagland Howard Carmichael,** born in 1899 in Bloomington, Indiana, was composing new ones that seemed like they'd been around forever: "Star Dust," "Lazy River," "Georgia on My Mind," "Heart and Soul." Hoagy Carmichael went to Indiana University to study law, but his love for jazz led him to direct the school dance band, the Collegians, and upon graduating he formed his own small group. He then tried law for a while, but that didn't take. He worked as a bank clerk for $12 a week while moonlighting as a dance-band pianist. Then he cast his lot, traveling to Hollywood, where he started composing for the motion pictures. This was kismet, and the songs—written in collaboration with great lyricists like Frank Loesser and Johnny Mercer—started to flow. Hoagy Carmichael had more than fifty hits, including his own renditions of his music and those of others. He appeared in several movies, usually as the saloon pianist (his interplay with Lauren Bacall in the 1944 film *To Have and Have Not* is representative), and on television, notably on the wildly successful Sunday-night variety show hosted by the former Broadway gossip columnist and fellow Irish American Ed Sullivan.

Our favorite version of Carmichael's "Blue Orchids," a truly wonderful melody, is by **Tommy Dorsey**'s orchestra. He was the younger of the two musical Dorsey brothers by a year: Jimmy had been born in 1904. Jimmy played saxophone, Tommy played trombone, and they formed the first of their swinging bands in 1920. They split, and found independent success throughout the twenties, thirties, and forties, working with a number of fine singers. Tommy's band was number one in the early forties after he hired a kid named Sinatra away from the Harry James band. (Tommy's famous comment to Frank when Sinatra went solo in 1943: "I hope you fall on your ass.") The Dorsey brothers reunited for a triumphant final tour in 1953. Both were dead within four years.

Frank Sinatra did not fall on his ass, of course, and the singer he replaced at the top of the polls and charts was **Harry Lillis "Bing" Crosby.** (Crosby's memorable quote: "A singer like Sinatra comes along once in a lifetime. Why did it have to be *my* lifetime?" Actually, he and Sinatra were fast friends, the only fallout occurring when

Sinatra raised with Crosby the issue of how Bing was treating his sons, which was poorly. Crosby was, indeed, a tyrant of a father.)

It's difficult to remember just how big Bing Crosby was. He made nearly nine hundred records and sold more than three hundred million copies of them. His version of Irving Berlin's "White Christmas" is the second best-selling disc of all time (Elton John's Diana tribute "Candle in the Wind" passed it in 1997). Introduced in a Crosby–Fred Astaire movie, *Holiday Inn,* it went on to float a film of its own, *White Christmas*, that had Irish-American all-star leads Crosby and Rosemary Clooney. Crosby made more than seventy other pictures, and won the Best Actor Oscar in 1944 for *Going My Way* playing a hip Irish American priest who was both teaching and learning from Barry Fitzgerald's old-but-wise priest. The crooner's versions of Irish songs and lullabies like "Too-ra-loo-ra" and "When Irish Eyes are Smiling" outsold those of McCormack or Kate Smith.

Bing Crosby was born in 1904 in Tacoma, Washington, to an Irish Catholic woman and her husband, who had converted from Protestantism to marry her. Catherine Harrigan Crosby was a piece of work, tough and domineering. When Crosby was on top, he marveled at his luck in her presence, and she shot back: "Your luck has been my prayers and the prayers I've asked the Poor Clare nuns to offer up for you." But luck did have something to do with Crosby's phenomenal success: He came along with his smooth, quiet baritone just when technology was transforming music.

Tony Bennett, no less, explained this for us in an interview during lunch in New York: "Bing Crosby actually invented the art of intimate singing. You used to have to belt it to the back row, or use a megaphone like Rudy Vallee. But Crosby realized what could be done by caressing the microphone, and talking to the listener. Talking the lyric. We all learned from him."

Bing Crosby died on the golf course, as he would have wanted, in 1977. As the century winds down it is clear that he was one of the greatest entertainers who ever lived.

Rosemary Clooney is still singing, and beautifully, as the century ends. Younger Irish Americans are making music that reflects the Irish renaissance. Black 47 rocks the house at Paddy Reillys in Manhattan, while Morning Star plays Celtic ballads and reels up at An Beal Bocht in the Bronx, melodies every bit as lovely as those coming from Irish Irish bands like Altan and Arcady. Two record companies based in the northeastern United States are thriving by putting their emphasis on the importing of Irish and Scottish music and on the production of Irish American music that is true to Celtic roots. In 1975 two Irish Americans based in New York City, Richard Nevins and Dan Collins, were lamenting the fact that they couldn't place the Irish music they loved with any mainstream record operations, and so they started their own independent label, Shanachie. Not long thereafter, a woman named Wendy Newton of Danbury, Connecticut, was vacationing in Ireland, and one night in a pub was serenaded for five hours by the fiddler Tommy Peoples. She returned home and found herself with a lament just like that of Nevins and Collins. She started Green Linnet Records. Overnight, bands like De Danaan (where Dolores Keane, Maura O'Connell, and Eleanor Shanley all started) and singers like Mary Black (who also had a spell in De Danaan) could find purchase in the States, and musicians in New York could get original material recorded. Growth has been better than steady, and today Shanachie and Green Linnet are real players in the music world

For all of this we thank the revivalists. We thank the Chieftains, and their leader Paddy Maloney; we thank Christy Moore, and his legendary band Planxty, which lasted from 1972 to 1975; we even thank such as Van Morrison and Sinead O'Connor, whose rock is infused with an Irish sensibility; we thank Mick Maloney, once an Irishman, now an American.

Any cultural flourishing needs a soundtrack, and they were the first to hum the new, old tunes.

Who is Mick Maloney?

Mick Maloney was a pioneer in his native land and is now a pioneer in the United States. He was born in County Limerick in 1944 and took up the guitar, tenor banjo, and mandolin in his teens. He learned from older, traditional players in neighboring County Clare. In and out of the Planxty scene, he came to America in 1973 and decided to stay. He formed a band called Green Fields of America in 1977 with musicians including Eileen Ivers (born of Irish parents in the Bronx), Jimmy Keane (born in Chicago), Robbie O'Connell (born in County Waterford), Seamus Egan (born of County Mayo parents in Philadelphia), and step dancers Donny and Eileen Golden (of Brooklyn). That band, whose earliest sides were on Green Linnet, now stands as an Irish American version of Planxty: authentic, leading the way, legendary, sadly bygone.

Mick went on to help organize Cherish the Ladies in the 1980s, which also recorded on Green Linnet and has now landed a contract with RCA. Eileen Ivers went on to fiddling fame with Riverdance. New bands began forming in America, and transatlantic distinctions began to blur, as they had in so many other aspects of the Irish American experience. Take Solas, which is as hot as any band on the Hiberno scene right now: Seamus Egan fronts it; three Irish Americans play in it. Who makes the rules? Who makes the distinctions? You need a musicologist these days to tell you that Solas is an American group, Clannad a wholly Irish one, and Cappercallie, Scottish.

In other words, you need a Mick Maloney, who eventually landed in Milwaukee as an ethnomusicology professor at the university. And in the summer of 1998 he sponsored a reunion at his college of the original Green Fields of America. Mick was able to look left and right at his now well-known colleagues, then glance back two decades, and see that he had been a vital cog in something that had grown very, very big.

And dance?

Talk about old and new!

The most dynamic, innovative popular dancer of the century was the Irish American **Gene Kelly** (1912–1996). His groundbreaking musicals *On the Town*, *An American in Paris*, and, especially, *Singin' in the Rain* are classics of the genre. It is often said that Astaire was more elegant, Kelly more virile—and this is true. But make no mistake, Kelly was a beautiful dancer, and his ideas on choreography and how to film a dance sequence changed moviemaking. (In some pictures, Astaire's feet are cropped from the shot!) Kelly was also a dramatic actor, singer, director, and producer.

In one of the sweetest ironies of the renaissance, the current stepdance craze ignited by the internationally triumphant Riverdance spectacle was fronted, in its first incarnation, not by young Irish dancers, but by two phenomenal Irish *American* dancers. Yes, certainly, the composer **Bill Whelan** is the driving force behind Riverdance itself—the music from which spent eighteen weeks at number one on the Irish charts in 1994, and the annual stage edition of which sells out Radio City Music Hall for weeks running. But the hard-driving dancers in the show's initial, innovative edition were **Jean Butler** from New York and **Michael Flatley** from Chicago.

Butler, a Maureen O'Hara–type beauty, started tap and ballet training at age four. Her mother was an immigrant from County

Mayo and viewed Irish dancing as a way to stay in touch with her roots. She enrolled her daughter at the Daniel Golden School, where such things were taught. At age ten Jean was a professional, and in her teens she and the aforementioned Donny Golden were winning national competitions. At seventeen Butler was the step-dancer interlude that always spices up a Chieftains concert, and in 1992 she represented not America but Ireland in performances at the Seville World's Fair. She performed for Diana, Princess of Wales, at the world premiere of Ron Howard's Irish film, *Far and Away,* and in 1993 for Irish President Mary Robinson. It was that last appearance that got her chosen by Flatley and Whelan for a taping of something called Riverdance that was to air on Eurovision. Butler choreographed her own solo. Few things are true overnight sensations, but Riverdance was—and so was Butler.

And so was Flatley, opposite her. His ride to the dance began on the Windy City's gritty South Side where he was the second of five children born to Irish immigrants Michael and Eilish Flatley. The boy took up step dancing at eleven and at seventeen became the first-ever American to win the All-World Irish Dancing Championship. He, too, appeared with the Chieftains in the 1980s. "From the start what Michael was doing was brilliant," said Paddy Maloney. "I could see he was not going to settle down with us." And Flatley did not. In 1987 he went to Ireland to enter a televised song contest, and his seven-minute Riverdance brought the house down. Flatley had taken the formerly rigid, up-and-down lines of step dancing and transformed them into wild, flailing, swirling curlicues: It was a mad Lughnasa dance, where once there'd been a simple jig. (Flatley "scares the bejesus" out of the Chandler character on the TV show *Friends* because his legs move independent from his body.) By 1993 the big, eighty-five-dancer, Whalen-scored extravaganza was ready for its close-up, and Flatley and Butler ready for theirs. "I flew to Ireland in 1993 with a standby ticket on Aer Lingus and I came back on the Concorde," Flatley told *People* magazine. "Not bad for a kid from Chicago who does the jig."

Neither Butler, who fancies a career as an actress, nor Flatley is with the show any longer. Flatley and Whelan battled over artistic control of Riverdance, and the dancer left with a huff and a lawsuit, and then formed his own forty-dancer troupe called Lord of the Dance. He appeared with it on the 1997 Academy Awards show, and his subsequent world tour was worth $60 million in tickets, perhaps another $100 million in CD and video sales. Flatley had pushed himself to become the world's highest-paid dancer by the time he collapsed after a show in Australia and had to cancel some of the tour's final dates. Five-foot-nine and 147 pounds, Flatley had simply run out of gas after months of eight-solos-a-night and an average weight loss of ten pounds per performance. The boy does work hard for his money.

Flatley's "Lord" is even sexier—some would say more salacious—than the plenty erotic Riverdance. It takes bare-chestedness an extra step. Critics say it ventures far too far from any Irish roots it might claim, but the brazen Flatley remains unapologetic: "What we do transcends dance. It's all about energy. We're making people feel things."

Perhaps. But Riverdance, originally, was about making people feel Irish. Jean Butler, in a spring 1996 interview with *The World of Hibernia* magazine, looked back to that first sensational performance: "Being American I was not particularly aware of the cultural sense of expanding and celebrating that Riverdance created. It took me quite a long time to understand the historical context of it." When the show was up and running on the stage, "I began to feel a part of it. I could understand the buzz in Dublin. I still think that is the best place to be. It is home for me now."

So America lost one of its own in a reemigration. Meanwhile, the dance classes in Queens are full of little girls who want to do what Jean Butler does.

What other Irish American contributions to the arts have there been?

One of the most influential painters of the twentieth century was **Georgia O'Keeffe** (1887–1986). She began painting at age twelve and, throughout a long career, became famous for her strong, sensual paintings of desert scenes and flowers near the New Mexico home that she shared with her husband, the photographer Alfred Stieglitz. In her life and work, O'Keeffe was a model for feminist women, as well as a great artist.

We've mentioned the architect Hoban, who landed the commission for the White House. We have also briefly mentioned, in chapter 8, **Louis Sullivan,** the Chicagoan who built the big buildings of the predominant Midwestern skyline after the Great Fire. He designed the Auditorium Building and the Gage Building. A pioneer of style and a turn-of-the-century radical, he was called the father of modernism in architecture. When he protested that the World's Fair of 1893 was being dominated by Beaux Arts neoclassicists, he received sympathetic backing from none less than the historian Henry Adams: "All traders' taste smelt of bric-a-brac; Chicago tried at least to give her taste a look of unity." Sullivan went on to revolutionize America's cities, and his legacy endured in the talent and style of the legendary Frank Lloyd Wright, who had learned at his knee.

Born one year before Sullivan, in 1855, was a New Yorker named **James E. Kelly,** who would eventually be called "the sculptor of American history." His bronze busts of Grant, Sherman, and Sheridan are considered masterpieces, as are larger works such as *Sheridan's Ride*, *Paul Revere*, and the equestrian statue of Teddy Roosevelt at San Juan Hill—all of which are in New York.

Kelly is not as famous or influential as **Augustus Saint-Gaudens,** who was born in a Dublin row house in 1848 to a French father and an Irish mother. Dad was a shoemaker and Mom the daughter of a County Longford plasterer. The Famine was in full cry, and the family decamped for America when the baby was only six months old. Augustus grew up in Boston and New York. By age thirteen he had decided to become an artist. At nineteen he went to Paris, then Rome, to study, and in the latter city met Augusta Homer from Boston. Gus and Gussie fell in love. Her father would not let the marriage take place until Saint-Gaudens was set in his profession, and the artist entered a competition for the memorial to Civil War hero Admiral David Glasgow Farragut, to be raised in Madison Square. He won the commission, built the statue, married the girl.

Saint-Gaudens captured his subjects' humanity in his art, not just their momentary bravery. Abraham Lincoln, head bowed, is deeply stirring in Chicago's Lincoln Park. So is the *Shaw Memorial*—Colonel Robert Gould Shaw at the head of the all-black 54th Massachusetts Infantry—the inspiration for the film *Glory*—on Boston Common.

Saint-Gaudens's designs were held by millions in his day and can still be had by anyone today: Go to your local coin shop and buy a century-old Saint-Gaudens silver dollar. His art was everywhere in America at the turn of the century, which is precisely when he was struck by cancer. Having received the diagnosis, he wanted to honor his mother and accepted a commission in Ireland. Today, two miles from where he was born in Dublin, Saint-Gaudens's memorial to Charles Stewart Parnell presides over the square. Saint-Gaudens died in 1907, in the Plainfield, New Hampshire, home that today is the only National Historic site dedicated to a visual artist.

*Is there a conclusion to be drawn about
all these Irish American artists?*

Perhaps that many of the things we now perceive as so thoroughly American—"Yankee Doodle Dandy," "My Old Kentucky Home," *The Great Gatsby,* the speeches of Ronald Reagan, John Wayne, a silver dollar, "Georgia on My Mind," a Gene Kelly musical—have a Gaelic heritage. Ireland's past seeps into the American consciousness. Listen closely. Do you hear the echoes?

ELEVEN

Sporting Irish

Did the Irish introduce any sports to America?

What is "hurling"?

What is Gaelic football?

Who were the first Irish American sports stars?

Who was John L. Sullivan?

What happened to Gentleman Jim Corbett?

Were there other great Irish American boxers?

What other games did Irish Americans
play, back then?

Who were some famous Irish American
baseball stars?

Who was Lefty O'Doul?

How do two Irish American catchers
figure in the Babe Ruth story?

Who were Johnny O'Hara and Babe O'Rourke?

Who was "Casey," of the bat?

What about Irish American Olympians?

So neither Johnny Kelley won the Olympic marathon?

When did the Irish take up the country club sports?

Any other games players?

Did the Irish introduce any sports to America?

Not by themselves.

Indigenous Irish games such as hurling or Gaelic football, while
played in the nineteenth-century Irish American enclaves (and even
today, by clubs and such), never gained popularity beyond the clan.
However, the Irish did much to popularize boxing in the United
States and were the greatest early contributors to the now-erstwhile
national pastime, baseball. Subsequently, Irish Americans have
starred in the Olympics—remember Grace Kelly's gold-medal dad,
Jack the sculler, from chapter 10—at golf and tennis, at just about
everything this side of luge. (Now that we think of it, Duncan
Kennedy, a World Cup luge star of the 1980s and 1990s, racked up
the best-ever record by an American male before hanging up his
sled in early 1998.)

Irish American patterns of achievement in sports have mirrored
Irish American patterns of achievement in society at large. When the

Irish were poor and downtrodden, they excelled at the games of the inner city (one of which was baseball, in its infancy). When they started to get a leg up, they formed their own clubs (you can look at the old Irish Athletic Association as New York's jockish Clan na Gael) and enjoyed broader success in sports. When they had been assimilated, you were just as likely to find them as anyone else playing the country-club games. Or sculling. Or riding down an icy chute on a luge.

Just a second! What is "hurling"? Sounds like a fraternity game.

Hardly. Hurling is a sport that demands the utmost skill. More than two thousand years old, it involves two teams of fifteen trying to score the most points in the course of two thirty-five-minute periods. A ball, or "slotar," is carried or bounced on the wide blade of a three-foot-long "hurley," a hockey- or lacrosse-type stick. The ball may be picked off the ground or struck along the ground with the hurley, or kicked by foot. Three points are scored when the ball is advanced under a crossbar at the goal; one point is registered for a ball going over the bar.

Have fun.

What is Gaelic football?

This game is even older than hurling. It started in the sixteenth century between Irish towns: a team from one town would try to drive a ball across the border and into the adjacent town, whose team was both resisting and trying to do the same. Nowadays, two teams of fifteen compete to score the most points by either kicking or punching the bladder between goalposts for a point, or under a crossbar for three. This game, too, is played in thirty-five-minute halves. It's hurling with a different ball and no sticks.

Who were the first Irish American sports stars?

Boxers were the first American-of-any-kind sports stars. They invented the idea of an American sports star.

The fight game had been introduced to the Irish by the English—no surprise there—and they took to it like tinkers to the road (the metaphor, if unfortunate, is not accidental; even today the original, bare-knuckle variety of boxing is still practiced, illegally, by the tinkers of Ireland, and the toughest among them is said to be the standing "King of the Gypsies"). When **Peter Corcoran** knocked out English champ **Bill Darts** on May 18, 1771, there was something approaching a frenzy about the sport in Ireland. Corcoran was followed by the storied **Dan Donnelly,** a carpenter by day and pub brawler by night. Donnelly was an Irish idol; on September 14, 1814, he drew forty thousand fans to a fight—a seventeen-round win over an Englishman. Donnelly spent his prize money within a week, it is said, something that would be impossible today, for such a king as Donnelly would be commanding purses in the tens of millions of dollars. Donnelly, a legend in his own time, remains one: There's an obelisk commemorating his feats at "Donnelly's Hollow" in Kildare, where he took on all comers from home or abroad.

This was not necessarily pretty sport, bare-knuckle boxing. Consider this contemporary account of Donnelly's bout against the Englishman Oliver: "Donnelly hit severely with his left. Several sharp exchanges occurred, till they both went down, grappling desperately. Oliver undermost. Five minutes had elapsed." There were no leather gloves, no three-minute rounds. The Marquis of Queensberry, who would be the bête noire of Irish writer Oscar Wilde (Queensberry wrote the "posing as a sodomite" note that got Wilde imprisoned in Reading Gaol), had not yet codified his "gentleman's rules" of boxing, and fisticuffs was not a game for the fainthearted. What rules were in place in the *finer* fights, the so-called London Prize Ring Rules, stipulated bare hands, an unlimited number of rounds, each round ending when one fighter went down. The fighter had thirty seconds to recover, or the bout was over. Tough stuff.

And in this brutal version, it had already been introduced to America, as it had been to Ireland, by the British. Redcoats had brought it across during the Revolutionary War. The colonial English and the Scotch-Irish were ready and waiting for the Catholics.

Donnelly, as prodigious a drinker as he was a fighter, died in 1820 at only thirty-two years old, and so an early death added to his heroic reputation. Certainly all but the most clueless Famine Irish immigrants knew of Dan Donnelly, and his fame traveled with them in stories true and false, long and short. **Mike McCool** and **Joe Coburn** were Donnelly acolytes, and the first Irish-born boxers to become boxing stars in the States. They fought in the 1840s, and were followed by **James Ambrose** of Cork, with his nom de ring "Yankee Sullivan." He became the American heavyweight bare-knuckle champion in the 1850s, then saw his career cut short when he was murdered in a California prison cell. (Boxing has never been a savory game.)

Tipperary's **John Morrisey** had already wrested Ambrose's crown by the time the old Yankee was done in. Morrisey had come to New York as a child and had been steeled by a youth in the ghettos, where he'd served as a "runner," meeting the boats and leading fellow immigrants to whatever rooms were available in the slums. Morrisey boxed under the nickname "Old Smoke": In a pub fight he'd been knocked against the stove, but had recovered and, with his coat on fire, had smoked the guy who'd popped him. He parlayed the fistic talent he had developed on the docks into an estimable career. He saved his prize winnings, pulled himself up, gained the respect of his peers—well, he'd always had that—won a seat in Congress, opened a gambling emporium in Saratoga Springs, New York, and died a millionaire: the American Dream.

The better circles looked down on all this, of course. When riots attended a Newport, Rhode Island, fight between two Irish Americans in 1856, the marble mansions fairly shook with indignation. Even as late as 1882, when **Paddy Ryan,** the Irish American from Tipperary, held the heavyweight crown, boxing was not a cross-societal game. The proletariat and below loved the fights; the middle class and above were scandalized by bare-knuckle boxing.

And then, as Paddy remembered later, "I thought a telegraph pole had been shoved against me sideways."

Who was John L. Sullivan?

John L. Sullivan was the Muhammad Ali, the Michael Jordan, the Tiger Woods of his day, all rolled into one massive man. (If you had used black men as metaphors to his face, Sullivan would have floored you; he was a terrible racist.) When he ruled the fight world he was a personality of immense fame and allure. He made sixteen times as much money in a year as the next biggest sports star in the United States, the Boston Irish American baseball player Mike "King" Kelly. For better or worse, Sullivan made boxing what it is today.

To first-, second-, and now third-generation Catholic Irish American immigrants, Sullivan was a source of immense pride. No Civil War hero had achieved this kind of fame. And his Irish American countrymen saw him as emblematic of what they were now (or wanted to be), and what they had so recently been (and wanted to remain). Consider the sweet, poetic schizophrenia of a popular lyric from 1890:

> *His colors are the Stars and Stripes,*
> *He also wears the Green,*
> *And he's the grandest slugger that*
> *The ring has ever seen.*
> *No fighter in the world can beat*
> *Our true American,*
> *The champion of all champions,*
> *John L. Sullivaaaaaan.*

The future "Boston Strong Boy" had been born in 1858 to immigrants. Boston today is seen as something of a bucolic Irish retreat, but in the nineteenth century the town hated its Irish. City fathers had tried to keep immigrant ships from docking by establishing prohibitive tariffs, and in one particular election the Know-Nothing Party, a nativist movement that featured immigrant-bashing (literal and figurative) as its principal plank, swept all Massachusetts offices, gaining its greatest-ever victory in the United States. Sullivan's father was a laborer, and his mother was a gentle woman who tried to steer her son toward the priesthood. But John was a baseball-loving, fight-loving boy, already sporting a chip on his shoulder. "My name is John L. Sullivan," read a note he wrote in school and passed among his classmates. "I can whip every kid in the room. I'm going to do it, too."

By the time he had finished with his Beantown school chums, he was seventeen years old and two hundred pounds. At twenty he fought his first exhibition bout and won easily. He was already fully formed as he would become known and notorious: huge, tough, ornery, inelegant, brash, proud, alcoholic. He started fighting for prize money soon after that first exhibition. By now, Englishman John Sholto Douglas, eighth Marquis of Queensberry, had drawn up his rules: twelve rounds, each three minutes long, ten seconds to recover after a knockdown, gloves on the hands. You could find either kind of action in America—London Rules or Queensberry—and

Sullivan sought out both, though he preferred the new format. He is remembered as the last of the great bare-knuckle brawlers, and the first of the great glovemen.

The enormity of Sullivan's contribution to American sport cannot be overstated. In 1880 prizefighting was illegal in thirty-eight states. It was impossible to foresee that Sullivan would become the country's first sports superstar. But the charismatic boxer and his sharp manager, the Irish American Billy Madden, had an idea. They challenged all comers and offered their own money to anyone who could best Sullivan. Few would take the offer, but the bravado of the boast drew large crowds for Sullivan-Madden sparring sessions. On his 1881 tour the boxer made $6,000, an immense amount of money. In 1882 Paddy Ryan took Sullivan on in Mississippi, and all of the country tuned in through the newspapers. After eleven minutes of fighting, Ryan ran into that telegraph pole, and Sullivan walked away with $4,500. Boxing and John L. Sullivan were on their way.

He defended his title ten times in the next year and a half, earning $40,000—a rich man's income. Sullivan's fame was knocking down not only men, but laws barring the fight game. Everyone wanted to see him, and John L. barnstormed the country: 195 exhibitions in twenty-six states. As Michael T. Isenberg wrote in his biography *John L. Sullivan and His America*: "John L. was literally challenging America to fight." The tour had a circus atmosphere, with Sullivan getting in drunken fights after the scheduled fights. He never lost, and on that tour made $80,000. Much has been made about Babe Ruth's quip when asked how he felt about making more money as a New York Yankee than President Hoover had made leading the country—"I had a better year than he did," said the Babe— but consider this: In his best year of touring, Sullivan made *four times* what the U.S. president earned. In 1887 Grover Cleveland was proud to shake the Strong Boy's mitt during a photo op at the White House. What American sport would become in the twentieth century—a multi-billion-dollar business of international force and standing—was making its bow. Isenberg wrote: "He was the most prominent sporting hero America had produced, and neither he nor anyone else knew quite how to handle the novelty of his fame. He had won no elections, no military victories; he was not in the forefront of any crusade. Yet there he was, arguably the most popular man in the United States.

"John L. Sullivan emerged as the first significant mass cultural hero in American life. He was not merely a celebrity, a person known for being known . . . Sullivan was, like earlier heroic figures, famed for his deeds. But his deeds were controversial and conversational at the same time. People *talked* about John L. Sullivan in ways that they had not talked about, say, Lincoln."

Sullivan's fame was not only nationwide, it was worldwide: He was an Irish American ambassador, fighting in his ancestors' homeland, also in England and Australia. He was larger than life, and things he either did say or didn't really say—"The bigger they come, the harder they fall"—were encrusted to his legend like barnacles. Music hall performers had a new staple: "Let me shake the hand that shook the hand of John L. Sullivan." Sullivan drank it in—and everything else, too—and he believed it all.

By the end of the 1880s Sullivan was out of control. The boozing caused his weight to balloon; his temper had cost him his marriage. Still he could fight: He won the last sanctioned bare-knuckle championship in U.S. history, a titanic two-hour, sixteen-minute, seventy-five-round struggle against Jake Kilrain in Mississippi. After that fight, Sullivan said he was through. He should have stayed true to his word.

In 1892 Sullivan, age thirty-four, fought in New Orleans against **Jim Corbett** before the largest crowd ever to see a prizefight in America. It was a $45,000 winner-take-all affair under modified Queensberry rules. Corbett, a stylish fighter known as "Gentleman Jim," became the only person ever to whip John L. Sullivan when he knocked him out in the twenty-first round.

Sullivan, well over three hundred pounds, returned to the ring years later, in 1905 at forty-six years old, and beat a man half his age. The fight proved to be an epiphany. He hung up the gloves and vowed to quit the sauce. He spent the last thirteen years of his life as a respected temperance lecturer. That's the good news. He also spent his time deriding blacks. As a fighter he had vowed, "I will not fight a Negro," which kept the formidable **Peter Jackson** from getting a title shot. As an entertainer he had appeared in a version of *Uncle Tom's Cabin* wherein Simon Legree came out the hero. Now, as a grand old man of the fight game, he led the search for a "Great White Hope" to beat America's first black heavyweight champion, **Jack Johnson.**

That's the ugly side of the legacy. The reason we go on at such length about Sullivan, the greatest-ever and certainly the most influential Irish American sports figure, is because, as Isenberg wrote,

"Without really intending it, he helped make boxing, and indeed American sport, both a cultural and commercial enterprise. Unknowingly he had become a grandfather to the modern sporting tradition in America."

What happened to Gentleman Jim Corbett?

The San Francisco–born Irish American held the title for five years before losing it to **Bob Fitzsimmons.** By all accounts, Corbett truly was a gentleman, and deserved the kind of popularity that had attended Sullivan. He never received it, and so he, too, plays a role in defining how the American sports-icon machine works. "You can't destroy a hero," Corbett said late in his life, "without it being resented." He died in 1933 at age sixty-seven.

Were there other great Irish American boxers?

Many, early on. Several, later. Few, today.

Two to remember had their most famous fights against each other.

Celia Dempsey of Manassa, Colorado, was, as it happened, reading an autobiography of John L. Sullivan as she waited to give birth to a child in the summer of 1895. **William Harrison "Jack" Dempsey** must have been soaking in the legend prenatally through osmosis.

The Manassa Mauler was the Babe Ruth of boxing (which is why we didn't call Sullivan that). In the Roaring Twenties, America was awash with glittering sports stars, raking in the dough in the sportsbiz Sullivan had created. Ruth was forcing the Yankees to build a stadium; Knute Rockne was transforming football with the Four Horsemen and other Fightin' Irish at Notre Dame; Red Grange was actually being paid to play the gridiron game; Bobby Jones was elevating golf as Arnold Palmer, Jack Nicklaus, and Tiger Woods later would do; Bill Tilden and Helen Wills Moody were stylishly dominating tennis; Johnny Weissmuller was swimming to Olympic gold; Man o' War was establishing himself as the safest bet in the land, and the exotic Dempsey—part Scotch-Irish, part Native American, a bit Jewish—was handsomely the king of the ring. He had defeated Jess Willard with dispatch to take the heavyweight crown in 1919—knocked him down seven times in the first round for starters, then finished him in three. It was said that no one, not even Sullivan, had ever thrown a punch as hard as Dempsey could throw a punch. He defended his title six times in the next seven years, and won them all, including the first $5 million bouts (one, in New Jersey in 1921, drew a crowd of eighty thousand; another at the Polo Grounds in New York attracted ninety thousand).

In 1926, 120,000 crammed into Sesquicentennial Stadium in Philadelphia to watch Dempsey take on New Yorker **Gene Tunney.** The ex-marine beat the Mauler in a ten-round decision. In their hotel room Dempsey's wife was horrified by Jack's beaten face. Dempsey smiled and said, "Honey, I forgot to duck." As Red Smith wrote later: "From that day on, the gallant loser was a folk hero whose fame never diminished."

Dempsey went away, KO'd **Jack Sharkey** to earn another shot, and traveled to Chicago's Soldier Field where 150,000 awaited the rematch (boxing's first $2 million gate). Dempsey nailed Tunney in the seventh round. The referee told him to go to the neutral corner. The rule was new, and Dempsey ignored it. The ref forced him, and five seconds went by. Tunney thus got fifteen seconds—not ten—to recover, and he needed it. He came back and won the "Long Count Fight" in another decision.

"Hiya pal" was Dempsey's calling card to everyone he met in his long life (he lived until 1983). Red Smith recalled a fellow sportswriter's opinion: "Grantland Rice said Dempsey was perhaps the finest gentleman, in the literal sense of gentle man, he had met in half a century of writing sports; Dempsey never knowingly hurt anyone except in the line of business."

Dempsey and Tunney were raised in an era when big, strong descendants of Irish immigrants all wanted to be John L. Sullivan. Later athletes—like **Jimmy McLarnin,** who won the welterweight title in 1933; like **Bill Conn,** the champ of the forties; like **Jerry Quarry,** who got some shots at the heavyweight title but never won it in the era of Ali and Frazier—had been raised to believe that they might be Ruth or Tilden or Jones or Grange. Or, indeed, Henry Ford or Al Smith or Red Smith. New avenues were opening to them in America.

The Irish were there when boxing was one of few options. They were there to help make boxing huge. It's still huge, but Irish Americans have largely departed the game.

What other games did Irish Americans play, back then?

Baseball, they loved baseball. They adopted this variation on cricket as their own and helped to form the character and style of what was, in the century following the Civil War, indisputably America's national pastime.

Even before that war, Irish were playing baseball in New York, New Jersey, and in places as remote as Iowa. (A period box score for a six-game series between Dubuque and Davenport shows a preponderance of Irish surnames. Charles Comiskey, of whom we'll learn more, was catching for Dubuque.)

By 1870 the game whose rules had been codified by descendants of English cricketeers—let's not get into the Doubleday/Cartwright who-invented-what debate; it's unimportant here—had spread well beyond its WASP origins. There were many professional baseball teams representing cities large and small, and American boys from the inner city—immigrants, sons of immigrants—could begin to see a career path forming. Most of the Irish who found their way onto the rosters of these pro clubs were not, indeed, Irish born. Ireland native **Edward Duffy** was a shortstop with Chicago in 1871 and, by 1876, catcher **Fergy Malone** was with Philadelphia and **Tommy Bond** was with Hartford. (In Boston a few seasons later, Bond became known as one of the very first pitchers to throw overhand and to master a curveball.) **Anthony Mullane** of Cork played in the 1880s, and **John "Dirty" Doyle** was a National League infielder in the 1890s. **Jimmy Archer** of Dublin caught for Pittsburgh and Chicago in the early years of the twentieth century. But it wasn't the same as with the boxers, since baseball wasn't indigenous to the Emerald Isle. The game had to be learned upon arrival if an Irishman was to have a chance.

Not so for the sons of immigrants. In the chapter "The Ballpark as Melting Pot" from *Diamonds in the Rough*, an exemplary book on the early days of baseball, writers Joel Zoss and John Bowman asserted, "The Irish ballplayers of the first decades were almost all American-born—the O'Briens who played for the Knickerbockers, the famous Peter O'Brien and Dickey Pierce of the Atlantics, and countless others with names that might not jump out as Irish but who were undoubtedly Roman Catholic Irish-Americans. The trouble with this version of baseball as an assimilator of a sequence of ethnic groups is that we simply do not know enough about most of these men—just who both parents were, how they were raised as boys, which group they identified with. A man could have an Irish name and parentage yet not be a Roman Catholic. Or be born in England, like Marty Hogan, and probably regard himself as Irish. Still, Irish Americans were an increasing presence in the large cities of the Northeast where baseball was also definitely on the rise, the same cities where signs that read 'Irish Need Not Apply' were appearing. Some of the many editorials criticizing baseball for harboring rowdies and worse were probably thinly veiled attacks on Irish-Americans; there was an old Puritan tradition of condemning public entertainments and this melded nicely with many Americans' distaste for the new urban immigrants. A *New York Times* editorial on September 3, 1897, went so far as to refer to baseball players as 'degenerates.' " So, at this time, Irish American baseball players were thought of as no better than Irish American boxers; the pastime was yet a low-class game.

And, as Zoss and Bowman indicate, a largely urban one—which may surprise you. In an interview for our book, the noted sportswriter Robert W. Creamer, author of the definitive biographies of Babe Ruth and Casey Stengel among several other books, shed some light on this: "Baseball's always thought of as being out in the cow pastures, with farmboys tossing the ball. But early on it was a city game. There were scores of games, amateur and professional, in any given week in New York or in Baltimore. And from the 1880s through the early 1900s, the Irish were really the dominant force. I don't want to say too much about the relationship between being poor and playing a lot of sports, but certainly it's there—perhaps because jobs were unavailable, perhaps because the other classes simply wouldn't engage in these games in order to protect their reputations. So the Irish flocked to baseball, which meant they didn't have to flock far if they were living in the urban slums. You could always get a game."

By 1890 at least one-third of major leaguers were Irish American; by 1915 eleven of sixteen big-league managers were Irish American. More important from sociological and Irish American perspectives, baseball was vying, in these decades, with the upper-class, thoroughly English, bat-and-ball sport of cricket for the hearts and minds of American men. That this new game, so heavily populated by Irish Americans, succeeded in driving cricket straight back to England stands not only as a nifty bit of revenge, but as a comment on the power of numbers, even if among the proletariat, in a democracy such as the United States. The Irish were a force in all things from politics to other forms of games-playing by the turn of the century.

One footnote to all this: Later on, Chicagoan **Albert Spalding** formed the Special Baseball Commission to investigate the origins of America's game, and it was this group that came up with the Abner Doubleday–Cooperstown story, a fiction that has long since been discredited (baseball was rampant well before Doubleday picked up a ball). Doubleday, with his Civil War pedigree, lent to the game an All-American image. Nowhere was British cricket cited in the commission's history, though certainly cricket is thickly entwined with baseball's roots. The name of Spalding's secretary, and the man largely responsible for guiding the commission away from English antecedents, was **James E. Sullivan**.

Who were some famous Irish American baseball stars?

The first great one, and one of the greatest ever, was **Michael J. "King" Kelly,** son of an immigrant papermaker from Troy, New York. "There have been a few larger-than-life characters in baseball," wrote Daniel Okrent and Steve Wulf in their *Oxford Book of Baseball Anecdotes*, "but King Kelly was the first." He was a catcher—the early Irish seem to have a lot of backstops among them—of power and consistency. In 1884 he hit .384 with twelve homers, quite a total in the dead-ball era. Kelly was the first catcher to use signs to call a pitch, and he invented the hit-and-run play. But Kelly became most famous for his sliding; the pop song "Slide, Kelly, Slide" was a major hit. Once, after the umpire Honest John Kelly called him out after a slide at home plate, King reached under and pulled out the ball he had knocked from the catcher's mitt. "John," he said, "if I'm out, what's this?"

King was an earlier version of Ty Cobb: He would trip runners with his catcher's mask. Off the field, he was an earlier Babe Ruth: Asked if he drank while playing baseball, King answered, "It depends on the length of the game." He was a dandy, according to a newspaper account of the day, "his cane a-twirling as though he were the entire population, his Ascot held by a giant jewel, his patent leather shoes as sharply pointed as Italian dirks."

When Spalding sold Kelly from Chicago to Boston in 1887—

"The Ten Thousand Dollar Beauty"—the Windy City was outraged; Clarence Darrow wrote a protesting letter to the newspapers. Kelly performed well for Boston, for a while. The nights of carousing were catching up with him by the time he was sold to New York in 1893. When he skipped a game to go to the track, he was fired. He started performing in burlesque with the London Gaiety Girls, reciting Ernest Lawrence Thayer's poem "Casey at the Bat" nightly. In 1894 he caught pneumonia, and on November 5 he whispered, "This is my last slide." The King was dead.

Ned Hanlon had already been a fine centerfielder with Detroit and Pittsburgh when he was brought aboard to manage Baltimore in 1892. By 1894 Hanlon had built a club of which seven of nine starters would ultimately make the Hall of Fame. Okrent and Wulf wrote: "Hanlon's Orioles quickly became mythic. 'Scrappy' would be the polite way to describe the way the Orioles played, but 'dirty' would be more accurate. With [third baseman John] McGraw showing the way, they would run into opposing first basemen, trip baserunners, and jostle the catcher when he was trying to make a throw. They even slipped their own fans dead balls to throw back onto the field in place of the foul balls that were supposed to be returned to the umpire." All to profitable effect: Hanlon's O's won back-to-back-to-back National League pennants in the 1890s, and two Temple Cups, awarded to the winner of a play-off between the first- and second-place teams.

John Joseph "Mugsy" McGraw, Hanlon's third-sacker and protégé, was the eldest of nine children in an Irish American family from a tiny village in upstate New York named Truxton. He was a small man who made up in quickness and aggressiveness what he lacked in size and strength. As we've seen, he starred for Baltimore on the field, but it was as manager of the New York Giants, a job he assumed on July 19, 1902, at age twenty-nine, that the Little Napoleon left a mark upon the game as great as anyone's this side of Ruth or Jackie Robinson. On July 19, 1927, all of New York would celebrate the twenty-fifth anniversary of McGraw's arrival.

McGraw brought with him from Baltimore some scrappy players he liked, brought in others from elsewhere, and was blessed with the arrival from Bucknell University of the great pitcher **Christy Mathewson.** In 1903 the club finished second, in 1904 it won 106 games and finished first. The next year the Giants mowed down **Connie Mack**'s Athletics in the nascent World Series, and in the next. . . . Well, suffice to say that when the tallying was done John

McGraw would have led the way to ten championship seasons in the National League and three World Series crowns (including two in the twenties over Babe Ruth's Yankees).

McGraw, ill, retired in 1932 and died in 1934. His funeral was held at Saint Pat's, and he was buried in Baltimore. His legacy is felt not only in America but throughout the world, for he had been a dedicated ambassador of the game. In 1913 he and Charles Comiskey, owner of the Chicago White Sox, had led an off-season world tour traveling west through Japan, China, Australia, Egypt, Italy, and France, playing baseball wherever they went. Their last game was staged before the king of England and thirty-five thousand other Brits in a London stadium: a nice audience for two brash Irish Americans.

In *The New York Times Book of Sports Legends*, Joseph J. Vecchione wrote, "Connie Mack, Joe McCarthy, and Casey Stengel are the only other leaders whose accomplishments are in any way comparable with those of the fiery McGraw." We'll tackle the first two, since they were Irish Americans.

Cornelius McGillicuddy was born in East Brookfield, Massachusetts, in 1862, and learned to play baseball while working in a shoe factory to support his mother, a widow. He was playing as a pro—another catcher!—in Connecticut in 1884. (His name was shortened so it would fit in the box scores of the day.) A decade later he took the helm of the Pittsburgh team and began what would become baseball's longest-ever managerial career. If McGraw reinvented the way the game was played, Mack revolutionized the way teams were built. He revered youth and was constantly tearing down championship clubs and constructing new ones. He took over the Philadelphia Athletics in 1901 and guided the club until 1950, winning nine American League pennants and five world championships along the way. Also along the way, in 1937, Mack became one of the original thirteen enshrined in the Baseball Hall of Fame. His bust in Cooperstown is entitled "Mr. Baseball." Enough said.

Connie Mack died in 1956; he was ninety-three.

Joe McCarthy was, like John McGraw, a stocky Irish American from New York state—McCarthy hailed from Buffalo—and was a martinet as a manager. Not that he needed to be, for his Yankee clubs of the 1930s and 1940s were blessed with Ruth, Lou Gehrig, and the other members of Murderers' Row. McCarthy had nowhere near the impact on the game that McGraw and Mack did, but he knew how to win, and win he did.

Charles A. Comiskey was the son of a Famine immigrant who'd come across in 1848 and had become a ward boss in Chicago. Charles apprenticed to be a plumber, but that didn't take; by 1875, at seventeen, he was playing third base for Milwaukee. He was an organizer of the American League, and owner of the Chicago White Sox until his death in 1931. Earlier, we celebrated McGraw and Comiskey's efforts to spread baseball throughout the world. It must be said that an uglier aspect of the men's personalities was evident in their own country. In 1901, when McGraw was trying to sneak a black ballplayer named Grant into a spring-training game by giving him the name Tokohama and passing him off as an Indian, Comiskey, then with the White Sox, railed, "Somebody told me that the Cherokee of McGraw's is really Grant, the crack Negro second baseman from Cincinnati, fixed up with war paint and a bunch of feathers." Grant did not play. Now, lest you think of McGraw as an enlightened sort—a Branch Rickey ahead of his time—consider that, thirty-two years later, Jimmy Powers of the *New York Daily News* conducted a poll of major league luminaries on the desirability of integrating baseball. Only one was against. McGraw.

In modern baseball there have been greats with Irish surnames—**Mike Flanagan** of the Orioles won the Cy Young Awards in the 1979; the greatest strikeout and no-hitter pitcher of all time is the Texan **Nolan Ryan;** the new home run champ is big, red-haired **Mark McGwire**—but the immense contribution of the Irish to baseball ended decades ago. Here are just a few more names from past eras, backtracking now toward the beginning: **George "Mickey" Cochrane** was one of the game's very best—what else?—catchers. **Joseph Jerome "Iron Man" McGinnity** was a fine pitcher who debuted as a pro in 1893 and lasted as one for thirty-two years. Five times in his career Iron Man pitched both ends of a double-header. In 1903 he pitched 434 innings, a National League record that will never be broken.

And then there were the **Delahantys.** "We were given bats instead of rattles," said Ed, and it may have been true: He and all four of his brothers made it from their Cleveland upbringing to the major leagues. In the 1890s Ed batted at or near .400 in seven different seasons. Frank, Jim, Joe, and Tom were good, but Ed was great. Sadly, like so many players of the time—kids from the lower classes, suddenly with money—Delahanty was a drinker. One night in 1903 he was aboard a train bound for Buffalo and he had too many whiskies. He started brandishing a razor and threatening the other passengers. The conductor threw him off the train, which disappeared across a bridge. Delahanty stumbled after it, pushing aside a watchman who tried to warn him that the span had just gone up to let a boat pass beneath. Delahanty plunged into the Niagara River, and over the falls.

Who was Lefty O'Doul?

A native San Franciscan who didn't reach the majors until he was thirty-one, **Lefty O'Doul** gained fame for a couple of sensational seasons—one in which he led the National League in batting and registered a then-record 254 hits—and also for one great crack. Asked years later what O'Doul's contemporary, Ty Cobb, would hit nowadays, O'Doul replied, "Oh, about the same as Willie Mays, maybe .340, something like that." The fellow who'd asked the question was surprised; O'Doul was always saying ballplayers were better in his day. And now he was saying Ty Cobb, who hit over .400 many a time, would only manage .340? What gives?

"Well," O'Doul said, "you have to take into consideration the man is now seventy-three years old."

How do two Irish American catchers figure in the Babe Ruth story?

Bob O'Farrell was the catcher who threw out Babe Ruth stealing to end the World Series in which the mighty Yankees fell to the surprising Cardinals. Here's how it happened:

It was the seventh game and, with three innings to play, Cardinals manager Rogers Hornsby sent Grover Cleveland Alexander in as his pitcher to protect a one-run lead. Now, Alexander, thirty-nine years old, had pitched the previous day (he'd won) and then, as was his habit, he'd gotten ferociously drunk. In the ultimate game, Alexander took the mound with the bases loaded and told his catcher, "no warm-up pitches." He struck out the great Tommy Lazzeri.

Alexander protected the 3–2 lead through the ninth when, with two out, he walked Ruth. Astonishingly, Ruth—the potential tying run in the last inning of the last game of the World Series—took off for second. O'Farrell nailed him. A couple of years later O'Farrell bumped into Babe and asked why he'd run. The Bambino said the way Alexander was pitching, the Yanks couldn't have moved him from first to home anyway.

Alexander's heroics were commemorated in the biopic *The Winning Team*. In it, the Irish American actor Ronald Reagan portrayed Alexander.

At the other end of Ruth's career, **Tom Padden** was the catcher who was largely responsible for Babe's 714th, and last, home run. Here's how it happened:

It was 1935 and Ruth was finishing his career as player-manager of the Boston Braves. They were visiting Pittsburgh. Catching for the Pirates was Padden, whose father Mike had emigrated from County Mayo to Manchester, New Hampshire, where young Tommy had learned to play (and where that Cy Young winner Flanagan would learn to play, a few decades later).

In his last at bat, the Bambino was struggling. Tommy Padden went to the mound. Guy Bush, Pittsburgh's pitcher, said, "I'm going to strike the big monkey out!" To which Padden replied, "They didn't come here to see you pitch or me catch. Give him something he can hit."

On the way back to the plate Tommy nodded to Babe, and the next pitch was down the middle. Ruth hit it completely out of Forbes Field, something that had never been done in twenty-six seasons of baseball there. Ruth's total of 714 career home runs stood as the "unbreakable" record until Hank Aaron broke it in 1974.

Who were Johnny O'Hara and Babe O'Rourke?

One was a World War II–era baseball broadcaster, the other was a stadium announcer at the same time. **Johnny O'Hara** used to call the St. Louis games over the air alongside Dizzy Dean, while **Babe O'Rourke** worked at Shibe Park in Philadelphia. Each was involved in an odd incident during the war.

Broadcasters were forbidden, at the time, from mentioning weather conditions to the audience lest they tip off enemy bombers. So one day during an hour-long rain delay, O'Hara and Dizz just chatted. Finally, O'Hara recalled later, they simply ran out of things to say. Exasperated, Dizzy announced this much: "If you folks don't know what's holdin' up this game, just stick your heads out the window."

O'Rourke was working a night game when the lights went off at Shibe; blackouts were routinely practiced during the war years. O'Rourke noticed the stands still aglow, and said patriotically over the loudspeaker: "You gentlemen who are lighting cigarettes and cigars, if you are Americans, you won't do it."

Who was "Casey," of the bat?

The man behind Casey was an old-school Yankee, **Ernest Lawrence Thayer,** classmate of William Randolph Hearst and George Santayana at Harvard, heir to the family mills in Lawrence, Massachusetts. Hearst had hired Thayer for his *San Francisco Examiner* after they'd left Harvard, and one slow morning the humor columnist had tossed off "Casey at the Bat, A Ballad of the Republic Sung in the Year 1888" in a few hours. The poem might have faded from view had not the actor William DeWolf Hopper taken it up as a staple in his stage show. "As the house, after a moment of startled silence, grasped the anticlimactic denouement, it shouted with glee," Hopper wrote in his autobiography, and he hit upon the point precisely: Because Casey strikes out, the poem has power. Pride hath gone before a fall. It's an epic thing.

Of course, Casey was bound to strike out—Thayer wouldn't have had it any other way. For while Tim Casey, a Boston shortstop of the era, claimed to be Casey, and while some folks said that Philadelphia's Daniel Michael Casey was a likely Casey, there *was* a real Casey, and he was no friend of Thayer's.

The poet had wanted to satirize not just the bustling, burgeoning world of nineteenth-century baseball, but the typical "big Irishman" athlete or laborer of the day. He recalled one **Daniel Henry Casey,** a classmate at Worcester Classical High back in 1881. Six-foot-two and more than two hundred pounds, Casey was Worcester's John L. Sullivan. Once, when Thayer had chided Casey in the school paper, Casey had threatened to knock the young poet's block off. When Thayer needed a model for a strong and headstrong athlete, he had a ready one.

D. H. Casey never played baseball, as far as we know. He became a teacher, was principal of Grafton Junior School in Worcester, and died in 1915. Yet he is immortal.

What about Irish American Olympians?

There have been many, most of them in the summer games. But one extraordinary athlete whose name was **Edward Eagan** remains the only person in the world to win a gold medal in both the summer and winter games.

Eagan was an extraordinary individual, and not only as an athlete. He was born into a poor family in Denver but applied himself and eventually was educated at Yale, Harvard Law School, and Oxford. His hero was Frank Merriwell, the athletic idol of the dime novels who, as we know, never existed. "To this day I have never used tobacco, because Frank didn't," Eagan wrote in 1932. "My first glass of wine, which I do not care for, was taken under social compunction in Europe. Frank never drank." As pleasant and mild a man as Eagan was, his sport was the old Irish American standby, boxing. He won the gold medal in the light-heavyweight division at the Antwerp Games in 1920. At the 1932 winter games in Lake Placid, New York, he was a rider aboard Billy Fiske's four-man bobsled that took the gold. Eagan applied himself as diligently to the law as he had to everything else in his life and became a success. Frank would have been proud.

There had been Irish American champions before Eagan, most of of them stars of track and field, and most of these stars of the field events.

Thomas Burke of Boston, a quarter-mile specialist, won both the 100-meter and 400-meter dashes at the very first modern Olympics in Athens in 1896, and **James Brendan Connolly** of South Boston won that year's triple jump. Burke became a successful lawyer and writer; he died in 1929 at age fifty-three.

Connolly had come from a poor family, but was self-educated and eventually attended Harvard. He was the national champion in his specialty when he read that the ancient games were being revived in Athens by the French Baron Pierre de Coubertin. He asked for a leave from school, and when Harvard refused, Connolly dropped out.

His wallet was stolen during the two-week voyage to Europe. At two in the afternoon of April 6, the modern games commenced. Connolly jumped last in the triple jump and the pit-raker said to him, "There's nobody within a yard of you." James Connolly thus became the first Olympic champion since Barasdates, an Armenian boxer who had closed the ancient Games with a win in A.D. 369.

Connolly won the silver medal in the triple jump at the Paris Olympics of 1900, finishing behind countryman Meyer Prinstein. Connolly, too, like his teammate and fellow Bostonian Burke, became a writer—of twenty-five novels, two hundred short stories, and volumes of lucid war correspondence. Harvard offered him an honorary degree, and he turned the school down. He died, at eighty-seven, in 1957.

John Flanagan, a New York cop born in Ireland, won the hammer throw at the 1900, 1904, and 1908 Olympics. **Martin Sheriden,** an Irish-born cop, won five gold medals and four silver in three Olympics beginning in 1904, successfully defending his discus title twice, adding a shot put crown, and a win in the Greek-style discus, which is no longer contested. **Matt McGrath,** an Irish American cop, threw the hammer fifteen feet farther than the second place finisher at the 1912 Stockholm games, and **Pat Ryan,** an immigrant—he'd arrived in 1910—threw the hammer to a world record in 1920 in Antwerp that would last for twenty-five years. These strong boys owe a great debt to **William Muldoon,** a big, tough Irish American character who went from being a New York bouncer to being a New York longshoreman to being a New York cabbie to, in 1876, being a New York policeman. Muldoon's sport was wrestling—he once wrestled Clarence Whistler for eight hours without a decision—but he founded the Police Athletic Association which, along with the legendary Irish American Athletic Club, was a breeding ground for such as Flanagan, Sheriden, and McGrath. " 'The Irish Whales' they were called," remembered Robert Creamer. "They were these captains on the police force, but amazingly rowdy. Matt McGrath was getting drunk and raising hell when he wasn't patrolling or winning medals. Some of those guys competed into their fifties. An amazing bunch!"

Frederick Kelly led a U.S. sweep of the 110-meter hurdles at Stockholm in 1912, and **Daniel Kinsey** won the race eight years later in Paris when the South African, Sydney Atkinson, clipped the last hurdle and fell. **Jack Kelly, Sr.,** whom we met in the last chapter as Grace Kelly's dad, won the gold medal in the single sculls at Antwerp in 1920. In 1928 **Helen Meany** became the first Irish American woman to win a gold medal by leading a U.S. sweep in springboard diving at Amsterdam.

In 1932 little **Thomas "Eddie" Tolan** won the 100- and 200-meter dashes at the first Los Angeles games. The five-foot-seven speedster had been America's dominant sprinter since 1929, but had recently been dethroned by Ralph Metcalfe. At the Olympic trials Metcalfe had beat Tolan at both distances. In the final of the 100 at L.A., Metcalfe caught Tolan at eighty meters and the two finished in a dead heat for a new Olympic record (10.3 seconds); several hours later, the photo-finish gave Tolan the gold. The following day Tolan set another Olympic record in the 200 (21.2 seconds), with Metcalfe finishing third. At those same Los Angeles games, **Edward Flynn** won the welterweight boxing class. After the Olympics he turned pro and earned enough money to finance his dental education, then opened a dentistry in New Orleans.

In a throwback to the great throwers, **Parry O'Brien,** a student at the University of Southern California—*not* a New York cop—won the shot put at the 1952 Olympics in Helsinki, then successfully defended his crown four years later in Melbourne, recording the five best puts of the competition. O'Brien revolutionized his specialty by starting with his back to the field, building all the momentum he could in the throwing circle. Meanwhile, O'Brien's dominance at the 1952 and 1956 games was trumped by that of **Pat McCormack**—also from southern California, a native of Long Beach. She won both women's diving contests, the springboard and the platform, at both Olympics. In 1956 she gave birth to a son only eight months before climbing the ladder at Melbourne. Think of her this way: She was an earlier, female version of Greg Louganis, and perhaps the best woman diver ever.

At those 1956 Olympics a third Irish American, **Harold Connolly,** prevailed in his competition, the hammer throw. But he prevailed in another arena as well, and this caused a much larger stir. Connolly fell in love in the Olympic Village with Czechoslovakian discus champion Olga Fikotova, and she with him. It was an impossibility, of course, the Cold War being in high fever. But the two strong and strong-willed youngsters simply would not be denied, and in a Romeo and Juliet story with international political ramifications, they wed—in a civil ceremony in Prague's Wenceslas Square before forty thousand well-wishers. (There were two subsequent, smaller ceremonies, one Catholic and one Protestant.) They settled in the United States and kept training; Harold competed in three more Olympics and Olga in four more. They divorced in 1973—some fairy tales do end unhappily—and Connolly married fellow U.S. Olympian Pat Daniels.

From the 1960s onward, the idea of Irish American Olympians—like that of Irish Americans—begins to blur. A lot of Irish blood has made it to the podium as the "Star-Spangled Banner" has played. For instance, there were Irish descendants on that miraculous 1980 gold-medal ice hockey team in Lake Placid; and Mary Meagher, Michael O'Brien, and Rick Carey won five gold medals among them—and that's just the swim team, and that's just in one Olympics, the 1984 games in Los Angeles.

But in the history of the games no Irish American had won the title of Best Athlete in the World, a title reserved for the winner of the decathlon, until **Bill Toomey** did it in 1968. Toomey, a twenty-nine-year-old English teacher from California, had overcome everything—hepatitis, mononucleosis, a broken kneecap, you name it—before he toed the line for the ten-event competition—pole-vaulting, discus throwing, mile running, dashing, you name it—in Mexico City. After two days of competing, he was the champion, with a new Olympic record. And twenty-eight years later, in Atlanta, he was followed as Greatest Athlete by a man named **Dan O'Brien,** who had more American Indian blood in him than Irish, but who looked like a perfect symbol of the melting pot as he accepted his medal.

An Atlanta postscript: The winningest swimmer in 1996 was a massively strong red-haired Irish woman named **Michelle Smith.** The fact that she had never swum so fast before nor would do so after, led to widespread suspicion that she had taken steroids. She did not test positive for drugs, and so took home to Ireland her several medals and newfound fame. Either Ireland's greatest-ever swimmer had gotten away with something, or she had been done dirty, for you couldn't mention Michelle Smith's name in swimming circles without eyebrows being raised. In 1998 she was found to have adulterated the sample she gave in a surprise test and was banned from international competition for four years. She denied the charges, and indicated she would appeal.

Welcome to the twenty-first century.

So neither Johnny Kelley won the Olympic marathon?

Neither came close, though John the Elder finished the race in both the 1936 and 1948 Olympics, the latter at forty-two years old.

But each Kelley did win the oldest and most famous annually run footrace, a race only a year younger than the modern Olympic contest, an event dripping in Green. We speak, of course, of the Boston Marathon, contested on the Monday called Patriots Day in Massachusetts, the Monday closest to April 19.

The first B.A.A. Marathon was won in 1897 by New York City's **John J. McDermott,** the second by the unfortunately named **Ronald**

McDonald of Cambridge, Massachusetts. Other early winners included a Caffrey, a Ford, a Morrisey, a Ryan, a Duffy—Sligo-born Jim Duffy, down from Ontario—a Kennedy, and a Henigan. But we'd like to scoot ahead to 1935 and the first of two wins by **John A. Kelley** of Arlington, Massachusetts.

He first tried the big race in 1928. He didn't know then that he'd try it fifty more times, and that he'd still be running a piece of it each April even as the millennium neared. He would finish in the top ten an astonishing nineteen times, and he would come in a frustrating second no fewer than seven times. "I love running," he said once. "It's free expression. I reaffirm myself. If I don't run for two or three days I feel as if something's been stolen from me."

Kelley, even in his prime, was a slight man and would often run out of gas in the late stages of the race—after the famous Heartbreak Hills leading out of Wellesley. But in 1935 he never wilted, even after he got sick near the end, and in 1945 the soldier-boy Kelley blew away the field. The later years, when he was no longer a challenger, were if anything more special. He became an institution, and the throngs waited to cheer him as he came through, nobody leaving the curbside until Johnny Kelley had passed. Kelley, who lived and ran on Cape Cod in his seniority, thought he knew the reason for his popularity, and shared it with Joe Falls for his 1977 book on the history of Boston's marathon: "The people are all so beautiful. I think I know why they like me. I'm local. That's number one. And it's my age. People can identify with me—people in their forties, fifties and sixties. And I'm Irish, and why kid about it: Boston is primarily an Irish city."

By the time he talked with Falls he was known to many as "John Kelley the Elder." John the Younger was the very next American to win the race after 1945, breaking a string of eleven straight wins by foreign runners in 1957. He set a course record, too: two hours, twenty minutes, five seconds for the 26.2 miles. Boston Celtics team owner Walter Brown was so pleased with the American victory, he gave Kelley a gold watch.

And, no, John A. Kelley of Massachusetts and **John J. Kelley** of Groton, Connecticut, were in no way related.

A final word and lament about the Boston Marathon: Another of the many Irish Americans whose names are linked to the race is Tommy Leonard. He ran it a few times, though God knows he was never close to the front. His distinction: He was the amiable publican at the Eliot Lounge in Boston's Eliot Hotel which, during the

1970s and 1980s, was the unofficial headquarters for the marathon during running's boom years. Tommy was the race's biggest booster, and when the elite hit town for the race, they'd head straight for the Eliot.

The lament is: The bar is shuttered.

When did the Irish take up the country club sports?

When they were allowed past the gates of the country clubs in America—either to work or to play.

In Ireland, at least one sport that we consider clubby is—or, at least, has been historically—a game of the proletariat. If you seek out golf's great links of Lahinch, Ballybunion, and Sligo (and in the North, County Down and Portrush), you'll be surprised to find them situated in the midst of villages. Over there, golf is—or was—a people's game. It was close at hand to the mills and shops, and a worker could get in a quick twelve or six before heading home, or even at lunchtime. The sportsmen would come out lively when the whistle blew, carrying their Sunday bags. (There are still no carts.) Even today, they fairly scurry around the course. There is none of the American habit of studying the green from six varied angles, or switching clubs again and again before swinging. The Irish whack the ball, trod on, then whack it again, trod on. They seem to pause but once in their round. That's at the ninth hole, where there's a wee hut. The grizzled gent at the hut has a few specialties to offer, but if it's a true Irish golf day—a day with a wind that's more than a breeze, and a spring rain slanting in sideways—then he'll push one particular restorative. It's a hot whiskey, lemon, and clove concoction. It's smooth and bracing. All Irish golfers are bold on the tenth tee.

But that's over there. Over here, golf has always been a game of the elite social classes. And it has always been tougher for minority ethnic groups to rise in a sport before they rise in society. Tiger Woods's success is all the more remarkable because he's mixed race; a half-century ago he wouldn't have been allowed on most of America's private courses, and even today many clubs have policies against blacks, other minorities, and women. Back at the turn of the century it would have been clear that, at most American clubs, people with Irish surnames need not apply.

Which makes it all the more delicious when a champion slips through the cracks, as did **Johnny McDermott** in 1911, becoming the first native-born American to win the U.S. Open. He was born in

Philadelphia in 1891 and learned the game as a caddy. In his first try at the Open, in 1909, he finished forty-eighth, but vowed to better himself. The next year he tied for first but lost in a play-off, and the year after that he tied for first again and won the play-off. In 1912 he won outright, proving emphatically that American golfers could hold their own with the English and Scottish. McDermott never won another national title, and in fact fell victim to mental illness not long after his successful defense. Though he lived until 1971, he had departed as a competitive golfer by 1915. But it was he who had set a standard for Americans and had shown the way: You didn't have to be a country clubber to be a champion.

Ben Hogan, whose ancestors were Irish, followed McDemott's lead with precision. Hogan, who with Bobby Jones and Jack Nicklaus, is considered one of the three greatest golfers of the century (yours will be the twenty-*first* century, Tiger), also came up by way of the caddyshack. He was born in the salubriously named Texas town of Dublin in 1912, even as McDermott was defending. He, like McDermott, was a small man, and he, like McDermott, was intensely driven. He was a no-nonsense golfer, a perfectionist and a fierce competitor. He won the Masters, the PGA and the Open in 1948, then, in 1949, he was involved in a terrible car accident that nearly killed him; had he not thrown himself across his wife's body to protect her, he would have been impaled by the steering column. There were fears that his career was done, but after rehabilitation Hogan asked for admittance to the 1950 Los Angeles Open as "an experiment" to see if he could hold up over seventy-two holes. He held up; he tied with **Sam Snead,** another American golfer with Irish blood. Months later he won his second of four U.S. Opens. In 1953 he added the British crown to his bag, making him one of only four (with Gene Sarazen, Gary Player, and Jack Nicklaus) to win all four of the world's major tournaments in a career, and one of a different set of four (with Bobby Jones, Sarazen, and Lee Trevino) to win the British and U.S. titles in the same summer. Hogan was among the most courageous, tenacious, and tough golfers of all time. He died in 1997.

Another country club game is tennis. It is instructive that it was the 1970s before two Irish American men came to dominate the game. **Jimmy Connors**'s mother, Gloria, was a strong woman from Illinois who had the money to buy her child lessons and to nurture him and his game through the junior ranks. **John McEnroe**'s father was a successful lawyer from Douglaston, Queens, New York, who also had the wherewithal to support the sporting pastime of his sons, John and Patrick. McEnroe and Connors had the talent, to be sure, but whether the opportunity would have been there for them a half-century earlier is questionable.

Is there anything to be said about the fact that in the era of McEnroe and Connors, their boorish on-court behavior spurred a general erosion in sportsmanship throughout this gentleman's game? Probably. Something about Irish tempers, or was it just an inevitable postmodern phenomenon linked to the decline of Western civilization at large? Whatever . . . It remains at least interesting that two Irish American athletes led the charge toward petulance, disregard for authority, and regular tantrum-throwing among professional and amateur athletes worldwide. The words McEnroe once used to an umpire in the Australian Open will not be reprinted here, but we would suggest that you can plot a chronology from what happened in tennis in the late 1970s and 1980s to the 1997 incident in San Francisco wherein Latrell Sprewell of basketball's Golden State Warriors found himself with his hands around a coach's throat. Sprewell's sentence for threatening mayhem on his coach was later lessened by an arbitrator, and that also says something about how standards have changed. We do not blame the whole situation on McEnroe and Connors. We remember Ilie Nastase, too.

Connors has always made little of his Irishness, McEnroe much. McEnroe also has made much of his Americanism, and indeed his record of service in Davis Cup campaigns is exemplary. Once, when America played Ireland in a Davis Cup tie in Dublin, McEnroe celebrated the event as a homecoming akin to those of JFK, Reagan, and Clinton.

Now, we do not mean to imply the matches *ended* in a tie. A Davis Cup competition is called "a tie." The outcome was: America whomped 'em. Irish tennis isn't very good.

Any other games players?

Plenty. An Irish American sporting miscellany would have to include, on its front end, **Michael Phelan,** who became America's first billiards champion in 1859 and whose concerns included the manufacture of "Phelan's Improved Billiards Tables and Combination Cushions" and the running of an emporium, Phelan's Magnificent Billiard Rooms, at Broadway and Tenth Street in Manhattan. Phelan, a fervent Irish nationalist, once visited Ireland ostensibly to play exhibitions but in fact to meet rebels.

On the far end of the sporting continuum—as outdoor as Phelan was in—would be **Al McClane,** the late, great Irish American sportsman and writer. As Arnold Gingrich wrote in *The Joys of Trout,* "Just as there were no tenors besides Caruso . . . to me, in my time, there were no anglers besides McClane."

TWELVE

The Road Rises: Irish Americanism in the Twentieth Century

What does "shanty Irish" mean?

What does "lace curtain Irish" mean?

What was the difference between the Irish Americans of 1800 and those of 1900?

Who was William Russell Grace?

Who was Henry Ford?

Who was Andrew W. Mellon?

Who was John R. Gregg?

Who were Howard R. Hughes and William Randolph Hearst?

Who was "honest" John Kelly?

Was Richard Nixon Irish?

Where was the largest political impact of Irish American activists felt?

Speaking of workers—Didn't Irish workers build Titanic?

Who were some other Irish American heroes of the twentieth century?

What does "shanty Irish" mean?

The term first described Famine immigrants who lived in the shanty towns of Seneca Village in northern New York City. This was a well-established minority community where Irish immigrants one step removed from the Five Points, lived side by side with German immigrants and black Americans, all of them occupying one- or two-story shanties surrounded by yards filled with pigs, goats, chickens, cows, and children. The village was, as it happens, the birthplace of two eventual Tammany Hall leaders; it was a place you could possibly climb out of.

Seneca Village was razed in 1857 to make way for Central Park. The term *shanty Irish* was more enduring, meaning to this day a poor, uncouth, even dirty, and certainly downtrodden soul.

What does "lace curtain Irish" mean?

The term was used in the old country and the new, and applied to those who had made it out: out of the ghetto, out of the shanty town, out of the lower class. You didn't have to be nouveau riche or *any* kind of rich to be lace curtain. You simply had to be respectable.

The term described a literal phenomenon: Families who could afford lace curtains—good ones or poor ones—immediately procured them, because in your window you could show this flag to the world.

You could be proud of your house and yourself, viewing your life from inside or out.

It's all a little sad, really, that those on the rise would be so quick to distinguish themselves, and that those who had not yet risen were reminded of their fate every time they passed a lace-curtained cottage.

At the turn of the century, there were millions of lace curtain Irish in the United States, but even more shanty Irish. The balance was soon to tip.

What was the difference between the Irish Americans of 1800 and those of 1900?

Everything, not least that they were from wholly different tribes.

Irish American had gone from meaning largely Scotch-Irish or Presbyterian people of Ulster heritage whose families may or may not have spent many generations on the Emerald Isle—remember, some of them counted as their Irish experience a few decades stealing or working farmlands in the North for English usurper landlords, and clearly had no attachment to the land—to being a mainly Catholic population who considered Ireland the homeland or the mother country. Moreover, these millions of people constituted a significant minority throughout the country and a majority in some urban sections. Generally downtrodden since their arrival as a huddled mass, they were sensing a change (folks such as John L. Sullivan, not to mention Louis Sullivan, were playing no small role in this shift in perspective). There were now Irish American contributors. There were now roads rising to meet the Irish, and roads they could travel that might allow them to rise. This encouraged many individuals to put their shoulders to the wheel with a new intensity, and it encouraged the community to take heart. Since the days of midcentury, when the Irish felt the lash of U.S. discrimination, there had been coming a general sense that it might be okay to be Irish—or might soon be—even in public. Irish Americans were growing loud and proud. They were behaving like the citizens they now were, in business, in trade, in sport, in culture, at the ballot box. In 1880 New York City elected its first Irish Catholic mayor (**William Grace**) and in 1882 Boston sent its first Irish Catholic congressman to Washington (**Patrick Collins**). Soon they would be leading the quintessentially democratic fight for better conditions in the workplace, and while their relations in Ireland would be debating whether to spill blood fighting alongside British soldiers, they would be shouldering a thousand rifles and would be fighting and dying for America.

You could have foreseen all this in 1900, for the Irish were coming out of their closet. Consider an institution that has been a useful bellwether for us in the past, from its birth as an Orange/Protestant/ English festival to its usurpation by Catholic Irish. We speak again of New York City's Saint Patrick's Day Parade. By the turn of the century the line of march would routinely include a platoon of policemen, several armed services regiments, dozens of divisions of the Ancient Order of Hibernians, parish benevolent societies too numerous to mention, bands from everywhere, temperance units (one year, as a for instance: "Father Mathew T.A.B. Society No. 2 of New York, 400 men")—thirty, forty, fifty thousand marchers in all. And by now, of course, not all of the marchers were Irish. Thousands were mongrel Irish, and thousands of others were sharing a day with the Irish— their countrymen. Their countrymen who, it was generally known, already had titans among them.

Who was William Russell Grace?

Born in 1832, **William Russell Grace** emigrated from County Cork to . . . Peru.

Yes, Peru, where he founded a shipping line, William R. Grace and Co. He relocated to the United States, and his interests thrived. At a time of great corruption, he was seen as an industrialist free of the taint. The enormity of his winning the mayoralty of New York in 1880 as a Roman Catholic born in Ireland was certainly no less and perhaps greater than that of John F. Kennedy winning the White House eighty years later.

Who was Henry Ford?

A son of Irish immigrants who came to Canada on a coffin ship and eventually found their way to Dearborn, Michigan, Henry was the eldest of the first generation of Fords born in the United States. He went on to become the greatest American automobile manufacturer. A pioneer, Ford used mass-production techniques in making the famous Model T and therefore could keep prices low. When Ford Motors made cars affordable to middle-class Americans, it spurred a social and economic revolution unlike any other. When Ford announced "the five-dollar day," Detroit became a mecca for laborers, the Irish chief among them. In 1920 Ford returned to Cork to open the first Ford Motor Company plant located outside the United States.

Other plants opened around the world, of course, and one that is at the center of a current controversy points up an unsavory aspect of Ford, the man. In March 1998 a lawsuit was filed in Federal Court in Newark, New Jersey, charging the Ford Motor Company of having profited from the forced labor of thousands of civilians at a truck factory of its German subsidiary during World War II. The factory was in Cologne, and the company has long maintained that it was under Nazi control and not in touch with corporate headquarters during the war. Present-day Ford executives are willingly cooperating in the discovery of whatever new facts there might be, but there must be nail-biting because Ford was flagrantly, even proudly, anti-Semitic. The suit filed in Newark went so far as to accuse Ford—the man and the company—of having received special treatment from Germany because of a personal relationship between Adolf Hitler and Henry Ford, who professed public admiration for the German government machine in the 1930s. The lawsuit said that Ford had sent annual birthday gifts to Hitler and had been decorated by him in 1938 with the Great Cross of the German Order of the Eagle.

Henry Ford died in 1947, having seen what came of Nazism.

Who was Andrew W. Mellon?

Born in 1855 to an Irish immigrant father, **Andrew W. Mellon** first started a successful lumber operation and then joined his dad's Pittsburgh bank. He was an astute judge of business ventures—his own and others'—and financially backed the start-up and growth of Aluminum Company of America, Gulf Oil, Union Steel, and other companies that came to rank among the nation's largest. While he was a fabulously wealthy man and one of the country's two or three major capitalists, Mellon was almost unknown to the public until he served as secretary of the treasury from 1921 to 1932. He guided the nation's financial affairs during the Roaring Twenties and, it must be said, into the Great Depression. He also served as ambassador to Britain. He was a philanthropist; he donated his huge art collection to his country, which led to the establishment of the National Gallery of Art in Washington, D.C.

Who was John R. Gregg?

Born in 1867, **John R. Gregg** emigrated from Rockcorry, County Monaghan, to the United States in 1893. We place him here as an example of an anonymous Irishman contributing something to American society—indeed, to the world—in an anonymous way. He developed the first practical, easily learned form of shorthand writing, which made office operations much more productive and practicable as the pace of twentieth-century America heated up. Gregg shorthand is still taught and widely used even in the era of dictating machines and computer word processors.

And while we're on the topic of language and communication, let's not forget that the teacher and friend behind the fantastic story that is Helen Keller—the great American hero who, though blind, became a leading writer, feminist, and antiwar conscience— was named **Annie Sullivan**. It was Sullivan who was "the miracle worker," helping bring Keller forth from the darkness.

Who were Howard R. Hughes and William Randolph Hearst?

Two very rich guys.

Two very rich guys with northern Irish blood in them, and we kept them off the list of Ulster Americans presented in chapter 6 because their stories seem so very twentieth century.

Howard R. Hughes was an aviation pioneer and industrialist who built one of the world's largest fortunes. Born in 1905, and a colorful, flamboyant playboy in his early career—Katharine Hepburn loved him dearly before going over to the Irish American Spencer Tracy, and Hughes taught Hepburn to fly—he became a reclusive eccentric in the post–World War II years. He lived at the top of a Vegas hotel and kept everyone at bay. Clifford Irving tried to write a book about him—long fingernails and hair, all that stuff—but it was merely weird. Far better is the whimsical film *Melvin and Howard*, concerning a gas-station owner's claim on the fortune that was represented by Hughes Aircraft and Hughes Tool Company. (Jason Robards played Hughes—and he was terrific. Paul LeMat was Melvin.) Howard Hughes died (we think) in 1976.

William Randolph Hearst was born in 1863 and grew to be an editor, publisher, and political kingmaker of renown. (*Citizen Kane*, a movie quite different from *Melvin and Howard*, was about the life of Hearst.) He created the nation's largest newspaper chain and served in Congress. He amassed an impressive (to say the least!) collection of art and antiques that are now on display at San Simeon, once Hearst's palatial estate in California (the model for Kane's Xanadu).

We raise Hearst's ghost here for an odder reason: When William Randolph's descendant Patty Hearst was going through her kidnapping-terrorist period in the early 1970s, the bank she pinpointed for robbery by her kidnapper-comrades was the Hibernia National in San Francisco. This institution had been founded by Irish Americans, for Irish Americans, in the gold-rush days. By 1860, according to *The San Francisco Irish*, by R. A. Burchell (1980), the boomtown Irish American community had established itself and was founding things—among them, banks—and **John Sullivan** (not the boxer) formed Hibernia National on April 12, 1859. The first office had been on Jackson and Montgomery Streets, upstairs.

The savings and loan took deposits of $2.50 or more (the Hearsts would have been appalled). By 1869 the bank had nearly fifteen thousand customers and assets of $10 million.

The Hibernia National Bank has been subsumed by Bank of America. However, the name is still on the building. And since we do love ironies, we'll tell you what Patty Hearst's building now houses: a police station.

Who was "Honest John" Kelly?

He was a nineteenth-century politician who provides a useful starting point for discussing the twentieth-century Irish American involvement in politics.

As we have seen in earlier chapters, William Marcy "Boss" Tweed was lord over a thoroughly corrupt New York Democratic club called Tammany Hall that dominated the city's politics in the post–Civil War years. Tammany had long depended on the Irish vote to get its candidates elected and hadn't minded using the Irish gangs to get the vote out, but it hadn't been led by an Irishman until Tweed was ousted in 1871, replaced by Kelly.

What had Kelly learned already, and what would become an adage of Irish politics? That the game was dirty business. All future political "machines" and many organized crime operations, including the Mafia, would take lessons from the Irish American school of political efficacy.

The Irish were the first to realize that the power of gangs could be used for purposes with a broader social significance. A gang meant numbers, and in numbers there was power. If violence or its potential were present or implied in those numbers—and in those gang faces—then the power was greater. If that power could be harnessed, then channeled to political purposes, the power would increase, and a system built upon a corrupt foundation could rule.

The gangs that worked New York in the post–Civil War years enjoyed the system. Money and even a certain amount of protection from authorities, who wouldn't dare cross Tammany, were the rewards for services rendered. There were colorful characters in gangland— some smart and some not so smart. **Richard Croker** of the Fourth Avenue Tunnel Gang was smart; he would rise to be a Tammany leader. **Maggie Carson,** a twelve-year-old girl who led Forty Little Thieves, was smart: She got herself adopted by a respectable family. **Martin "Bully" Morrison,** the huge red-bearded Orangeman called The King of Hell's Kitchen, wasn't necessarily smart, but he was scary—which could be just as effective. He hated Irish Catholics and would guzzle beer from chalices stolen from church just to incite them. He ruled until Irish Catholic numbers overwhelmed the slum, then power was transferred: Bully Power was out, Green Power was in. Politics at its most irresistible. Hell's Kitchen was still an Irish Catholic domain— think of it as one of those ancient Celtic kingdoms—during Prohibition, and its chieftain was **"Mad Dog" Call,** who was said to scare even the underworld.

The gangs were the hot center, the boiler room, of political machines. More intelligent and sophisticated players of the political game than the gang members reaped proportionally richer rewards, and the biggest were reaped by the politicians themselves and their handlers—in New York and elsewhere.

James Michael Curley, born in 1874, walked onto the Boston political landscape at a time when the Irish of the city were still a detested lot, and the office holders were Republican, most of them descended from old, established Yankee families. A common sense of exclusion bound the town's outsiders, and Curley and his cronies realized that they could capitalize on this resentment. They also skillfully interwove the needs of the neighborhood with the day-to-day machinations of the local Roman Catholic churches. They brought religion in as a political adjunct, just as John Kelly was bringing in gang violence.

Some brief background: Curley was the son of an immigrant and was fatherless by age ten. He foraged for coal while his mother was a washerwoman downtown. Once, when he bent over to pick up some found coins, an uncle kneed him in the groin and took the money. His was a hard-bitten youth. He dropped out of school in the eighth grade, thought about a career as a fireman, finally figured politics was the way out—and up.

By the turn of the century Curley had acquired a reputation in the neighborhoods as one who cared, one who might be able to provide needed services and who would dole out jobs through patronage—a good thing, if your man got elected. He was seen as the ultimate populist: The civil-service exams of the day were seen by immigrants as elitist, as they were based on a proficiency in grammar and arithmetic. Curley, an "educated" man, once took the mail-carriers test for a friend named Fahey, and Curley got caught. His constituency loved it; the night before he was sent to prison for sixty days, hundreds cheered him in the streets. Curley was reelected as alderman as he sat behind bars at the Charles Street Jail and hailed as a hero upon his release.

Curley had to beat the bosses to become the boss, and he was eager to do it. He always remembered that, upon the early death of his father his family had received no help from Ward 17 boss "Pea Jacket" Maguire. He wanted to dismantle the ward system and run things—as a boss—from city hall. The ward bosses saw the handwriting on the wall and convinced their more decorous Irish American mayor, a man named Fitzgerald (of whom you'll hear more later), to run again. An Irish American one step ahead of Curley, Honey Fitz had held office for six years. Curley, the congressman from Roxbury, grew impatient: In November of 1913 he said he was running to run the city. He claimed publicly that Fitzgerald had promised he wasn't going to run again. This didn't budge Fitzgerald, but something else did: Curley's threat to expose the mayor's affair with a cigarette girl named Toodles Ryan. With the field clear of formidable Democrats, Curley ascended.

The Republican state legislature hated Curley and passed laws against a mayor succeeding himself. So Curley went on to four *un*-successive terms and dominated city hall politics for decades. He changed the city, directing millions of dollars to infrastructure.

Out of office so much because of the new rules, he lost often: five times for mayor, twice for governor, once for the U.S. Senate. But he won a lot, too: He was a congressman (from Fitzgerald's district!) and many times a mayor. His excessive use of patronage and penalty—he taxed the Yankee property owners wherever he could find them—did nothing to advance the cause of amicable relations between the Irish and other Boston citizens. Curley was charming, and a corrupt bully. His legacy is mixed at best. His second jail term was not as winning as his first: During World War II—Curley lent his name to a company that claimed, fraudulently, that it could help land war contracts. Curley was in prison for five months before Truman freed him in 1947. Curley lost his last hurrah in 1950 and he died, poor, in 1958 at eighty-four years of age.

Others also realized that politics was a way to rise. The governor of New York from 1919 to 1929 and the Democratic nominee for president of the United States in 1928 was a man named **Al Smith,** and he was considered the most famous Irish American of his day, a quintessential Irish Catholic urban politician and a product of generations of Irish mastery of Tammany techniques. Appearances are deceiving, and in recent years Al Smith's heritage has come into question. It seems that when his father died in 1886 at the age of fifty-one, the death certificate listed his name as Alfred Emanuel Smith, born in New York City. It also shows that his father, Emanuel, had been born in Italy and that his mother, Magdalena, had been born in Germany. New York State census records confirm that the same Emanuel Smith was born in Genoa in 1813 and naturalized in the United States in 1825. Emanuel's mother, Catherine, was most certainly Irish on her father's side, but by some accounts her mother had been English.

So, Al Smith may have been one-quarter Irish. An astonishing fact, when you consider how much was made of it, and how much it both gained and cost him.

But he certainly identified himself as Irish. His upbringing in a New York neighborhood had been undeniably Irish. His social, religious, and educational background had been thoroughly Irish Catholic. His political influences (and his political handlers) were Irish. And he was perceived by others as Irish.

In the final analysis, blood is thinner than choice. This famous Irish American politician, the precursor to John F. Kennedy, is Irish because he himself chose to be Irish.

The Irishness didn't hurt him in 1928 against Herbert Hoover so much as did the Catholicism. That's what finally sunk him like the *Titanic*. America wasn't ready for a Catholic president—yet.

Now, **James Aloysius Farley** was the epitome of the New York Irish politician, and the real thing. In Grassy Point, New York, he began his career by getting himself elected district committeeman. He served eight years as town clerk and was made supervisor. He was elected to the New York State Assembly and became head of the state's Democratic Committee in 1930. Two years later he successfully pushed the presidential nomination of Franklin Delano Roosevelt. Becoming chairman of the Democratic National Committee, Farley managed FDR's campaign with obvious success and landed in the cabinet as postmaster general. He dropped out of public service to mastermind Roosevelt's 1936 campaign after which he stepped right back into his old cabinet job. By 1940 Farley had presidential aspirations of his own. But they weren't to be: Roosevelt decided he wanted the job for yet a third term, and Farley dropped out of the cabinet and the party leadership.

The massive general mail facility in New York City is named in his honor.

Richard J. Daley of Chicago, born in 1902, is called "the last of the bosses." He grew up in the Irish working-class neighborhood of Bridgeport on Chicago's South Side and derived both his hard-core political support and his personal emotional strength and sense of self from his Irish community. His ethnic focus and system of patronage built a political machine that could "deliver votes to order." It not only reelected him mayor every four years from 1955 to 1975 but also provided critical support for the presidential nominations and campaigns of Adlai Stevenson, John F. Kennedy, Hubert Humphrey, and Jimmy Carter.

Daley earned an unsavory reputation across the country when Chicago police "rioted" against anti–Vietnam War demonstrators during the 1968 Democratic National Convention. It was a sign that he (and such as he, such as Curley) was beginning to be viewed as an anachronism, After his death in 1976, the old machine lost to African American Harold Washington in what seemed a symbolic shift in urban political power. But following Washington's death, Chicago voters picked, first, the Irish American Jane Byrne, and then none other than Richard M. Daley, son of the old boss, to be their new boss.

Curley was revered and Daley was feared, but **Thomas P. "Tip" O'Neill** was beloved. He held the Eighth Congressional District (the number kept changing) that had already been a launching pad for John Fitzgerald and John Fitzgerald Kennedy, and that would be so for Joseph P. Kennedy II. And he held it, and he held it—from 1952 through 1986. Tip's adage was "all politics is local," and the man from Cambridge and Boston College lived that way, taking care of his own when he could, meanwhile glad-handing the enemy.

Thomas P. O'Neill was born in 1912, and those who would look back on him as a fogey are mistaken: He fought to have all House votes publicly recorded (no small matter, and no easy victory) and his early opposition to the Vietnam War stood out. Tip loved his state, he loved his wife, he loved his party, he loved the Cape, he loved golf (he wasn't much good), he loved life, he loved being Speaker of the House—and he was loved in turn. He wanted the country to keep progressing and so, as a conciliator, he was a major reason the Reagan presidency moved forward and did not stall. Two Irishmen, talking.

Joe McCarthy had been born four years before O'Neill—in 1908—and his image and legacy could not be more different. If one was from Mars, the other was from . . . Pluto.

It's a true shame that most Irish American anthologies, histories, and guides that celebrate forebears such as Andrew Jackson and Ben Hogan—and Tip O'Neill—do not acknowledge Joe McCarthy. It's the Irish way to wish a thing would just go away (like, for instance, the British). But coming to terms with one's heritage—confronting the racism of the nineteenth century, confronting Joe McCarthy—is part of process.

Tailgunner Joe. Born in 1908 in a farming area near Grand Chute, Wisconsin, that was called the "Irish Settlement," he was the son of Bridget Tierney, a native of Ireland, and Timothy McCarthy, of mixed Irish and German ancestry. He worked his way through Marquette University and practiced law until 1939, when he was elected a judge. He resigned his position to serve in the Marine Corps during World War II. After the war he campaigned as "Tailgunner" and won his seat in the Senate.

He gained no large notice until 1950, when he claimed to have a list of fifty-seven employees of the State Department who were Communists. That particular claim and others were never substantiated, but it was the start of a frenzy of accusation the like of which hadn't been seen since the Salem Witch Trials (a point seized upon by the playwright Arthur Miller in his allegorical drama *The Crucible*).

McCarthy was named chairman of the Committee of Government Operations, and from that position he probed allegations concerning Communist activity in the United States Information Agency. The Central Intelligence Agency, the Government Printing Office, the United Nations, and the U.S. Army also came under the scrutiny of Tailgunner Joe. But there were no Communists to be found there. Finally, at long last (and too late for too many), his behavior during the televised Army-McCarthy Hearings led to his being "condemned" by his fellows in the Senate. After that, his influence steadily declined.

President Harry Truman gave a definition to McCarthyism, a phrase that persists: "The corruption of truth . . . the abandonment of . . . fair play and due process of law . . . the use of the 'big lie' and the unfounded accusations, . . . in the name of Americanism and security." President Eisenhower, slow to figure out McCarthy, finally denounced his tactics and assailed "the book burners" in his commencement address at Dartmouth College in 1953.

A sterling contrast to Joe McCarthy as a senator was **Michael J. Mansfield**, a leader of the august body from 1961 to 1977. Though regarded as a Montanan—that's the state he represented—he was born in New York City on March 16, 1903, very shortly after his parents had emigrated from Ireland. The family shuffled off to Great Falls, Montana, in 1906.

Mike Mansfield left school at fourteen to join the Navy and serve as a seaman during World War I. He went on to serve in the Army and the Marine Corps. When he left the service he went to work as a miner in Butte, Montana (of course), and attended the Montana School of Mines. He earned a bachelor's, then a master's degree from Montana State University, despite the fact that he had never finished high school. After teaching Hispanic and Far Eastern history at MSU, he won election to the House in 1943 and moved on to the Senate a decade later. He left his post there in 1977 to become U.S. ambassador to Japan, and he was so effective and popular that he continued to serve in the post from the Carter through the Reagan administrations (1979–1989). The longest-standing ambassador to Japan in U.S. history, he was given the Presidential Medal of Freedom (the nation's highest nonmilitary honor) by Ronald Reagan and the Grand Cordon of the Order of the Rising Sun by Japanese Prime Minister Takeshita.

Mike Mansfield continues to work. He is an adviser for Far Eastern affairs at Goldman, Sachs and Co. in Washington, D.C.

Born three years later than Mansfield (in 1906) and just across the river (in Newark, New Jersey) was **William J. Brennan.** His father had been a metal polisher and brewery worker in Ireland who, once arrived, became active in the trade-union movement and state and local politics. It's fair to say William was schooled as much in the Irish-dominated precinct politics of Newark as he would later be at Harvard Law. He served as a justice of the United States Supreme Court from 1956 to 1990. He wrote nearly as many dissents as he did majority opinions, but his keen intellect, forceful personality, and gift for building coalitions often produced narrow majorities that kept the court's liberal vision alive well beyond the Warren years. He was fond of saying that the most important skill for the nine members of the Court was "counting to five."

His most important decisions laid the groundwork for modern voting-rights law; upheld the power of Congress to enforce the Voting Rights Act of 1965 against race discrimination at the polls; made clear that the right to criticize government is "the central meaning of the First Amendment"; enforced school desegregation; found sex discrimination unconstitutional; and extended due-process rights with the result, in this case, that the government was stopped from taking away welfare benefits without giving recipients an opportunity to be heard. Brennan was also a steadfast opponent of the death penalty and railed against its discriminatory nature as much as he did its barbarism.

When Justice Brennan passed away in 1997 at the age of ninety-one, having sat on the bench during eight presidencies, Bill Clinton hailed him as his "hero." Professor Kathleen M. Sullivan of Stanford Law School wrote in an op-ed piece in the *New York Times*: "Justice Brennan maintained that the Court was the only branch of government that could speak for minorities, dissidents and underdogs. He saw protecting them from the tyranny of political majorities as his duty."

One colleague from Brennan's last years on the bench was **Sandra Day O'Connor** who assures, with Justice **Anthony Kennedy,** that the panel maintains an Irish face. Of course, that's not an important thing. What is significant regarding O'Connor is that she is the first woman to serve as one of "the brethren." It's another nice irony that a very conservative president, Ronald Reagan, appointed the first woman to the bench (in 1981). The Texas-Irish O'Connor traces her lineage on her father's side to the great clan O'Dea. Reagan and

Bush thought they were getting a safe vote in O'Connor, but she has surprised many with her moderate decisions and clearly has a mind of her own. Recently, she has also become more outspoken than Supreme Court justices are wont to be: Since being diagnosed with breast cancer, she has made public her trials and has sought to help other women and aid in the fight against the disease.

Not all Irish Americans are liberals. O'Connor isn't, and certainly Richard Nixon and Ronald Reagan weren't.

Was Richard Nixon Irish?

Yes, without a doubt. His great-great-great-great-grandfather, Thomas Milhous, was from Timahoe, a village twenty miles outside Dublin. They were Quaker Irish. It is believed that a generation further back they had been in Carrickfergus, the hometown of Andrew Jackson's parents—something of a breeding ground for American presidents. Thomas moved to Pennsylvania with his family in 1729.

When **Richard Nixon** visited Ireland in October of 1970, they couldn't find any Milhous relations for him to greet. They did, however, come up with several Ryans related to Nixon's wife, Thelma "Pat" Ryan Nixon, whose nickname derived from being born on Saint Patrick's Day.

Ronald Reagan was descended from a Famine-era immigrant. Michael Reagan had left Ballyporeen in County Tipperary in or about 1850. Reagan revisited the area during his presidency and found several distant relatives. He recounted in his memoirs that he "got a shock" when they brought before him "a man in his middle twenties who caused me to do a double take. It was amazing how much he and I resembled each other—his eyes and hair, the whole facial structure resembled mine. Since it had been over a century since my great-grandfather had left Ballyporeen for America, it was an eerie experience.

"Although I've never been one for introspection or dwelling on the past," Reagan continued, "as I looked down the narrow main street of the little town from which an emigrant named Michael Reagan had set out in pursuit of a dream, I had a flood of thoughts. . . . I thought of Jack [the president's grandfather; Michael's son] and his Irish stories and the drive he'd always had to get ahead; I thought of my own childhood in Dixon, then leaving that small town for Hollywood and later Washington."

During that extraordinary journey of Ronald Reagan, the Irish heritage got blurred a bit. As was not the case with, say, the Kennedys, the Reagan family's important postimmigration marriages in America were not necessarily Irish-to-Irish, and certainly the religion aspect was not a factor with the electorate. But by the time he was in the White House, Reagan seemed to regain some hard-to-put-your-finger-on-it Irishness. Maybe it was just the game of politics that seems so innately Irish to us now. One commentator, watching Reagan and Tip O'Neill tussle, said, "Once the politics is over with, it's just two old Irish pols swapping stories."

Bill Clinton never has and never will seem like an old Irish pol. In fact, his Irish heritage is more muddled than Reagan's, and the religion question more blurred as well. But he, too, has a line that can be drawn—to County Fermanagh—and so he, too, like Kennedy, Nixon, and Reagan, made the pilgrimage back home during his presidency and was warmly greeted. That was in December of 1995, and the trip was just as sentimental as the others had been, although it had a sharper edge as well. For Clinton went North and South—he was the first sitting president to go to Northern Ireland—and pointedly kept talking about peace.

This is how contemporary Irish American politicians will finally be remembered as Irish heroes: If they can help pull the rabbit from the hat in the peace process. Clinton has involved himself. He very purposefully approved the controversial visa that allowed Sinn Fein leader Gerry Adams to visit the United States for the first time in 1994, and he entertained Adams at the White House in 1995. But he was quick to rebuke Adams and his associates when the IRA cease-fire was broken in 1996. Since then, Clinton has met with the Irish Taoiseach Bertie Ahern, SDLP leader John Hume, Ulster Unionist Party leader David Trimble, and, of course, British Prime Minister Tony Blair. The progress of the peace talks was always a central point of these meetings.

Throughout the process, Clinton has been fast with words of encouragement for any breakthrough, and first with words of condemnation for any acts of violence. That seems to be the modern Irish American stance; Senators **Ted Kennedy** and **Daniel Patrick Moynihan** have behaved the same way. There is very little sitting on hands.

Moynihan was born in Tulsa, Oklahoma, but was raised above a family pub in New York's Hell's Kitchen where Irish dockworkers drank. The future ambassador and U.S. Senator from New York (since 1977) learned much about the urban problems that would become his signature issues. Abandoned by an alcoholic father, he became a shoe-shine boy in Times Square and worked as a long-shoreman and bartender before he went off to the fancy schools to which his intellect allowed entrée. He earned a Ph.D. and taught at Harvard and MIT before drifting into politics. He served as assistant secretary of labor in the John F. Kennedy administration, then was appointed ambassador to India by President Nixon, then served as the U.S. ambassador to the United Nations. He has written a dozen books and has delivered a thousand speeches, but many Irish re-member best his words on the occasion of President Kennedy's as-sassination. He's the one who said, "To be Irish is to know that, in the end, the world will break your heart."

Which brings us back to the peace process, whence we've strayed.

Clinton continually pledged America's support for a settlement and has emphatically urged all paramilitaries to lay down their arms. Other Irish quarrel with this view; they see it as pacifist and too trusting of British motives. But it's the president's position, and he has put this country's might and persuasiveness behind it.

Within two weeks after the IRA shattered its seventeen-month cease-fire with the Canary Wharf bombing in London on February 9, 1996, the Irish government got Britain to agree to come to the bar-gaining table for peace talks that would be mediated by an Ameri-can on loan for the purpose. **George Mitchell,** the former senator from Maine, would direct the talks that would ultimately lead to an interim government for Northern Ireland, and agreement on how to structure relations between Northern Ireland and the Republic in sharing "cross-border institutions," and how to build relations of any new sort between Britain and Ireland.

Mitchell is the grandson of Irish immigrants to Maine, a state he served for fourteen years as senator. Mitchell became Senate leader, then declined to run for reelection in 1994. Some were touting him as commissioner of baseball before he was appointed as Presi-dent Clinton's special adviser on Irish economic initiatives. Mitchell organized the highly successful Irish Economic Conference in Washington in 1995, then agreed to chair the International Body on Decommissioning in Northern Ireland that Clinton himself was sponsoring.

As the independent chairman of the Northern Ireland all-party peace talks, Mitchell was praised for his evenhandedness and steady leadership. He delivered a compromise few thought was possible. He did a good job for his ancestral land.

Before we leave the grand topic of the Irish American rise through political ways and means—a march that, like the others, starts out looking so starkly Irish and ends up looking so broadly American—we must discuss **Paul O'Dwyer,** whose efforts and energies were ceaseless through much of the century. O'Dwyer, a New York lawyer and civil rights advocate who died in 1998, stands as one of the most beloved and inspiring Irish Americans of modern times.

Born in County Mayo in 1907, he came to New York at eighteen with a commitment and dedication to justice, civil rights, and humanity that had been forged in the Irish civil war. He worked his way through Fordham University and Saint John's University Law School, and in 1935 established the law firm O'Dwyer and Bernstein, which continues today its involvement in civil rights and civil liberties litigation both at home and abroad. In the thirties, O'Dwyer served as counsel for several trade unions. In the forties, as chairman of the Lawyers Committee for Justice in Palestine, he pleaded before the United Nations for the establishment of a sovereign state of Israel. (There's our hundredth irony: An Irish-born American helped another native people found its nation. O'Dwyer was awarded the Jerusalem Medal by Israel in 1976, and in 1980 received recognition from Israeli Prime Minister Menachem Begin as a founding father of the Jewish state.)

The fifties found O'Dwyer battling the unconstitutional activities of the House Committee on Un-American Activities (intra-clan squabbling between O'Dwyer and Tailgunner Joe). O'Dwyer represented Martin Popper, former president of the National Lawyers Guild, who had been indicted for contempt of the House Un-American Activities Committee, and also Pendar O'Donnell, the Irish writer whom the State Department had refused to allow into this country.

O'Dwyer formed the Committee for Democratic Voters with Eleanor Roosevelt and Senator Herbert Lehman and served as co-chairman of the Committee for Kennedy-Johnson in 1960.

The sixties found him working tirelessly to establish and defend the civil rights of African Americans and to end the war in Vietnam. He defended, on a pro-bono basis, civil rights demonstrators in the federal courts of Mississippi and Georgia. At the 1964 Democratic National Convention he led the fight to seat representatives of the Mississippi Freedom Democratic Party ticket in lieu of the all-white state delegation. He campaigned for black candidates in the Mississippi Delta region, and his efforts were rewarded with the election of the first black county officers since Reconstruction. In 1969 he helped elect the first black mayor of Fayette, Mississippi, in one hundred years.

He became the leader of the peace forces at the Democratic Convention in Chicago in 1968, and addressed the delegates on the issues of civil rights and the Vietnam War. He served as counsel for many peace activists, including **Father Philip Berrigan** and **Sister Elizabeth McAllister,** two of several famous Irish American activists to wear robes.

During the early seventies, O'Dwyer founded the American Committee for Ulster Justice, which sponsored the Kennedy-Ribicoff Resolution in the Senate and the Carey Resolution in Congress. In 1974 O'Dwyer was elected president of the New York City Council, and it was in that capacity that he appointed David Dinkins as city clerk. This boost would help Dinkins go on to become, with Paul O'Dwyer's support, the first African American mayor of New York City. Dinkins returned the favor by selecting O'Dwyer as the city's representative to the United Nations.

Between and amidst his political appointments, O'Dwyer served as counsel for Irish Northern Aid and founded the Brehon Law Society to help not only Irish Americans who were being harassed in American courts but also victims of discrimination in Northern Ireland. He personally represented Kevin Lynch, a hunger striker in Northern Ireland's Long Kesh prison, and attended Lynch's funeral after he died of starvation in 1981. O'Dwyer also guided Representative Gary Ackerman and State Senator Jeremy Weinstein on a tour of inspection of Northern Ireland, and through the influence of the legislators he was able to expose the flagrant abuses and discrimination exercised by American-financed manufacturers there. This had tangible results, as we will see in this book's final chapter.

O'Dwyer also founded the Irish Institute and served as its first president. The Institute raises money to support libraries, schools, artists, and writers in Ireland, and seeks to preserve Irish landmarks.

But enough about Paul O'Dwyer. Let's talk about his older brother, **William O'Dwyer.** He had preceded Paul to the States, was a unionist in New York City, used the support of labor to win election as mayor (he succeeded Fiorello La Guardia in 1946), which office he would resign to accept President Harry Truman's offer of the ambassadorship to Mexico.

Why all this about the O'Dwyer boys? Because it illustrates how, not always loudly—not always with the splash of a Curley, a Daley, a Kennedy, a Reagan, or a Clinton—Irish Americans were contributing to their new land and, indeed, to the world in ways that did not always have an Irish slant. We are, too often, proud only when an effort abets our particular cause. The O'Dwyers stand simply as good world citizens, and that the Irish had grown to become such in this century says something. Heretofore, it was difficult for someone from that small island to have an international impact. With the United States as avenue, conduit, soapbox, and backup, a good Irishman could now have a mighty effect indeed.

Where was the largest political impact of Irish American activists felt?

Probably in the labor movement.

It's hard to decide who was the most noteworthy, influential, or even heroic of Irish American labor leaders as the union movement revolutionized how America thought about and treated its workers. **Terence Vincent Powderly** was born in Carbondale, Pennsylvania, in 1849 to poor Irish immigrant parents. Powderly became a railroad laborer at the age of thirteen and later a machinist, which job he held for many years. In 1871 he joined the Machinists and Blacksmiths' national union and before long was its president.

He also joined a secret organization known as the Knights of Labor. Although bitterly opposed by owners and managers, the Knights soon developed into the largest and most influential force in the American labor movement. Powderly rose to head this organization, too, as "General Master Workman" from 1883 to 1893, a period during which he toured the nation to advance the workingman's cause.

Powderly's approach to labor issues was conciliatory. He rejected the concept of a class conflict that pitted owner against worker, and rejected the call for a new political party to exclusively represent labor interests. Under Powderly's moderate stewardship, the Knights of Labor reached a peak of power and influence; its membership rose to nearly a million.

Powderly was respected not just by his colleagues. He served for a time as mayor of Scranton, Pennsylvania, and President McKinley appointed him commissioner general of immigration in 1897 (figuring the Irish knew something about immigration). But it is as a labor leader that he is remembered. When industrial magnates responded to growing resentment of deplorable work conditions by tightening the screw, Powderly's Knights went through a tough period. At the turn of the century a new and mightier organization, the American Federation of Labor, emerged. AFofL leader Samuel Gompers took a moderate line with management that quite resembled Powderly's. The old Knight could be comfortable in such an organization, and in fact spent the years before his death in 1924 working for the AFofL in a variety of positions.

Mary Harris arrived in America from County Cork at age five in 1835 to join her father, a railroad worker who had emigrated earlier. She became educated, taught for a time in Michigan, and wound up in Memphis, where she married in 1861. **Mary Harris Jones** was thirty-seven when yellow fever wiped out her family (a husband and four children) in 1867. She moved from Memphis to Chicago and opened a dress shop. Devastation struck again in 1871 when she lost everything in the Chicago Fire.

From the window of her dress shop she had taken note of "poor, shivering wretches, jobless and hungry." She started attending meetings of the Knights of Columbus, an early labor organization. She found her calling, and her purposeful, strident voice. (She can be seen as an early feminist, if you like, but she felt that the suffragettes were concerning themselves with trivial matters compared to the widespread suffering caused by industrial capitalism.) She hit the road and would spend the rest of her one-hundred-year life traveling with her Crusaders from mine to mill, organizing workers, exposing the horrors of child labor, the evils of scabs, the dangers of manual labor, and the need for a strong union. She faced confrontation at the labor riots in Pittsburgh in 1877. She was in Chicago for the Haymarket riot in 1886. She was in Birmingham for the American Railway Union strike in 1894. She was at the Copper Mine strike in Colorado in 1913, and was jailed for her trouble (the charge: conspiracy to commit murder). The U.S. Senate freed her that time, but there were several other instances when Mother Jones found herself in lockup. It only added to her legend. "She was born a crusader, a woman of action, fired by a fine zeal, a mother especially devoted to the miners," wrote Clarence Darrow. "Wherever fights were fiercest and danger greatest, Mother Jones was present to aid and cheer. She had a strong sense of drama. She staged every detail of a contest."

Mother Jones addressed the AFofL in 1923 at age 93. She died seven years later and was eulogized by the Reverend J. W.

McGuire of Kankakee, Illinois: "Wealthy coal operators and capitalists throughout the United States are breathing sighs of relief, while toil-worn men and women are weeping tears of bitter grief. The reason for this contrast of relief and sorrow is apparent. Mother Jones is dead."

Elizabeth Gurley Flynn, born in New Hampshire in 1890, is a second feisty Irish American woman who expressed courage of conviction and thus affected the labor movement. She would become the first woman to head the Communist Party in America.

Flynn was born into a family of socialists, an odd thing in the Granite State, then or now. Her mother had emigrated alone from Ireland in 1877 to join a sister who'd left earlier. The family moved to New York in 1900, and by age fifteen Elizabeth was giving street-corner speeches for workers' rights. In 1906 she joined the radical labor group the International Workers of the World and was a leader during several bloody strikes. In 1920 she cofounded the American Civil Liberties Union and, in the same year, joined the American Communist Party. Over the next two decades the "rebel girl" rose to be the head of the organization and, in 1955, went to jail for violating the Smith Act, which forbade the advocacy of a violent overthrow of the United States government. In 1957 the United States Supreme Court ruled that teaching communism was not in and of itself illegal, and Flynn was set free. She died in self-imposed exile in the Soviet Union in 1964.

By now, you might be tired of our passion for irony, but this is irresistible: America and American democracy had given the Irish so much elbow room for philosophical expression that, by the 1950s, the most virulent anti-Communist ever (McCarthy) was an Irish descendant, as was the leader of the country's Communist Party. By 1960 the irony would deepen: The leader of the free world would be an Irish American named Kennedy, while the woman leading the Communist opposition in Kennedy's own country would be an Irish American named Flynn. The Irish were not necessarily clannish in their views.

Michael Joseph Quill was born in 1905 in Kilgarrin, County Kerry, and became a volunteer in the Irish Republican Army at the age of fourteen. He served through the War of Independence and the civil war, then came to New York in 1926. He found work there in the expansive and expanding subway system. In 1934 he was one of the founders of the Transport Workers Union of America, which elected him its president. For three decades to follow, Quill would be

MAY THE ROAD RISE TO MEET YOU

active in local and national union affairs. He became president of the International Transport Workers Union, which affiliated with the Congress of Industrial Organizations in 1937.

During the 1930s, approximately 50 percent of the TWU's members were natives of Ireland. Many had been recruited from over there by Clan na Gael, the secretive American branch of the Irish Republican movement that is discussed in chapter 9. Throughout the first half of the twentieth century, motormen, conductors, and change-booth attendants on the New York subways were more likely than not to have an Irish accent. (The Interboro Rapid Transit system was sometimes called Irish Rapid Transit.) The Transport Workers Union, under Irish-born leaders like Quill, still seemed like a Celtic club long after the composition of the rank and file came to reflect the city's population shifts.

Quill, who had once had Communist leanings à la Flynn, became, over time, an anti-Communist, and tried to root the Communist influence from the U.S. labor movement. He was seen in New York as a respectable and respected man: He served, off and on, as a member of the New York City Council. Then, in 1965, he led a tumultuous strike against New York's bus and subway lines, a strike that paralyzed the city for twelve days. Quill was sent to prison for refusing a court order to end the strike; he was also indicted for criminally libeling a member of the Transit Authority. In jail he suffered a heart attack, which in all probability hastened his death the following January.

In the time of great progress for American labor—the time of Gompers and Jones and Quill—many Irish Americans worked from inside government to speed reform. **Maurice J. Tobin** was the U.S. secretary of labor from 1949 through 1953, and for a short time **Martin Durkin** took over; **James Mitchell** succeeded Durkin and served until 1961; **Peter J. Brennan** would hold the post for a year during the Nixon and Ford administrations, and **Raymond J. Donovan** for a time while Reagan was in the White House.

But it was the outsiders, the agitators, the leaders of the movement itself who had the big impact. Safe to say, no one played a larger role in bettering the lot of the working man in the twentieth century than did **George Meany.**

Born in New York in 1894, he was the grandson of Famine refugees. He began his career at sixteen as an apprentice plumber and soon became active in his union. By 1952 he had been elected president of the American Federation of Labor and was instrumental in its 1955 merger with the Congress of Industrial Organizations. The new AFL-CIO, a national labor organization of unprecedented size and strength, was ruled by Meany until his retirement in 1979. He worked vigorously to reduce corruption in labor and orchestrated the expulsion of the powerful Teamsters Union from the larger organization in 1957 after charges of unethical conduct were brought against Teamsters leaders. Meany also worked to strengthen U.S. labor's stand against Communism at home and abroad (opposing Flynn, of course), and strongly backed the U.S. war effort in Vietnam (opposing Robert Kennedy, the Berrigan brothers, and many others).

In 1963 Meany was at John F. Kennedy's side during the president's historic visit to Ireland. He was introduced to crowds in Wexford by JFK as head of the American labor movement. He received a hero's welcome. George Meany, a coalition builder, a negotiator, a conciliator *par excellence*, died in 1980, one year after leaving the movement.

Speaking of workers— Didn't Irish workers build Titanic?

Well, yes, sort of. In fact, Irish and Irish Americans have more than a few links to the ill-fated ship.

Titanic was built in Belfast's Harland and Wolf shipyard. Moreover, Ireland was *Titanic*'s last port of call for the passengers before heading west over the Atlantic (final embarkation was at Queenstown, now Cobh, in County Cork). Lawrence Beesley, who survived the sinking, wrote one of the first of scores of books about the tragedy, *The Loss of the SS Titanic*. In 1912 Beesley remembered, "The last we saw of Europe was the Irish mountains dim and faint in the dropping darkness."

More than two hundred members of the Ulster Titanic Society still meet regularly to discuss a range of *Titanic*-related topics. Older members recall their first glimpses of the ship and recount tales handed down from their fathers and grandfathers who worked on her construction. The society also holds a commemorative dinner every April 2 to salute the day *Titanic* left Belfast, and to remember the many Irish who perished on board.

The ship's designer was Belfast-born **Thomas Andrews,** and the movie got it right: Andrews was the first to realize that *Titanic* was doomed after its encounter with the iceberg. There were many other

Irish aboard, most of them down below. Of those passengers in steerage, 113 had joined *Titanic* at Queenstown, among them Flynns, Connollys, Foleys, Gallaghers, Morans, Bourkes. Just 39 survived. As is famously known, more than 1,500 of *Titanic*'s 2,223 passengers and crew were lost at sea, but more than two-thirds of those traveling first class were saved, while three-fourths of those in third class died (only 23 of the 73 children in third class survived). Dying—or living—was not an egalitarian proposition on the Night to Remember.

One of the steerage passengers who managed to survive was twenty-one-year-old **Daniel Buckley** from Cork. He was able to break through a gate locking the third-class travelers out of first class, and then jump into a lifeboat. Buckley's reprieve was short-lived; he died in 1918, fighting in World War I. Another survivor was sixteen-year-old **Kate Gilragh** from Longford, who later became a member of Titanic Enthusiasts of America.

Among Irish Americans aboard the ship, the most famous was certainly **"Molly" Brown,** the unsinkable one, memorably portrayed in the 1997 film by Kathy Bates. Whether she helped Leonardo DiCaprio with his girl problems or not, she was by all accounts an irrepressible presence on board. And, again by all accounts, she behaved valorously during the terror.

Margaret Tobin's father had emigrated to America before the Famine, and Margaret, who would go by "Maggie" but never "Molly," was born in 1867 in Hannibal, Missouri (she later claimed to have known Mark Twain, but she claimed a lot of things). Her mother, the former Johanna Collins, had also been an Irish immigrant. By 1886 Maggie was in Leadville, Colorado, where her siblings were hoping to strike it rich. She was working in a dry goods store when she met James Brown, who did indeed find gold shortly after he and Maggie were wed. The Browns moved into an expensive house in Denver, and Maggie started building her pile of jewelry and clothes. But there was her mitigating personality— sunny, down-to-earth—that kept others from disliking her. James suffered a stroke in 1899 and was forced to quit mining. Maggie, for her part, took to being transatlantic; she wanted her children educated abroad, and she liked boating back and forth herself. On one of her European tours she learned that a grandson back home had taken ill, and she hurriedly booked passage on the new luxury ship *Titanic*.

As was true everywhere, people aboard the ship loved her company and her unpretentious, plainspoken manner. The legend goes that, upon being told that the ship was sinking, she declared herself "unsinkable" and tried to rally others to think the same way. In all probability the unsinkable part came to the fore in the United States when, explaining her good fortune after the sinking, she spoke of "typical Brown luck . . . we're unsinkable!"

In any event, she did end up in a lifeboat (she claimed she was pushed in) and did essentially take charge of the vessel from an ineffectual *Titanic* crewman. Her fierce self-confidence buoyed her boatmates; they later hailed her as a heroine. She was the first to spot the lights of *Carpathia*, the liner that rescued *Titanic*'s survivors. Once on board that ship she compiled a survivors' list, saw that the information was transmitted to New York, then went among her fellow wealthy passengers and collected $10,000 as a fund for the less well-off. Upon reaching America she became an instant celebrity, and since she wasn't shy about telling the tale over and over—Maggie wasn't shy about much—her fame endured. Well before James Cameron made his titanic *Titanic* there was a Broadway and movie musical based on the unsinkable Molly Brown.

She was a feminist. She ran for the U.S. Senate in 1914 but lost; women didn't have the vote yet, so that didn't help. She lobbied with President Calvin Coolidge for an Equal Rights Amendment, to no avail.

She couldn't conquer her high-living ways. James died in 1922, and in the next decade before her own death Maggie squandered most of what remained of the lucre from the gold strike—which had been the first but hardly the most famous instance of typical Brown luck.

Who were some other Irish American heroes of the twentieth century?

During World War I there were some, and World War II produced a passel of them.

Many Irish Americans were against U.S. intervention in World War I, as we learned in chapter 9. But others felt it was time for the clan to show its patriotism in the New World.

The 69th New York National Guard Regiment, which saw service in the erstwhile war to end all wars, was alternately called the Fighting 69th and the Irish 69th. Poet **Joyce Kilmer** was a sergeant in the unit: "It was desired to enlist strong, intelligent, decent living men,

men whose sturdy Americanism was strengthened and vivified by their Celtic blood, men who would be worthy successors of those forgotten patriots who at Bloody Lane and on Marye's Heights earned the title of 'The Fighting Irish.' " In service of this "desire," the regiment's machine-gun trucks toured Irish sections of New York displaying a placard reading DON'T JOIN THE 69TH UNLESS YOU WANT TO BE AMONG THE FIRST TO GO TO FRANCE. This appealed to Irish pride and pugnacity both. The Catholic clergy was asked to refer good men from the parish athletic clubs to the 69th.

One priest directly affiliated with the regiment was the Canadian-born **Father Francis Patrick Duffy**, always beloved and ultimately heroic. (His statue now commands Duffy Square, just north of Times Square in the Hell's Kitchen parish of Holy Cross Church, where he served as pastor.) Father Duffy observed of the 69th: "An Irish regiment has its trouble in time of peace. But when the call to arms was sounding we knew that if they would let us, we could easily offer them an Irish Brigade for the service." There were numbers of French, Italians, and Poles in the unit as well, drawn by its Catholic character. "The 69th never attempted to set up a religious test," Father Duffy maintained. "It was an institution offered to the nation by a people grateful for liberty, and it always welcomed and made part of it any American citizen who desired to serve in it. But, naturally, men of Irish birth or blood were attracted to the traditions of the 69th, and many Catholics wanted to be with a regiment where they could be sure of being able to attend to their religious duties." As it turned out, he said, only about 5 percent of the regiment was Irish "neither by race or racial creed."

The 69th was, as promised, among the very first fighting units sent overseas in World War I. After training at Camp Mills on Long Island, the regiment was shipped to France in two transports. All told, it was in direct contact with the enemy for 180 days, the most of any U.S. unit. The records show that it changed its headquarters eighty-three times, and gained in battle a total of fifty-five kilometers. It went overseas with some 3,500 men, and it suffered exactly 3,501 casualties—644 killed and 2,857 wounded.

The regiment was gassed only a short time after reaching France, but it survived and went on to distinguish itself in the Aisne-Marne push, the St. Mihiel offensive, and the crucial Argonne-Meuse drive. The heroic deeds of the 69th's brave soldiers are too many to catalog here, but they were recorded with care in one of Father Duffy's diaries, which was published after the war. In his remarkable volume

Father Duffy wrote of the curious blend of piety and pugnacity that went into making the fighting Irishman. "The religion of the Irish has characteristics of its own," he said. "They make the Sign of the Cross with the right hand, while holding the left ready to give a jab to anybody who needed it, for his own or the general good. I cannot say that it is an ideal type of Christianity; but considering the sort of world we have to live in yet, it is as near as we can come at present to perfection for the generality of men. It was into the mouth of an Irish soldier that Kipling put the motto, 'Help a woman, and hit a man; and you won't go far wrong either way.' "

Father Duffy—and Kipling, for that matter—might as well have given a name to the soldier, for he was epitomized in the man who rose to become the unit's leader and, subsequently, to be awarded the Medal of Honor: Colonel **William J. "Wild Bill" Donovan.** A Buffalo lawyer, Donovan had gained his nickname not in fighting but as a college football star. In his diary, Father Duffy maintained: "The richest gain that I have gotten out of war is the friendship of William J. Donovan."

Donovan, as a boy, had reveled in stories of the great deeds of Meagher's Irish Brigade during the Civil War, and he'd dreamed that someday he too might command such a force in service to his country. As it turned out, his dream came true in spades, for the 69th was larger than the Irish Brigade ever grew to be. Donovan arrived ready to take charge. "He is always physically fit," wrote Duffy, "always alert, ready to do without food, sleep, rest, in the most matter of fact way, thinking of nothing but the work at hand. He has mind and manners on varied experience of life and resoluteness of purpose. He has kept himself clean and sane and whole for whatever adventure life might bring him."

The adventures were ferocious. With "Front Line" Duffy as confessor and inspiration to the men, and "Wild Bill" spurring them on, the 69th performed with a gallantry that was truly astonishing. What survivors there were returned as heroes; Father Duffy was awarded the Distinguished Service Cross and the Croix de Guerre. He returned to his work among the poor, and when he died in 1932 of colitis, Bill Donovan saw to it that his statue was erected in New York. In the bronze, the priest is not in robes but in his doughboy's uniform.

Donovan, meanwhile, ran for governor of New York, then hooked up with Franklin D. Roosevelt and, when FDR ascended to the White House, he went to London as the president's confidential agent. He came back convinced that America needed an intelligence organization similar to that of Britain. The upshot was the cloak-and-dagger Office of Strategic Services, which under General Donovan's command proved vital to Allied operations during World War II.

The range of OSS activities in the realms of espionage and sabotage was wide and impressive. The United States emerged from the war firmly committed to spying as a way of life in the nuclear age. Among the many bright, ruthless young Irish Americans who Donovan recruited into his apparatus was **William Casey,** who, under President Reagan, would direct the Central Intelligence Agency, the successor service to the OSS.

And you say there were also Irish American heroes from the Second World War?

Yes. In this war, with the American operation so immense, the Irish were fairly well dispersed throughout the fighting forces. There was no Irish brigade. But there were individual Irish Americans who distinguished themselves.

- Captain **Colin Kelly** was the pilot of a bomber that destroyed a Japanese warship in the Philippines on December 9, 1941. When his plane was damaged by enemy fire, he ordered his crew to bail out while he flew on. The plane crashed. He was posthumously awarded the Distinguished Service Cross and became the first American hero of the war.
- **Edward H. O'Hare** was born in St. Louis in 1914 and graduated from the U.S. Naval Academy in 1937. Early in 1942 he was serving as a naval aviator on the carrier *Lexington* when the ship was attacked by Japanese bombers. The rest of his squadron was heavily engaged, and O'Hare found himself alone, opposed by an entire enemy squadron. He attacked the nine heavily armed bombers single-handedly, shooting down five and damaging three. The surviving attackers fled. O'Hare had saved the *Lexington*, and had become the navy's first ace of the war. He was awarded the Medal of Honor and promoted to lieutenant commander. By November 20, 1943, he had shot down a total of twelve enemy planes; on that date he was listed as missing in action. O'Hare International Airport in Chicago is named in his honor.

- Lieutenant **Audie Murphy** was born in 1924 to a poor Texas-Irish sharecropping family. He enlisted in the army in 1942 and during the next thirty months rose from private to lieutenant, serving in Tunisia, Sicily, Italy, France, and Germany. Wounded three times, he was repeatedly cited for gallantry in action. He won the Medal of Honor for single-handedly holding off a German force of half a dozen tanks and two hundred men. With a total of twenty-eight American and foreign medals, he was the most highly decorated U.S. serviceman of World War II. And he made the most of it: After the war he played himself in *To Hell and Back* and became a movie idol. His film career included starring roles in *The Red Badge of Courage* and a series of low-budget westerns. He died in a plane crash in 1971.

- General **James M. Gavin** was the intrepid leader of the great new development in warfare, the paratroopers. His efforts in the European theater during D-Day and the Battle of the Bulge helped turn the tide. Later, Gavin was a confidant of fellow war hero John F. Kennedy and served his country as ambassador to France.

- General **Anthony McAuliffe** was the Bulge leader who uttered the single most significant word of the conflict—"Nuts!"—to the Germans demanding surrender of the beleaguered American forces at Bastogne. When the tide did turn, McAuliffe was ready.

- Major **Thomas B. McGuire** was born in New Jersey in 1920 and entered the U.S. Army Air Corps in 1941. During his service in the Pacific he shot down a total of thirty-eight Japanese planes, making him the second-highest-ranking American fighter ace of the war. On January 7, 1945, while aiding a comrade under attack, Major McGuire crashed in the Philippines. He was awarded a posthumous Medal of Honor, and McGuire Air Force Base in New Jersey is named for him.

- The **Fighting Sullivans** were more than just a 1944 film of that title, they were the goods. George, Francis, Joseph, Madison, and Albert Sullivan of Waterloo, Iowa, boarded the USS *Juneau* when it was commissioned at the Brooklyn Navy Yard at the outset of the war. They had enlisted in the navy after Pearl Harbor and had received permission to serve on the same ship, despite a navy prohibition against assigning brothers together. The cruiser joined the Pacific fleet in August of

1942 and was assigned to task forces operating with the aircraft carriers *Wasp*, *Hornet*, and *Enterprise*. The *Juneau* helped sink several Japanese ships and brought down dozens of aircraft with her guns. On November 13, 1942, she was hit by a Japanese torpedo off Guadalcanal in the Solomon Islands, where she had been part of a protective screen around troop transports and cargo vessels unloading on the beaches. She went down with most of her crew of seven hundred. Among the victims were all five of the Sullivans. In 1977 U.S. Senator Daniel Moynihan commissioned a new naval destroyer named the USS *Sullivan* in New York harbor—the same bay whence the brave brothers had sailed to one of the great American tragedies at sea.

Those, obviously, are but a few who fought courageously. And by ending our consideration of Irish American war heroes of the twentieth century here, we in no way mean to slight the heroes of the Korean and Vietnam conflicts. But there were external considerations at hand in the world wars—the mother country, Ireland, was saying "Don't go"—and so the American patriotism shown by these fighting men was complex indeed.

How did Irish Americans impact religion in the twentieth century?

Well, certainly, Father Duffy wasn't the only man of the cloth to have an effect. **Edward J. Flanagan** was born in County Roscommon in 1886 and came to the United States in 1904, where he soon entered the seminary. After continuing his studies at the Gregorian University in Rome and the University of Innsbruck in Austria, he returned to the United States and was assigned to a parish in Nebraska. He took an interest in social service and founded a hostel for workingmen in Omaha. Eventually his compassionate nature turned to helping disadvantaged boys who had broken a law or come from a broken home. He began appearing at juvenile court hearings, insisting that "there is no such thing as a bad boy." Usually, he could persuade the judge to turn the youthful offenders over to his care for "another chance." But what to do with the boys? In 1917 Father Flanagan established Boys Town U.S.A., which became a haven for hundreds of boys of all religions and races. (The statue and the slogan say it: "He's not heavy, he's my brother.") Father Flanagan's work was immortalized in the 1938 movie starring two who could play Irish, Spencer Tracy and Mickey Rooney.

Fulton J. Sheen was born in El Paso, Texas, in 1895 and ordained a priest in 1919. He, too, studied in Europe: philosophy at the Catholic University of Louvain, Belgium. He returned to the United States in 1926 and began a quarter-century teaching career at Catholic University of America. He could write, too: *God and Intelligence in Modern Philosophy* was only the first of some fifty books. And could he speak! Beginning in 1930, his *Catholic Hour* radio programs were luring millions, inside and outside the faith. In 1950 he was named director of the Society for the Propagation of the Faith in the United States, and in that post he used his talent for fundraising. Millions were given for mission work abroad. During the 1950s he also became a familiar television personality with his program *Life Is Worth Living*. Not only effective with mass audiences, Sheen acquired a reputation as a personal proselytizer, converting a number of well-known Americans, such as Claire Booth Luce. In 1966 he was named bishop of Rochester, New York, but Archbishop Fulton J. Sheen was never elected cardinal. Small matter. He might have been too American—too mass media—for Rome, but he was what the modern country wanted, perhaps needed, in its twentieth-century spiritual adviser.

Francis Spellman was born in 1889 to Irish immigrant parents in Massachusetts. He earned a B.A. at Fordham University and entered the priesthood in 1916. After service in Boston, he was assigned to the Papal Secretariat in Rome from 1925 to 1932. When he returned to the United States he served as auxiliary bishop of Boston before being named archbishop of New York in 1939. He was elevated to cardinal in 1946.

Cardinal Spellman was the apostolic vicar to the U.S. armed forces during World War II and made several visits to the battle zone. His friendships with church leaders around the world led to several missions as envoy for Presidents Roosevelt and Truman. His influence abroad was immense: He was sometimes called the American pope.

His power at home was even larger.

When Bishop Spellman took over in New York he inherited an impressive army of more than 2,500 priests, 10,000 nuns, and 2 million parishioners, but the whole operation was more than $25 million in debt. He immediately set about reversing the financial situation. He cultivated ties to prominent Catholic public officials,

Irish and otherwise, as well as with the city's growing middle and upper classes. Under Cardinal Spellman the church raised considerable sums overnight and began expanding its schools, charities, and parishes.

But Cardinal Spellman was interested in things other than parish affairs and church building, and he began to play a prominent role in public life. His critics charged that he exercised undue influence in city politics, while his supporters saw his activities as proper exercises of concern for the spiritual and moral welfare of the citizenry. Cardinal Spellman sought to censor movies, gain public funds for parochial schools, and blur the distinction between church and state. At a controversial breakfast sponsored by the New York Police Department's Holy Name Society in April 1953, Cardinal Spellman gave his support to the anti-Communist efforts of Senator Joe McCarthy, much to the delight of thousands of cheering police.

Not all Catholics agreed with the cardinal's political positions, nor were they in agreement with him when he criticized the reformers of Vatican II in the early 1960s. But Cardinal Spellman continued to go his own way, alienating whomever he might, making friends where he would. When he died in 1968 there were nearly as many political leaders as clergy at the funeral, including Lyndon Baines Johnson, who was, perhaps, thanking the cardinal for his long and ardent support of the U.S. role in Vietnam.

If you see harbingers in the careers of Bishop Sheen and Cardinal Spellman, so be it. Undoubtedly, the former taught all future charismatic church leaders that the media could be the message, and certainly the latter taught that politics and religion could and do mix. Pat Robertson, Jerry Falwell, even Ralph Reed, the young lion of the religious right, learned from these masters.

And then there was modest Tom Dooley.

Thomas Anthony Dooley was born in 1927 and seemed headed for a lucrative medical practice before he dedicated his life to serving the suffering in Southeast Asia. His first experience there had been as a navy doctor in 1954, aiding refugees who were fleeing Communist North Vietnam. In 1956 he began a medical mission in the jungle of neighboring Laos. His first book, *Deliver Us from Evil*, which recounts his naval service in Vietnam, was published that year, and it gave Dooley some fame and a bit of fortune. He used the money from the book and nearly three hundred lectures to establish the Laos hospital. In 1957 Dooley was instrumental in founding the Medical International Cooperation Organization, which he used to channel money from more speeches and other books into good works abroad. He built two more hospitals in Laos, three more elsewhere in Southeast Asia. Dooley died of cancer at the age of thirty-four in 1961 and was posthumously honored with a Congressional gold medal.

Did Irish Americans contribute anything else to the country in the twentieth century?

Oh, certainly. Just as an example: Irish coffee. Perhaps.

Pardon me?

Irish coffee is a concoction invented either in 1946 in the Shannon Airport bar in western Ireland or in 1953 at the Buena Vista Cafe in San Francisco. This is according to *Philadelphia Inquirer* food columnist Bill Collins, who researched the controversy for a Saint Patrick's Day column in 1980 and published his conclusion "to end controversies [but] in full awareness that it will only start new ones."

The Irish argument: On Saint Pat's day in '46 a bartender at the airport needed—*needed*—something in his coffee to help him past the previous evening, and he tried a shot of whiskey. It worked, and he offered it to his earliest customers. It kept working. Seven years later, Stanley Delaplane, travel writer for the *San Francisco Chronicle*, had a drink—*that* drink—at Shannon and brought the recipe home to his friends at the Buena Vista. The Buena Vista had an American knack for marketing and successfully promoted the coffee as its signature drink. But the Delaplane link seems to indicate that the concoction was, indeed, born back home.

Want one? Boil some water. Get a teaspoon of brown sugar, an ounce and a half of Irish whiskey, five ounces of hot, strong coffee, and some softly whipped cream. Into a clear eight-ounce glass put a spoon, so the glass won't crack. Fill it halfway with the water, then remove the spoon and dump the water. Pour in the coffee, then the brown sugar, then the whiskey. Top with the cream, poured in lightly over the back of a spoon so it floats on the surface like an iceberg. Drink through the cream—don't stir the stuff in. And *please*, skip the green garnishings. *Slainte!*

THIRTEEN

From County Wexford to Camelot: A Family Saga

Who was Patrick Kennedy?

Who was Bridget Murphy?

How did the family begin?

What happened to Irish-born Bridget Kennedy?

Who was James Fitzgerald?

How did Rose Fitzgerald meet Joe Kennedy?

What were the ambitions of the
Joseph Kennedy family?

Who were the children of Rose and Joe?

How did the Kennedys conquer the country?

What did Bobby do first after his brother's death?

What did Ted do after his brother's death?

*Are there other Kennedy politicians
today, besides Ted?*

*So what does this amazing Kennedy
saga really mean?*

Who was Patrick Kennedy?

He was a Famine immigrant and patriarch of what grew to be certainly the most remarkable (adherents would argue, greatest) of all Irish American families.

Who was Bridget Murphy?

She, too, was a Famine immigrant—from the same county, Wexford, as Patrick Kennedy. She traveled to America aboard the same ship in 1849. She would become the matriarch of that family.

How did the family begin?

Eighteen forty-nine, not Black '47, was in fact the worst year of the Famine. Patrick Kennedy, twenty-six, was part of a family that farmed twenty-five acres in Dunganstown. His elder brother, John, had died years earlier, and Patrick left behind his parents, one brother, and a sister—who would be evicted from the farm by the landlord. Patrick made his way to Liverpool and there boarded the *Washington Irving*, a good ship named for the first American writer of international reputation. On board, Patrick met Bridget, and they found that they had a month to kill and much in common to discuss. By the time the boat reached Boston, they were in love.

The Kennedys did not arrive in any way rich. Patrick and Bridget married and took quarters in the East Boston slum—they probably couldn't afford the two-pennies ferry fare to cross the harbor into downtown—a place where, as Terry Golway put it in *The Irish in America*, "children were born to die." The conditions in "Paddyville," in "Mick Alley," were deplorable. Golway pointed out that 60 percent of those born in Boston at that time didn't live to see their sixth birthday, and "adults fared little better, for the average Famine immigrant lived no longer than five or six years after stepping foot on American soil. The Irish lived in shanties and basements, breeding grounds of disease and despair. A Boston doctor was visiting a patient lying ill in a bedroom filled with water when a tiny coffin floated by. It contained the body of the patient's child."

Patrick became a cooper. Bridget bore three daughters and a son in eight years (a pace that would seem sedate when compared with that of Robert and Ethel Kennedy, more than a century later). In doing his research, Golway found a public health commission report from approximately the time when Patrick and Bridget were raising their children: "huddled together like brutes, without regard to sex or age, or sense of decency; grown men and women sleeping together in the same apartment, and sometimes wife and husband, brothers and sisters in the same bed . . . self-respect, forethought, all high and noble virtues soon die out [replaced by] sullen indifference and despair, or disorder, intemperance and utter degradation." It wasn't a technical report, and all the more vivid for it.

Cholera hit these Irish slums at that time, killing five hundred. There was little sympathy on Beacon Hill, since the Irish were not only resented but hated in Boston. There was no mourning beyond the family when, late in 1858, the immigrant Patrick Kennedy died of cholera. He had left behind one son to carry his name, his last child born—Patrick Joseph Kennedy Jr.

The boy, "P.J.," went to school under the Sisters of Notre Dame, worked in Boston Harbor as a stevedore, saved some money, borrowed some from his mother, got a dilapidated saloon—in Haymarket, not far from where The Black Rose is today. He worked hard, his saloon prospered, and, still in his twenties, he was able to buy two more bars. By the age of thirty he had formed his own liquor-importing business, P.J. Kennedy and Company. In 1887 he married up in class, catching Mary Augusta Hickey, the daughter of a businessman and sister of a police lieutenant, a physician graduated from Harvard, and a funeral director.

P.J. and Mary would have two sons (the second would die in infancy) and two daughters. Their firstborn, in 1888, was given an inversion of the family name: Joseph Patrick Kennedy. He would grow up to be a real piece of work.

What happened to Irish-born Bridget Kennedy?

After her husband's death, she was nearly destitute. She clerked in a notions store in a building near the ferry, while neighbors helped the children stay alive by bringing them soup during the day. She saved and eventually bought the store. P.J. assisted her there before departing for the docks, the saloon, and the small fortune that made Bridget's last years more comfortable.

She lived to see her grandchild Joe born on September 6, but died before the year was out, at age sixty-seven.

Who was James Fitzgerald?

Like Bridget and Patrick, he was a Famine immigrant. Unlike Bridget or Patrick, he did not come alone, but was accompanied by an uncle and a cousin. He was a forerunner for his own immediate family, arriving sometime in (or just after) 1848. Shortly thereafter his three sisters and his widowed mother, Ellen, arrived and finally an older brother, Thomas, who, according to Fitzgerald family tradition, tried to work the land in Ireland until there was no hope. Thus were the Fitzgeralds uprooted as a unit of some size in Ireland and transplanted in America.

James was but a boy when he emigrated—ten or eleven—and in his uncle's care. He got terribly sick on the crossing and was sheltered by his kin under a blanket lest the captain think he had typhus and throw him overboard. A ferocious storm battered the ship as it neared the U.S. coast, turning it northward. The ship may have been heading for New York and was blown to Boston; fate may have played a larger role than is evident in the powerful coming together of the Fitzgeralds and the Kennedys (and, by the way, our synopsis of the Fitzgerald part of the tale, at least, owes much to the wonderful book of that name by the Pulitzer prize–winning historian Doris Kearns Goodwin).

The first intrepid three settled in the North End, and the rest of the clan followed. When Thomas arrived, he and a cousin and her husband moved out to Acton, west of Boston. He worked as a farmer for a while, then moved back to Boston and worked as a street peddler. He married Rosanna Cox, daughter of Irish immigrants, in

November of 1857, and after five years the couple had four sons. Thomas had eyes for the Midwest, and now was the time for the move. But James enticed his brother to stay in Boston and join him in his fledgling grocery business on North Street. The Fitzgeralds stayed whole in Boston. Thomas later said that he stayed for his family, his wife, and his Church, and Goodwin pointed out that at the time this was in no way surprising. The Church was bedrock and solace for a struggling community; John Boyle O'Reilly and his *Pilot* were glue for Boston's underclass. They were hope.

Whether or nor Thomas was ever truly happy about remaining in Boston, he had backed a solid horse in James. "Of all the Fitzgerald children, [he] adapted most readily to the challenge of life in the New World," wrote Goodwin. "Whereas his sisters and brothers retained all their lives many characteristics of western Ireland, James, with his ready will and raw intelligence, made himself thoroughly comfortable in the city." James had clerked in the store he eventually bought, and during a half-century he would turn it into a great success. At twenty he married up in class, wedding Julia Adeline Brophy. (Was James the first of the charming, seemingly irresistible members of the great family? Details elude us; we can only speculate.) Once James had brought Thomas into the business, he was able to expand his store to stock liquor and open an adjunct saloon. The Fitzgerald place at 310 North became the neighborhood local as well as the country store.

Tom and Rosanna both worked in the store, meantime having twelve children in all; they, too, stand as early American role models for such as Bobby and Ethel. **John Francis Fitzgerald,** the fourth boy, the one whose birth had prompted thoughts of exodus to the Midwest, later remembered that he, too, loved the store, "loved the sense of being right in the middle of everyone, where everything was happening." James's family slowly became one of the very wealthiest in the North End, while brother Tom's grew to be stable and safe— no small victory. "John Fitzgerald long relished the memory of eating fish as well as meat and of having fresh vegetables every day," wrote Goodwin, "and he particularly remembered Sunday nights when his mother made flapjacks which he loved to drown in butter and syrup or molasses.

"If the store did well by day, it thrived by night as the neighborhood men, home from a long day of hard work, began to drop in for drinks."

Thomas was able, by 1866, to buy a three-story tenement for his burgeoning family in Hanover Street (cost: $6,550). He became a landlord, and, on the ground floor, opened his own grocery. He bought two more tenements; he was now quite a slumlord. And the family grew—nine boys in all, three of whom would prosper as their father had in the liquor business, three of whom would die young from drink. "The curse of the liquor money" became a family mantra.

John was the healthiest and happiest of boys; he would remember much later, "We used to run on the sidewalks and cobblestones of Hanover Street and I could always beat any of the boys. I could also sprint around the loop of old Fort Hill in a shorter time than any competitors. As a sprinter my distance was from 120 to 150 yards. I won the half mile distance cup in Boston one year. I was a champ." We cite this with emphasis: Between James's charm and now Johnny's vibrancy, it becomes clear that many of the instinctual traits that the great family is famous for were formed early on the side of the clan not named Kennedy. The Fitzgeralds had good teeth, too.

John, not his two older brothers, emerged as a leader: "For some reason, it was my trust to boss the family." He was remembered by his kin as "the one who taught the others how to swim, how to play ball and how to whistle through their fingers." He was the one "who kept the whole family together."

In 1877 fourteen-year-old Johnny was selling newspapers on Boston's streets, not a bad business: He could make $2.50 a week. Arriving in the predawn to pick up his papers, he fell in love with the business and bustle of the newsroom. He made friends there, and throughout the city. Everyone loved seeing Johnny Fitzgerald. Everything was grand.

In 1879 his mother, Rosanna, died after a seizure at age forty-eight. Things got serious. Thomas Fitzgerald, having lost a young daughter to cholera, another in infancy, and now his wife to a brain disease, determined that one of his nine sons should become a doctor. So it was that John, the leader, was sent to Boston Latin School and then to Harvard Medical School. In 1885 Thomas Fitzgerald died of pneumonia at age sixty-two ("He was a plain, frank, noble hearted man, open of speech and upright in his dealing," read the obituary). By now, John was a man. He was starting to get involved in ward politics; he was not only liked but respected. And, he was in love.

And the circle comes 'round: Remember that cousin Thomas had ventured to Acton with, years earlier? She had stayed. Mary Ann

Hannon and her husband had made a go of the farm, and so of course the Fitzgeralds would occasionally visit—as they did in 1878, when John had first become aware of Mary Josephine Hannon ("Josie") thirteen to his fifteen. She was beautiful even then and would grow lovelier.

The Hannons had had a difficult time. Five of nine boys had died before making a mark as adults—alcohol was a problem in this family, too—leaving three girls and a crippled boy. Josie, therefore, loved her visits in Boston with John. For second cousins to marry in the Catholic Church, dispensation was required. The Hannons were against the match, fearing more weak or crippled children, and pressed the priests to stall. But, finally, on September 18, 1889, according to the *Concord Enterprise*, "The marriage of Miss Mary Hannon . . . and Mr. J. F. Fitzgerald, president of the Neptune Associates of Boston, was solemnized in Concord on Thursday last. The wedding party was confined to the relatives and intimate friends on account of a recent death in the bride's family. Elegant wedding gifts were presented by Mr. Fitzgerald's associates in the Customs House, from the Neptune society and classmates in the Boston Latin School. The bridal party left immediately after the ceremony for an extended tour of the White Mountains."

Two months after the honeymoon, Josie was pregnant. They would name this first daughter, born on a hot and steamy July 22, 1890, **Rose Elizabeth Fitzgerald,** in memory of her grandmother Rosanna and Josie's little sister Elizabeth. The Hannons' fear about the constitution of John and Josie's offspring were, in this case, wildly unfounded: Rose would live a century plus five years, surviving more triumph and torment than a hundred other women. The writer Brad Darrach would, upon her death, be able to look back and claim without undue hyperbole, "She was the Queen Mother of Camelot. A tribal matriarch as formidable as the iron-willed dam of the Bonapartes, she bore and nurtured America's most dazzling political dynasty. Yet she saw, one after another, five of her nine children—three of her four sons—struck down in a family tragedy as grim as any Shakespeare contrived."

But that was yet to come.

How did Rose Fitzgerald meet Joe Kennedy?

John Fitzgerald did exceedingly well. He had an innate talent for politics and soon the press was calling him the Little Napoleon of

Ward 6, as he consolidated not only his Irish support but that of newer Italian and Russian immigrants who had followed into Boston. His personal machine was called the Jefferson Club, and it helped him get elected, first, to the state house of representatives, then to the state senate. The *Boston Daily Advertiser* cited him as "the most called for man at the state-house." In 1894 Fitzgerald set his sights on the U.S. congressional seat from the Ninth district—now famous as the district of JFK, Tip O'Neill, and Joe Kennedy, Jr. It was, in Fitzgerald's day, the only Democratic district in Massachusetts, and he would have to beat a fellow Irish American, Joseph O'Neil, a favorite of city boss P. J. Maguire's. The Wall Street panic of 1893, however, had created unrest, and all incumbents were vulnerable. Fitzgerald appealed to the poor and unemployed, and the depression carried him to Washington. "Now that the fight is over, P.J., let's shake hands," a tired Fitzgerald offered on the morning after election. They did, and Fitzgerald got the Boston machine behind him.

Fitzgerald's family stayed in rural Massachusetts while he went to Boston. The brood had grown—Rose had a sister Agnes and a brother Thomas by now—and Josie coped by moving them all to West Concord. "Those were wonderful years," Rose would recall, "full of the traditional pleasures and satisfactions of life in a small New England town: trips with horse and buggy to my grandparents' house, climbing apple trees, gathering wildflowers in the woods behind the house." John Francis Fitzgerald, Jr., and Eunice Fitzgerald were born in these years.

There were vacations north of Concord. The Fitzgeralds encamped each summer in a cottage in Old Orchard Beach, Maine, one of the Irish Rivieras—like Spring Lake, New Jersey, and Hampton Beach, New Hampshire—that were being established on the Atlantic seaboard by families on the rise. There, in 1895, Rose met a seven-year-old named Joseph Patrick Kennedy, who was also vacationing with his parents. There's a group photo that proves it, and there is nothing at all surprising about the fact that two large, energetic, Irish American families from Boston would come together in this way. Though the amazing results of their intersection seem to have been determined by the fates or the furies, the Fitzgeralds and the Kennedys were, in fact, bound to bump into each other.

John Fitzgerald came home for good in 1900, saying he didn't want to run for Congress again. He had bought a Catholic weekly newspaper earlier and it had done well, so now he had the money for a mansion in Dorchester. The family moved back in toward Boston and, in 1905, after the incumbent had died on vacation, Fitzgerald entered a three-way horse race for mayor of Boston and won.

Rose would turn sixteen in the summer of 1906, and she again met Joe Kennedy at Old Orchard Beach. Joe and Rose were their fathers' children, as smart, confident, energetic, and optimistic as either P. J. Kennedy or John "Honey Fitz" Fitzgerald, and that's saying something. Rose remembered later that young Joe—a top scholar at Boston Latin, captain of the baseball team—had "the most wonderful smile that seemed to light up his entire face from within and made an instant impression on everyone he met." Hers wasn't bad either. As Darrach wrote: "At 16 she was a magical creature—elegant, spirited, well read." But summers never last forever. Joe went on to Harvard, Rose to a convent school in the Netherlands. Her father proceeded down the road that would end with James Michael Curley, the clan's first taste of defeat, its first roadblock in America.

Rose had been nicknamed "Father Says" for her often-repeated phrase, but she disobeyed the elder Fitzgerald by secretly dating Joseph Kennedy when she was home (the Kennedys weren't high society enough, Honey Fitz insisted). But Rose profited by her father's errant ways. After news leaked about Dad's dalliance with a Boston cigarette girl named Toodles, Rose wed Joe in 1914—and who was to say anything about it? Rose's life was being formed in both her parents' images. From the Boston pol she got brains and charm, from the matriarch she got her Black Irish loveliness, her genes for longevity (Josie would live to be ninety-eight), and her avid Catholicism, reinforced by her convent training ("Freed from all worldly thoughts, I was able to find in myself the place that was meant for God"). This last would see her through when Joe, too, found his various Toodles.

What were the ambitions of the Joseph Kennedy family?

To conquer the country, perhaps the world. In these ambitions Rose and Joe were united, and ambition was the cement that would hold this troubled marriage together.

Their firstborn, Joe Jr., was to be president. He was raised that way by Rose, as Joe Sr. was often away, making the family millions in the stock market, in Hollywood (that's where the affairs come in, including the well-publicized one with Gloria Swanson), and in the age-old Kennedy-Fitzgerald concern, liquor. "The molding of the family was largely left to Rose," wrote Darrach, "and she did an astonishing job. She organized the household like a small town and ran it like a mayor, supervising a staff of cooks, nannies, maids and secretaries. She was the health department: She made sure teeth were brushed after every meal, drove the gang to the dentist every few weeks and kept a medical history of each child on file cards. She was the police department: She regularly whacked backsides with a coat hanger, as well as with a ruler. She was the religion teacher: She tried to take at least some of the kids to church every day and, after Sunday service, quizzed them about the sermon. She was the school system: She hired tennis, golf, swimming, skiing and skating instructors and gave tests at mealtimes ('What does the word "Florida" mean? When is the longest day of the year?'). Above all, she taught responsibility (quoting Saint Luke, 'To whom much has been given, much will be required') and the supreme importance of winning ('No matter what you do, you should try to be first')."

Meanwhile, for herself, Rose went to Mass every day (she would continue to do so until crippled by a stroke at ninety-three). Boston civic leader Marie Greene, her lifelong friend, told Doris Kearns Goodwin that during the marriage to Joe, Rose adhered to a strict interpretation of Church teaching that defines the principal purpose of sex as procreation. According to this doctrine, sex is forbidden during pregnancy—and for seventeen years Rose was pregnant at least half the time. She had her last child at forty-one and at that point, according to Greene, told Joe, "No more sex." But long before then, Darrach wrote, "the fire had surely gone out: Rose and Joe took separate vacations and stayed in different hotels when they did travel together. Joe became a chaser—a fact he kept secret from no one, including his sons." We mention these things only by way of explaining the difficulties within this magical family, a family that kept its focus and its dignified front even as there were problems within the walls.

Who were the children of Rose and Joe?

In order of birth, they were:

- **Joseph P. Kennedy, Jr.,** even more handsome than his father, as dazzlingly so as the next oldest brother, John, would prove to be. Joe, born on July 28, 1915, was the chosen one. His father had dreams of the White House for himself, but scandal and bad politics—he was seen as soft on fascism in the 1930s; he was anti-Semitic; he was terribly slow to come around regarding America's intervention in the war—doomed him. So it would be Joe Jr., in every way raised to be a junior Joe. Within the family, he was designated the leader, and it was a role he wanted and protected. Jack would tease him, and there was a lot of tussling between the two older boys. Jack refused to obey Joe's commands; Bobby remembered later that the others would cower as the two brothers went at it. (Joe, stronger, would win the battles, but Jack was undeterred.) Joe might well have made it to the White House, but his plane was shot down on August 12, 1944, and he was dead at twenty-nine. Robert F. Kennedy, Jr., told us in an interview, "That was always portrayed, in our family, not as the ultimate sacrifice, but as the ultimate extension of a life—to give yourself for our country. We were taught in our family to envy Joe."

- **John Fitzgerald Kennedy,** who grew up free of the pressure. Born on May 29, 1917, he had to confront no great expectations for twenty-seven years, and so was free to form himself as a fun guy, a fair scholar, a lover of books (he listed toward adventure stories), and a willing supplicant to the fates. (The hand they would deal him!) Joe Jr.'s domination of Jack caused the second child to become something of an anti-Joe: sloppy in his bedroom where Joe was orderly, lazy at school where Joe was industrious, carefree where Joe was intense and impulsive. JFK did all the right things, however: Harvard, the service. He, like Joe, turned out to be a World War II hero (his valor aboard PT 109 is unquestioned, no matter how his father subsequently blared the news). Then he turned out to be an impossibly charismatic congressional candidate. Then he turned out to be an electrifying president. Then he turned out to be the greatest American martyr since Abraham Lincoln.

- **Rosemary Kennedy,** born on September 13, 1918, a happy girl with a story that now reads sad. She had followed her two brothers to the Devotion School for kindergarten, but the teachers could not recommend her for first grade. She was a lovely and sweet young girl, but all were quickly saying that she was "mentally retarded." Had she suffered from the flu epidemic of 1918? Perhaps, but no matter. She was a Kennedy and would receive the best care money could buy. By age twenty-one, she had received all of that and was perhaps the most beautiful of any Kennedy girl before or since. And so her parents were concerned for her and about her increasingly violent moods. In the 1920s and 1930s the understanding and treatment of retardation was woefully unsophisticated. The Kennedy parents despaired. They worried for Rosemary's choices and her safety. Joe took matters into his own hands and, without telling Rose or anyone else in the family, had Rosemary lobotomized—then a new treatment for mental illness. "He thought it would help her," Rose would say, when she herself was nearly ninety, speaking with bitterness. "But it made her go all the way back. It erased all the years of effort I had put into her. All along I had continued to believe she could have lived life as a Kennedy girl, just a little slower." Rosemary still lives in the institution to which she was assigned after her operation.

- **Kathleen Kennedy Cavendish,** marchioness of Hartington, born on February 20, 1920, married at twenty-four and dead at twenty-eight. "Kick" will be remembered as forever young. She was the spark, the kick, of the Kennedys. Wrote Goodwin: "What set Kathleen apart from her siblings was the fact that she more than they maintained a sense of wonder at how lucky she was to be born who she was in her family and in the world." According to Goodwin, Joe Jr., Jack, and Kick were "a family within the family . . . the golden trio." Kick and JFK were especially close. Kick was a female version of Joe Sr., Joe Jr., or John Fitzgerald (either JFK or Honey Fitz). All the men loved her, and when Joe Sr. was posted as ambassador to England early in the war, she was, perhaps, the most sought-after woman on the island. (This is, admittedly, a small comeuppance, but worth noting, that a lovely Irish girl should be the toast of the British Isles.) Kathleen dearly loved England (we're sorry), and whether that increased her affection for William John Robert "Billy" Cavendish, ninth marquess of Hartington, cannot now be said but only speculated. Billy died during the war, and Kick in 1948, with her new love, in a plane crash. The word arrived first in the States at the office of Congressman John F. Kennedy, his sister's favorite.

- **Eunice Mary Kennedy,** born on September 10, 1921, a smart and sensible Kennedy, but nonetheless strong and vibrant.

Though Kick was her idol—everyone loved Kick—young Eunice was caught between older and younger siblings and found herself more often aligned with Pat, Bobby, and, later, Jean and Teddy. Her health wasn't the best; she was plagued by chronic stomach troubles. But she had, like her brother Jack, a capacity to ignore pain, and she didn't think of herself. "Somehow," a family friend told Doris Kearns Goodwin, "Eunice seemed to develop very early on a sense of special responsibility for Rosemary as if Rosemary were her child instead of her sister. There was an odd maturity about Eunice which was sometimes forbidding but which clearly set her off from all the rest." The trait would underlie the great accomplishments of her life. At twenty-six she was working for the Juvenile Delinquency Committee of the Justice Department and saying things like "substantial efforts must be made to keep adolescents from quitting school at fourteen or fifteen and to give them a chance to learn a trade or develop special skills." She was the strongest-minded of her generation, and an instinctive politician (she was a great aid in her older brother's national campaign). In May of 1953 she married Robert Sargent Shriver after a seven-year courtship. Shriver, who ran Joe Sr.'s Merchandise Mart in Chicago, also was instrumental in forming the Peace Corps. For her part, Eunice Shriver founded the Special Olympics one summer on the lawns of their estate and has seen the organization grow to mammoth size, helping mentally handicapped children around the world. As we'll see, the five children of Sarge and Eunice Shriver have inherited their mother's instinct for reaching out and giving back.

- **Patricia Kennedy,** born on May 6, 1924, a Kennedy in all ways, but quieter. She was taller, more lovely, more athletic than her sisters, but as Rose once observed she never seemed "particularly ambitious or enthusiastic or keen about anything. . . . She would never make the effort to achieve distinction." Perhaps she was overwhelmed by all the achieving of distinction going on around her. She found her own friends outside the clan and enjoyed their company. In June 1954, Pat, age thirty, married the English actor Peter Lawford, and the following year they had the first of four children. The Lawford link is an interesting one: He was about to become a core member, along with Dean Martin, Joey Bishop, and Sammy Davis, Jr., of Frank Sinatra's wild-and-woolly Las Vegas–based Rat Pack. John F. Kennedy, never one to pass up a fun time, would become an orbital associate of the Pack— "Chickie Baby," Sinatra called him—and would meet women through his association. He would also, as we'll see, gain needed assistance from these show-business stars during the run for the White House: both onstage and behind-the-scenes assistance. Ultimately, Bobby Kennedy would counsel his brother to cut ties with Sinatra and Co., as there were unsavory things concerning the mob being said about the group. JFK would heed his brother's advice, and that would be it for poor Peter Lawford: banished from the Pack forever. No one could hold a grudge like Sinatra. Years after the snub by the Kennedys, he refused to take the stage at the Sands Hotel one night because he spotted Peter Lawford in the audience. Not until the actor was removed would Sinatra sing. As for Pat Kennedy, she divorced the actor in 1966 and raised the children through their teenage years herself. Peter Lawford died in 1984; Pat never remarried.

- **Robert Francis Kennedy,** born on November 11, 1925. He always wanted to be bigger, older—always wanted the chance to do what Joe demanded of Joe Jr. and then Jack. In certain ways, he was the beneficiary of the rivalry between the two older brothers: Joe Jr. would lightly toss the football with Bobby for hours, and so would Jack, but between themselves a game like football would turn from touch to tackle, with no one announcing that it had. While Joe sensed a challenge from Jack (and the fun-loving Jack did nothing to dissuade him), Rose made sure her eldest sons treated the younger siblings with gentleness and compassion. Nevertheless, Bobby, smart and ambitious, applied himself with an intensity that was greater than even Joe Jr.'s, and arrived at all the pre-ordained stops, if a step behind: Harvard (where he, little Bobby, played football, as neither of the older boys had); the service (he entered the navy's V-12 training program at Harvard in the spring of 1944 when he was nineteen, and later served on a ship named for his oldest brother); finally politics. At one thing, he was first among the boys—by a mile. On June 17, 1950, he married Ethel Skakel and they started a family reminiscent in size of the turn-of-the-century Irish Catholic households we met earlier. Bobby and Ethel would have eleven children in all before he was assassinated in 1968.

- **Jean Ann Kennedy,** born on February 20, 1927, the little sister. She followed behind Eunice and Pat wherever they went. In London, when Joe was ambassador, the girls would trot off to convent school at Roehampton every Monday—Rosemary was at a special school in the English countryside at this time—and return to the official residence every Friday, happy with themselves and all the attention their comings and goings generated (the Kennedy kids were treated as celebrities during Joe's ambassadorship). In 1955 Jean married Stephen Smith, an executive with his family's New York transportation firm. As would the Shrivers, Lawfords, and, of course, the various Kennedys, the Smiths pitched in energetically in JFK's presidential campaign. In fact, Steve Smith became something of a rock for the Kennedy family, handling problems as they arose in any of the households, being the stable, trusted uncle to all the many nephews and nieces. Jean and Steve had or adopted four children of their own before Steve's death in August 1990. Jean Smith retired in July, 1998, as U.S. ambassador to Ireland, having used her influence to forward the cause of peace.

- **Edward Moore Kennedy,** born on February 22, 1932, the little brother. To look at Ted Kennedy now, the elder statesman, is to view the far end of a most remarkable transformation. He was the boy in short pants, the puppy dog, the chubby-cheeked one in the corner of all the pictures. Then he was the handsome young man, but still quiet. Then he was the one who had to shoulder the cross. Then he was the one who seemed not quite up to it—the one who had problems with liquor, whose wife had problems with liquor, who was cheating and carousing in ways unseemly even for a Kennedy. Then he was the patriarch by default. Then he was on the verge of a Last Hurrah, and he thundered back. Now he is the country's last liberal, and as a Kennedy he is the unquestioned head of the family. He is a large, weathered man who looks to be in his seventies but isn't yet. He is barnacled like no one else in the country.

How did the Kennedys conquer the country?

That was Joe Sr.'s doing. Many books have been written about it; our job here is to briefly synopsize.

Joe Jr. was gone, Joe himself was unelectable, and so Joe would steer Jack's machine. He got support, of course, from John Fitzgerald, who knew a thing or two about politics—but Joe was the boss. In 1945 JFK and his father were eyeing the Massachusetts lieutenant governorship when, all of a sudden, Honey Fitz's old congressional seat became available. How? James Michael Curley had won election to the mayoralty of Boston and had forsaken his seat in Congress. In the streets of Boston, Cambridge, Somerville, and Dorchester, John F. Kennedy's remarkable charm and charisma were first put on display. Young men signed up to support him, young mothers swooned. In 1946 Jack beat many comers, and ascended to the same congressional seat his grandfather had held a half-century earlier.

Years later JFK would visit Ireland and be received as a triumphal general. Less well remembered, except by the family, was a trip he made there in 1947 to visit his sister Kathleen, who was staying at Lismore Castle in County Waterford. This was an estate belonging to the family of Kick's late husband, and a place the widow considered "the most perfect" in the world. Goodwin quotes from Rose's diary, and paints an image of the setting: " 'a picture book castle' with its gray walls covered on one side with soft green moss and on the other with reddish ivy." Then "the steep straight down drop to the quickly running stream . . . the artistic bridge over the stream with a few figures fishing and the winding road beyond where the children walk along from school in their bare legs and shabby shoes and torn coats but shining rosy faces."

We quote at a little length to make a point here: Almost precisely a century after P. J. Kennedy trudged the roads of Wexford, leaving an island of poverty, despair, and death, P.J.'s descendants, now the ruling class in the world's suddenly ascendant nation, were able to revisit the homeland and see it as a pastoral idyll. Things had changed quickly for the Kennedys and the Fitzgeralds.

Jack thoroughly enjoyed his stay at Lismore, and one morning enlisted Pamela Churchill to accompany him on a pilgrimage after ancestors in the village of New Ross, fifty miles east. His aunt Loretta had given him directions to the old family home. Goodwin again: "They motored through the soft green countryside along the southeastern coast of Ireland and across the bottom of Kilkenny

County, past wooded valleys and ruined castles, along roads so bumpy that it took more than five hours to reach the little market town of New Ross, settled on the banks of the Barrow River. At the outskirts of the town Jack stopped the car and asked a man where the Kennedys lived. 'Oh, now, and which Kennedys will it be that you'll be wanting? David Kennedys? Jim Kennedys?' a very Irish voice replied. Jack explained about being from America and looking for his relatives, and the man told him to drive to a little white house on the edge of the village."

The found the thatch-roofed house, and, Churchill reported later, "a tough-looking woman came out surrounded by a mass of kids, looking just like all the Kennedys." The woman finally softened, and the afternoon was spent in reminiscence and trying to figure out the relationship. (Third cousins was the upshot.) The family graciously offered butter and eggs, which certainly would have been dear to them. Jack, leaving, asked if he could do anything for them in turn. The woman asked if the children could have one ride around the village in the splendid station wagon. Jack obliged, and it certainly must have been one of the happiest, most moving times of his life.

During this visit to Ireland, while they walked by the banks of the Blackwater River, Kick confided to Jack that she had fallen in love with a married man, Lord Peter Fitzwilliam. That she carried on an affair with him, that Peter was with her in the plane when she died, in no way lessened her brother's grief for his dear sister when she was gone less than a year later. Friends of the family were always happy for both Kick and Jack that they had had that special time together at Lismore in 1947.

JFK dutifully served a couple of terms in Congress—he didn't seem engaged by the job, particularly, and spent more time socializing than legislating in Washington—and then, in 1952, he ran for the Senate. His father had been building a formidable statewide machine in Massachusetts, and Jack knew the Senate was a place where he could better exercise his interests in foreign affairs. His opponent for the seat, the incumbent, stands as symbolic in much the same way as the Ireland visit: as an indicator of how things were changing so quickly. When the Kennedys were downtrodden in the North End of Boston along with all the other Irish, the Lodge family was already ensconced atop Beacon Hill. The isolationist **Henry Cabot Lodge** had defeated John Fitzgerald for the U.S. Senate thirty-six years earlier. Now it was grandson against grandson—John

Fitzgerald Kennedy versus **Henry Cabot Lodge II**—and things were different.

Still, JFK entered the contest a heavy underdog. Joe Kennedy poured great amounts of his own money into the campaign and took over much of the decision making, sometimes to the consternation of his son. Suddenly arriving in Massachusetts was Bobby, who gave up his job at the Justice Department to join the campaign. He worked as a mediator between Joe and Jack, and as a sparkplug. He demonstrated previously unseen political instincts and energies. Kenny O'Donnell, a member of JFK's inner circle, told Goodwin: "Those of us who worked with him over the next few months are convinced that if Bobby had not arrived on the scene and taken charge when he did, Jack Kennedy most certainly would have lost the election."

But he didn't, and overnight this young prince was seen nationwide as a man who could be king.

Except . . . he was Irish Catholic. The country would never elect a Catholic president.

Times were good in America and John Kennedy looked like good times. As a Most Eligible Bachelor—sort of the precursor title to *People* magazine's Sexiest Man Alive, a mantle that JFK's son would wear for a year—Jack was right in tune with the Sinatra-soundtracked ring-a-ding era. Ike was in the White House and that was okay—stability, after all—but much of America found itself gently swinging. Jack Kennedy looked like what they wanted to see in the mirror, and when he married the beautiful **Jacqueline Lee Bouvier** on September 12, 1953, the country had to concede it had never set eyes upon a more attractive, more enviable couple. Image counts much in politics, and no newlyweds have ever projected such an image as the John Fitzgerald Kennedys. Drink them in for just a second, add a couple of impossibly cute children to the picture, and then think of Richard Nixon. That's what the country was faced with in 1960.

Again, of course, Kennedy was the underdog. Ike was popular, it was thought the Republicans would steer more cautiously through the nasty waters of the cold war world, and JFK was Catholic.

Joe, who always played rough, played as rough as ever this time. One example shows how emphatically and desperately he wanted the White House, and it didn't involve any Irish mafia of O'Donnell, Donahue, and Powers—it involved the real deal. JFK was struggling in the Democratic primaries and it looked like Texan Lyndon Johnson or some other candidate would be the nominee. The West Virginia primary would be crucial, and things didn't look good for Jack there—particularly because of the Catholic question in a non-Catholic state. Joe went to his son's friend Sinatra, and asked if Sinatra could seek help from *his* friend, the mobster Sam Giancana. Sinatra said sure and intervened with Giancana. No quid pro quo, just a favor. Giancana got on the horn with the labor unions in West Virginia and, voilà, Kennedy won the primary and was on his way. All such machinations were covered, of course, by the high gloss of the campaign—Jack and Jackie smiling out front, as the theme song "High Hopes" blared in the background, Frankie Boy singing a Kennedy-specific verse that he had asked his pal, the lyricist Sammy Cahn, to customize for the cause.

It all worked, and history was made. In January of 1961 a son of a Famine immigrant family was inaugurated as president of the United States of America. He became the de facto leader of the free world. "Ask not what your country can do for you," said John Fitzgerald Kennedy on that frigid day in Washington, "ask what you can do for your country."

Joe Kennedy, the father, was witness to the glory. Later that year he suffered a stroke. In a paralyzed state he would witness the murders of his second and third sons before dying on November 16, 1969, at age eighty-one.

They are well known, the salient details of JFK's presidency: His growing reliance on Bobby, Bobby's battles with labor and the Mafia (*that* certainly made Giancana and Sinatra grateful), the Bay of Pigs fiasco, the Cuban missile crisis triumph, the Peace Corps, the beginning of a civil rights movement, and so many other things that transpired in those few hundred days. And there's little point in recounting here the terrible events of November 22, 1963, and even less point in talking about conspiracy theories. The young president was killed, and his life passed into history and legend. What this chapter of our book is about is the climb of an Irish American family. The family had climbed as far and high as one can in this history, lifting its people's spirits as it went. Another shining son of the family had been taken, and now the family marched on.

What did Bobby do first after his brother's death?

He picked up the mantle.

Or, at least, he tried to—hesitantly at first. He challenged Republican Kenneth Keating for the New York Senate seat in 1964, suffering attacks from liberals such as Gore Vidal (who has a drop of Irish blood in him) who labeled him a carpetbagger and formed Democrats for Keating. Bobby's heart wasn't in it at first, then Keating attacked him before an audience of Jews as linked with a "Nazi cartel," obviously trying to paint him as Joe's Jew-hating son. (The Justice Department under RFK had settled claims regarding the assets of General Aniline, a chemical company that had once had ties to the Third Reich.) Keating's charge was a cheap shot, as was immediately evident to all, and Bobby shot back that one who had lost a brother and a brother-in-law in World War II could never be soft on Nazism. "Outrageous," said Bobby of the charge. Now he was engaged, and he was on his way. That he won by seven hundred thousand votes when Lyndon Baines Johnson defeated Barry Goldwater in New York State by more than three million is more a comment on Goldwater than on Bobby Kennedy.

Still, after JFK's vivacity, made larger by memory, Bobby seemed serious, pointedly ambitious, hard. Fortunately for him, the times were about to get intense, even angry, and he would do more than tap into this, he would become a champion. Civil rights was already a significant issue to him, and after the Watts riots of 1966 he began a crusade for improvements in the inner city. As his Bedford-Stuyvesant Development and Services Corporation began to achieve tangible results, one black leader spoke for others: "Kennedy puts money where his mouth is." RFK's Migratory Labor Subcommittee looked into not only poverty in Appalachia but also the farm workers' plight in California. The committee became activist, and laws were changed. He became aware of the plight of New York State Indians and helped them. He became aware of the plight of Delta laborers in Mississippi and helped them. As Peter Collier and David Horowitz wrote in *The Kennedys: An American Drama*: "He went from one powerless group to another like a detective obsessively following clues to a mystery which he knew was inside himself. What was his responsibility to these people?"

He was becoming a liberal shining star. Coming up on the outside as the liberal's principal cause—overtaking civil rights and the War on Poverty—was ending the war in Vietnam. Bobby took it up, and this put him in opposition to the Democratic president, his brother's former vice president, Lyndon Johnson. When Democratic Senator Eugene McCarthy, riding the antiwar sentiment that was growing in the land, made headway in the early 1968 primaries by challenging

LBJ, forces within the party started pressuring Kennedy to enter the race, saying that McCarthy was all well and good, but not electable, while Bobby was very, very electable. Finally RFK did throw his hat into the ring—those charges of opportunism were heard again—and his campaign was on the upswing when, after taking the crucial California primary, he said to Kenny O'Donnell from his suite at L.A.'s Ambassador Hotel, "You know, Ken, finally I feel that I'm out from under the shadow of my brother. Now at least I feel that I've made it on my own. All these years I never really believed it was me that did it, but Jack."

After making his victory speech at the Ambassador he was ushered through the hotel kitchen and, for reasons still unfathomable, a man named Sirhan Sirhan gunned him down.

Another shining son of the family had been taken, and now the family marched on.

What did Ted do after his brother's death?

He picked up the mantle.

Or, at least, he wanted to.

He had been a senator (from Massachusetts) even before Bobby had joined Congress. Now he was the surviving son in a political dynasty, and even the leader, since Joe had been taken from the field by his stroke (he would die a year and a half after Bobby). The next generation, those who were now being called the Young Kennedys, were not yet of age. (For politics, anyway. They were proving plenty old enough to start getting into trouble—of both the misdemeanor kind and of more serious consequence.)

At the tumultuous Chicago Democratic convention of 1968 Ted gave his first political speech since Bobby's death and offered candidly, "Like my brothers before me I pick up a fallen standard." There was talk of a draft at that convention, but Hubert Humphrey was the ultimate candidate (he would lose to Richard Nixon). Things began to get strange. Jackie married the Greek shipping magnate **Aristotle Onassis,** and the outcry in America was startling. Ted Kennedy returned to the Senate, but he was a troubled man: drinking too much, losing the focus that had made him a superb legislator. His wife, Joan, was also drinking. Still and all, Ted was regarded as the all-but-anointed 1972 Democratic presidential nominee.

Then, on July 18, 1969, after a party for many of his brother's former campaign workers, the senator drove his 1967 Oldsmobile off Dike Bridge at Chappaquiddick on Martha's Vineyard and, though he escaped, his passenger, Mary Jo Kopechne, drowned in the bay. Kennedy was never found criminally responsible for the death, but Chappaquiddick would haunt him for the rest of his life and serve to derail his presidential aspirations.

It took a trial balloon or two for Kennedy to realize this truth, but truth it was. Still, among the Massachusetts electorate, he was unbeatable, and so Ted Kennedy would evolve over many years into the old liberal lion of the Senate and the patriarch of the country's most famous family. Ted and Joan divorced in 1983. It took several more years, but Ted finally calmed down. In 1992 he married a smart lawyer named Victoria Reggie, and she helped him get in fighting trim for what promised to be a tough 1994 reelection campaign against the smooth, attractive Mitt Romney. It turned out to be another Kennedy landslide, not least because Ted's increasingly strong record as a legislator and public advocate was unassailable before the people of the Bay State.

Ted Kennedy's hair is white now, and he looks the part that has fallen to him, but that he never would have chosen. He presides at the weddings and wakes. He's seen it all, and the amazing thing is that all of it hasn't simply been too much for him.

Are there other Kennedy politicians today, besides Ted?

Yes, and many activists and public servants. The Young Kennedys have arrived.

There were thirty offspring born to or adopted by six of Rose and Joe's nine children (Joe Jr., Rosemary, and Kathleen never had children). Of the thirty, three have died: Jack and Jackie's third child, in infancy; David Anthony Kennedy (1955–1984), Bobby and Ethel's fourth child, by drug overdose; and Michael LeMoyne Kennedy (1958–1997), Bobby and Ethel's sixth child, who was killed in a ski accident at Aspen, Colorado, after a particularly troubling year that saw him accused of an affair with his family's fourteen-year-old babysitter. The remaining twenty-seven have so far survived all that America could throw at them in terms of trial, error, tragedy, divorce, and scandal. They have also experienced great success, joy, and triumph. As a group, they have exhibited remarkable generosity, self-sacrifice, and public-spiritedness. As a group, they have contributed. They have achieved success to a far greater degree than they have failed.

The late president's surviving children thrive. **Caroline Bouvier Kennedy,** born on November 11, 1957, married Edward Arthur Schlossberg in 1986 and the couple has two daughters and a son. Caroline has written books and been involved in good works; she and her husband, who live in New York City, are instrumental in running the Kennedy Library in Boston. **John Fitzgerald Kennedy, Jr.,** born on November 25, 1960, married Carolyn Bessette in 1996. He is the editor of the political magazine *George*, which he helped found.

Jackie had a third child, **Patrick Bouvier Kennedy,** who died two days after being born in April 1963.

The **Shrivers** thrive. The four boys—**Robert III, Timothy, Mark, Anthony**—are, like their parents, involved in various philanthropies (Bobby and Timothy with Special Olympics; Mark with Choice Program, which provides supervision and counseling for troubled adolescents in Baltimore, and with another operation that provides Catholic school education for the mentally retarded; Anthony with Best Buddies, another program for the retarded). **Maria Shriver** is married to actor Arnold Schwarzenegger and raises their three children while continuing her two-decade journalism career with NBC's *Dateline*.

The **Lawfords** thrive. **Christopher** has been a lawyer and substance-abuse counselor (he beat his alcohol and heroin addictions), lecturing at Harvard. He is now trying his father's profession, acting. **Sydney Lawford McKelvy** and **Victoria Lawford Pender** both live in the Washington, D.C., area where their families—four and three children, respectively—often gather for Kennedyesque outings. **Robin Kennedy Lawford**—"Your entrance is timely, as we need a new left end," JFK wrote to her upon her birth in July of 1961—is a wildlife conservationist living in New York, and raises funds for the Kennedy Child Study Center, a school for the developmentally disabled.

The **Smiths** thrive—even Willie. **Stephen Jr.,** a former assistant D.A. in the Bronx and then a political-ethics instructor at Harvard, now works for Conflict Management Group, teaching diplomats and gang members the value of negotiation. **Will** completed his residency at Northwestern University after his acquittal on rape charges in the infamous Palm Beach incident of 1991. He's a physician specializing in rehabilitation therapy, a specialty he was drawn to by his cousin Ted, who had lost a leg to cancer. Will helped found Physicians Against Land Mines, which provides service world-wide. **Amanda** lives in Boston, where she works on a book about her grandfather Joe. **Kym** lives in New York and has spent much time in recent years with her mother in Dublin.

The **Ted Kennedys** thrive. **Kara** married architect Michael Allen in 1990 and they have two children; she works with her aunt Jean Smith's Very Special Arts, a program that helps the disabled express themselves through the arts. **Ted Jr.,** who lost his leg as an adolescent, has spent more than two decades as an advocate for the physically disabled, and, subsequent to completing his law degree, he formed a nonprofit organization in New Haven that provides transitional housing as well as medical and social services to families in homes where lead levels exceed safety standards. He married Katherine Gresham, a psychiatrist at Yale Medical School, in 1993 and they have a daughter. **Patrick Kennedy** became, at twenty-one, the youngest Kennedy ever to hold public office when he was elected to the Rhode Island legislature in 1988. Six years later he ran for Congress and won, becoming the youngest representative in Washington. Barely in his thirties, he is said to be eyeing the Senate. "I'm using my name, but hopefully I'm using it in a way that it was meant to be used, trying to further the interests of those who don't have a voice."

And then there are the Bobby Kennedys. Two have died, and of the nine who live, most now thrive. The eldest, **Kathleen Harting-ton Kennedy,** certainly does: She has a prosperous marriage to university professor David Lee Townsend (four children, one of whom attends her mom's alma mater, Harvard) and, as the first Kennedy woman to hold public office, is the lieutenant governor of Maryland, where her causes are education reform, community service, and crime prevention. **Joe Jr.** has had a tumultuous go. He married Sheila Rauch in 1979 and they had two children, but the union ended in divorce in 1991. After he tried to have it annulled upon marrying Anne Elizabeth Kelly in 1993, Sheila contested it in private and in public. Her book about Joe's betrayal only added to Joe's *annus horribilis* in 1997. That year, Joe's younger brother Michael, thought by many to be the best and brightest of his generation, became embroiled in the baby-sitter scandal. Michael had been planning to run Joe's campaign for the governorship of Massachusetts, but with the incessant media glare, Joe dropped the idea of running. At year's end, Michael, who was chief executive of the Citizens Energy operation that Joe had founded—a firm that supplies fuel at cut-rate prices to low-income families—was tragically killed in Aspen. In March 1998 Joe announced that he would not run for re-election to the congressional seat he has held since 1986—and that JFK and Honey Fitz had held before him—but would retake the helm at Citizens Energy and spend time with his family. He'll be back, but where or when is uncertain.

Bobby Kennedy Jr. now thrives, but he, too, has had a bumpy ride. He was very close to David, who died of an overdose in 1984. Losing David stunned Bobby, but he was luckier and overcame his own addiction. His first marriage ended in divorce, but his second, to Mary Richardson, appears strong. (Bobby has two children from each.) Always the outdoorsy Kennedy, he teaches environmental law at Pace University in White Plains, New York, and heads legal efforts for the extremely successful Hudson River Fishermen's Association, whose Riverkeeper program seeks to clean up the Hudson.

Mary Courtney Kennedy is once divorced and now married to **Paul Hill.** He is the Irishman wrongly imprisoned fifteen years for IRA terrorism. (He was freed when the conviction was overturned, and the story is central to the film *In the Name of the Father*.) Ethel Kennedy met Paul at a congressional hearing on human rights and introduced him to her daughter. The couple's first child, **Saoirse Roisin** (Gaelic for "Freedom Rose"), was born in May of 1997. Courtney, formerly a representative for a United Nations AIDS foundation, is staying home to care for the baby at Hickory Hill. Paul works against land mines through Operation USA.

Mary Kerry Kennedy married **Andrew Cuomo,** Mario's son, in June of 1990 and instantly became a member of a political power couple. He has served in the Clinton administration as Secretary of Housing and Urban Development. She battles torture and abuse on behalf of Amnesty International and the RFK Center for Human Rights, which she founded after law school. They have twins.

Christopher Kennedy, married and the father of three, runs the family business, Merchandise Mart, the design and wholesale trade center in Chicago that Joe Sr. got up and running. **Max Kennedy,** married and the father of two, is in business school at UCLA and has compiled a book of his father's favorite quotations, "the words that inspired me." **Douglas Kennedy,** born the year before his father was killed, is a Manhattan-based television journalist; under-cover stories he produced in 1995 on Medicare fraud helped spur legislative reform. **Rory Kennedy,** born months after her father died, grew up steeped in social activism. She and Doug were arrested for protesting apartheid in front of the South African embassy when they were still in their teens. Rory is now a documentary filmmaker. Her 1995 film *Women of Substance*, about pregnant drug addicts, won several awards. Her next is about rural children living in poverty in Appalachia—the same issue that had been dear to her father.

So those are the Young Kennedys. That's how they're contributing today. Say what you will about them, they are—as were their forebears—an extraordinary bunch.

So what does this amazing Kennedy saga, from Patrick and Bridget through Honey Fitz and Joe and Rose to JFK and RFK to John-John, really mean?

To look at it as an epic, it can only mean disproportionately, unrealistically much. It's like one of the great Celtic cycles, with heroes and villains, impossible tragedies and impossible triumphs. All of this couldn't possibly happen to one family.

So don't look at it that way. Don't put a symbolic weight on it that it cannot bear.

But don't treat it as fiction, either. It did happen, and in America.

Listen to Rose, talking to her twenty-nine grandchildren long ago, trying to put it simply, attempting to humanize the whole:

"I hope that they will realize where they came from and how they happen to be where they are. They came—on the Kennedy-Fitzgerald side—from ancestors who were quite poor and disadvantaged through no fault of their own but who had the imagination, the resolve, the intelligence and the energy to seek a newer, better world for themselves and their families. . . . In a short time, just a few generations, these beleaguered Irish immigrants had produced a family to whom many in the world looked with admiration. It was an inspiring story. They are the continuing part of it, and I hope they will try always to be worthy of it."

As do we all.

There are fifty great-grandchildren of Rose and Joe in America. More on the way.

FOURTEEN

The Road from Here

Are the Irish still coming to America?

How many Americans have some Irish blood?

Have many Irish Americans returned to Ireland?

Will Ireland ever be as big as it once was?

Who should we be watching as the
road continues to rise?

Are other Irish Americans rich? Are they generous?

What is Ireland House?

Guess who else is Irish?

What are the MacBride Principles?

*Why do many Irishmen drink Jameson
Whiskey and shun Bushmill's?*

Is there one more story to be told?

Are the Irish still coming to America?

Not so much. Not like they used to.

Irish immigration fell off after the turn of the century, although it picked up again briefly in the 1920s after Ireland had achieved independence from Great Britain. But during the Great Depression, few Europeans, Irish or otherwise, came to the United States. The same held during World War II, and then immigration began again, but in far fewer numbers than those of the nineteenth century. Some fifty thousand Irish arrived during the 1950s and another thirty-two thousand in the 1960s. As was traditional, about a quarter of these settled first in New York City.

In 1965 Congress passed an immigration law that scrapped the national-origins provisions favoring northern and western European nations. Although Ireland actually saw its quota increase from seventeen thousand to twenty thousand, the rules for getting in changed; preference was now given to potential citizens with close family ties in the country, or those who had skills that were needed in the United States.

Equally significant to the falloff in Irish immigration was the situation in Ireland during the sixties, seventies, and eighties. Economic expansion and participation in the European Common Market had caused the Irish economy to grow at a relatively brisk rate, with the result that few young Irish needed to emigrate, and fewer than before chose to.

New York City saw fewer than seventy-five hundred Irish settle there between 1965 and 1980, and Irish immigration to the city averaged fewer than two hundred a year between 1982 and 1985.

When Ireland's economy stagnated and unemployment rose in the 1980s, the Irish hit the road again. Between 1980 and 1990, outward migration totaled 216,000, or 6 percent of the population. Few of the émigrés had the necessary family connections to make a landing in the States, but they came anyway, usually as tourists, and stayed on as their visas expired, living and working illegally. It is estimated that as many as twenty thousand were so situated in New York alone. The men found work in construction; the women in child care.

With the Immigrant Reform and Control Act of 1986, forty thousand special (NP-5) visas were offered between 1987 and 1990 to immigrants from thirty-six countries that had been traditional sources of citizens for the United States. The visas, known as "Donnelly visas" after the congressman who had initiated the scheme, were offered to randomly selected applicants. Unlike normal visas based on family reunification or other factors, the Donnelly visas carried no stipulations. In all, 16,329 of these visas were issued to Irish applicants.

The Immigrations Act of 1990 established a second lottery that would distribute 120,000 visas to thirty-four countries over a period of three years. Under the terms of this act, Ireland was guaranteed 16,000 so-called "Morrison visas"—again, after the sponsoring congressman—each year for three years, a total of 48,000 in all.

Bruce Morrison's contribution is significant: From 1983 to 1991 he represented his Connecticut district in the U.S. House of Representatives. As chairman of the House Immigration Committee, he instigated a program that granted residency to thousands of undocumented aliens from Ireland. He also served as cochair of the Ad Hoc Committee on Irish Affairs. An Irish American, Morrison considers Ireland his thing. When he returned to private practice, he founded Americans for a New Irish Agenda and joined an American delegation meeting in Northern Ireland with leaders from both sides of the conflict. In 1992 he was chairman of Irish Americans for Clinton (the president had been a classmate of Morrison's at Yale Law), and then was a behind-the-scenes negotiator on the talks that led to the IRA's 1994 cease-fire. He continues to serve on the U.S. Commission on Immigration Reform

Morrison and others want to see more Irish over here, if more Irish want to come. But there's only so much they can do. These are not good times for supporters of large immigrations, and sentiments on the issue do not appear to be changing.

Not all Irish who wished to come to America were lucky in the lotteries, of course, and a high level of illegal Irish immigration has continued throughout the 1990s. These undocumented aliens try to blend into the "New Irish" communities that emerged in the old Irish cities: New York, Boston, Chicago, and San Francisco. Whether they will ever become U.S. citizens, or whether they will stay just a while, try to earn some money, and then return home, is yet uncertain. They don't have their forefathers' desperation. They don't have need or cause.

A book published in early 1998 focuses on this point. Joan Mathieu's *Zulu: An Irish Journey* takes its title from a comment by Giorgio Joyce, James's son, who called his countrymen Zulus, presumably because of their tribal wanderings. Mathieu points out that while scholars have traced the movements of Indo-European tribes and the wanderings of the Jews, the dispersal of the Irish has gone largely unstudied (Tom Keneally is at work on that as we speak). From 1815 to 1915 more than 4.5 million people left the island: That is one of the greatest population scatterings in the history of the world. What has been its impact? What is the status of the diaspora today? Those are questions that we have tried to address in *May the Road Rise to Meet You*, of course, and they interest Mathieu as well.

She is a Zulu—actually, a kind of reverse Zulu. Born in Brooklyn, where her Irish grandmother settled early in this century, she emigrated from New York to Roscrea, the County Tipperary town of her ancestors. Her book is about this migration home. She finds the Irish welcoming, after a fashion. Then she realizes she's not comfortable, so she tries Brooklyn again. She's distressed by the new Irish community there: young people unsentimental about their own heritage and about any promise of a new life in America—people without optimism. Finally it's back to Roscrea, where little happens, but life seems to make more sense.

It's a tough time for Zulus.

How many Americans have some Irish blood?

It is a figure that is growing through child-bearing, but the massive Irish American population is simultaneously thinning its sense of Irishness. The clan is a manifestation of the past, not a phenomenon of the present. It's not centered. It's large, diffuse, and growing.

The cities mentioned above still have many Irish among their citizenry, but these great towns have *seemed* more Irish in the past than they do today; other ethnic groups that are currently part of America's polyglot urban scene also influence the cities' culture and style. In addition, following classic social patterns, there has been a large Irish exodus to the suburbs. The rise of the Irish has been accompanied by not only greater affluence and assimilation but also more intermarriage and secularization. These are not bad things, although they seem so to some romanticists.

To be sure, the current renaissance in Irish culture—the return of traditional music and dance, the bracing new literature—seems to fly in the face of any feared "death of Irishness." And also, Irishness has cropped up in many places where least expected. Because there are so many Irish Americans, their influence and culture are everywhere. Let us quickly paint for you some surprising Irish scenes.

> *It's a wonderful city in Georgia*
> *Where on March the seventeen*
> *Ev'ry mother's son and daughter*
> *Will be wearin' of the Green . . .*

Largely overlooked in the best-seller *Midnight in the Garden of Good and Evil* is the large Irish population of Savannah, Georgia, which thrives amidst the azaleas, cypress, and elms. The Irish came in the 1830s to help build the canals and the railway; the relative shortage of free black or slave labor in the city created employment opportunities that the unskilled immigrants eagerly took up. The railroad was completed in 1843, but the workers stayed on in large numbers. By 1850, 10 percent of Savannah's population (19 percent of its white population) was Irish born.

Savannah's commemoration of Saint Patrick's Day dates back to 1813, when the oldest Irish society in the South, the Hibernian Society, was founded by thirteen Irish protestants who are believed to have been United Irishmen refugees from the 1798 rising. In 1814 the society gathered for a private procession to the Independent Presbyterian Church. The first public parade took place on March 17, 1824. The Irish Jasper Greens, named for Irish American Sergeant William Jasper, who was killed during the 1778 siege of Savannah, provided escort and fired a salute at the parade's end.

Today Savannah begins its Saint Patrick's Day celebration well before March 17 with the Savannah Irish Festival, which focuses on the arts and on educating people about Irish culture. When the day itself finally comes, an estimated half-million Georgians gather to enjoy some three hundred parade units marching by the city's shaded squares and pastoral parks in one of Irish America's premier celebrations of its heritage.

Far less decorous but no less surprising is what goes on in New Orleans.

Certainly this city is better known for its French and Sp
ture, but a case can be made that it was the Irish who really
town what it is today. Irish immigrants brought with them to the
mouth of the Mississippi much of the heart and soul—and perhaps
the conscience—of New Orleans.

Irish immigration to the city began as early as the 1700s, but it
was in the early nineteenth century that the Irish arrived in vast
numbers. As many as thirty thousand came into town between 1832
and 1838. At the time, the port of New Orleans was the second
busiest in the country, after New York. The Irish flocked south in
hope of good wages, but so did every other ethnic group; the Irish
usually found work at the basest level.

One of the largest employers of the Irish was the New Orleans
Canal and Banking Company. In 1832 the company planned a sixty-
foot-wide canal to link the waters of vast Lake Pontchartrain north of
town with the Mississippi on the western edge. Thousands of Irish
enlisted for the brutal digging in hundred-degree heat and overwhelming humidity. The workers lived in ramshackle tent cities
along the canal, communities bare to the swarms of disease-carrying
mosquitoes. With poor sanitation, they fell victim to killer sick-
nesses: typhoid, yellow fever, cholera. So many Irish died that the
canal bosses gave up on carting the bodies away for proper burial.
Instead, they ordered the dead buried where they had worked,
along the banks of the muddy, stagnant canal. (The canal was later
filled in, and atop it was built West End Boulevard. To this day, when
improvements are made to that street, bones sometimes surface.) No
clear record exists, but it is believed more than eight thousand Irish
immigrants perished digging the canal.

Still, for 50 cents a day, the survivors persevered. They finished
the canal and went on to other things. As was happening elsewhere,
the strongest of them were rising. By the mid-1800s, the Irish of
New Orleans were a cohesive, self-supporting community. They
helped each other gain employment on the docks and aboard ships
that brought goods up the river. They opened their own shipping
companies and stevedoring firms. An early founding family of immigrant Irish from Dundalk was the clan of **James Gallier, Jr.** (the
name may originally have been Gallagher). Gallier's sons designed
some of New Orleans' best-known buildings: the old city hall on
Saint Charles Avenue, the interior of Saint Patrick's Cathedral, the
family home which is today a museum on Royal Street in the French
Quarter. The Irish were having an influence. In 1892 the city saw fit

to elect an Irish mayor. By this time the Irish had their own quarter on Magazine Street, a narrow, unruly, winding path. The Irish opened small shops and pubs, and the area became known as the Irish Channel. Saint Alphonsus' Cathedral, with towering walls and Gothic spires of dark brick, was built at the foot of the Channel.

There is no record of when the first Irish Channel Saint Patrick's Day parade was staged, but it is believed that it dates from a time in the nineteenth century when the Irish needed a private celebration, since they were still not welcome at the city's pre-Lenten Mardi Gras bash. Today the Saint Pat's blowout includes a dozen floats, hundreds of Irish Channel parade groups, and a morning Mass at Saint Alphonsus' to ask forgiveness for sins soon to be committed. To mock the French tradition of throwing baubles and beads from Mardi Gras floats, masked riders hurl the makings of a good Irish stew: cabbages, potatoes, onions, and turnips. It's a mess. We recommend you miss it. Go, instead, to West End Boulevard for a moment's contemplation. There's a granite Celtic cross near the lake that was erected in the 1980s, when New Orleans finally came to terms with who had built the city, and what had been done to these poor men. That, more than anything, speaks of the Irish experience in New Orleans.

So, clearly, the Irish are living not just in New York, Boston, Chicago, and San Francisco, or in former mining meccas like Butte and Denver. They are everywhere, sometimes where you least expect to find them.

Have many Irish Americans returned to Ireland?

Many have to visit, but there is no evidence of any large reverse migration.

Interestingly, in most cases anyone with a parent or grandparent born in Ireland is eligible for derivative Irish citizenship. To start the process, you'll need to register yourself in the Irish Foreign Births Entry Book. The necessary papers and information can be obtained from the Irish Consulate (in New York, 212-319-2550). The packet is very complete and detailed as to the required documentation: parents' or grandparents' birth certificates, parents' marriage certificate, and so on. These documents will be checked very carefully before the application is processed, because the right to hold an Irish passport is highly coveted these days, particularly with European union on the horizon.

Becoming an Irish citizen will have no impact on your U.S. citizenship: You may also hold an Irish passport; however, when entering or leaving the States, you are required to use your American documents.

Will Ireland ever be as big as it once was?

That depends on how you define Ireland and on how you define big.

Geographically, of course, that is precisely the hope of nationalists: For Ireland to be once again as big as it was before the British had their way.

As far as population goes, there have never at any time been close to as many people living in Ireland as there were just before the Famine. The Republic today has 3,525,719 citizens, and the six counties of the North have 1,569,971. That total roughly mirrors the population on the island in, say, 1890: There has been little change in a century.

But what of greater Ireland? Forty-four million Americans, to start. And estimates of thirty million more throughout the world, constituting the greatest spread of any ethnicity in the history of the planet. It is clear: Ireland will forever live largely outside its own borders.

In *The Lie of the Land*, a collection of essays published in 1998, Finton O'Toole, an Irish journalist living in New York, observed: "Emigration means, quite simply, that the people and the land are no longer co-terminous. In this sense, the map of Ireland is a lie. The lie of the land is that there is a place called 'Ireland' inhabited by the Irish people, a place with a history, a culture, a society. Yet the central fact of that history is that, over 150 years, much has happened elsewhere, in Chicago and Coventry, in Boston and Birmingham, in Hell's Kitchen and Camden Town. The central fact of that culture is that it knows no borders. The central fact of that society is that it is porous and diffuse, that its apparent stability is maintained only at the cost of the continual export of its instabilities. . . .

"It was an Irishman, Oscar Wilde, who wrote that 'a map of the world that does not include Utopia is not worth even glancing at, for it leaves out the one country at which humanity is always landing. And, when humanity lands there, it looks out, and seeing a better country, sets sail.' In a more downbeat mood, one cay say that a map of Ireland that does not include its elsewheres is not worth even

glancing at, for it leaves out the places where Ireland is always landing and returning from."

Who should we be watching
as the road continues to rise?

Here are a few:

- **Patrica Ireland,** whose Irish roots are actually on her mother's side. As president of the National Organization for Women since 1991, this lawyer is one of the most influential feminist leaders in America.
- **Bill Flynn,** who as a businessman has led Mutual of America up from a struggling existence, and who as a world citizen has contributed to the peace process in Northern Ireland. His National Committee on American Foreign Policy was instrumental in Clinton's granting a visa to Sinn Fein leader Gerry Adams in 1994. Flynn also sponsored trips to the United States by leading loyalists, and it is this kind of evenhanded approach that is carrying the day. Flynn, chairman of the Irish Chamber of Commerce, received the Initiative for Peace Award from the National Committee on American Foreign Policy for his efforts.
- **Peter King,** who as a three-term Republican congressman from Long Island has represented Irish American interests in Washington. He is cochair of the Congressional Ad Hoc Committee for Irish Affairs and speaks out constantly for progress in Northern Ireland. With ancestors from Counties Limerick and Galway, and with a law degree from Notre Dame, King was a natural choice as grand marshal of New York City's Saint Patrick's Day Parade in 1985.
- **John J. Sweeney,** who as president of the AFL-CIO carries forth the legacy of Mother Jones, Mike Quill, and, particularly, George Meany. Sweeney's parents emigrated from County Leitrim and settled in the Bronx; his father was a New York City bus driver and a member of the Transport Workers Union. Sweeney worked his way through Iona College, then got his first union job—as a gravedigger. He worked for IBM before starting to ply the waters as a labor leader (garment workers, service employees). He is trying to modernize the labor movement and hopes to make it a friendlier place for

minorities. If he can accomplish his goals, he will be remembered as a titan of labor, just like those earlier Irish Americans.

- **Claudia J. Kennedy,** who in 1997 became a lieutenant general in the army, the first woman ever to wear three stars. Kennedy joined the service in 1968 at age twenty—and at the height of the Vietnam War. During her two decades in the army she has been decorated with four Legion of Merit awards, the Defense Meritorious Service Medal, four army meritorious service medals, four commendation medals, and the Army Staff Identification Badge.

- **Dennis Mulcahey,** a native of Cork and now a senior member of the New York Police Department Bomb Squad, who in 1976 founded Project Children, an effort to teach kids about living in peace. The organization has brought more than ten thousand Catholic and Protestant children from Northern Ireland to vacation together in the United States with volunteer host families. The experience is designed to show the youngsters that people from different religious and cultural backgrounds can not only get along but also be friends. Mulcahey has been nominated for the Nobel Peace Prize.

- **Charles Feeney,** the Elizabeth, New Jersey, native who in 1997 gave away so much money that he became the greatest American philanthropist of all time. Feeney made his billions by founding and operating a multinational duty-free-shop empire. While much of his giving has been to educational institutions in the United States, particularly his own alma mater, Cornell University, he has given generously to the land of his ancestors, who came from County Fermanagh. He has donated more than $100 million to Irish institutions from the University of Limerick to Trinity College, Dublin. A quiet, private man—there's no Ted Turner flash about him—Feeney has served as a member of the American peace delegation that helped secure the 1994 cease-fire and has helped fund Sinn Fein's office in Washington.

How the world found out about Feeney's beneficence is as fascinating as the generosity itself. He had donated anonymously almost all of his personal fortune to the charitable Atlantic Foundation and Atlantic Trust. It was only when the sale of his remaining shares in the duty-free shops was publicly disclosed that it became apparent what had transpired. Feeney, a bit embarrassed, urged that others with means be more charitable: "You can only wear one pair of shoes at a time."

Are other Irish Americans rich? Are they generous?

Some are. And some are.

There are at least one hundred Irish names on the annual *Forbes* list of the four hundred wealthiest Americans (no matter when you're reading this). That said, Irish Americans have never been famous for their philanthropy. That said, things may be changing.

Donald R. Keough, former president and chief operating officer of Coca-Cola, has given huge amounts of money to Irish cultural causes and other charities. **John Burns,** the big-bucks financier from San Francisco, has done the same. **A. J. F. O'Reilly,** the Irish-born chairman of H. J. Heinz, founded the Ireland Fund in 1976 (with Daniel M. Rooney, president of the Pittsburgh Steelers football team). This international fund has raised $55 million for Irish education and the arts. (Meanwhile, O'Reilly has continued investing in his part-ownership of Waterford and Wedgwood.) **Loretta Brennan Glucksman,** president of the American Ireland Fund, and her husband, **Lewis L. Glucksman,** vice chairman of Smith Barney, have given $4 million to the University of Limerick and $2 million to Ireland House at New York University.

What is Ireland House?

Founded in response to the remarkable resurgence in Irish culture and scholarship, the center is housed in two adjoining landmark buildings at Number One and Two Washington Mews, in New York's Greenwich Village; its sole focus is on things Hibernian. Ireland House plays host to visiting scholars and dignitaries and has become something of an Irish hub in New York; when it opened in 1993, no less than Irish Taoiseach Albert Reynolds was on hand for the ribbon cutting. It has been called "the most important center for Irish culture in the U.S."

Guess who else is Irish?

Colin Powell, retired four-star general, who led American forces during the Gulf War, who has received an honorary knighthood from Queen Elizabeth, who is perceived not only as a great American but as a potential president, has Irish blood in him, and it's blue at that. The authority on such matters, *Burke's Peerage,* pegs him as a direct descendant of Sir Charles Coote of Leitrim, who forced thousands of Irish into slavery in the seventeenth century. One of the Cootes, General Sir Eyre, fathered a child with a black slave girl while he was serving as governor of Jamaica; this daughter turned out to be Powell's great-great-grandmother.

What are the MacBride Principles?

They are a set of guidelines for firms operating in Northern Ireland. They were promulgated in 1984 by the late Irish statesman and Nobel Prize laureate **Sean MacBride** and several of his associates.

Sean MacBride was born in 1906, the only son of John MacBride, who would become one of the executed rebels of 1916, and **Maud Gonne,** Yeats's famous muse. Sean was a resolute Republican from the first and accompanied Michael Collins to the treaty negotiations in London. He split with the IRA after its 1939 bombing campaign in England. As a lawyer and politician MacBride continued to work for the rights of political prisoners, and in 1961 he founded Amnesty International, serving as its head for thirteen years. Clearly, he was the man to draft the principles.

The MacBride Principles call on firms in the North to increase employment opportunities for members of underrepresented religious groups, bar the display of provocative sectarian emblems in the workplace, promote security for minority employees, and abolish hiring criteria that discriminate on the basis of religion or ethnicity. The campaign has made steady progress, both in the United States and in the North. Bernadette Devlin McAliskey has called it "the most important human rights initiative in Northern Ireland since the Irish civil rights movement of the 1960s."

In the United States the campaign has focused on securing commitments from firms doing business in Northern Ireland to abide by the principles. Some fifty American companies, employing thousands, have significant operations in that country. One half of these have agreed to implement the fair-employment standards of the MacBride Principles and to accept independent monitoring. There is a drive on to get states and municipalities to enact laws tying their investments and procurement policies to corporate agreements that they will abide by MacBride.

Economic pressure such as this worked wonders in the campaign against apartheid in South Africa. We'll see what happens in Ireland.

Why do many Irishmen drink Jameson whiskey and shun Bushmill's?

John Jameson Irish Whiskey, along with Tullamore Dew, Paddy, Dunphy's, Power's Murphy's, and other fine whiskeys, is made in the Republic. Old Bushmill's—arguably the finest potion made on the island, especially in its top-shelf Black Bush brand—is distilled in the far North at the world's oldest licensed distillery, in operation since 1609. That would be reason enough for some to boycott it, but there's more: Bushmill's long discriminated against Catholics in its hiring practices. It is said you can taste the bigotry in every dram.

Now having said all that, if you buy either in the States these days, your dollar goes to the same distillery company. So choose your poison.

Is there one more story to be told?

There is. It's the tale of the "Irish adoptees," and we feel it says something about the Ireland of the near past, regrets of the present, the certainty that such a thing will never happen again—and how very lucky Ireland has been that America was there for her.

Between 1949 and 1973 at least twenty-two hundred future American citizens were born out of wedlock in Ireland, then shipped off for adoption in the United States so as not to suffer as outcasts in their homeland. The Ireland of the time was rigidly Catholic, of course, and both premarital sex and the use of birth control were forbidden. In Catholic Charities homes, young women would give birth, then be pressured to give up their infants and return to the community with their reputations reasonably intact. Unfortunately, there weren't enough homes in Ireland to adopt the two thousand infants left in the wards annually, and so the Church looked to the United States, where the demand for babies was greater than the supply.

It was a shabby business: Life in the mother-and-child homes was miserable; the girls scrubbed floors for their keep, and the nuns showed little sympathy, allowing the mothers hardly any time with their newborns. Some girls were so unhappy that they tried to run away, but they were caught by guards and returned.

So great was the sense of shame attached to the practice, that precious little documentation concerning the babies exists (in many cases, they were said to be orphans). As a result, there are Americans today who don't know that they are Irish.

That's okay. They're here now. They're American. And as for the Irish American part: It's in their blood. All of us carry the old country with us, whether we know it or not, think of it or not. Every day. Today. Tomorrow. The road goes on.

Sources

General

John A. Barnes. *Irish-American Landmarks: A Traveler's Guide.* Detroit: Visible Ink, 1995.

Ronald H. Bayor and Timothy J. Meagher, eds. *The New York Irish.* Baltimore: Johns Hopkins University Press, 1996.

The Book of Irish Weirdness. New York: Sterling, 1997.

Leslie Conron Carola, ed. *The Irish: A Treasury of Art and Literature.* Hugh Lauter Levin Associates, 1993.

Michael Coffey and Terry Golway. *The Irish in America.* New York: Hyperion, 1997.

Brian E. Cooper, ed. *The Irish American Almanac and Green Pages.* New York: Harper & Row, 1990.

Aubrey Dillon-Malone. *The Guinness Book of Humorous Irish Anecdotes.* Enfield, Middlesex, England: Guinness Publishing, 1996.

Marjorie R. Fallows. *Irish Americans.* New York: Prentice-Hall, 1979.

Constantine FitzGibbon. *The Irish in Ireland.* New York: W.W. Norton, 1983.

Andrew M. Greeley. *The Irish Americans: The Rise to Money and Power.* New York: Harper & Row, 1981.

William D. Griffin. *The Book of Irish Americans.* New York: Random House, 1990.

Robert Kee. *Ireland: A History.* London: Weidenfeld and Nicholson, 1980.

SOURCES

Thomas Keneally. *Now and in Time to Be*. London: Ryan, 1991.

The Macmillan Atlas of Irish History. New York: Macmillan, 1997.

Pat McArt and Donal Campbell, eds. *Irish Almanac and Yearbook of Facts*. Derry, Ireland: Artcam, 1997.

Mary A. McCaffery, Henry M. Quinlan, and Michael P. Quinlan. *Irish Trivia*. New York: Wings, 1990.

Peter Neville. *A Traveller's History of Ireland*. New York: Interlink, 1993.

Maire and Conor Cruise O'Brien. *A Concise History of Ireland*. New York: Beekman House, 1972.

Kevin O'Rourke. *Currier and Ives: The Irish and America*. New York: Harry N. Abrams, 1995.

Charles Sullivan, ed., *Ireland in Poetry*. New York: Harry N. Abrams, 1990.

J. F. Watts and Sandra Stotsky, general eds. *The Irish Americans*. New York: Chelsea House, 1996.

Carl Wittke. *The Irish in America*. Baton Rouge: LSU Press, 1956.

Ernest Wood. *The Irish Americans: How the Irish Arrived and Became Part of America's Heritage*. New York: Mallard, 1992.

Chapter Two—Ancient Ireland

Barry Cunliffe. *The Ancient Celts*. New York: Oxford University Press, 1997.

———, ed. *The Oxford Illustrated Prehistory of Europe*. New York: Oxford University Press, 1994.

Alfred Perceval Graves. *The Irish Fairy Book*. New York: Greenwich House, 1983.

Chapter Three—The Middle Ages: Christianity Comes to Ireland, and the Vikings Invade (Meanwhile, the Irish Discover America)

Thomas Cahill. *How the Irish Saved Civilization*. New York: Doubleday, 1995.

Chapter Four—Troubles Brewing

Peter Berresford. *Hell or Connaught! The Cromwellian Colonisation of Ireland 1652–1600*. Belfast: Blackstaff, 1975.

T. A. Jackson. *Ireland Her Own: An Outline History of the Irish Struggle*. New York: International, 1970.

Seamus P. Metress. *Outlines in Irish History: Eight Hundred Years of Struggle*. Detroit: Connolly, 1995.

Chapter Five—Fighting Irish, Founding Irish

D. N. Doyle and O. D. Edwards, eds. *America and Ireland, 1776–1976*. New York: Greenwood, 1980.

Chapter Seven—Boston Bound (or, Philadelphia Here I Come!)

Hasia R. Diner. *Erin's Daughters in America: Irish Immigrant Women in the Nineteenth Century*. Baltimore: Johns Hopkins University Press, 1983.

Edward Laxton. *The Famine Ships*. London: Bloomsbury, 1996.

F.S.L. Lyons. *Ireland Since the Famine*. New York: Oxford University Press, 1971.

Lawrence McCaffery. *The Irish Diaspora*. Washington, D.C.: Catholic University Press, 1984.

Eileen McMahon. *What Parish Are You From?* Lexington: University Press of Kentucky, 1995.

Kerby Miller. *Emigrants and Exiles*. New York: Oxford University Press, 1985.

——— and Paul Wagner. *Out of Ireland: The Story of Irish Emigration to America*. Niwot, Colo.: Roberts Rinehart, 1997.

Joel Mokyr. *Why Ireland Starved*. London: Routledge, Chapman and Hall, 1985.

Robert Scally. *The End of Hidden Ireland*. New York: Oxford University Press, 1995.

Cecil Woodham-Smith. *The Great Hunger: Ireland 1845–1849*. London: Penguin, 1991.

Chapter Eight—The Fightin' Irish in the Wild, Wild West

Iver Bernstein. *The New York City Draft Riots: Their Significance for American Society and Politics in the Age of the Civil War*. New York: Oxford University Press, 1990.

David M. Emmons. *The Butte Irish*. Chicago: University of Illinois Press, 1990.

Oscar Handlin. *Boston's Immigrants*. New York: Athenaeum, 1968.

Noel Ignatiev. *How the Irish Became White.* New York: Routledge, 1995.

Arthur H. Lewis. *Lament for the Molly Maguires.* New York: Harcourt, Brace and World, 1964.

John Bernard McGloin. *Eloquent Indian: The Life of James Bouchard.* San Francisco: Stanford, 1949.

James M. Moynihan. *The Life of Archbishop John Ireland.* New York: Harper & Brothers, 1953.

Peter Quinn. *Banished Children of Eve.* New York: Penguin, 1994.

Ellen Skerrett, ed. *At the Crossroads: Old St. Patrick's and the Chicago Irish.* Chicago: Loyola Press, 1997.

Chapter Nine—Irish Nationalism: The American Role

Thomas N. Brown. *Irish-American Nationalism.* New York: Greenwood, 1980.

Tim Pat Coogan. *De Valera.* London: Hutchinson, 1993.

———. *The IRA.* London: Fontana, 1971.

———. *The Man Who Made Ireland: The Life and Death of Michael Collins.* Niwot, Colo.: Roberts Rinehart, 1992.

———. *The Troubles: Ireland's Ordeal and the Search for Peace.* Boulder, Colo.: Roberts Rinehart, 1996.

Peter De Rosa. *Rebels: The Irish Rising of 1916.* New York: Fawcett Columbine, 1990.

T. Ryle Dwyer. *De Valera: The Man and the Myth.* Dublin: Poolbeg, 1991.

Terry Golway. *Irish Rebel: John Devoy and America's Fight for Ireland's Freedom.* New York: St. Martin's, 1998.

Robert Kee. *The Laurel and the Ivy.* London: Hamish Hamilton, 1993.

Eoin Neeson. *The Civil War 1922–23.* Dublin: Poolbeg, 1989.

Conor O'Clery. *Daring Diplomacy.* Boulder, Colo.: Roberts Rinehart, 1997.

Frank O'Connor. *The Big Fellow.* Dublin: Poolbeg, 1979.

Jill and Leon Uris. *Ireland: A Terrible Beauty.* London: Andre Deutsch, 1976.

Chapter Ten—The Lit'ry Life
(and Other Artsy Pursuits)

Van Wyck Brooks. *The Confident Years: 1885–1915.* New York: E.P. Dutton, 1952.

———. *The Flowering of New England.* New York: E.P. Dutton, 1936.

————. *New England: Indian Summer.* New York: E.P. Dutton, 1940.

Bob Callahan, ed. *The Big Book of American Irish Culture.* New York: Penguin, 1987.

Joseph M. Curran. *Hibernian Green on the Silver Screen.* New York: Greenwood, 1989.

Charles Fanning. *The Irish Voice in America.* Lexington: The University Press of Kentucky, 1990.

Alfred Kazin. *A Writer's America: Landscape in Literature.* New York: Alfred A. Knopf, 1988.

Frank McCourt. *Angela's Ashes.* New York: Scribners, 1997.

Michael Meyer. *The Bedford Introduction to Literature: Reading, Thinking, and Writing* (4th ed.). Boston: Bedford Books, St. Martin's, 1996.

Eugene O'Neill. *Complete Plays* (3 vols.). New York: Library of America, 1988.

Robert Welch, ed. *The Oxford Companion to Irish Literature.* Oxford: Oxford University Press, 1996.

Note: John O'Hara's novels are generally available (most published by Random House), as are F. Scott Fitzgerald's (most published by Scribners). The fiction of Flannery O'Connor, Thomas Flanagan, Mary Gordon, Elizabeth Cullinan, William Kennedy, Anna Quindlen, and Jimmy Breslin (his journalism, too) is generally available from a variety of publishers.

Chapter Eleven—Sporting Irish

Dave Anderson. *The Story of Basketball.* New York: William Morrow, 1988.

Robert H. Boyle. *Sport: A Mirror of American Life.* Boston: Little, Brown, 1963.

Jerry Brondfield. *Rockne.* New York: Random House, 1976.

Bob Carroll. *When the Grass Was Real.* New York: Simon & Schuster, 1993.

Robert W. Creamer. *Babe: The Legend Comes to Life.* New York: Penguin, 1974.

Stan Fischler. *Those Were the Days.* New York: Dodd, Mead, 1976.

David Gallen, ed. *The Baseball Chronicles.* New York: Carroll & Graf, 1991.

William Grimsley. *Tennis: Its History, People and Events.* Englewood Cliffs, N. J.: Prentice-Hall, 1971.

Allen Guttman. *The Olympics: A History of the Modern Games.* Chicago: University of Illinois Press, 1992.

Brad Herzog. *The Sports 100.* New York: Macmillan, 1995.

Ralph Hickok. *A Who's Who of Sports Champions*. Boston: Houghton Mifflin, 1995.

Michael T. Isenberg. *John L. Sullivan and His America*. Chicago: University of Chicago Press, 1994.

Peter Levine. *A. G. Spalding and the Rise of Baseball*. New York: Oxford University Press, 1985.

Robert Lipsyte and Peter Levine. *Idols of the Game: A Sporting History of the American Century*. Atlanta: Turner, 1995.

Daniel Okrent and Steve Wulf. *The Oxford Book of Baseball Anecdotes*. New York: Oxford University Press, 1989.

George Peper. *Golf in America*. New York: Harry N. Abrams, 1988.

David L. Porter, ed. *Biographical Dictionary of American Sports* (3 vols.). New York: Greenwood, 1989.

Lawrence Ritter and Donald Honig. *The 100 Greatest Baseball Players of All Time*. New York: Crown, 1986.

R. Wayne Schmittberger. *Test Your Baseball Literacy*. New York: John Wiley & Sons, 1991.

Harold Seymour. *Baseball: The Early Years*. New York: Oxford University Press, 1960.

John L. Sullivan. *Life and Reminiscences of a 19th-Century Gladiator*. Self-published, 1892.

Joseph J. Vecchione, ed. *The New York Times Book of Sports Legends*. New York: Random House, 1991.

David Wallechinsky. *The Complete Book of the Olympics*. New York: Penguin, 1988.

Alexander Wolff. *100 Years of Hoops*. New York: Time Magazine, 1991.

Rick Wolff, ed. *The Baseball Encyclopedia*. New York: Macmillan, 1992.

Chapter Twelve—The Road Rises: Irish Americanism in the Twentieth Century

Oliver E. Allen. *The Tiger: The Rise and Fall of Tammany Hall*. New York: Addison-Wesley, 1993.

Gerald Astor. *The New York City Cops*. New York: Scribners, 1971.

Jack Beatty. *The Rascal King: The Life and Times of James Michael Curley*. New York: Addison-Wesley, 1992.

James Michael Curley. *I'd Do It Again: A Record of My Uproarious Years*. New York: Prentice-Hall, 1957.

T. J. English. *The Westies: Inside the Hell's Kitchen Irish Mob*. New York: G.P. Putnam's Sons, 1990.

Nathan Glazer and Daniel Patrick Moynihan. *Beyond the Melting Pot: The Negroes, Puerto Ricans, Indians and Irish of New York City.* Boston: MIT Press, 1970.

Frank Graham. *Al Smith, American.* New York: G.P. Putnam and Sons, 1945.

Edwin O'Connor. *The Last Hurrah.* Boston: Little, Brown, 1956.

George Reedy. *From the Ward to the White House.* New York: Scribners, 1991.

William Riordan. *Plunkitt of Tammany Hall.* New York: Signet, 1995.

William V. Shannon. *The American Irish: A Political and Social Portrait.* New York: Macmillan, 1966.

Al Smith. *Up to Now: An Autobiography.* New York: Doubleday, 1929.

Chapter Thirteen—From County Wexford to Camelot: A Family Saga

Peter Collier and David Horowitz. *The Kennedys: An American Drama.* New York: Summit, 1984.

Doris Kearns Goodwin. *The Fitzgeralds and the Kennedys.* New York: Simon & Schuster, 1987.

Theodore C. Sorenson. *Kennedy.* New York: Harper & Row, 1965.

Richard J. Whalen. *The Founding Father: The Story of Joseph P. Kennedy.* New York: New American Library, 1964.

Chapter Fourteen—The Road from Here

Samuel G. Freedman. *The Inheritance: How Three Families and America Moved from Roosevelt to Reagan and Beyond.* New York: Simon & Schuster, 1996.

Rosemary Mahoney. *Whoredom in Kimmage: Irish Women Coming of Age.* New York: Houghton Mifflin, 1993.

Joseph O'Connor. *Sweet Liberty: Travels in Irish America.* Boulder, Colo.: Roberts Rinehart, 1996.

Paul O'Dwyer. *Counsel for the Defense.* New York: Simon & Schuster, 1979.

Ray O'Hanlon. *The New Irish Americans.* Niwot, Colo.: Roberts Rinehart, 1997.

Richard Powers. *Not Without Honor.* New York: Free Press, 1996.

Index

317

Fitzsimmons, Bob, 216
Fitzwilliam, Lord Peter, 286
Flaming Corsage, The (Kennedy), 184
Flanagan, Father Edward J., 266–67
Flanagan, John, 228
Flanagan, Mike, 223
Flanagan, Thomas, 183
Flannery, Michael, 165
Flatley, Michael, 203, 204–205
Flood, James, 97
Flynn, Bill, 304
Flynn, Edward, 229
Flynn, Elizabeth Gurley, xiv, 257
Football, Gaelic, 209, 210
Ford, Henry, xiv, 82, 97, 239–40
Ford, John, 194–95, 196
Forsaking All Others (Breslin), 188
Foster, Stephen Collins, 80, 199
Four Cohans, 193
Fredericksburg, Battle of, 104, 105
Free State of Ireland:
  becomes Republic, 2, 164
  civil war, 156, 161, 165
  founding of, 2, 154, 161
  neutrality in World War II, 162–64
French Revolution, 66
Friel, Brian, 21, 172, 173
Friendly Brothers of Saint Patrick, 58

Gaelic, 14–16
Gaelic American, 152
Gaelic League, 15, 153
Gallagher Brothers, 129
Gallier, James, Jr., 301
Gangs, 119, 243
Gang That Couldn't Shoot Straight, The
  (Breslin), 188
Gardner, Alexander, 107
Garrett, Pat, 128
Garrity, Judge, 114
Garson, Greer, 82
Gavin, General James M., 265
George III, King of England, 63
George IV, King of England, 99
Georgetown University, 65, 112
Gerard, John, 23
Gettysburg, Battle of, 107–108
Giancana, Sam, 288
Gift, The (Hamill), 188
Gilragh, Kate, 260
Ginger Man, The (Donleavy), 182
Gingrich, Arnold, 235
Glaciers, 7
Gladstone, William, 150
Glaven, Darbie, 46

Gleason, Jackie, xiv, 193, 197
Glenn, John, 82
Glorious Revolution of 1688, 53
Glucksman, Lewis L., 306
Glucksman, Loretta Brennan, 306
Glynn, Frank, 31
God and Intelligence in Modern Philosophy
  (Sheen), 267
Goidelic, 14–16
Going My Way, 201
Golden, Donny, 202, 204
Golden, Eileen, 202
Golden Age of Ireland, 27
Golden Bowl, The (James), 174
Goldwater, Barry, 289
Golf, 232–33
Golway, Terry, 147, 161, 187, 188,
  194, 272
Gompers, Samuel, 256
Gone with the Wind (Mitchell), 179
Gonne, Maud, 307
Good, Mary O'Neil, 113
"Good Country People," 181
"Good Man Is Hard to Find, A," 181
Goodwin, Doris Kearns, 274, 279, 281,
  282, 285–86, 287
Goodwin, William, 30–31, 32
Gookin, Vincent, 51
Gordon, Mary, 183
Grace, William Russell, xiv, 238, 239
Grange, Red, 216
Grant, Ulysses S., 3, 79, 103, 143
Great Britain, *see* Britain
Great Famine, The (Williams and
  Edwards), 94
Great Hunger, The (Woodham-Smith), 87,
  94, 96, 114
Great Indian Council of 1851, 125
Great Potato Famine, 4, 76, 87–98, 117
  aid from America, 92–94
  aid from Choctaw Indians, 92–93
  British attitude toward, 88–91
  lasting effects of, 98
  monument commemorating, 98
Greeley, Rev. Andrew M., xiii, xiv, xv, xvi,
  173–74, 182–83, 199
Greeley, Horace, 78, 110, 120, 147
Greene, Marie, 279
Green Fields of America (band), 202
Green Linnet Records, 202, 203
Greens, Jasper, 300
Gregg, John R., 241
Gresham, Katherine, 293
Gribbin, Emmet, 112
Griffin, John Howard, 113

Index

Griffin, William D., 117–18, 128–29
Griffith, Arthur, 154
Group, The (McCarthy), 182

Hall, A. Oakley, 146
Hamill, Pete, xiv, 111, 188
Hanlon, Ned, 221
Hannon, Mary Ann, 273, 275–76
Harper's Weekly, 120, 126
Harrington, Michael, 113
Harrison, Benjamin, 3
Harvard College, 50
Hawthorne, Nathaniel, 95
Hayes, Helen, xiv, 192
Healy, James, 112
Healy, Patrick, 112
Heaney, Seamus, 172–73
Hearst, Patty, 242
Hearst, William Randolph, xiv, 226, 241–42
Henry, Augustine, 81
Henry II, King of England, 41–42
Henry VIII, King of England, 44, 45
Hepburn, Katharine, 195, 241
Herbert, Victor, xiv, 199
"Hermit's Song, The," 27–29
Hibernia National Bank, 242
Higgins, George V., 183
Hill, Mary Courtney Kennedy, 294
Hill, Paul, 294
Hill, Saoirse Roisin, 294
Historical Relics of the White Mountains (Spaulding), 36
History of Essex County (Paradise), 51
History of the Ginger Man, The (Donleavy), 182
Hitler, Adolf, 163, 240
Hoban, James, 65–66, 205
Hogan, Ben, 233
Hogan, Marty, 219
Holiday Inn, 201
Holland, John Philip, 144–45
Holland, USS, 145
Homer, Augusta, 206
Home rule, 149, 150–51, 152, 153
Hopper, William DeWolf, 226
Hore, Father Thomas, 97
Hornsby, Rogers, 224
Horowitz, David, 289
House of Gold (Cullinhan), 183
Houston, Sam, 48, 71, 73, 80–81
Howells, William Dean, 174, 175
How the Irish Became White (Ignatien), 101
How the Irish Saved Civilization (Cahill), xii, 25–26

Hudson River Fisherman's Association, 294
Hughes, Howard R., xiv, 241
Hughes, John, 79–80
Hughie, 190
Hume, John, 167–68, 251
Humphrey, Hubert, 290
Hurling, 290, 210
Huston, John, 158

Ice ages, 7
Iceman Cometh, The, 190
Idaho, 130–31
Ierne, the word, 16
Ignatien, Noel, 101
Illinois and Michigan Canal, 121
Immigrant Reform and Control Act of 1986, 298
Immigrants, Irish, *see* Emigration from Ireland
Immigration Act of 1990, 298
Indian Civilization Act of 1819, 124
Indians, American, *see* Native Americans
"Instruction of a King," 12–13
International Workers of the World, 257
"Interrupted Native, The," 188
In the Name of the Father, xv, 185, 294
Ireland:
  ancient, 7–16
  deforestation of, 7
  described, 4–5
  history of, 2, 7–55
  the Middle Ages in, 17–39
  unification under Henry VIII, 45
  weather in, 5, 68
  see also Free State of Ireland; Northern Ireland; Republic of Ireland
Ireland, Father John, 105
Ireland, Patricia, 304
Ireland House, 306
Ireland's Liberator, 150
Irish America magazine, 123, 158
Irish American Athletic Club, 228
Irish American Landmarks (Barnes), 196
Irish Americans:
  of 1800 versus 1900, 238–39
  scope of the term, 1–3
  see also specific categories, e.g. Music; Sports
Irish Americans: The Rise to Power and Money, The (Greeley), 183, 199
Irish Athletic Association, 210
Irish Bridget, 106
Irish Brigade, 104–106, 108, 148
Irish coffee, 269

Index

Irish Emigration Society, 75
Irish Gaelic, 14–16
Irish in America, The (Coffey and Golway), 187, 188, 192, 272
Irish in Ireland, The (FitzGibbon), 164
Irish Institute, 254
Irish language, 14–16
Irish Lesbian and Gay Organization, 74
Irishman's Story, An (McCarthy), 93–94
Irish nationalism, 66–68, 91, 118, 164–65
    American role in, 139-69
Irish Northern Aid (NORAID), 165
Irish People, The, 141
Irish Rebellion of 1848, 91, 139
Irish Republican Army (IRA), 118, 154, 158, 161, 164–66, 167, 168, 169
    cease-fires, 166, 167, 251, 252, 298, 305
Irish Republican Brotherhood, 91, 140, 141–42, 143–44, 148, 149
Irish revolt of 1798, *see* United Irishmen's Rebellion of 1798
Irish Sweepstakes, 97
Irish Times, 157, 160
"Irish Voice in American Fiction, The," 174–75
Irish Volunteers, 153, 154, 155, 165
    see also Irish Republican Army (IRA)
Irish War of Independence, 154, 155–56
Irish World, The, 150
Ironweed (Kennedy), 184
Irving, Clifford, 241
Irwin, James B., 82
Isenberg, Michael T., 214, 215–216
Iserninus, 18–19
Ivers, Eileen, 202, 203

Jackson, Andrew, 3, 48, 69, 70, 78, 79, 124
Jackson, Peter, 215
Jackson, Stonewall, 79, 103
Jackson, Thomas Alfred, 163
Jackson, William, 67
Jail Journal: On Five Years in British Prison (Mitchel), 79, 139
James, Henry, 174
James, William, 174
James I, King of England, 46
James II, King of England, 52, 53
Jeter, Derek, 113
John L. Sullivan and His America (Isenberg), 214
Johnson, Andrew, 3, 81, 140, 143
Johnson, Jack, 215
Johnson, Lyndon B., 268, 287–88, 289–90

John Wayne's America: The Politics of Celebrity (Wills), 196
Jones, Bobby, 216, 233
Jones, Mary Harris (Mother Jones), xiv, 256–57
Jones, Michael, 51
Jordan, Neil, 157-60
Joyce, Giorgio, 299
Joyce, James, 172
Judgment Day (Farrell), 178

Kazin, Alfred, 179
Keane, Dolores, 202
Keane, Jimmy, 202
Keating, Kenneth, 289
Keaton, Buster, 193
Kehoe, John, 133–34
Kelley, John A., 231
Kelley, John J., 231
Kelley, Colonel Patrick, 104
Kelly, Anne Elizabeth, 293
Kelly, Captain Colin, 264
Kelly, Emmett, 193
Kelly, Frederick, 228
Kelly, Gene, xiv, 203
Kelly, Grace, 187
Kelly, "Honest John," 120, 242
Kelly, Jack, Sr., 198, 209, 228
Kelly, James E., 206
Kelly, Michael J. "King," 212, 220–21
Kelly, Walt, 189
Kelso, J. J., 146
Keneally, Thomas, 90–91, 94–95, 105–106, 160, 172, 299
Kennedy, Anne Elizabeth Kelly, 293
Kennedy, Justice Anthony, 249
Kennedy, Bridget Murphy, 271–72, 273
Kennedy, Caroline Bouvier, 292
Kennedy, Carolyn Bessette, 292
Kennedy, Christopher George, 294
Kennedy, Claudia J., 305
Kennedy, David Anthony, 291, 294
Kennedy, Douglas Harriman, 294–95
Kennedy, Duncan, 209
Kennedy, Edward M. "Ted," xv, 251, 282, 284, 290–91
Kennedy, Edward M. "Ted," Jr., 293
Kennedy, Ethel Skakel, 283–84, 294
Kennedy, Eunice Mary, 281–82, 284
Kennedy, Jacqueline Lee Bouvier, 287, 288, 290
Kennedy, Jean Ann, 282, 283, 284, 293
Kennedy, Joan Bennett, 290, 291
Kennedy, John F., 113, 164, 247, 252, 257, 259, 277, 280, 281, 283, 285–88